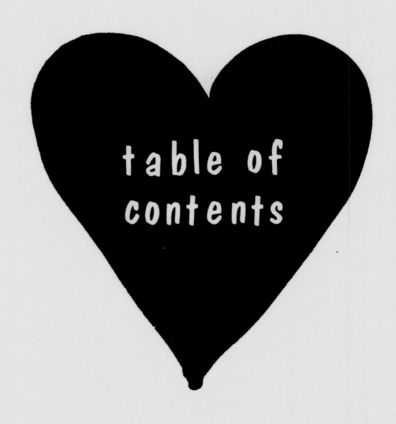

table of contents

introducing the collection LISA DARMS

"Riot Grrrl is because I believe with my wholeheartmindbody that girls constitute a revolutionary soul force that can, and will, change the world for real." —Bikini Kill 2

Frustration with the white-centered culture of riot grrrl was very apparent by 1995. Mimi Nguyen, in a call for submissions to her zine Evolution of a Race Riot, writes pointedly of the need for "taking back the conversation @ race & re-centering it around ourselves, not as voiceless victims or objects-to-be-rescued of white punk antiracist discourses." Some narratives attribute the dissolution of the movement to such rifts, and indeed, challenges to racism and class bias within riot grrrl did prompt existential crises for some local chapters. But these necessary growing pains were paired with fatigue: From early on, distorted portrayals of riot grrrl in the mainstream press drew converts as they narrowed its image—showing the movement as both homogenous and hierarchical, always focusing on a few predictable "leaders." Complicated and seemingly intractable personal-political dynamics arose in part from this disconcerting attention. For many of the young women initially involved with riot grrrl, the result was their unsentimental shedding of the term "riot grrrl."

In 1994, I escaped the Northwest to attend art school in New York. My first friends in the city were Ramdasha Bikceem, author of the zine Gunk, and some of the women who had been active earlier in Riot Grrrl NYC. In this new circle of artist friends, I felt a post-riot grrrl sense of possibility—a shared drive to make politically engaged work in a DIY spirit, but not only for an insular punk scene. From this came my zine Artaud-Mania: The Diary of a Fan, in 1997 a work indebted to Kathleen's My Life with Evan Dando, Popstar for its conceptual confessional tone, and its use of ironic fandom as a vehicle for cultural critique. Artaud-Mania is evidence that, by this time, even if my commitment to radical feminism hadn't faded, I approached my riot grrrl past with a measure of self-parody.

Reading through this collection, though, I'm brought back to the time when each girl's photocopied missive was a revelation, and much of riot grrrl's meaning was derived from the simple fact of its existence. As a teen, it astounded me to discover that girls were organizing to fight their exclusion and silencing, and that they were doing it with intoxicating subcultural style. Two decades later, the imprisonment of members of the Russian feminist band Pussy Riot, who—also astoundingly-cite riot grrrl as an inspiration for their punk music and guerrilla performances, drives home the breadth of the movement's influence. For those who love riot grrrl for its music, or know it only from journalistic accounts, this book will give its legend some missing detail: Here are some of our souvenirs from a bold experiment, the cursive letters we turned into knives in the 90s.

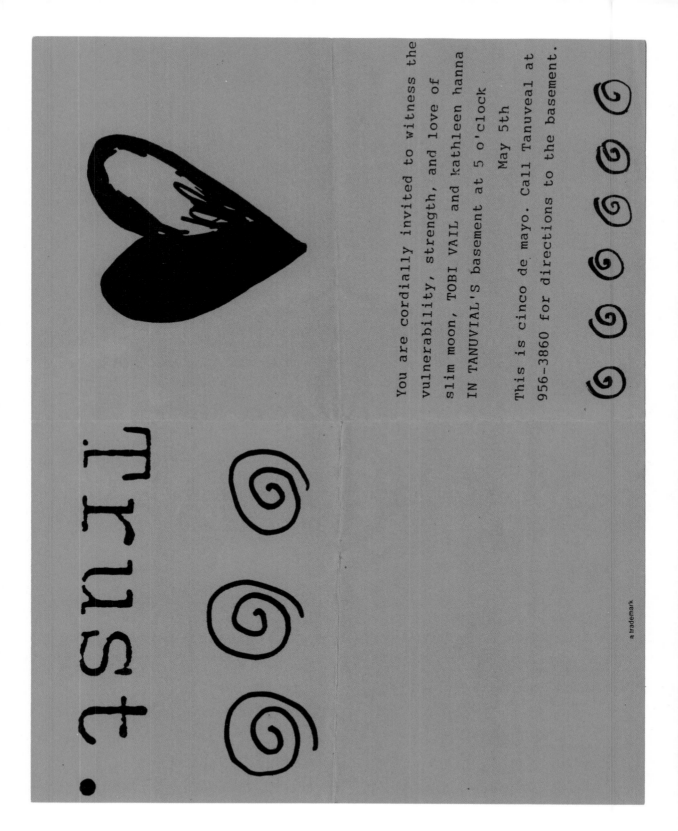

Trust.

You are cordially invited to witness the
vulnerability, strength, and love of
slim moon, TOBI VAIL and kathleen hanna
IN TANUVIAL'S basement at 5 o'clock
May 5th

This is cinco de mayo. Call Tanuveal at
956-3860 for directions to the basement.

a trademark

FLYER

The Revolution starts here + now within each one us.

Burn down the walls that say you can't:

Be a dork, tell your friends you love them.

Resist the temptation to veiw those around you as objects + use them.

Recognize empathy and vulnerability as positive forms of strength.

Resist the internalization of capitalism, the reducing of people + oneself to commodities meant to be consumed.

Resist psychic death.

Don't allow the world to make you into a bitter abusive asshole.

Cry in public.

Don't judge other people. Learn to love yourself.

Acknowledge emotional violence as real.

Figure out how the idea of competition (winning and losing) fits into your intimate relationships.

Decide that you'd rather be happy than be right all the time.

Believe people when they tell you they are hurting or are in pain.   Trust.

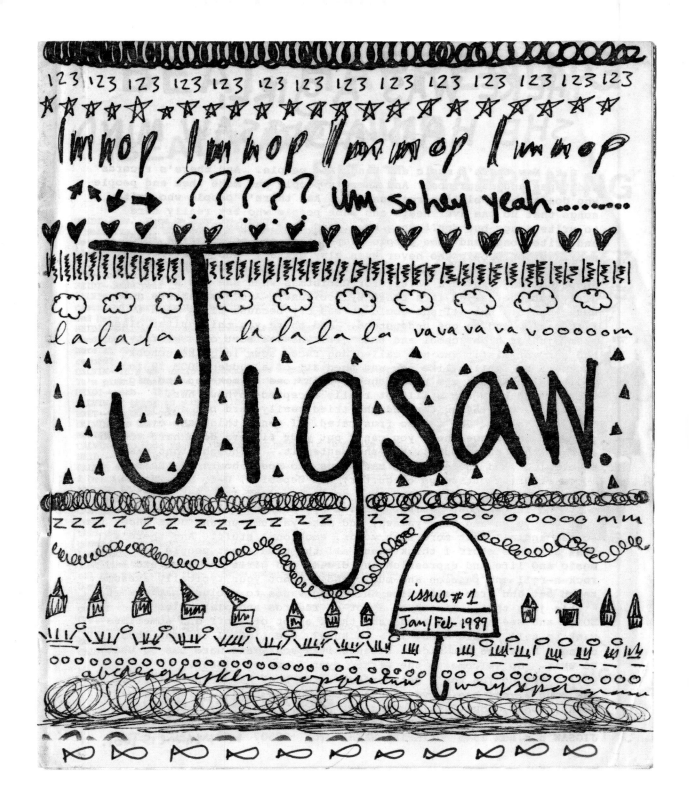

JIGSAW 1 (EXCERPT)

THERE WAS A GIRL,
SHE HAD A JIGSAW MIND

O.k. Now there's music and bands and people. And there's records and tapes and magazines. And there's people who make them and people who don't and a billion reasons why. And there's people who write songs that no one ever hears and some people who try really hard to write songs but don't know how...and some people play guitar and write songs and some people play guitar and never write songs and a lot of people who never even play guitar. And a lot of them want. To But for some reason they never do. My mom tells me a story about how she wanted a guitar for Christmas when she was a little girl, but she called it a banjo by accident. And her parents got her a banjo. But all she could do was cry because Elvis didn't play banjo, and no one understood. And there was this guitar class at my junior high school and this girl who was sort of a misfit-the sort of misfit who got called dog faced scum in grade school and sort of smelled like pee and then all of a sudden BOOM YR in junior high school and there she is with tons of make up and cig-arettes and boys but still not really accepted-anyhow, her.
She wanted to play guitar and she tried really hard but she just couldn't do it. She was so frustrated. I don't think she ever got past the stage where you can't put your fingers down hard enough to stop that buzz sound...but she wanted it. I thought that was so tragic. And there are so many kids who spend hours in their rooms figuring out songs on guitar, Led Zeppelin, U-2, DRI, Beat Happening; you name it. And they don't even get it! But some go on to be in the most soulful passion WOW rock-n-roll bands that really move ya and blow ya away and make ya jump up and down and scream and all that more than words, emotional stuff. And there's just all this stuff I think about all the time about people and music and life and expression and dreams and girls and boys and rock-n-roll and passion and music and I'm not your typically awesome reach out and grab ya fanzine Chick who wants to decide what's what
It's just that I listen to a lot of records and play a lot of SONGS and see a lot of bands and think a lot of stuff and sometimes want to tell people about it. YA know? One time I thought about doing a magazine but didn't because it's scary and hard but so what. SO what. So welcome to the first ever issue of Jigsaw.
Um....just so you won't get confused, the beat happening interview was done a year ago, live on K.A.O.S. Thanks Heidi! Also thanks to Al, Donna, Joe, Calvin, Candice, Laura, Bill, Tam, Jenny, Beth and Louise. Oh yeah and NIRVANA RULE. Stay tuned for next issue!
JIGSAW p.o.box 2345 OLYMPIA, WASHINGTON 98507 My name is Tobi.

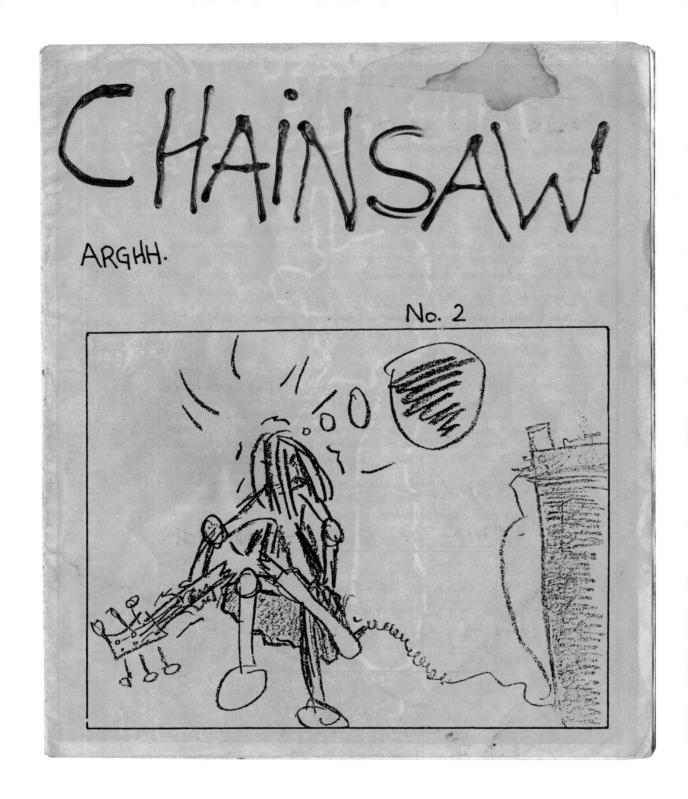

CHAINSAW 2 (EXCERPT)

CHAINSAW Two.

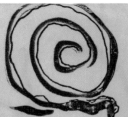

Right now, maybe CHAINSAW is about Frustration.
Frustration in music. Frustration in living, in
being a girl, in being a homo, in being a misfit of
any sort. In being a dork, you know, the last
kid to get picked for the stupid kickball team in
grade school. Which is where this whole punk rock
thing came from in the first place.
NOT from the Sex Pistols or L.A. But from the GEEKS
who decided or realised (or something) to "turn the
tables" so to speak, and take control of their
(our) lives and form a Real underground.
Which is ALSO where the whole heart of CHAINSAW
comes from.

CONTRIBUTERS: GB JONES AND BRUCE LABRUCE WROTE
THEIR OWN STORIES — CANDICE DREW HER SELF POTRAIT —
BILL DREW AMY CARTERS HEAD — JOHN H. WROTE THE AMY
TENNIS CAMP STORY. I DID EVERY THING ELSE. I NEVER
DREW ANYTHING BEFORE CHAINSAW AND NOW I'M AN
ARTIST. STAY FREE — DONNA

♡ A BIG THANKS AND A BIG KISS TO LAURA ♡

"Rock and roll is the nerds revenge" - george smith 1989

☎ 415-776-9668 — DONNA'S #:

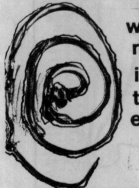

W
r
i
t
e

MAKE TOAST NOT WAR
2336 MARKET № 128
SF, CA   94114

Make Toast Not War

W
r
i
t
e

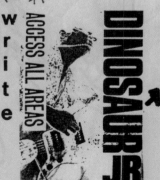

ACCESS ALL AREAS

DINOSAUR JR

I CAN'T DRAW
NEW ZEALAND

Here is a little introduction. I joinedthis band, see, Dinosaur J? I flew to massachusetts, they flew to San Francisco, we practiced a few times played our first show (with me) at the kennel club with the Melvins and then we flew to Aukland, New Zealand (stop No. 1) and then to a bunch of cities in Australia (stops 2 through 14). So, anyways I'm just trying to get to the beginning of this "thing But I figured it would be best if you had at least one little clue of what was happening.

AUKLAND

Chainsaw is a "magazine" that is pretty much formatted along the lines of this radio show that Rich Jensen had a long time ago in Olympia Called "Snapshot Radio" which was bits and pieces of whatever Rich had on tape at any given time. You know, a picture on tape. Chainsaw is the same way but I transcribe it all on paper so everyone can read it over and over and over. Snapshot magazine.

If I happen to meet someone or some thing that I might want to use for Chainsaw, there is no stopping me. No matter how understandable it is. So take heed this is my warning.

Back to the tour. O.k. now pretend your sitting at a table in a pub in Aukland New Zealand with David the bass player/singer in the Jean Paul Sarte Experience and Bridgett our New Zealand tour manager.

-click-
Topic: Jean Paul Sarte Experience's record called "the size of food" on Flying Nun records.
David: It should be out by now.
Bridgett: It's Bullshit.
Donna: It's Bullshit?
B; No, no, thre's no copies of it in New zealand supposedly- but it's been released in the states. It's been out a month and it hasn't been seen he
David: we recorded it in november of lastt year and just the way Flying Nun operates, on a shoe string budget, it's been a year.. it'll prob ablly be out at the end of this m (October)
Donna: becuase they don't have any money?
David: yeah, they have a deal with fundament who takes care of it in the states.
Donna: sort of a production and distribution deal?
David: yeah. and Flying Nun don't pay anyth forit, they get given a certain amount of m for the rights of it. So by that side of i gets done a lot quicker than it does h
Bridgett; why did you call it the size food?
David: It was going to be called "The Moth disk" but we decided it sounded too Freudi
B: Who was going to call it that?
David: Me. Because I've got a bit an obsessi with mothers and things like that.
Donna: are you a Mama's boy?
David: I don't like to think of myself as a mothers boy...maybe I am...I'm definately more of a mothers boy than a fathers boy, tha for sure
Donna: Bridget, do you think you're a dork?
B; It depends on what your defination of a dork is. Here it's quite derogatory.
D: It is in the states too. But it's due tim to take back the rights of the word. you know. ..outcast.
David: a creep. D: not a creep like an asshol people think people are creeps because they a freaks... B: but they are actually just doing their own thing...D: O.K. maybe FREAK is better word.
B: I did things different than most kids.
D: so how 'bout you J? are you a dork?
J: yeah D: see, that's why I wanted to join band.

WITH: BRIDGET AND THE
GUY FROM the JEAN PAUL
SARTRE EXPERIENCE AND J. MASCIS

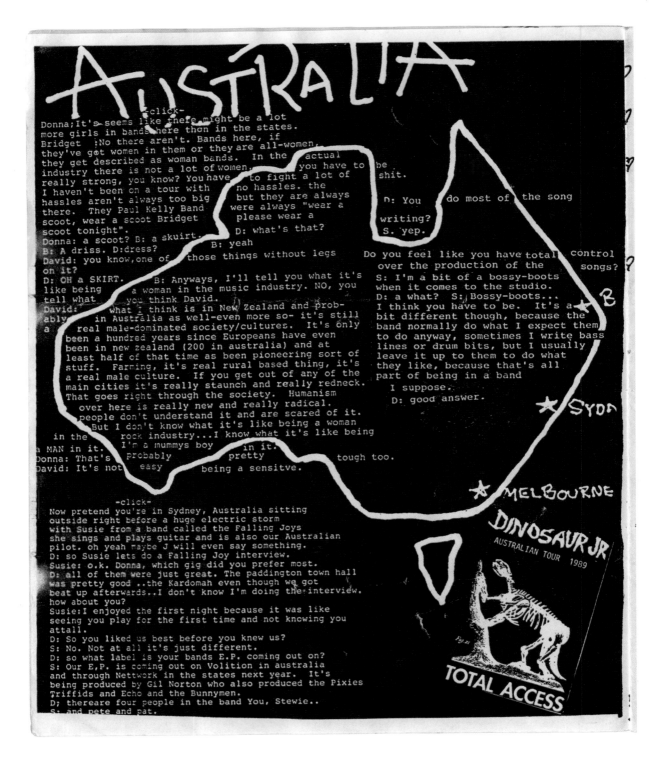

AUSTRALIA

-click-

Donna; It's seems like there might be a lot more girls in bands here then in the states.
Bridget ;No there aren't. Bands here, if they've got women in them or they are all-women, they get described as woman bands. In the actual industry there is not a lot of women, you have to be really strong, you know? You have to fight a lot of shit.
I haven't been on a tour with no hassles. the hassles aren't always too big but they are always there. They Paul Kelly Band were always "wear a scoot, wear a scoot Bridget please wear a scoot tonight".
Donna: a scoot? B: a skuirt. D: what's that?
B: A driss. D:dress? B: yeah
David: you know,one of those things without legs on it.
D: OH a SKIRT. B: Anyways, I'll tell you what it's like being a woman in the music industry. NO, you tell what you think David.
David: what I think is in New Zealand and probably in Australia as well-even more so- it's still a real male-dominated society/cultures. It's only been a hundred years since Europeans have even been in new zealand (200 in australia) and at least half of that time as been pioneering sort of stuff. Farming, it's real rural based thing, it's a real male culture. If you get out of any of the main cities it's really staunch and really redneck. That goes right through the society. Humanism over here is really new and really radical. people don't understand it and are scared of it. But I don't know what it's like being a woman in the rock industry...I know what it's like being a MAN in it. I'm a mummys boy in it.
Donna: That's probably pretty tough too.
David: It's not easy being a sensitve.

D: You do most of the song writing?
S. yep.

Do you feel like you have total control over the production of the songs?
S: I'm a bit of a bossy-boots when it comes to the studio.
D: a what? S:;Bossy-boots... I think you have to be. It's a bit different though, because the band normally do what I expect them to do anyway, sometimes I write bass lines or drum bits, but I usually leave it up to them to do what they like, because that's all part of being in a band
I suppose.
D: good answer.

★ B
★ SYDN

-click-
Now pretend you're in Sydney, Australia sitting outside right before a huge electric storm with Susie from a band called the Falling Joys she sings and plays guitar and is also our Australian pilot. oh yeah maybe J will even say something.
D: so Susie lets do a Falling Joy interview.
Susie: o.k. Donna, which gig did you prefer most.
D: all of them were just great. The paddington town hall was pretty good ..the Kardomah even though we got beat up afterwards..I don't know I'm doing the interview. how about you?
Susie:I enjoyed the first night because it was like seeing you play for the first time and not knowing you attall.
D: So you liked us best before you knew us?
S: No. Not at all it's just different.
D: so what label is your bands E.P. coming out on?
S: Our E.P. is coming out on Volition in australia and through Nettwork in the states next year. It's being produced by Gil Norton who also produced the Pixies Triffids and Echo and the Bunnymen.
D; thereare four people in the band You, Stewie..
S: and pete and pat.

★ MELBOURNE

DINOSAUR JR
AUSTRALIAN TOUR 1989

TOTAL ACCESS

25

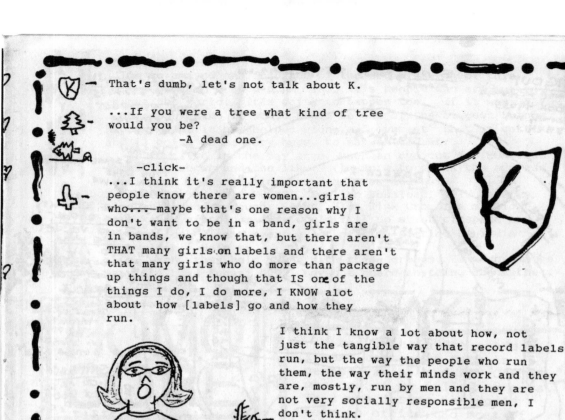

- That's dumb, let's not talk about K.

...If you were a tree what kind of tree would you be?
        -A dead one.

-click-
...I think it's really important that people know there are women...girls who....maybe that's one reason why I don't want to be in a band, girls are in bands, we know that, but there aren't THAT many girls on labels and there aren't that many girls who do more than package up things and though that IS one of the things I do, I do more, I KNOW alot about how [labels] go and how they run.

I think I know a lot about how, not just the tangible way that record labels run, but the way the people who run them, the way their minds work and they are, mostly, run by men and they are not very socially responsible men, I don't think.
I think the whole thing between K and SUB-POP really exemplifies that for me. You know, Bruce thinks I answer the PHONE not anything else. It's really important for people to know that there are girls out there makin' decisions and doin stuff.
    -click-
Candice
c/o K
pobox 7154
Olympia, Wa
98507

CANDICE

CHAINSAW 2 (EXCERPT)

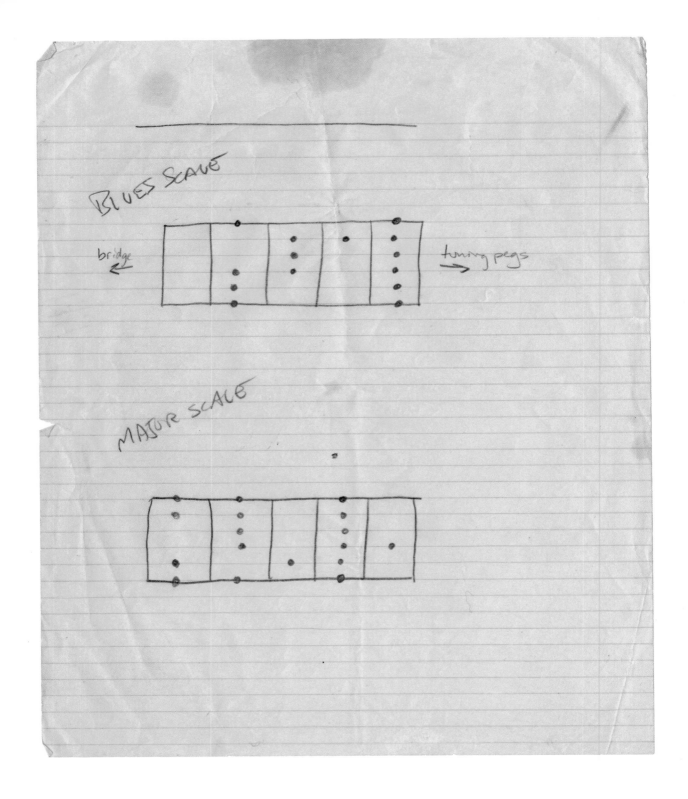

BLUES SCALE

bridge

tuning pegs

MAJOR SCALE

May 9, 1990

Molly--- now, thanks for writing! It's really inspiring to find out that there are actually people in the world who are thinking about the same sort of things I am... sometimes I feel kind of isolated I guess.

I used to live in Eugene... it was kind of really cool and kind of a real drag. The times I've been back there since I moved I went to shows @ WOW HALL and it seems like things have totally changed for the better... like there was a place to have shows + tons of kids that were pretty into it... I saw Vomit Launch and then I played w/ some Velvet Sidewalk when they opened for Dead Moon.

You should definitely do the radio show thing. I tried to get a show at KRVM - a 'women in rock' show and they were totally not into it and way into professionalism and they were dicks.

Intimidating and stupid know-it-alls. So I will send you a tape when it's done... but it probably won't be done until the end of the summer... I am doing another issue though - #2½ and that should be out in June or July. There's also a DORIS Bootleg tape that will be out as soon as my tape deck is fixed - for only $2.

So maybe we could trade tapes of bands we like sometime... I don't know very much about RAP music but the girl stuff seems pretty fucking great.

Do you play an instrument? Aaron said he was in a band with you + Allison.

maybe you could review some stuff for jigsaw? →

or maybe he said he was in a club
w/ you. I can't remember.

It's cool that you're studying about
sexism + racism in school. I wanted
to take a class at Evergreen this
quarter called something like 'Race +
the Politics of Racism' but instead I
took 'Freud, Feminism and the Social
Construction of Sexuality' and it's
been totally blowing me away. It's
psychology, philosophy and social and
political theory. I guess what we are
studying is called 'post modern' feminism
-- whatever that means. All I know is
it seems totally new and exciting to
me. I should have some good articles
coming up from my class, who knows.
Next year I'm going to take 'Political
Economy and Social Change' which
focuses on race, gender and class;
politics; economics and forces of power
embedded in social and cultural
institutions. Evergreen is cool.

It's exciting to study about sexism in
school because it gives you a feeling
of power just to actually be able to
admit that things like oppression actually
do exist and affect your life -- which is
something you have to deny a lot in real
life.

Maybe I'll see you at Fugazi! Thanks
again for writing!! love, tobi vail

ohh -- I'll make a list of bands or something... I have to
find out record labels too... you should send 'Bitch' and
'Chainsaw' and 'Sister Nobody' -- addresses listed in Postlude
section of Jigsaw... (Julie also knows a lot of bands.

hair on your face and glasses that hide your eyes
you slow down at the stop light
you start to stare at me
and this happens, a thousand times
and this happens, a thousand times

why is your favorite pasttime
making me feel like i'mm pinned to wax
why is your favorite hobby
reminding me that i'm being watched

your eyes
and your half smile
look like
they will eat me

your eyes
and your half smile
look like
they will eat me

(i tell my boyfreind and he says
and this happens, a thousand times i take things much too seriously)
and this happens, a thousand times

maybe you think it makes me happy
that look in your eyes
maybe you think that looking
cuts me down to size
i don't wanna be don't wanna be
your prize
just want a place to live, i
can call mine

DRAFT LYRICS

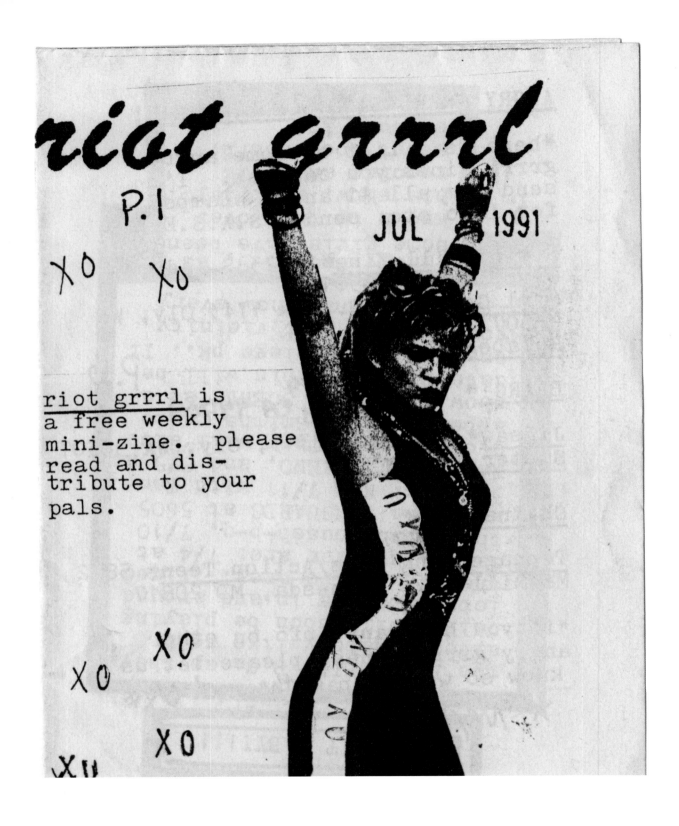

riot grrrl

P.1

XO XO

JUL 1991

riot grrrl is
a free weekly
mini-zine. please
read and dis-
tribute to your
pals.

XO

XO

XO

XO

there has been a proliferation of
angry grrrl zines in recent months,
mainly due to the queezy feeling we
girls get in our sto..machs when we
contemplate the general lack of girl
power in society as awhole, and in
the punk rock underground specifica-
ly. In this long hot summer we are
presently experiencing, sme of us
girls thought it was time we put .
our collective angry heads together
and do a mini-zine, and put it out
as often as possible. Hey, theres
also a sale on at kinko's now, so
if you know anyone who would want
one of these, it would only cost
¢6 to copy it for them. We'll try
to keep everyone posted on all the
rockin' girl events that are gonna
happen as the summer progresses, and
maybe we'll spotlight 1 or 2 special girls who make our lives a
little easier to stand. we would
of course appreciate suggestions
or comments. Please send to:
        RIOT GRRRL
1830 Irving st. NW, W.D.C. 20010
P·3   XXOO,
            The riot girl gang

RIOT GRRRL 1 (EXCERPT)

Love, Allison

-O.K.. this is gonna be my weekly section on the latest cool scams/ideas I've scavenged for the good of the people. As we all now know, Robin Hooh is definately not no Kevin Kostner- Robin Hood is a girl &she is your friend.

1. Riot Trick: When you need to slash/pop some fucker's (cops) car tire,and don't wanna get caught, you can just get a piece of wood w/ a nail coming up through it perpendicular and position it behind tire of said parked vehicle. They'll back into it & tire can slash itself when you're long gone. (courtesy S. GAMBOA)

2. Stamp Scam: I just found out about this one and cant figure out where I've been all these months... rub bar soap (dry?), over your stamp on letters to friends & be sure to mention in the letter that you

cont. p. 5

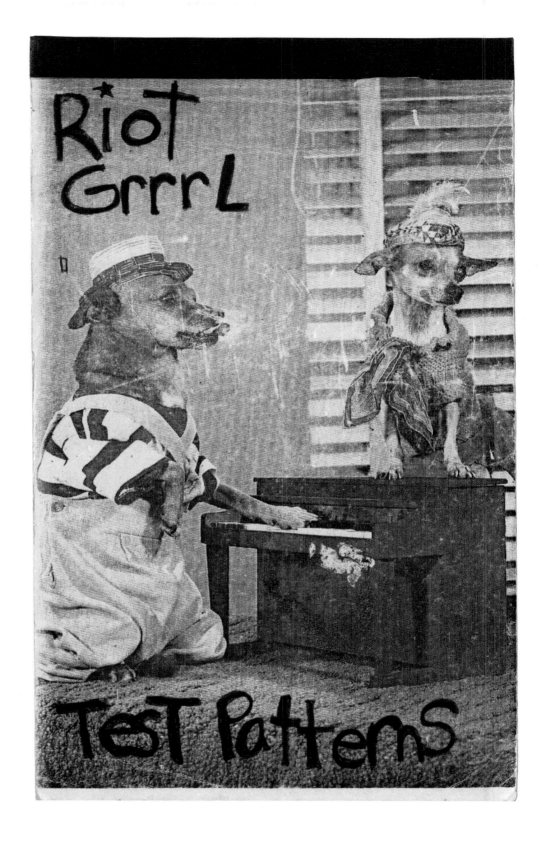

Riot GrrrL

TeST PatternS

Some important questions facing girl-punks in the 90's....

- How can we make our scenes less white in both numbers + ideology?

- How can we boot support/educate + non-punk feminists? Should we draw from

- How can we draw up a program (fluctuating) that encompasses Race, class + gender relations (species too?) w/out have any be seen as central or MOST PRESSING.... ie) for expediency sake NOT doing outreach w/ punks of color, NOT including music/zines by lesbian punks, NOT having vegan food available at functions etc. ... THESE ISSUES MUST BE INCORPORATED FROM THE BEGINNING, anti-racist
  - speciest
  - heterosexist
  - classist

  work can not be written in the margins, they MUST BE CENTRAL

What is riot grrrl???.....

we don't know yet.... you tell us. Here are some questions we came up w/ that face us.

[ie this is what _we_ wanna do ①, how do you think we should do it, ② What do ya think is good/bad, should be added/changed about our goals ③ How do you think you could ~~help~~ be RIOT G?

A) print fliers for, set up, house, feed shows for girl bands.

B) Help spread word of R.G. by ~~xer~~ zeroxing on letters + dist. or word of mouth/media pub.

C) start holding R.G. meetings in your town.

D) Start a band/solo project + send tape to R.G. (we may want to use specific songs for compilation tapes or make a record)

E) make a zine

F) buy R.G. products

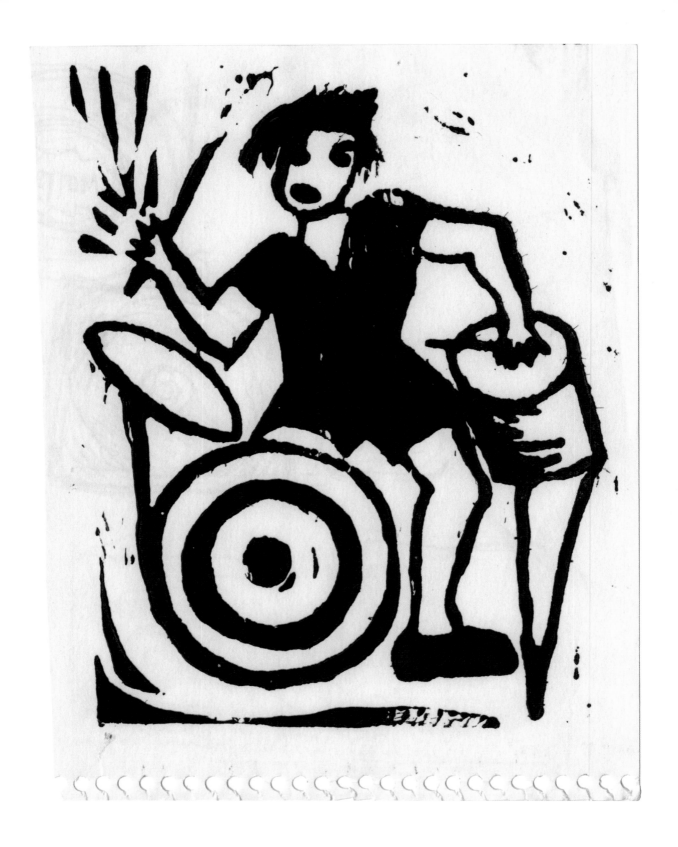

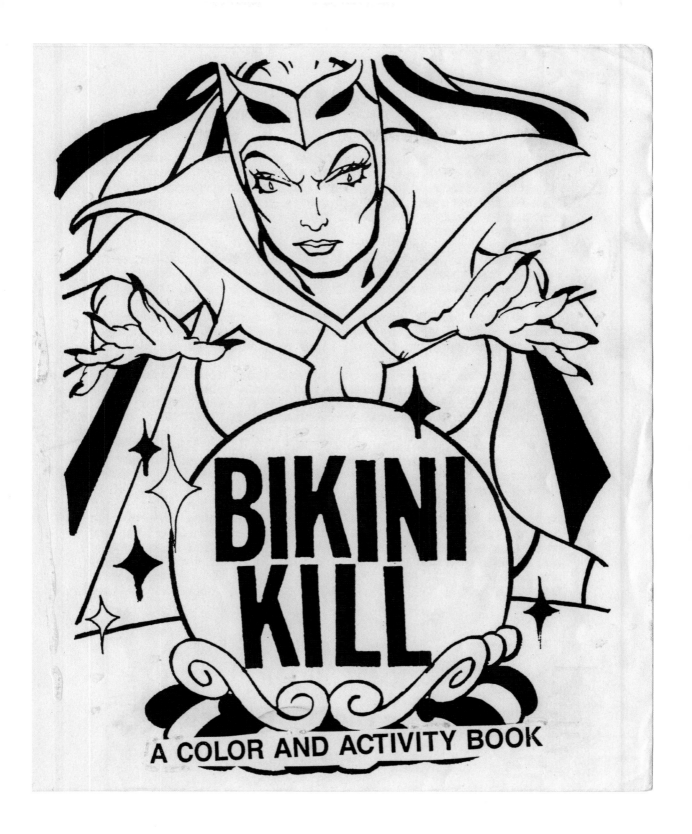

BIKINI KILL 1 (EXCERPT)

Bikini Kill is a band and this is our little thing to give out at shows etc...AND THEN THERE'S THE REVOLUTION.

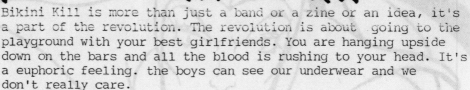

Bikini Kill is more than just a band or a zine or an idea, it's a part of the revolution. The revolution is about going to the playground with your best girlfriends. You are hanging upside down on the bars and all the blood is rushing to your head. It's a euphoric feeling. the boys can see our underwear and we don't really care.

I'm so sure that lots of girls are also in revolution and we want to find them. Sure our revolution has a lot to do with making ourselves important enough to start a revolution, but we also don't care about this....Because what makes us feel good without hurting others IS good. This society isn't my society cuz this society hates women and I don't. This society doesn't want us girls to feel happy or powerful in anyway.

My girlfriends help me stop crying and start looking towards whats important (revolution) my girlfriends know the revolution (sex) my girlfriends aren't owned by me BUT have cringing and choking on boy cum in common (revolution) MY GIRLFRIENDS WANT REVOLUTION GIRL STYLE NOW.

Being a sexy and powerful female is one of the most subversive projects of all. (we are the preistesses of a new kind of power oh yeah.)

We know we are not like this due to any weird gene formation or luck or trick. We are how we are from working together with our eyes open and having experience and getting help from out Moms and friends. We vow to struggle against the "J" word (jealousy) the killer of GIRL LOVE. We are not specail, anyone can do it. ENCOURAGEMENT IN THE FACE OF INSECURITY is a slogan of the revolution.

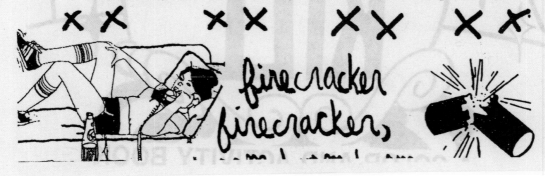

BIKINI KILL

anthem

```
justin likes surf music
justin likes surf music
justin likes surf music
justin likes surf music
it killed my friends
it killed my friends
it killed my friend,
it's happening again
REPEAT

in the trailer when Chris is gone
turn on the radio to here his
favorite song
turn on the radio to here his
favorite song

hardcore generation
hardcore generation
hardcore generation
hardcore generation
teenage boy generation
teenage boy generation
not my generation
not my generation

it doesn't speak to me
no not at all
I don't see anything
there's something wrong
I can't understand
you're favorite song

you will never hear surf music again
```

writing and words
by Tobi Vail

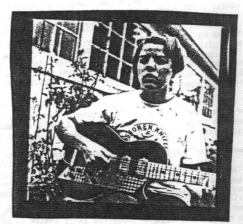

This is a picture of TOBI.
She is BIKINI KILL's
drummer. She also
sings and plays guitar.

BIKINI KILL 1 (EXCERPT)

So okay, I want to write about anthem...one time when I
was sitting in the smithfield giant henry boys vern and
justin came up to me and asked if I wanted to go play
drums with them in their practice space and so, thinking
that maybe the cute one (chris jordan, naturally) would
stop by, I agreed.After a while of practicing at an incredible volume and trying to figure out which songs were Black
Flag covers and which songs were Giant Henry songs I started
to feel classic dork girl symptoms coming over me. I mean,
think about it...what if they <u>were</u> playing a Black Flag
song and I was playing drums that were totally else?!!!
Then I would be a complete jerk...and I kept psyching
myself out over this and then when we finally switched
instruments I was relieved and decided to sing into the
microphone. The words that came into my head= anthem.

But one thing that I want to make clear is that the names
have been changed to protect the innocent. Which means only
just that the words are more about what happened to me as
a teenage punk rocker in love hanging out with my boyfriend's
crowd and its a true story and it all has to do with....YOKO.
um...so if you have ever gone out with anybody in a band
then you have been most likely been made to feel unimportant
or excluded at least once or twice. I know when I was in
highschool I spent way too much time trying to figure out
how to fit in to the guy scene instead of realizing that
my band and my songs and my whole thing was just as cool,
just as interesting, just as valid, just as important as
theirs. And maybe it did just so happen to be that way
and maybe that's just the way it was and maybe nobody was
trying to make me feel left out but all of that doesn't
really count because, in effect, I was paralyzed. ANd
the more I think about it the more it tells me about how
underground music can be really just as oppressive, and
in a lot of the same ways even, as anything else. I mean
if you look at the fact that most bands are mostly or all
guys and then look at how if you are a girl who is hanging
out with a band you have less say then they do because
everything is totally based on what their band is doing
then you start to see how the whole thing is sort of structured
to make girls feel dumb. From band practice schedules to
various band projects to shows to tours to recording to
everything revolves around the band...boys. And I think
most girls know what it feels like to sit around in your
boyfriend's bedroom, talking about records with all of his
friends and having a lot of what you say (that is if you
even bother to say anything) either dismissed or misunderstood.

And a lot of guys give their girlfriends rock lessons so that they can learn and memorize the important details for future reference. Don't get me wrong, talking about bands is one of my favorite pass times, I just think that alot of times it is done in a way that makes other people feel left out and that all too often its us girls who feel like we don't know anything worthy of mmention***REMEMBER*** --there's nothing wrong with being a dork unless you don't have other dorks to bond with and all too often us dork girls live in isolation, like donna says: misfits unite!-- um...and well it all comes down to YOKO ONO. You see, part of the revolution(GIRL STYLE NOW) is about rescuing our true heroines from obscurity, or in Yoko's case, from disgrace.

So part of what your boyfriend teaches you is that Yoko ONo broke up the Beatles. And as his girlfriend, according to this, you could very easily do the same thing to him and he has to be careful that this doesn't happen. In essence, besides being completely unfair to both you and yoko this works in a way that makes you into the opposite of his band and its that whole western duality thing about women and also about forbidden fruit and all that bullshit and when you are being made into the opposite of his band you are sort of being relegated to the audience and it takes that much longer for it to become a real idea that you could participate instead of just watch. One way that this is evident is in the movies. Name one movie about a band in which the girlfriend is not made into the evil diversion. There are two that I can think of off the top of my head.(and they always want to know why I hate the movies) But besides being the victim of the girlfriend-is-distraction thing Yoko was so fucking ahead of her time. I mean in a lot of ways she is the first punk rock girl singer ever. What she was doing was so completely unheard of and she needs to be recognized for what she did, provide a true alternative to the corporate bullshit john lennon was faced with in the beatles at that time. Not to mention that the Plastic No Band was totally subversive politically, in form and content. ...those early records are absolutely incredible nd name another asian woman in rock...I can't think of ny...um so let it be known, from now on, that Yoko Ono aved the way, in more ways then one for us angry grrl ockers and maybe in the future girls will learn to question he motives behind the need in music for so many standards. for one refuse to be the opposite of any band and encourage hers to do the same.

BIKINI KILL 1 (EXCERPT)

so i guess anthem is just about me sitting on my boyfriend's
bed in highschool and having an argument with his friend
About jimi hendrix 'you will never hear surf music again'
and how hardcore had become just as stupid and tame as surf
music was in the '60s and that it was time for something new.
I think maybe Bikini Kill is going to write your favorite
song.

ANGRY GRRRL ZINES

jigsaw fanzine issue #3 is going to be out shortly, available
for $1 and two stamps from: Jigsaw PO Box 2345
Olympia, WA 98507

The New episode is all about NEWmodrockers and the Jigsaw
underground. Jigsaw fanzine is an ANGRY GRRRL ZINE. This
is one of many...Girl Germs is Molly and Allison's fanzine.
They are in a band called Bratmobile together with Michelle
and Julie sometimes. The first issue came out a few months
ago, around X-mas and was full of local scene info and the
usual angry grrrl talk about REVOLUTion. My favorite part
is Allison's editorial about the Lodge and Molly's thing
about girl rappers...it's fun, intelligent and completely
on the mark. Send stamps to.... Girl Germs PO Box 3060
Eugene, OR 97401.

Word has it that Laura of SISTER NOBODY is putting out a
new issue featuring an in depth article on PATTI SMITH.
Also, last I heard, Donna Dresch was on the verge of
going to the printers to do the third issue of chainsaw
when she got a phone call from Maria of Holy Rollers drum
goddess fame begging her to make room for a couple of
short stories she had just written. So write and see if
they made it in or not. Both sister nobody and CHAINSAW
are availble from:
send stamps and a dollar Donna/Laura 2336 Market
#128 SF CA 94114

oh yeah and BIKINI KILL is an angry grrl zine too and
we are gonna do more so stay tuned. Also, Tamra, of
Doris fame used to do a zine called Someone Said that
was totally inspirational and paved the way for years
to come and I just heard that she is singing in a band
again..YAY!!! which makes me SO happy, and they are
called THIRTEEN and are going to be playing in SeattlE
on February 28.

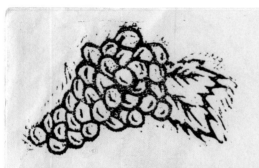

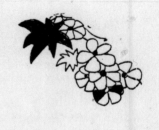

STOP the J word jealousy from killing girl LOVE

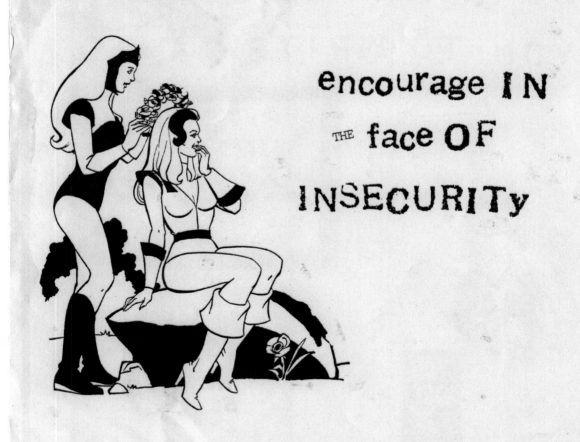

encourage IN
THE face OF
INSECURITy

BIKINI KILL 1 (EXCERPT)

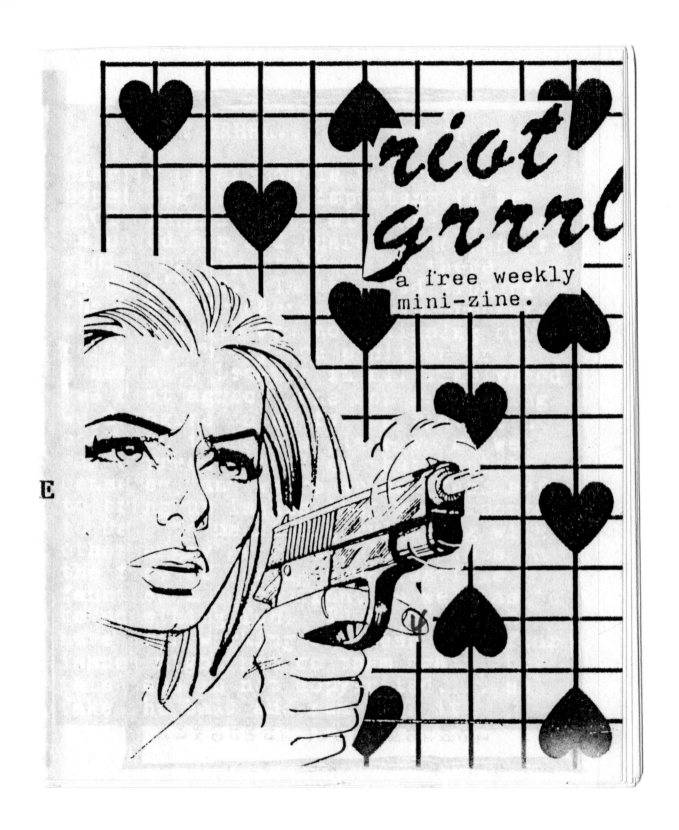

RIOT GRRRL 4 (EXCERPT)

RIOT GRRRL... believe in me!

Clarity of agenda is not really something that is important to me. RIOT GRRRL is a total concept. there is no editor and there is no concrete vision or expectation, or there shouldn't be. In the tradition of the NEW Modrockers and Hypocrobrats, we riot grrls are not aligning ourselves with any one position or consensus, because in all likelyhood xwe dont agree. One concrete thing we do agree on so far is that it's cool/fun to have a place we're we can express ourselves that wont be censored, and we're we can feel safe to bring up issues that are important to us. To me riot grrrl along with other angry grrrl zine's, exists in the face of boring nowheresville fanzinedom to confront as well as to be something fun. Those of us who have been working on these past four issues might not do them again, but this name is not copywrited.... so take the ball and run with it!

RIOT GRRRL 4 (EXCERPT)

AND THINK

ABOUT WHAT YOU DO
ABOUT WHY YOU DO WHAT YOU DO
ABOUT HOW IT AFFECTS OTHER PEOPL
ABOUT HOW IT AFFECTS YOU

Contact **riot grrrl!** HQ at:
1830 Irving St. NW 20009
202-332-3119

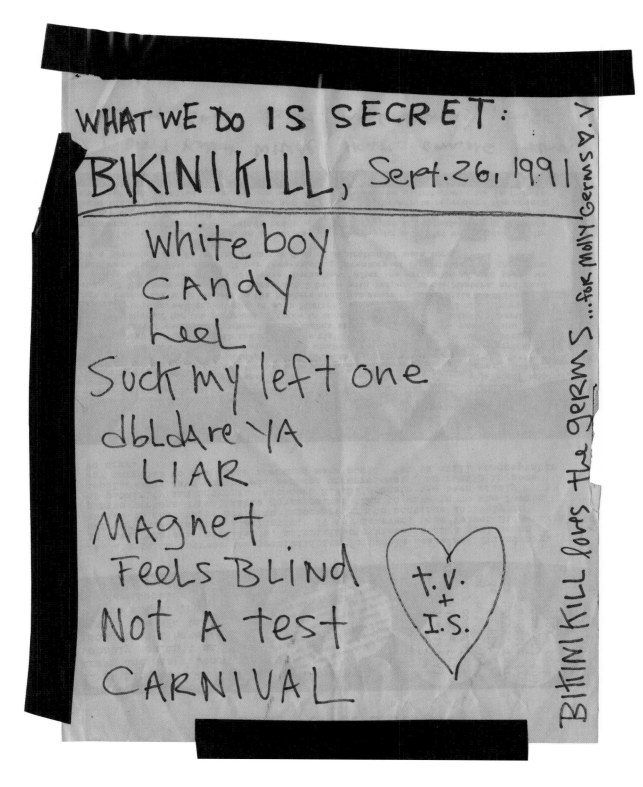

BIKINI KILL SET LIST

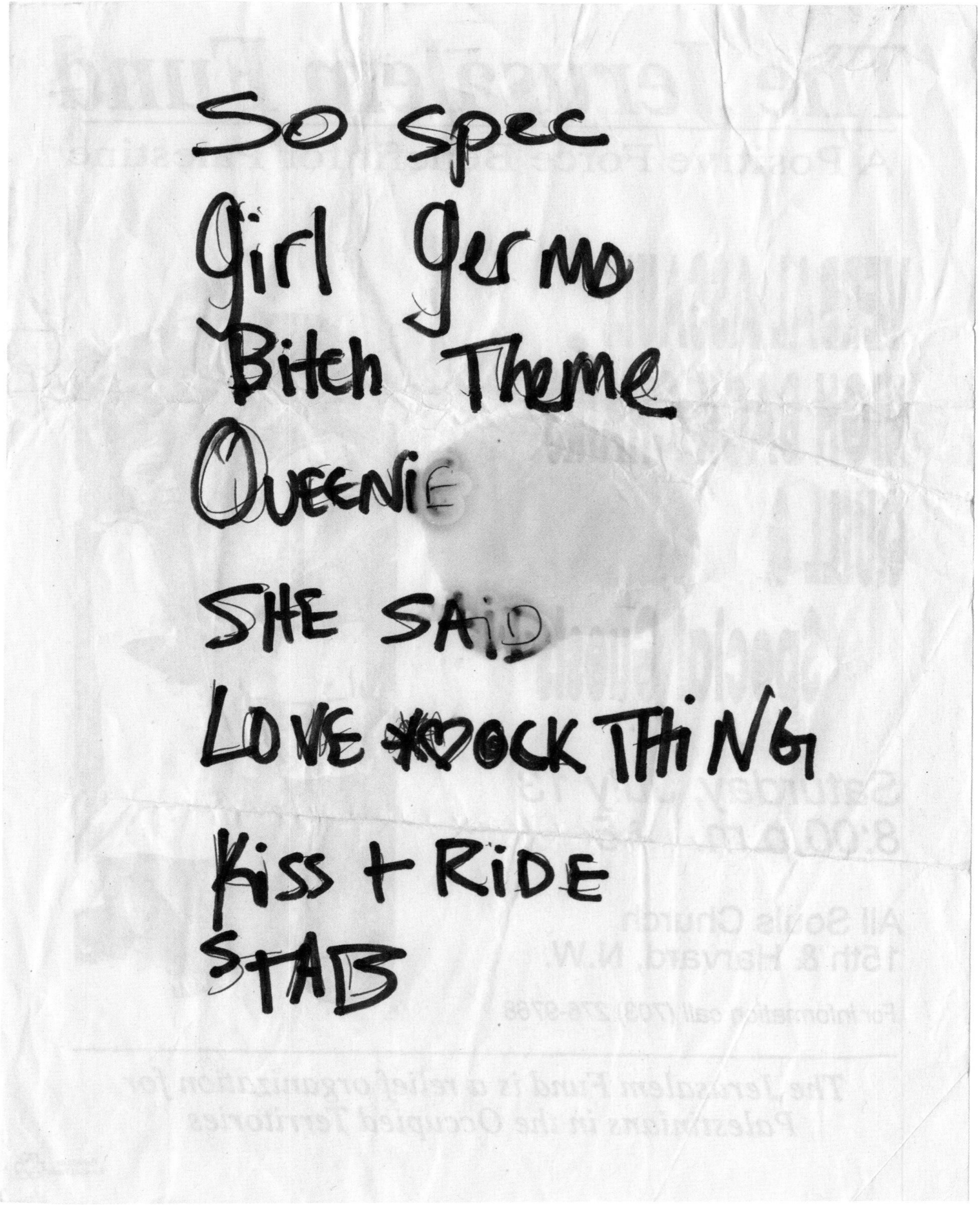

So spec
Girl Germs
Bitch Theme
Queenie

She Said

Love *♥Ock Thing

Kiss + Ride
Stab

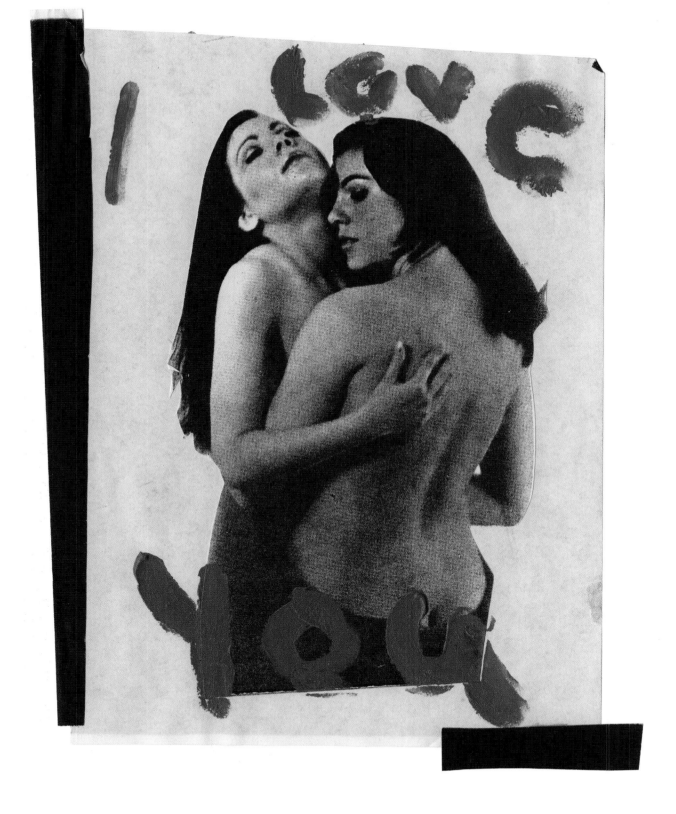

ARTWORK

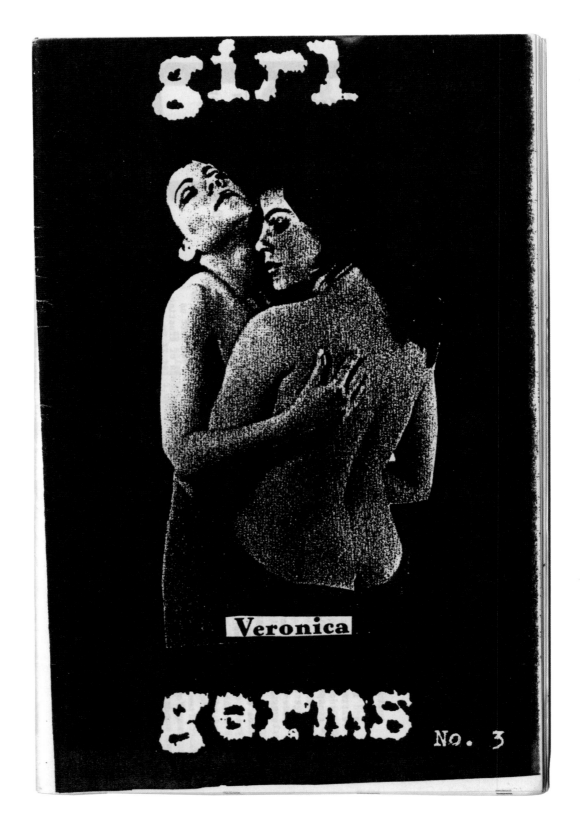

girl

Veronica

germs No. 3

Chapter I
THE RAPTURE

"Round in knowledge and square in dealings..."

sQUARE aND cIRCLE cLUB

Hanging out homeless with Lainga all day is the safest place to be—buttoning each others' undershirts and sharing lipstick popcorn sodapoppin around. Here we can be the hipocribrats that we are because loud is real and laughing is crying is laughing. We're so hungry, and we never stop eating. We're antipatient we're suckers. If you're not a sQUARE you're not a sucker. W're sQUARES. We're gullible 'cause we believe. But we know the conspiracy we feel it in our spit and we wish to spit on The White Boy with no shame...and we call him W-H-I-T-E B-O-Y (and he calls us "baby") and we do together what we can't face apart. We try to stalk Him down and brat in His face when He suckers our sQUAREness. We are sQUARES for sure, but we are cIRCLES too. Don't forget it by mapping us two-dimensional or by setting His cock standard of anti-SQUARENESS which makes us deny and shame that part in us so dear. "Dare to be a Dork." We see and constantly must struggle to see the connectedness of all His actions— of all action and inaction we must connect the dots so bad. This circle, our desire and necesity for total rev-o-lution totally, must acknowledge all want and hate as valid and utterly real-istic. Still, we must love too, and somehow we do, somehow. As hets, we so often compromise and love (pour/give/invest energy into) those who hurt us and/or perpetuate what hurts us. The sQUARE is our awkwardness of trusting under the spell of this annhilating system/society.

"Don't let life turn you into an asshole" but remembering that "violence in self-defense is called intelligence"—

cIRCLES exist within sQUARES, and sQUARES exist within cIRCLES. We're struggling and scheming in vicious circles, we're dying to survive emotionally (and also physically). We must protect ourselves and each other from emotional death.

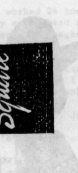

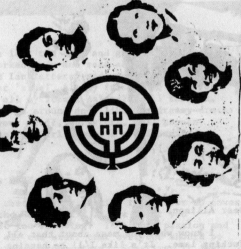

SQUARE AND CIRCLE CLUB

dARE tO bE a sQUARE

'cause Cool won't spare anyone, 'cause Cool kills. We will deal with you straight up with love with hate with all the fucked up shit we've been taught and bombarded with. And it will be awkward it will come out "wrong" it might sound ridiculous overreacting and irrational it will be vindictive "unfair" and inarticulate. Cause sQUARE and cIRCLE don't cross each other out and this is the REALITY of our lives. We are totally goofy one minute and screaming blue murder the next... He calls us hipocrit He doesn't get it He expects an explanation articulation justification rationalization maybe He expects us to kiss his ass and suck His dick--and believe me, we have and we do but maybe we don't really want to. Maybe we want the Best, but we know how to get by, how to pass, how to survive. There's a price to pay and He wants us to know how lucky we are. Our security = compromise and we deal with these circumstances 24 hours a day, whether we're on the front line or not. In our cIRCLE we recognize oppression and privilege and how it affects everything and everyone-- including ourselves and our friends and our scene. We draw it on our skin we paint it on the wall we cry it over the phone we eat it for dinner we slap it in faces. We battle systematic sleep techniques and refuse to kill the messenger who brings bad news. And we try so fuckin hard to see past our hate to sift through the fuck so we can love each other. Oh sQUARES and cIRCLES!, believe that we're all in a process and that we're trying and living at the same time.

Round in knowledge and square in dealings, i love Lai-nga.

♥a.

2

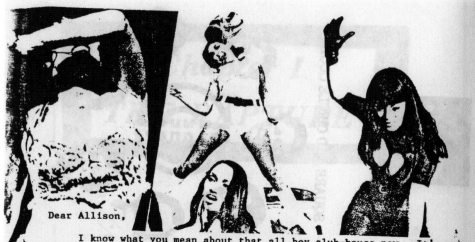

Dear Allison,

I know what you mean about that all boy club-house now. It's so
fucking lame. It's like I'll be hanging out with boys and all, then
they'll just disappear and I won't see them until the next show or
whatever. And whenever I see them they're all together. If I catch
one alone they aren't all that interesting, probably because they don't
have the security of their boyfriends. What is up? It's so hard to
have pals in Olympia! When I'm outside Olympia it seems I have people
to hang out with, it's just in Olympia...

So what are we going to do about the all-boy club house? I think
we should bomb it. Jealous? Well, I don't know, I just think they're
dumb for being so exclusive. We aren't that way. We include the boys.
We must be better than them. I think you're right, the boys are
insecure, or no, you say 'girl intimidation.' Whatever. I feel left
out. It sucks. Let's kick their ass. I can't wait til you and Molly
revisit Olympia.   See you love,

Dana

P.S. That boy in DC never wrote back. BOY CONSPIRACY.

Dear Molly and Allison

I've just finished reading your fanzine and I have to say that
you are all very strong and cool women! Never be afraid of being
misunderstood by anybody, because if they can't take the truth as
you girls tell it...well fuck them!

I've been to too many shows where the crowd was such that me and
my girlfriends were afraid to even get near the stage. I mean, even
if you are able to control the space around you and defend yourself,
usually some big stage diver (who is male and taller than you!) will
boot you in the head! I know that people use the music to get out
their anger and frustration, but what about our anger and frustration!
You are so right, we have to reclaim the music on and off the stage.

I know that our world is a really twisted one, I mean, I just
read yesterday that some dude wants to blow up the moon with a nuclear
device! His theory is that it would give the earth perfect weather
by eliminating the lunar gravitational pull on our planet. Since the
moon has always been a symbol for women in particular (like the
goddess Diana) this is just another 'fine' example of what our world
thinks of us. But voices like yours can't be stopped, and we in turn
will keep writing and working on our own revolution.

Love,

Beth Waldron
Lansdoune, PA

—3—

Molly and Allison

I worked 24 hours in the last two days and grabbed Girl Germs with my empty head and overworked body and read about my girl Maria on a couple of pages, Guy and Ian letters, and every good-damn page (in the bathtub). Really great 'zine! All my friends at Food For Thought will see it tonight, all my lezzie gal-pals will tune in, all their housemates will pass it around and, like the dreamy-dreams extolled on pages 1 and 29, your stuff, our stuff, will happen. Beautifully... Thanks Big-Time for Girl Germs. I'm all excited.
    Gravity,
          Juliana

Hey it's me, your step-sister MARY--

WOW!!!! I've just been reading your fanzine from cover to cover. what's goin on out there in the Northwest? I rave about you 'cause I think it's great what you're doing. It's pure passion and ideas and anger and love and all the stuff that everyone should be feeling every day about everything around them. Sometimes it just seems like there's not enough time but I know that's bullshit. Thanks so much for the FANZINE and keep me posted man. When I have more time I'll tell you ALL--Keep rockin and I'll do my part too.
    Step Blood Love--
          Mary

Molly and Allison,

This is Laura. We never found the bass player. The band is screwed. We decided to kill it since it didn't work out. Depressive. I mean-- none of us really knew how to play music. We played by ear. None of us ever took a lesson in our lives. It has a homemade taste too. How did you start Girl Germs? How do you get it printed, mailed out, etc? Where do you get your info? I freaked out at the mailbox wondering who the hell Molly and Allison are, but it finally hit me.
    Lates,
          Laura
P.S. Things suck and hopefully in college I'll start a new wave band called 40 Flamboyant Godfast Days. Think it'll work? Heck, if my sister's friends didit, I can too!

Dearest Allison and Molly,

Issue #1 is sooo cool. You can do no wrong. I love your editorials. I especially dig the Bikini Kill lyrics. Do they have a record or any music available to the public? Suggestion for Girl Germs #3: the strict abortion laws that recently have been passed in some states and how the gov't is slowly taking women's rights away-- what rights we have left! I know it has nothing to do with music but it pertains to the lives of girls/women everywhere. I'll lend my services any way possible. Some of my female influences are: Bangles, Go-Go's, the Runaways, STP, Lunachicks, Kim Gordon, L7, Babes in Toyland, Yo-Yo, and Madonna (she's beautiful and headstrong).
As for Kerri, Kerri is Kerri. Kerri is wack. She'll be 18 in August. Kerri is really beautiful. she is my friend and I love her. I guess Girl Happy! is o!k. Erin Smith thinks I should call my band Leather Market, after my street name. What do you think?
    Best,
          Anna Garza

Chapter II
THE TRIBULATION

But you told me to!?! an excerpt from 1989 by julie

Cigarette pot smoke beer wine whiskey armpit sweaty moldy mildewy punk rock house. here we are again. same people, they're always the same, ever since oh, 1984 or so. they come and go but basically stay the same HE's got a case of schmidt altogether plus a half rack of some other shit. it don't matter, it'll never be enough. HE'll be back at the store before 9:00 p.m.. we always get there early and watch cops on the Fox network and laugh about how wouldn't it be funny if we were watching it and the cops were coming into the house on the screen and it was the house where we were. ha ha ha. i'll bet i'm the only one wishing that would happen. i mean i'd probably go to jail but at least i wouldn't be getting my head knocked in by HIM again. so tonight i don't wanna drink and as usual HE says drink and so i do, not wanting to be hit and humiliated in front of them again. and anyway if i drink enough it won't hurt 'til morning. but if i drink i won't have my wits about me if tonight's the night. i make a run for it. ahh, who the fuck am i kidding i don't have anyplace to go that HE wouldn't find me. so later on about a half rack in my body later i'm sitting around talking to matt and he likes me and everyone knows it. but we're only talking, i know better and besides i don't like him anyway.

"BITCH, PUT YOUR HAND ON HIS DICK!!" "fuck you, no way!" it's a feeble reply i know but i also know it's not going to do me any good and i better just deal with it. i guess tonight is the night i am prostituted. matt says "hey, no don't make her do that, she doesn't want to, besides she's your old lady and you'll kick my ass"

"NO FUCK YOU BOTH, DO IT NOW AND KEEP IT THERE!!!!!" i don't move and so HE does it for me. now my hand is in a forced position on matt's half hard pants covered (thank god) dick. "SO BITCH IS IT HARD?" i say nothing, i'm humiliated, i am shrinking. HE tells everyone to come and look. i am not really even there anymore but i am. my hand doesn't want to be there and neither do i but both of us know better than to get up and run. i am scared to do anything and matt knows better too. he's not enjoying it even though he likes me. everyone knows how it is but they all humor HIM and laugh, they know better too.

much later, oh 2:00 or 3:00 a.m. we're on our way home. HE's driving even though i begged HIM to let me drive, you see i haven't been drinking for hours. HE's still plugging away i mean as much as you can plug when you've been swilling since 5:00 or so. we get on to the highway and I can feel it coming. i can't run, i can't hide.

"FUCKING SLUT YOU FUCKING SLUT YOU PROBABLY WANT TO FUCK HIM YOU FUCKING SLUT BITCH" and then it happens ***** the first blow is administered to the left side of my head. "what was i supposed to do you told me to, you made me????" i don't know why i even bothered, HE didn't hear me.

"YOU FUCKING SLUT! YOU ARE A WORTHLESS PIECE OF SHIT!" the last phrase is one of HIS favorites in fact HE makes me say it about myself sometimes "i am a worthless piece of shit" i believe it sometimes, most of the time. as if the words weren't enough i

5

get hit smashed smacked punched the whole way home. it's a long way home. i wanna go home. where is home? home's supposed to be safe.

Then, HE passes out thank god. i carry HIM into the house. my five foot three 118 pound body carries HIS dead weight drunk six foot three 145 pound asshole self to bed. just like i did so many times. we're home. i go home. but i'm not home. home should be safe. i don't have home.

You know, it didn't happen every day, but it didn't have to. once should've been enough. I WASN"T DUMB! I TRIED TO LEAVE. A LOT! you fucking try to leave with a gun at your head. i dare you. it came to the point where i didn't have to get shot. I DIED. INSIDE. i walked and talked and breathed and shit but i was not living anymore. now i am trying to be alive but i'm still afraid. i don't even know if it's worth it. i've been away from HIM and alcohol for over a year. HE left ME, finally. but HE still exists, in reality and in my mind and i'm terrified. HE is out of proportion and above the law. it's all i can do to wake up and that's only one person one time in my life and there are more where that came from. and i wanna be - sedated,related,elated past high,great,a date,eight plus sixteen,better,get a letter,wear a sweater tight,thrive,drive,be alive and o.k.,see a show,tie a bow,let it go away,panty raid,good grade,and mostly UNAFRAID.

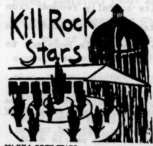
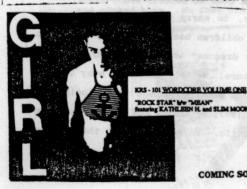
contribute please,
issued i
experie
re is (

— 6 —

57

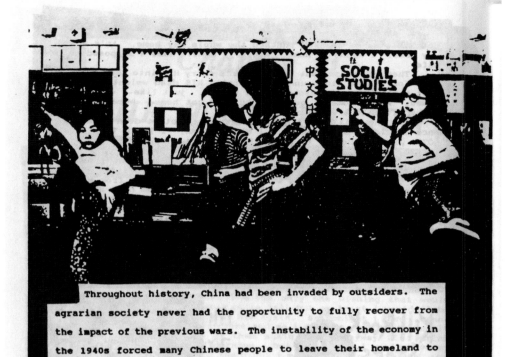

Throughout history, China had been invaded by outsiders. The agrarian society never had the opportunity to fully recover from the impact of the previous wars. The instability of the economy in the 1940s forced many Chinese people to leave their homeland to seek work in the nearby colonies.

Ma Choy, my mama, remembered that many of the people from Taishan, a small village near Guangzhou, journeyed to Hong Kong to escape hunger and starvation. The Taishan people migrated to Hong Kong for it was relatively close to their village. The people who stayed in Taishan were subject to work from dawn to dusk and rationed to one bowl of rice a day. During these years, many people died from starvation than killed in previous battles. The government confiscated all the agricultural goods produced by the people and exported them to raise capital to reconstruct the economy.

As China continued to be torn by internal upheaval, my grandmother encouraged her daughter, Ma Choy, to accept Tin's proposal of marriage. Ma Choy left China in 1949, shortly before the Communists came to power, to marry Tin in Hong Kong. My parents wanted to have seven children because a family with nine members symbolized the "nine dragons" which meant strength and prosperity in the Chinese culture. We only wanted to stay in Hong Kong long enough to save enough money to escape the colonization under the British empire. In 1977, my family and i left Hong Kong and traveled all over the Pacific. We immigrated to the U.S. in 1980.

It has been a continuous struggle to retain our cultural identity in a society which denies non-anglos their identity. Although the dominant group has emphasized "assimilation" into the

mainstream culture, our family has resisted the ideology of the melting pot. It is important to emphasize the physical differences between the Chinese and whites, thereby, "assimilation" has been difficult for non-anglos. Besides, we are very proud of our Chinese heritage and would like to maintain our cultural identity.

My mama has played a very important role in preserving and retaining our Chinese traditions. She would only allowed us to speak Taishan and Guangzhou language in her house. Her teachings were centered around collectivity rather than individuality. My mama maintained our Chinese culture through the vibrant folk tales; celebration of Chinese New Year and Moon Day; Budda religion; herbal medicine; food; and crafts which have been passed down from mother to daughter in China.

One of the family traditions in Ma Choy's family has been to serve dong with all Chinese holidays. Dong is made from sweet rice, beans, sun-dried sausage, salt-cured egg, peanuts, and black mushrooms---then wrapped carefully with bamboo leaves and secured with strings. The women and children in the family would gathered around the dining table to prepare dong and tell each other stories about their experiences in China.

> The Taishan people were given few days notice before Japan's invasion of China. The peasants worked vigorously night and day to prepare for their hide-outs in the hills. The women and children were given the responsibility to make dong. While the women prepare the rice, beans, cured eggs, etc., the children gathered and washed the bamboo leaves. Later, the women threw batches of dong into the boiling water and cooked them. Ma Choy was allowed to eat one dong each day during the war.

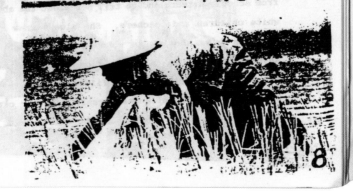

8

My grandmother taught mama how to prepare dong in China.

Ma Choy was very close to her mama. The bonding of mother and daughter relationship made it very difficult for either person to part from one another. When my grandmother urged Ma Choy to go to Hong Kong to marry Tin, the decision was made out of the love she had for Ma Choy. The political-economic turmoil during 1949 in China was unsafe for many Chinese people. Ma Choy also realized the instability of her homeland, thereby, followed her mama's wishes.

My relationship with mama is also very close. She has made many sacrifices with her own life so that i can have a college education. My way of thanking and appreciating her has been to excel in school. I think my good grades has made her and the Chinese community very proud. I don't get good grades for myself but for others who had sacrificed their personal goals to help me get where i am today.

ONLY SHE SAID SHE LOVED ME
SHE ONLY SAID SHE LOVED ME
SHE SAID ONLY SHE LOVED ME
SHE SAID SHE ONLY LOVED ME
SHE SAID SHE LOVED ONLY ME
SHE SAID SHE LOVED ME ONLY

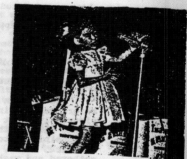

Mama have never complained about discriminatory practices in the work force or white world. Yet I remembered i used to run home from school in tears and to tell her about the abusiveness from the white children and teachers. She always knew and understood the problems i was having in school. Mama taught me never to say anything that would take attention away from the white children. She told me to keep a low profile and an over-achiever, minority student would only alienate herself from her classmates. Mama's advice was for my own safety in the white world.

9

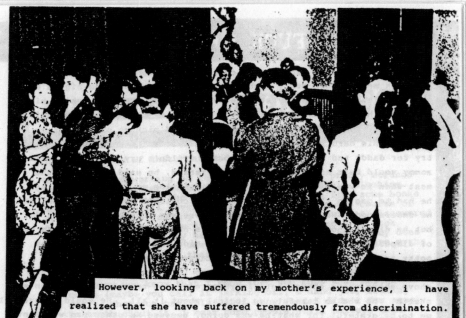

However, looking back on my mother's experience, i have realized that she have suffered tremendously from discrimination. The reason for this has to do with the fact that even though she was educated in China, the only employment mama could attain was a dishwashing job. I remembered she used to work anywhere from 10 to 16 hours a day. She was denied economic mobility due to her English proficiency. As i get older, i understood the terrible discriminatory practices she went through and the sacrifices she made for her family.

Lainga

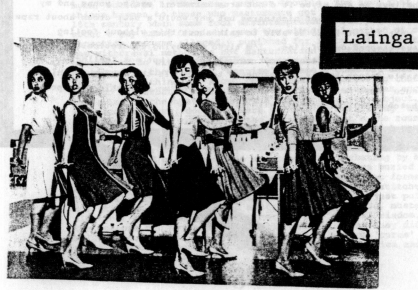

FUCK OFF MAN!

When I was little my dad used to come into my room to read me stories and tuck me into bed every night. I remember now; on some nights he would smile in this really strange way, and shut the door behind him. Sometimes he would masturbate on the edge of my bed, or on the chair by my crib, sometimes. Other nights he would pick me up and put my mouth on his hard penis and I couldn't fit it all inside but I had to try for daddy and it hurt so much but I couldn't cry 'cause if I did mommy would hear and she wouldn't understand, he said. It hurt the most when he would try and put his penis inside my infant vagina and he had to gag me then, because he knew I couldn't help but scream, and he understood. He told me he wished there was something he could do, but he didn't know what since my diapers had to be changed., I was out of diapers much earlier than most other kids, my mom told me. I was potty trained but that didn't help because my dad had to change me into my nightie anyway. So he would rub his penis around and then shove shove shove shove, but always careful not to make me bleed on my sheets. he was so careful, so logical about it all. He would always tell me to be grateful for what he was doing, because no other man would ever want me. AS IF I knew what all this meant when I was fucking two years old anyway.

So now I'm older and men do want me but the way they want can be so sick, and my insides are twisted. I never talk about what my dad did to me; I used to but my friends acted so strange about it all. It wasn't treated like an event in my life, it was treated like a stigma, a tragic handicap I can never overcome. It was a big deal to me, but I don't wand to be treated as an object to be pitied. Sometimes my friends don't believe me and maybe it's not true because I was so young and my dad said I had a lot of nightmares but why would a baby dream about rape rape? What I want is to be able to talk about this without feeling like I've stepped out of line. I'm tired of having theoretical, philosophical conversations about sexual assault but not feeling comfortable enough to say "it happened to me? All the burden of this experience must be mine alone. So now that you've read this my experience belongs to you, so deal with it.

think again.

Chapter III

IN THE WILDERNESS

The Many Myths of Masturbation

When I started working on this story I got some pretty strange
reactions. My sister blushed. My boyfriend is still blushing.
And the nice lady at the library, who helped me find some books
on the subject, will never be the same again. In the course of
my sometimes embarrassing research into masturbation I discovered
three things: only diehard Dr. Ruth types seem able to look
you in the eye when they say the word; virtually everybody does
it (though virtually no one admits it); and there are more myths
about masturbation than there are about Zeus.

By Karen Catchpole

Okay. I know you know that I know that you know what masturbation is (maybe you call it jerking off, a hand job, beating
off etc.). What you probably don't know (and I didn't for ages)
is the truth about it. I mean some people still believe that
if you masturbate, terrible things will happen to you-- real
wrath of god stuff. And these are the '90s (that's the 1990s,
not the 1790s). So, once and for all, here's the truth about
masturbation.

FIRST MYTH: Masturbation causes blindness/epilepsy/barrenness/
impotence/fainting fits/hairy palms/madness/schizophrenia/dry
brains (I kid you not)/homosexuality/softness of the spine/
lethargy/dark circles under the eyes (and you thought it was
lack of sleep)/laziness/loss of pubic hair/tumors/constipation/
even death.

If this were true, most of the people on the planet(see next
myth) would be in serious, serious trouble. The idea that bad
things happen to those who masturbate got started during the
18th century when some fool misinterpreted a story in the Bible
about a guy named Onan who used the withdrawal method of cont-
raception and was allegedly punished for it by god. Even though
the withdrawal method is not masturbation and the story had
nothing to do with masturbation (masturbation is never even
mentioned in the Bible), 'Onanism' became a commonly used term
for it. Next thing you know, people started believing that anyone who masturbated would be punished by god, and that accounts
for a lot of the hysterical myths surrounding the subject.
Soon doctors (yes, doctors) were performing horrifying 'cures'
like the complete removal of the clitoris (that's the round,
bulby, sensitive part of the vagina right at the front near the
pubic hair) and blistering of the thighs and genitals with hot
tongs. One particularly gory story goes like this: In 1894 a
seven year old girl from Ohio was caught masturbating by her
parents. They took her to a hospital where doctors buried
her clitoris inside her labia (the flap of skin that forms the
outer lip of the vagina) with four sterling silver stitches.
The girl--following her natural sexual instincts--just pulled
the stitches out and started masturbating again. So, mustering
all their up-to-the-minute, authoritative "medical wisdom,"
the doctors cut her entire clitoris out. (I guess they didn't
malpractice back then.) The scary thing is, these 'cures' were
still being recommended in medical journals in America and
Europe as late as 1940.

12 —

SECOND MYTH: Masturbation is rare.

The next time you've got nothing better to do--like in between copies of
Girl Germs--look around. Most of the people you see--including your Spanish
teacher, your brother's girlfriend, your boss at work--masturbate. Research
(yes, they pay people to ask questions about this stuff) shows that 95
percent of males and at least 70 percent of females masturbate and 90 percent
of the overall population have done it at least once by the time they're 21.
Women generally masturbate more after the age of 30-- the fact that the
female sex drive peaks between age 25 and 35 probably has something to do
with this. But how frequently you do it depends on how strong your personal
sex drive is and how comfortable you are with the idea of masturbating.
Some girls told me they do it almost as often as they brush their teeth (that's
three times a day for those of you who haven't been to the dentist lately).
"I masturbate every day before and after school," says one 15-year-old. "I'm
addicted." On the other hand, some girls never masturbate. "Every time I
try to masturbate I'm dry and unstimulated," 13-year-old Erin said. "I don't
like it." Either way you're okay because there's no rule that says how much
or how little you should masturbate-- or whether you should do it at all.
Just make your own decision based on what you think is right.

THIRD MYTH: Masturbation is bad for you.

Masturbation is only bad for you if you feel so guilty about it that you
develop an unhealthy attitude toward it. In reality, masturbation can be
one of the best ways of getting to know your body. A lot of women who have
trouble having an orgasm (the physical and mental sensation you feel when you
reach a sexual climax) with a partner during intercourse are actually encouraged to masturbate by doctors and psychologists so they can teach themselves
how to have one. Doctors (they've come a long way in the last 200 years or so)
also recommend masturbation to relieve menstrual cramps and as a way to get
rid of sexual tension without having actual intercourse which can result in
getting pregnant or perpetuating a sexually transmitted disease.

FOURTH MYTH: If you masturbate you're not a virgin.

Sixteen-year-old Telita wrote us a letter saying: "I want to masturbate,
but I'm worried I won't be a virgin anymore." Take it from me Telita (and
all the rest of you who are worried about this): Masturbation is not the
same thing as intercourse. So even if you insert fingers or dildos (the
fake plastic penises advertised in the back of those magazines under your
big brother's mattress) or vibrators (battery operated dildos) or whatever (within reason girls) you're still a virgin. Sometimes masturbating
stretches the hymen (the thin membrane that covers the entrance to the
cervix), but it's probably already stretched or even broken from sports
(like horse back riding or gymnastics or circus contortionism) or just from
using tampons. And even if you break the hymen, that doesn't mean you've lost
your virginity.

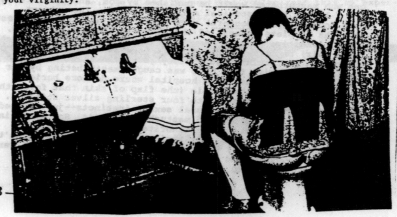

—13—

FIFTH MYTH: You don't have a real orgasm when you masturbate.

Wrong. Research shows that women reach orgasm more often through masturbation
than through intercourse and many say those orgasms are much more intense.
But no matter how great it feels, masturbation probably won't make you want
to give up sex with another person. It will just help you learn about your
body-- what feels good and what doesn't (you know, all that stuff your health
teacher skips over).

SIXTH MYTH: You can hurt yourself masturbating.

"I've been masturbating for two years," writes another worried reader. "Am I
hurting myself?" The truth is, you'd have to be forcing sharp or very big
objects into your vagina before you'd do any damage. Most common forms of
masturbation-- like touching and rubbing the clitoris and/or inserting fingers,
vibrators or dildos-- are very unlikely to cause any kind of damage no matter
how often or vigorously you do it.

SEVENTH MYTH: There is only one way to masturbate.

There are as many ways to masturbate as there are people who do it. (In other
words, a lot). Most girls (according to our fearless researchers) masturbate
by rubbing the clitoris with their fingers or a pillow, by applying pressure
to it with a stream of water, or by squeezing their thighs together. Three-
fourths of women who masturbate prefer to lie on their backs while rubbing
the clitoris with their hands. The rest prefer to do it while lying on their
stomachs, and 20 percent insert fingers, vibrators or dildos into the vagina.
But you won't find any summer school course in masturbation technique. It's
just one of those things that comes naturally. Fantasies are usually part of
masturbation too, in fact some women can have an orgasm just by having a
fantasy without touching themselves at all. Fantasies can be about anything
or anybody that may turn you on. A girl I talked to liked to fantasize about
sex with an older man; another imagined being with a teacher. Some girls
think about having sex with a girlfriend. These fantasies don't necessarily
represent your character (I don't care what Freud would say). So don't freak
out if you fantasize about getting raped* or about having sex with your
brother-- it doesn't mean you really want that to happen.

I'd bet money that none of you will be rushing off to school to tell all your
friends about whether or not you masturbate. And that's fine. I'm not planning
any public speaking tours on the subject either. But at least you know enough
not to fear it, or feel guilty about it and not to do it if you don't want to.
But if you feel like doing it (or if you already are), now you've got the truth.
Mission accomplished.

**How girls around
the country are spending
their free time**

*Karen
Catchpole*

* Editor's Note: "Fantasizing about getting raped" doesn't equal rape in that
rape is about power/control over someone (usually a woman), and when a person
is fantasizing, they are in control of the situation-- she is in control of
the fantasy. Obviously, this type of fantasizing says a lot about our culture/
society, and you may not agree with the point just made so we welcome any
confrontation/debate from readers on this subject. Cool.

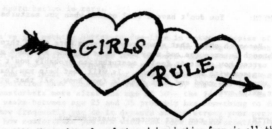

A shout out to the Soulforce...

W. LuV - Jen Smith

One thing that I am finding a lot of comfort and inspiration from is all these girls, states-wide, that have surfaced. These women are young and down with the kids, down with the revolution. But I find their version of the revolution promises something to me that hither to has been ignored. Blatantly, these girls are demanding gender conciousness from both men and women. These women are saying to me (and I am saying to you): I AM NOT going to take shit fr. "the man" where ever "he" manifests "himself," either in the outside world (the square world) or in my friends I think of as good boys or cool boys or good girls or cool girls. I am saying I AM NOT going to scratch yr. eyes out in the girls room when the boys aren't around so that I won't be called a bitch. I AM NOT going to judge you because the jerky sweet boy I used to date, dates you now. Or because you unwittingly fucked him because maybe he didn't tell you the whole truth. I AM NOT going to talk about you behind yr. back because I don't know you. I AM NOT a fucking cat... I AM NOT going to call you the blonde groupie of yr. friends' band. I AM saying (and they are saying) that I am going to respect you from the start and make the assumption that you have a brain and a heart and that because yr. a girl, you know about the fight- OUR FIGHT with "the man." I am not a square and I don't think like a square and I don't bite like a square becuase I am out for the righteuous fight. I will fight the good fight and not tug at yr. fur. And I fight hard to not be a jealous girl or a malicious girl. And I mean to make this a pushy point... revolutionary girl soul force... I said FORCE, mother fucker, I want to FORCE the issue. This injustice has been unsung too long. It's important that this revolution, this addressing of the issue is done because the rhetoric can shy one away from it's necessity. It's important to not be afraid when the rhetoric can seem alienating and hostile. But I am not hostile because I don't blame anyone, in particular. And I won't be hostile because I have to live and produce in this world: a world which I didn't create but am trying to find a place in. I don't think I'm irrate. But I am angry and I am aware. I don't feel inclined to point the finger but I am not afraid to give the finger when need be and if that's alienating than that's really tuff shit because somethings need to be done. And it is my intention to put this issue right up in yr. face, SEE, so we'll be face to face, SEE, with the fact, SEE, that sometimes, we stand against one another wrongly... And by seeing and saying: I WON'T-- when it may seem trite or hostile or obvious or self conscious, it creates the possibility of a time when we can leave these things be. But for now I take this ardent stand, to stand by my woman: to be for her and then maybe she can be for me. And I hear these girls, girls I don't know, girls I have never met, make these same promises and these same threats. They speak to me and I speak to you and I know our time has come... revolutionary girl soul force... wow.

15

I was a very dykey-looking 13-year-old, with my short haircut, plain blouses, and knee-length skirts. (This was when very long hair and very short skirts were fashionable.) On my way home from school, sometimes groups of high-school boys would stop me, demand to know whether I was a boy or a girl, and threaten to rape me in order to find out.

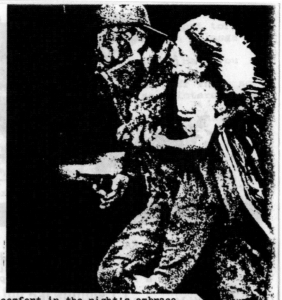

Sleep little one sleep, take comfort in the night's embrace cause the morning sun will open your eyes and you'll see that you live in a fucked-up place. Sleep,little one,sleep,take comfort in any kind of embrace,the morning sun's gonna open your eyes and you live in a fucked-up place.

Oh,baby,I was like you once;I slept in a crib with yellow sheets. Now the sand in my eyes and the dirt on my feet and the sand in my mouth,and everyone just dreams of themself anyway,don't they? No,you never asked no one for life but here you are in somebody else's world. And they'll say that the change can come through you but it should've come long ago. And how can things change when all of our dreams are unfurled?

The stars in your eyes are just shattered glass, and the dolls on the shelf will become the men in the gutter. And veryone dreams of somebody else.
Baby,I'll never sleep that way again until I die.

-Anna Springer(Blatz)

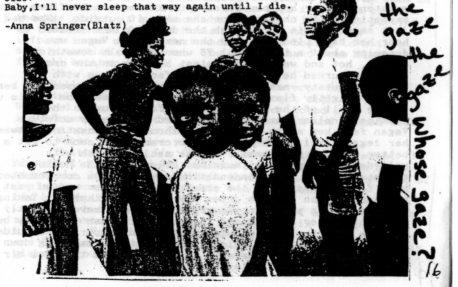

the gaze
the gaze
whose gaze?
16

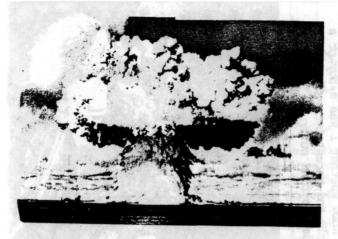

Dana
Younkins

A TOWN CALLED KALI FLOWER
A Continuing Saga

Here's a rundown of what happened in the second
episode:
Milton lets on that he's interested in Vegan and they
make goo-goo eyes over a wheatgrass juice.
Bill tries to get his cousin Daffodil to invest in
stock for the Moola Boobyard, a farm growing organic breasts
for transplants.
Phyllis shows Malcom the paper route and discovers he
has a crush on Daffodil and that she may be falling for him
herself.

****

The guitar feedback from the last note of the set rang
in everyone's ears as they exited through the door to get
some air and dry their perspiration. Vegan had peeled her
sweater earlier and now carried it in the crook of her elbow
expecting to be chilled once she made it outside. She had
just seen Phyllis go through the door and was excited to
hear her band Linoleum play the next set. Vegan was
dreaming about a tall, cool V8 when she felt something
smooth, hot and wet press against her arm in the crowd.
She turned her head and came face-to-face with a
vibrant, sweaty, naked torso. The bicep was closest to her.
It was slightly flexed and she visually traced the muscle up
to the swell of the shoulder, then farther up to the
prominent collar bone that glistened with salty moisture.
Vegan felt her mouth water and a throbbing sensation between
her legs. As if in a trance, she craned her neck to get a
better look at the chest. It was satiny smooth with
well-developed pectoral muscles; below them the hollow of
the sternum and faint indendation of ribs were complemented
by a flat stomach. As the scent of male torso waffed past
her nose, Vegan felt so drawn she nearly collapsed. Taking
advantage of a shift in the crowd the torso moved directly
in front of her and exposed its back. It wasn't a back, but
a piece of art. Wide shoulders accented by perfect shoulder
blades, wrapped in two thick slabs of muscle tapering down
to a trim waist. She made it to the door and the cool air
cleared her head a little.

17

"Hey Vegan, what's up?" asked Phyllis.

"I'm on the brink of an orgasm. Check out that torso, can you believe it actually belongs to a man? It belongs on my wall, or maybe mounted above my bed."

"It's ok, I guess. That last band rocked. Have you seen Malcom? He said he was coming-"

"Ah, Phyllis, would you mind if we stood over there so I could get an unobstructed view of the torso," interrupted Vegan.

"Sure. I thought you had a thing for Milton, what's with all this torso lust?"

"I don't know, it's a lust-inspiring torso. I find objectifying men strangely empowering. Milton's different. I mean, I like his body, but he's a complete individual. He's here somewhere, by the way. I convinced him to come see your show, are you nervous?"

"I'm not sure my voice sounds all that good, I've had this cold, and I passed a dead bird on the way to the club-"

(Then there was the guy
with the Bat attitude.)

"Vegan!" Bill waltzed over. "Nice nipples, ever hear of a bra?" he said smirking.

"Yeah, I just burned it." There was no way a lame ass like Bill was going to make her feel self-conscious about wearing a halter top, thought Vegan. Without a second glance Bill left to talk to his brother Milton.

"Hey Bill, I thought you were too smooth for shows," said Milton.

"Sweating like a pig with hyper freaks isn't my idea of a good time. I'm cruising on three legs for buxom blond teenage girls, if you know what I mean. I've been putting up these flyers for the Moola Boobyard, there's an informational meeting next week and I'm hoping to attract some potential investors. You want to hand some flyers out for ol' brother Bill?"

"No."

Bill turned to go and said, "Whatever. See ya."

Milton searched the crowd and caught sight of Vegan. He moved towards her in a way he hoped looked cool and indifferent. She looked strangely flushed and seemed to be hanging on to Phyllis for support.

"Vegan. Hi. Are you all right?"

"Milton, yeah, I'm fine. Just catching my breath. I thought I'd go get a V8, want to come?" Vegan gave him a big smile, hoping she wouldn't have to deal with any kind of jealousy scene. Milton really was a dreamboat, she liked his boyish looks.

"Ok, but I'll probably get a Jolt. I had a vegetable serving yesterday. Hey Phyllis, see you in a couple of minutes." Vegan and Milton strolled off into the darkness and Phyllis saw their arms entwine, then she absentmindedly glanced around for Malcom.

18

"So, are we in tune or what?" asked Phyllis. The
Linoleums were onstage and she hated delays; standing around
under the lights, doing nothing, waiting for the band to get
their shit together. "How do I turn this amp up?" she
asked, not really expecting anyone to answer.

Phyllis talked into the mike, "Are we ready? Ok. Ah-
we're Linoleum, thanks for coming out." She glanced at the
bass player who started strumming a deep, harsh rhythm
sounding like death itself. The drummer started thumping
and a cymbal shimmered in time with the bass. Phyllis
slowly gyrated, holding the mike with both hands, her head
slightly bowed to avoid the bright lights. Her mouth
opened:

"This is warning
For the pimps to move on
'cause the new woman is too strong
She's had enough of rape and misery
It's time to kill the patriarchy," Phyllis could feel the
sweat beading up around her eyebrows.

"Slavery started with Eve so
learn a lesson from goddess Kali
Eat their blood or drown in the cum
---of an all male kingdom
Kill the patriarchy! " The band laid into the beat and the
crowd began screaming and writhing. The center of the club
was taken over by the mosh crew. Phyllis lost herself
pounding out lyrics-

"Free your mind from sexist oppression
and set yourself for the girl revolution
Don't diss me cause we won't be thwarted
A set back 'cause our sister it's plain to see
--is lost in a male supremacy

You won't see me get played
I've got an Uzi to make him spade
He kills for sport or lust or greed
I kill to fuck the patriarchy
Dead men don't rape you see
We spill your guts to be free
Kill the mother-fuckin' patriarchy!"

Phyllis was hot and everyone knew it. Malcom stood at
the back of the club watching her. Then he glanced over at
Daffodil who had just walked in the door. He wasn't sure
what to think.

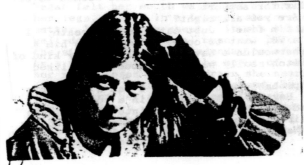

you know
there's got to
be another
one.....

Let's just be friends
friends
just exactly what does that motherfuckin word mean?
Let's not-- and say we are
Let's not-- and i'll make you pay and pay and pay
Now i know why you kept us so far apart
kept us at a heart's length
Me and my new girlfriend
a real friend
and not just your ex-girlfriend(s)
not just your fuckin "let's be friends" girl(s)
And together we see the clues
We know the clues like the claws on our skin
Yet we still believed that you made us special
that somehow "you're the one, girl"
And we knew the clues like the claws on our skin
but somehow we died to let you in
Without girl-held-hands
how're we sposed to know
what crashed in us
and why we pay and pay in pain and pay
So "let's just be friends"
Let's just not, let's just rot
and pay and pay and pay

Chapter IV
THE GREAT TRIBULATION

Allison and I had a conversation with Rebecca Odes of the band LOVE CHILD on saturday July 27th, right before we played a show in New York. We had seen Love Child play the week before in d.c., and we were going to do the interview then, but things like this are really hard to get organized. So when we got to New York, we called her and we met before the show. Since there was no place to do the interview at the club, we went out on the street to talk about stuff. It was cool to listen to the tape of our conversation 'cuz there's all this new york noise in the backround. Dogs barking, car radios blaring, horns honking, and shithead harrassing. Rebecca is an artist who went to college at Vassar, and last semester she was in a graduate painting program in chicago. Love child has been a band for like four years, and they are completely great. They have this song called "know it's alright" that Allen sings thats so awesome, it goes::'what you gonna say when i'm out of your way...and i blow you away, and i blow you away...it's alright...it's alright...' there are also these incredible screams..This song, along with the 6 incredible ones that Rebecca sings are on their new record "OKAY?" on Homestead. I would advise you to check it out. Okay?

gg: WHen we interview girls in bands we like to ask them questions about their experience in music, but also, since you're in a band with boys, maybe you could talk about that too.

Rebecca: Well, I don't know. I mean, theres definately things, ideas that girls have about music that are different from boys. I mean I haven't played with that many girls so I don't really know, but I feel like since boys have been playing music for their whole lives; I mean Allen has been playing guitar since he was 10, and he thinks he Knows every thing. I mean I never tried and that's why I didn't play music before, because when I would try to practice something, it was just much to much work, and I would just rather draw or something that wouldn't require to much practice for me. And I just wasn't in to the monotony of learning scales or even hurting my fingers to learn chords when I started. I tried to play guitar when I was 12, but it was too much trouble. Sometimes Allen gets frustrated at how I can just not remember how the song went. We hardly ever practice, we try to practice before every show if it's been more that two weeks since the last show. We're completely lax, and then he gets really mad if I forget how a song went especially if I wrote it. He thinks it should be ingrained on my skull.since I wrote it. ...I just don't think that girls are encouraged to pursue it when they're younger, so I think it's a totally different way of looking at it when you're older and you pick it up. You're more conscious of the idea that you don't need to learn to play to do it. So you don't really go through intensive training or lessons. I mean, I never had lessons or anything; someone taught me how to play "wild thing" and that was it and then I taught myself listening to records and the boys in my band abusing me in practice to learn our songs so... I had some problems with the guy who use to be in our band, and I guess isn't really anymore (Will), 'cuz he's constantly moving to different cities. He used to sort of try to control me in weird ways, like what I wore and shit. The first show we played they told me I couldn't wear what I was wearing 'cuz I was wearing a dress & they thought it was too fancy and "we're not a fancy band, we're a Punk rock band". I mean not that I should put sugar water in my hair or anything, but they didn't want me to wear this cocktail dress. It was really irritating, I don't know what his problem was, we had a lot of difficulties in general. Hey, we're gonna ne playing with Shonen Knife at CBGB's in august.

21

gg: NO WAY!

R: yeah, august 16. it's the best show we've ever been on. Shonen Knife is my mom's favourite band. She's gonna be totally dying.

gg: Do you have any ideas on how womens issues like rape etc. enter in to the arena of music, experiences, whatever.

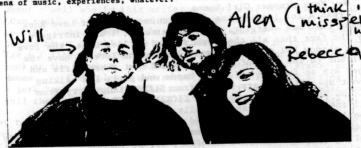

Will →
Allen (I think misspelled his name)
Rebecca

R: well, I guess my most specific experience has been with my parents and their reaction to things like the way I dress, and the way I conduct myself, in that they think it's gonna somehow fuck me up later in life. ...the first thing that ever happened with this was like when we played at CBGB's like 3 years ago and I was wearing a short mini-skirt and my dad had come to pick up my sister 'cuz she had just seen us play, and my dad started yelling at me while I was standing outside of CBGB's that my skirt was too short, and there were like 15 people standing around and he's yelling at me; and he's not even that dictatorial or anything, I guess he was just worried about it. This was actually when Tobi, and Billy, And Calvin were staying at my parents house in N.J. 'cuz we had just played with the Go Team, and my dad called me into his office to talk about it. He said:" I just want to let you know that it's not that I don't trust you.it's just that I think you are too trusting. You know you just can't walk around like that". And I got so angry that he was just buying into the whole 'asking for it' thing. That's when I wrote this song that's now called "asking for it", thats sort of about being harrased. I sort of tried to tell him that, although I'm not quite sure it's true, but that when you're on stage, its sort of a safe place to be. where you're not at risk in such a real way. It's hard 'cuz there are times when I feel so hysterical about the idea of being raped that I just don't want to leave the house. But I feel like sometimes you just have to ignore your hysteria and go out or you wont be able to function. It's just not cool. It's fucked up.

gg: since you guys don't practice that much, how much of the songwriting do you do. Does Allen write what he sings and you write what you sing?

R: Well, mostly thats what's been happening recently. In the beginning I Hardly even knew how to play bass, so I wasn't big in the song writing thing. Then, I started writing songs. At first I sang two songs that Will wrote, and then I started writing some songs and singing them, and on the album that just came out I wrote like 4 songs I think, and then there's the two songs that Will wrote that I sing. And then I guess recently since Will hasn't really been in the band Allen and I have written a lot of songs together, which is pretty good I guess.

Oh yeah it's good. You can write Rebecca and LOve Child c/o Homestead Records, P.O. Box 800, Rockville Center, NY 11571-0800. Their lp is probably $7 if you can't find it at your local record shop.

LOVE CHILD

22

This is my TOP 10.   extended dance remix.
produced by revolution (summer) girl style now.

1. New York Drummer Girl Scene
   I read a lot last spring a bout this east coast Love Rock
scene that was emerging, skepticism aside, I was intrigued
by the fact that all the bands forced to live under the love
rock shadow had girl drummers. Two months later I have the
fortune to see most of these bands and meet these girls and
they are so fucking rad. The bands and girls I'm talking
about specifically are Rachel from SLEEPYHEAD, Torry from
FLYING SAUCER, and Rachel from KICKING GIANT. They are
all incredibly cool, and actually three of the nicest
people I've ever met.
Kicking Giant and Sleepyhead have a split E.P. comming out this
fall on Shimmy Disc (JAF Box 1187; NY, NY 10016).
Flying Saucer has a single coming out on Teen Beat (P.O. Box 50373
W.D.C. 20091), as well as an EP on Homestead (P.O. BOx 800
Rockville center, NY 11571-0800).
It just seems like a really cool thing that all these girls
are in bands and they're all friends, and that there is
something cool & exiting going on in New York. I really
like New York.

2. International Pop Underground + I.P.U. convention.
   Things about this convention thing that exite me include:
a- Girl day... 'cuz it is the revolution!
b- Rich Jensen live at the capitol theater.
c- Spoken word scene
d- Sleepyhead--Shadowy Men on a Shadowy Planet--Melvins
e- Mecca Normal
f- Thee Headcoats
g- Unwound
h- Courtney LOve
i- P.O.T.A. (all 5, even though I'm already an orangatan and
have been for some time now).
j- Kill Rock Stars LP-- the real soundtrack to revolution
   with such shining stars as Jad fair, N.O.U., Bikini KIll,
   Withchypoo, bratmobile, NIrvana, the list goes on dude.
   Can you even believe it?
                  P.R.D.C.T.
   (PUNK ROCK DREAM COME TRUE)
   get this record from Kill Rock Stars c/o Slim Moon
   1123 s. adams No. 418, Olympia, WA 98501 $8 (i think)

 —> Box 7154, Oly WA 98507 USA

International Pop Underground Convention
August 20-25, 1991, Olympia, Wash., U.S.A.

23

3. KICKING GIANT

K.G. was in <u>SASSY</u> the same month as <u>G.G.</u> was reviewed and
they had a girl in it so I was interested but the blab said
something about Love Rock, and even though the woman who wrote
it Christina is my friend now, then i had this really bad attitude
about :"well who is this writer anyway, what does she know about
LOve rock", it bums me out in retrospect. Anyway, Allison writes
to K.G., because she thinks they sound cool & I'm still kind of
ho-hum about it all. She gets their cassette in the Mail from
Tae & I like it alright. Their Harmonies are so great, and I
look at the cassete, and I see it was recorded by kramer and I'm LIke
Hmmmm...   God, please understand I was feeling and acting like
a jerk last spring. Production values (I think thats what you
call them really mean nothing to me.) Anyway, the K.G. are all

set to play this NO Nukes benefit here in d.c. w/Courtney Love,
and Jonny Cohen, and TSUNAMI in june. so I'm stoked and Allison
writes them letters and Tae writes her & he comes to visit & I
like him & then Rachel comes & she's sooo cool & we hang out &
I see them PLAY & my life is changed.
no lie.
...Then next month we (bratmobile) have a show in NYC w/ K.G.
and CHIA PET and we all hang out for two days and nights and
its incredible fun and just incredible. (see more on this night
in Tae & Rachel's new fanzine I don't know the name of yet, you
can write us here for more info.)
Anyway, our show was really great, and Erin runs into allison
during our lastsong because I think they both had their eyes
closed (I did), and All this exiting stuff happens. And then
I get my tape of Kicking Giant's new Demo with GIRLY SOUNDS on
it as well as book of Love's girl power anthem "BOY", and I go
home to d.c. to listen to this tape & play a show w/ fugazi (also
awesome to me); and I realize that Kicking Giant & bratmobile
are soul bands to be together. Their new song "this sex says"
is one of my true favourites and has a line that goes: " I can't
touch my skin... it means everything.... please don't touch my
skin... it means everything. PLEASE don't touch <u>MY</u>!"
Rachel plays standing up, is part of the NYC drummer girl scene,
and sings a beautiful acapella song that consistently makes
me tear up.
Tae pretends to be James brown by also pretending to faint and
freaking the audience out. He can also balance his guitar on
his nose like a circus seal.
Some people say they sound like Some Velvet Sidewalk, which is
o.k. by me as they are one of my favorite bands; but I think
this fact might bug some people. oh well.
K.G. break form & confront issues & are corny & sincere and in
your face. I believe in KIcking Giant. FOREVER.

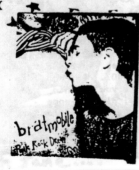
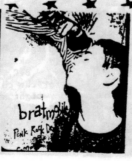
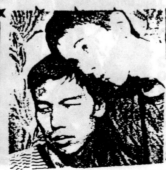

24

4. GIRLY SOUND

Girly Sound is this girl who is a band by herself. The first
tape I heard of her was Allison's made by Tae who knows her. It
was just voice and acoustic guitar & allison said she asked Tae if
she (G.S.) was folk and hewas like: "Oh no, she would not be into
that idea at all." But then Tae made me a cassette a couple of weeks
back & he put 2 G.S. songs on it 'gigolo' and 'flower'; these songs
are voice with electric guitar and they became my favourite songs.
gigolo goes:" ...and it gives me something to laugh about, 'cuz
my real life ain't fuckin funny. ....OOOOOh lord... why...have...
you... forsaken ...me?" So awesome and flower my extra special
favourite song goes: " every time I see your face i get all wet
between my legs. ....I want to fuck you like a dog I'll take you
home and make you like it."
This song sounds like a round with two vocal tacks completely
different from each other, and it's like nothing else I've ever
heard. Totally inspirational. Infact it inspired me to start my
new band Cruella de Ville, which is just me as of yet but I'm
open to suggetsions. As far as I know G.S., has only been
writing songs si nce the war, she lives in chicago now, but will
probably be moving to somewhere else (texas?) 'cuz she is sick
of the concrete jungle. If I could remember her name or find
her address I would ask her to move to Olympia & be in a band with
me. But it's o.k. cuz I'll sit in my apartment & write songs & someday
maybe we can trade tapes, or send eachother songs and record tracks on
eachothers tapes & never meet face to face. but still be a band. Is
this even feasible?
Maybe I should explain that her Voice + her words+ her melodies & guitar
is what makes her songs so great. Tae says:"they are so honest &so true."
and there is no fear in her voice or her words.

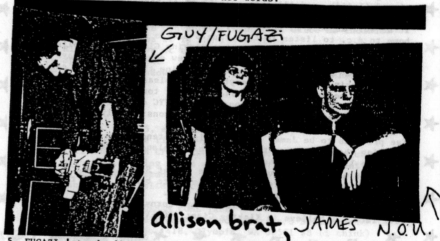

GUY/FUGAZI

allison brat, JAMES N.O.U.

5. FUGAZI 'staedy diet of nothing' LP/ Nation of Ulysses 13 pt. program to
destroy America' LP

THese are two new records being released this month or next month
(august & september). They both totally fucking rule. they are
on Dischord Records-3819 Beecher st. NW, W.D.C., 20007. $7 each
for the cassette or record, some more for the cd if you're into
those. both of these bands are on tour right now, playing some
shows together, and will also be playing at the I.P.U. convention.

25

GIRL GERMS 3

6. Sean Young

Should have been cat woman in Batman II. she didn't get the part, but she is a total fox, and one of the coolest chicks in Hollywood.

7. HYPOCROBRATS

I am a hypocrobrat. I think I am a hypocrobrat because I really believe in a lot of things, but living is really hard for me, and somtimes to slow down the process of impeding psychic and physical death, I contradict myself, am a hypocrit or do other fucked up things. I don't feel like contradicting myself is a good thing, but I do feel that circumstances in my life can help me rationalize something that others might construe as hypocritical. Some people call it 'falling off the edge', and that hurts me because I see a lot of my actions as survival techniques that I have developed naturally. I think feminist sex trade workers are hypocrobrats. It's like using the tools that are already existing, to help revolution; which won't happen in a day but can happen everyday... maybe if I can figure this out, I'll explain more later. One total hypocrobrat mantra is :"well sure I <u>could</u> do that,...BUT I DON'T <u>HAVE TO!</u>"

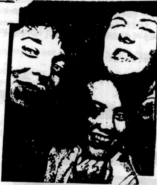

TABATHA
+
Bratmobile
=
hypocrobrats 0069

8. JEZEBEL 69

is a band that doesn't exist physically yet, but in five years time they will blow your mind. Details are still hazy, but more will be reported as the specifics are worked out.

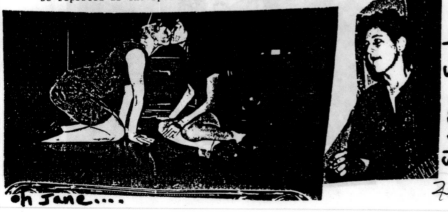

oh June....

Sharon Suture

26

9. RIOT GRRRL

Riot Grrrl is so much. It will end up being so much I am sure. right now it isn't anything concrete, it's not a fanzine or a group or anything specific, although it is also all of those things. As of now, it has been a mini fanzine, and there have been some girls who met once a week calling themselves riot grrrls, talking about issues in and outside of punk rock that are important to us. But I know, and I'm sure some of youknow that it is gonna be something BIG.

... but we keep talking about what is riot grrrl and it's so hard to say 'cuz as far as I'm concerned all it really is, is an idea that could go far. There's no copywrite on the name so if you are sitting ther reading this and you feel like you might be a riot grrrl then you probably are so call yourself one.

Major influences is me being a riot grrrl are:

-Olympia girl day girls
-candice
-Jenny & Kristin
-angry girl zine scene

-and all the girls I've met & hung out with this summer
-and my band.
....there's more too, boys & girls who make this world easier to exist in. Recognizing influence and importance in my life and trying to understand how big an impact the people in my life make and help me to understand the world and soul force and Love and myself. It's good for me to see that although I am completely fucked up as an individual, I can also see that everyone else I know is probably fucked up in some way too, & that fact I dig sooo much.
Sometimes I get mad too though. See Hypocrobrats.

10. = Revolution (summer) riot grrrl style now!

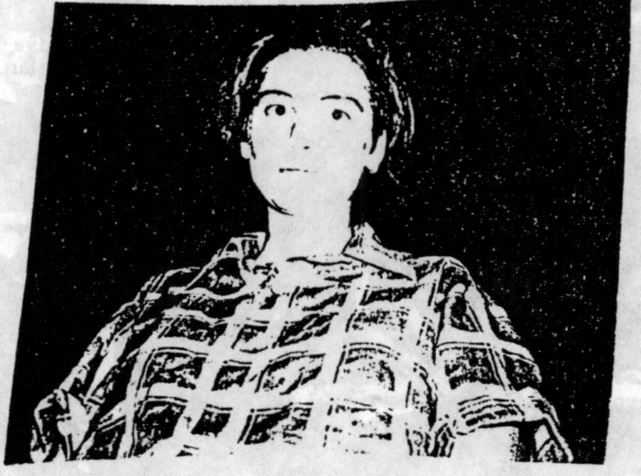

27

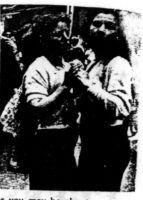

WHEN YOU MEET A LESBIAN: HINTS TO THE HETEROSEXUAL WOMAN

Do not run screaming from the room -- this is rude.

If you must back away, do so slowly and with discretion.

Do not assume she is attracted to you.

Do not assume she is not attracted to you.

Do not assume you are not attracted to her.

Do not expect her to be as excited about meeting a heterosexual as you may be about meeting a lesbian -- she was probably raised with them.

Do not immediately start talking about your boyfriend or husband in order to make it clear that you are straight -- she probably already knows.

Do not tell her that it is sexist to prefer women -- that people are people and she should be able to love everybody. Do not tell her that men are as oppressed by sexism as women and women should help men fight their oppression. These are common fallacies and should be treated as such.

Do not ask her how she got this way -- instead, ask yourself how you got that way.

Do not assume that she is dying to talk about being a lesbian.

Do not expect her to refrain from talking about being a lesbian.

Do not trivialize her experience by assuming it is a bedroom issue only -- she is a lesbian twenty-four hours a day.

Do not assume that because she is a lesbian she wants to be treated like a man.

Do not assume that her heart will leap with joy if you touch her arm (condescendingly? -- Flirtatiously? -- Power-testingly?). It makes her angry.

If you are tempted to tell her she is taking the easy way out, think about that . . . .

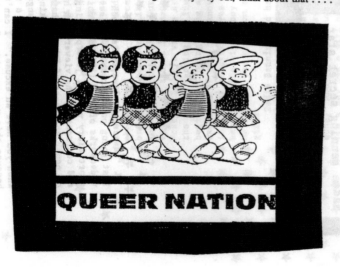

QUEER NATION

28

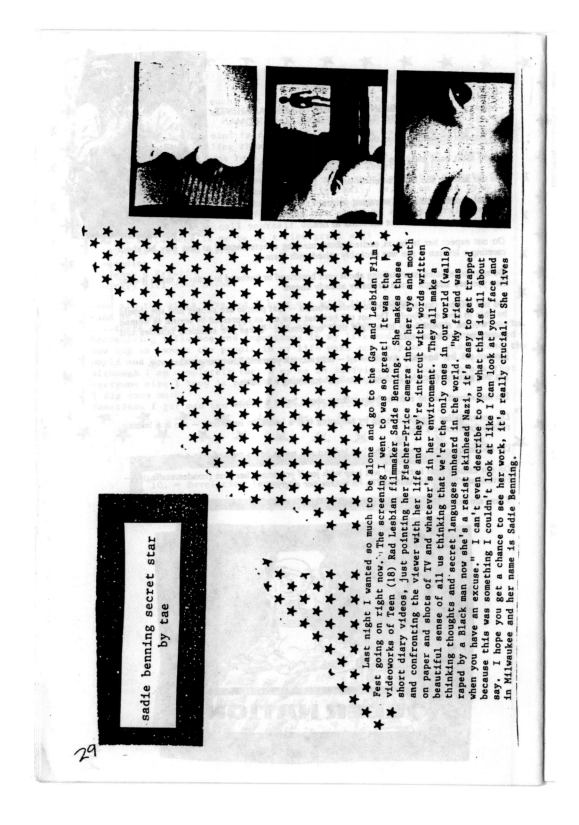

sadie benning secret star
by tae

Last night I wanted so much to be alone and go to the Gay and Lesbian Film Fest going on right now. The screening I went to was so great! It was the videoworks of Teen (18) Rad Lesbian filmmaker Sadie Benning. She makes these short diary videos, just pointing her Fischer-Price camera into her eye and mouth and confronting the viewer with her life and whatever's in her environment. They all make a beautiful sense of all us thinking that we're the only ones in our world (walls) on paper and shots of TV and they're intercut with words written thinking thoughts and secret languages unheard in the world. "My friend was raped by a Black man now she's a racist skinhead Nazi, it's easy to get trapped when you have an excuse." I can't even describe to you what this is all about because this was something I couldn't look at like I can look at your face and say. I hope you get a chance to see her work, it's really crucial. She lives in Milwaukee and her name is Sadie Benning.

29

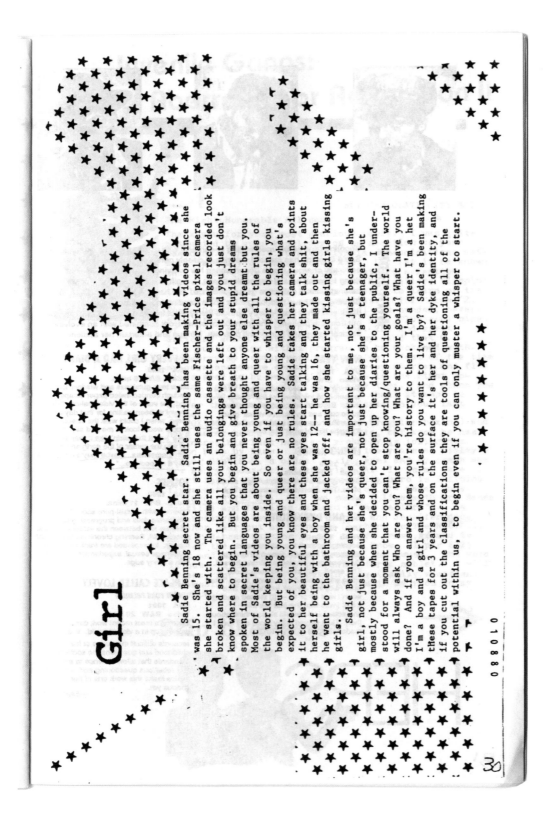

Girl

Sadie Benning secret star. Sadie Benning has been making videos since she was 15. She's 18 now and she still uses the same Fischer-Price pixel camera she started with. The camera uses an audio cassette and the images recorded look broken and scattered like all your belongings were left out and you just don't know where to begin. But you begin and give breath to your stupid dreams spoken in secret languages that you never thought anyone else dreamt but you. Most of Sadie's videos are about being young and queer with all the rules of the world keeping you inside. So even if you have to whisper to begin, you begin. But being young and queer or just being young and questioning what's expected of you, you know there are no rules. Sadie takes her camera and points it to her beautiful eyes and these eyes start talking and they talk shit, about herself being with a boy when she was 12— he was 16, they made out and then he went to the bathroom and jacked off, and how she started kissing girls kissing girls.

Sadie Benning and her videos are important to me, not just because she's girl, not just because she's queer, not just because she's a teenager, but mostly because when she decided to open up her diaries to the public, I understood for a moment that you can't stop knowing/questioning yourself. The world will always ask Who are you? What are you? What are your goals? What have you done? And if you answer them, you're history to them. I'm a queer I'm a het I'm a boy and a girl and whose rules do you want to live by? Sadie's been making these tapes for 3 years and on the surface it's her and her dyke identity, and if you cut out the classifications they are tools of questioning all of the potential within us, to begin even if you can only muster a whisper to start.

★ ★ ★ ★
★ ★ ★ ★
★ ★ ★ ★
★ ★ ★ ★
★ ★ ★ ★

0 1 0 8 8 0

30

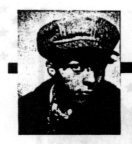
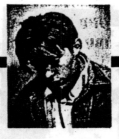
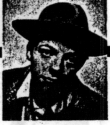

Sadie Benning

WITH SADIE

Shooting (and sometimes editing in-camera) with a cheap plastic video camera, Sadie Benning has created a series of deeply personal, artistically deft and politically charged works documenting her evolving state of mind. Her work, rising from the soul of her adolescence, is a gift to her audience. Recent videos resonate with a collective gay experience. We have all been young and, like Benning, we have had to fight for understanding in a homophobic world. Her black and white pixel-poetry speaks loudly—not from a distanced reminiscence but from the present. The immediacy of her work combined with an evolving political savvy and humor will provoke, intrigue and entertain her audience.

NEW YEAR

USA 1989
Video B/W 4 mins.
Benning's first video made at age 15 is a testament to the power of the "cheap and dirty." Beyond conscious glitches, raw audio cuts and an intuitive visual grace lies a stunning piece of truth and art. And it's just a hint of what's to come.

LIVING INSIDE

USA 1989
Video B/W 4 mins.
Benning has a way of capturing a sense of place. This short is her farewell to high school.

ME AND RUBYFRUIT

USA 1989
Video 4 mins.
Benning captures the intensity and pleasure of Rita Mae Brown's *Rubyfruit Jungle* as passionately as Brown herself. This emotionally charged coming-out video was inspired by Brown's book: "I had read *Rubyfruit Jungle* for the first time when I was 13 or 14 — [I] started reading it and I was like, 'I'm just like this character,' and I would always think about [her]. I just stayed in my room and then I made ME AND RUBYFRUIT."

IF EVERY GIRL HAD A DIARY

USA 1990
Video B/W 6 mins.
More teen gutsiness and wisdom told through handscrawled paper scraps and the voice of the videomaker: "You know I've been waiting for that day to come when I could walk the streets and people would look at me and say, 'that's a dyke' and if they didn't like it they would fall into the center of the earth and deal with themselves. Maybe they'd return, but they'd respect me..."

JOLLIES

USA 1990
Video B/W 11 mins.
Opening with a pixel-porn scene between two Barbie dolls and progressing to a close-up kiss between the videomaker and another girl, Benning chronicles her sexual history. Interspersed are frank re-tellings of teenage sexual experiences—all told with a funny edge.

A PLACE CALLED LOVELY

NEW YORK PREMIERE
USA 1991
Video B&W 20 mins.
Benning's most recent work deals with growing up in a violent world. In it, she recounts difficult memories of her childhood and questions the societal standards that allow violence to exist. Her rebellious questioning and desire for justice make this work one of her most serious yet.

—Ellen Spiro

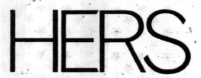

Juvenile Gangs:
Aberration or Adaptation II

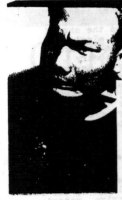

HOT CHOCOLATE CITY 1991

The Right Honorable Allison:

Thank you for your most gracious reply. I was quite
astounded by your knowledge of my reaction to your
postcard. The D.C./Oregon/Olympia communications network is truly _of_ this rocket age. But let it be known
that I was quite taken by your postcard selection
(what could be more Ulyssean than kid sailors flippin'
the bird?!) and was extremely pleased to learn of the
success of the tape I sent you kids. Girl Germs '2,
Punks Dead! NOT was the whirlwind, two-handed, never-
stop attack I always expect it to be. Plus cool pics
of E.D.C. and The N.O.U. kids (pg. 26) and great
articles which leave no doubt in my mind that G.G.
is a publication with a program to be reckoned with.
I'm sorry my letter perplexed you so. Most of the time
my correspondence consists of made-up stories and fibs
(it's good to be enigmatic). This is the first coherent letter I've written in some time. And since you
wish to be a girl in the know - I shall attempt to
answer the burning questions enclosed in your last
letter.
ON BOXING: I box Queensbury Rules (regular boxing) and
have never heard of Kao-Sai Galaxie, but know he has
an incredible last name and probably _is_ losing his
brain blow by blow. I boxed for two years at Finley's
Boxing Club(D.C.'s oldest boxing gym) and my coach was
Mr. Henry Thomas of Alexandria, VA. It is my fave
sport in all the world and my boxing hero is Filipino
flyweight, Pancho Villa (1920's) of P - power fame.
ON 1830 IRVING ST: The two girls I live with are Renee
Tantillo and Jennifer Ballard ("the mallard"). As
you observed, Renee is skate-rock and Jennifer _does_
get her hair cut at Tropea's (barbers to The N.O.U.),
_is_ a red-head walking in the truest sense, and is
one of the coolest girl rockers I know. I pay $225
rent and have the coolest room in the house. The word
is out. I have scouts searching for a sublet. I will
be away for the first week in July (family vacation)
and would be honored if you stayed in my room in my
absence.

Skip likes boys

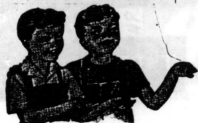

32

83

ON JOINING YOUR GANG OF DRAPES FOR REVOLUTION: My
services are rendered freely and voluntarily as a love-
offering to my beloved compatriots. For that matter,
I need not be compensated nor pensioned.
ON GAMBOAS: I am of ~~Kritik~~ Keith Gamboa and Teresita
Amos. My Grandfathers were Melquiades Gamboa and
Felipe Amos. My Grandmothers were Tina Jensen and
Pilar Acuña. I have two sisters named Jennifer and
Kathleen who are both younger than me. My Great Great
Aunt was a hero during the War for Independence from
the Spaniards. Patrocinio Gamboa outsmarted the shrewd
Spanish Cazadores of Iloilo in her voluntary mission
of taking safely the Philippine flag to Santa Barbara
in time for the inauguration of the revolutionary
government of the Visayas in 1898. She served as an
indefatigable rebel, intelligence worker and was in-
strumental in getting the Iloilo Chinese to support the
common cause and was a campaigner for food, medicine,
arms and ammunition for the revolutionists. During
the revolution against the Spaniards and later the
Americans,Gamboa led the women volunteers to the battle
fields where they undertook Red Cross work, nursed the

wounded and comforted the sick. She remained single until her death on
Nov. 24, 1953.

We begin our American Campaign ~~III~~ 1991 in a few weeks so please alert
the kids. Please communicate express of tender feelings to our future
battery mates - Bikini KillandFuel up,for soon we arrive, notorious.

                                        love/rock/revolution
                                        yours truly,

                              S GAMBOA
                                        Steve
                                        Gamboa XoXo

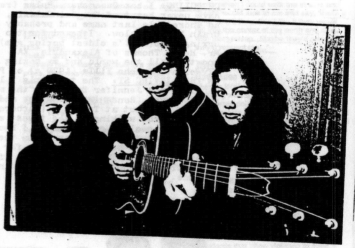

33

PURELY

CIRCUS LUPUS

Circus Lupus are one of my very favourite bands right now. At our
last show at d.c. space allison said: "oh, by the way bratmobile
hearts the Circus Lupus". I looked over to Chris Thomson and he
looked like he was BLUSHING!! hopefully anyway.

x xx

Circus Lupus are: Chris Hamley- guitar
Seth Lorinczi- bass
Chris Thomson- vocals
Arika Casebolt- Drums

3906 Benton NW
Washington, D.C.   20007

x xx

They used to live in Madison Wisconsin and they just moved to d.c.
this summer. This band is completely incredible, and I can't really
figure out why, but one reason is that everything about them, as
individuals is completely different, and everything sounds completely
different if you try to listen to the individual instruments, but
sounds totally great together. Allison and I did a 2 hour interview
with them at food for thought, but it was so long I just couldn't
begin to transcribe the whole thing to get it done on time. The
interview was really great though, and I promise it will be in the
next issue. (this is good because it guarantees that there will be
another issue.)   x xx

Anyway, word has it that they will be releasing an lp on a very nice
label based in d.c. hopefully around december or january. They also
might be going on tour sometime this fall. you might want to write
them and ask them to play in your town.
x xx

Circus Lupus also released a single I believe last spring or so, on
the Cubist Label, which is that punk rock scientist scene in pittsburg.
I dont have that address so please write to the band to find out if
there are any left or how to pressure a second pressing.

XOXOXO

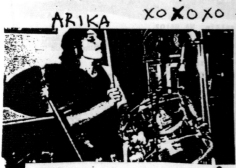 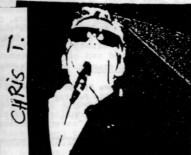

ARIKA

CHRIS T.

the girl germs ♥'s the Circus Lupus

34

Love will tear us apart....
again

Here is a section on cool publications and record company things that deserve some attention. if you write for info it would probably be wise to send along a stamp to encourage a reply (punk rockers are poor), and if you write for a fanzine send a dollar and some stamps just to be nice. Maybe tell them where you heard about it. I always like this.

NOT EVEN ZINE- 8709 Fenway dr., Bethesda, MD 20817
Daisy is a cool straight edge riot grrrl who has done two of these zines so far, and the third one is almost done. It's gonna be mainly about issues of religion in punk. Born Against, Shelter, etc.. Write her, she's rad.

QUIT WHINING- P.O. Box 2154, Mt. Holyoke, S. Hadley, MA 01075
Margaret is Daisy's sisterand she is working on her first issue of this fanzine. MAybe write her for info first. She's cool man. A riot grrrl.

BIKINI KILL ZINE- 3217 19th St. NW, Wash DC 20010
if you're a regular girl germs reader, or into the jigsaw scene then you will know that this is the literature that goes along with the Bikini Kill band. Kathleen is busy at this very moment working on the second issue, and i've been cheating by taking a few peeks here and there; and it looks fucking rad. There is also another issue that will be kept in print so try and get both.

PEBBLES 2000- P.O. BOx 2273, Olympia, WA 98507
This is my friend al + Stella's thing that right now is making thousands of t-shirts. Send some stamps for their catalog. I think they are called 'love rock t-ees'. "Kitten w/ a whip" is my fave.

ACTION TEEN- 5812 MIdhill st., Bethesda, MD 20817
So yeah, this is Don and Erin of TEENAGE GANG DEBS's, new fanzine. And by the way this is a real fanzine along the lines of TIGER BEAT & SIXTEEN. Theres interviews, exposes, and fabulous pin ups too. Ever scince TGD has taken off by being blabbed about in SASSY, the VILLAGE VOICE, d.c.'s CITY PAPER, THE WASHINGTON POST, and ugh... spin, old Erin and Don haven't been the same. ...but they're trying to do some penance by making a punk fanzine. (there also might be something like a 15 page Beat Happening interview, and nude photo's of Mark E. Robinson as King Oil, but i didnt tell you..)

L I F E A N D D E A T H- 617 high ave, Bremerton, WA 98310
   i n t e r t w i n e d
... this is Skippy's fanzine and it's about revolution, and punk and veganism, and straight edge and lots of other stuff. The first issue had an article written by my girlfriend Julie, and an interview with Ian Mackye. I think No. 2 has a jawbox interview. cool.

BRING IT BACK- P.O. Box 20224, Seattle, WA 98102
I haven't actually seen this fanzine but it is done by a guy named Ron, and the next issue has the theme of 'not just boys fun'. sounds good to me.

JANE AND FRANKIE- P.O. Box 55, Postal STN. E, Toronto, ONTARIO, CANADA
               M6H 4E1 (send extra 'cuz it's from canada)
this is done by the brother and sister team of Jena and Klaus Von Brücker. it is totally fucking great, with high queer scene influence. It is really beautiful too. G.B. Jones and 5th Column are discussed lots. Ummm... just get it o.k.? I love this. (21 people who should be queer is the best!)

35.

SISTER NOBODY-
Laura's fanzine that has two issues that I know of although, I am sure
both are out of print. Try her anyway. The next issue is going to be
almost entirely on Patti Smith i understand, which should be good as a primer
for those of us who have fallen behind on our punk rock history, (herstory?).
When i read S.N. #1 i was so happy. Laura used to live in Eugene and she
tells great stories and it looks cool too. This is a queer girl zine as
well as a girl zine. try and get it dude.

HOLY TITCLAMPS- P.O. BOx 3054 Minneapolis, MN 55403
A boy named Larry-Bob makes this fanzine and it is a cool zine cuz it is
real inclusive on issues of gender, has lots of contributers, as well as
lots of writers (and i assume readers) in prisons. He is also real nice.
We are kind of pen pals.

CHAINSAW-
Chainsaw is a true inspiration. I feel dumb talking about it. It is Donna's
"homo-dork-girl-freak-queer-punk type fanzine thing". it is rad. it is real.

JIGSAW- 3217 19th St. NW Wash. D.C. 20010
If i prayed i would pray that i will see a copy of JIgsaw in my hands
cuz i dont know where they go. If you want to, write Tobi and ask
her about it. Some day they will be available. Back issues and all, i have
some weird faith or something. i'll try and be patient. you too, just
don't forget that it does exist, and people still contribute. it's actually
kind of phenomenal.

SIMPLE MACHINES- 3510 N. 8th st., Arlington, VA 22201
   In case you missed July SASSY, there was a little bit
of information on how to get a booklet that Jenny And Kristin
put out on how to start and maintain record companies.
Simple Machines, their record company is forging onward
at full speed with the recent release of Screw with Jawbox,
Velocity Girl, GEEK, and Candymachine. It's really great.
They also have released the first TSUNAMI single with 5
songs on it. A total bargain at $3 dollars I'm sure.
Get their catalog & if you want the booklet send two
extra stamps or .50c.

SLUMBERLAND RECORDS- P.O. Box2741; College Pk., MD 20740
   I believe this address has changed, but it's the only
one I could find. Slumberland is Archie from Velocity
Girl record releasing scene, although i think others are
involved too. There are about 7 records in their catalog
now so write and get it. I haven't actually heard it,
but I understand the Black Tambourine single is major.

TEENBEAT RECORDS- P.O. BOX 50373, Wash., d.c. 20091
   one monkey dont stop no teenbeat!

FADE OUT

      Natasia J. Chan, a 21 year old American woman of Chinese
descent currently resides in Portland, Oregon. She is
            a. working on her screenwriting portfolio
            b. planning super-8 documentaries in her head
                about Chinese-American culture
            c. on sabbatical
            d. an unemployed University of Oregon
                graduate.
      While living in Northwest middle-class limbo this summer,
Natasia is striving to learn how to be a perfect radical, a need
brought on by frustrations with "pseudo-hippies" she met in Eugene
and with the growing awareness of hate crimes in the state of
Oregon through racist incidents caused by skinheads and the
costumed racist (ie. those in suits, blouses, jeans, dresses,
etc).
      Through her work, Natasia plans to discuss these issues while
still trying to have fun. Alas, someday....

36

87

Maybe you should take all this

Do you know what it is like
to walk down the street at night?
Do you know what it is like to feel the threat
The threat that fills the streets as the sun goes down?
    THREATENING,THREATENING,THREATENING

My aloneness has become an isolation
An isolation that is nothing but fear
Fear of who might be out there
Fear of becoming the next statistic
 Streets that seem so safe at day
  At night take on a meaning I've learned to hate
All the bushes,shadows,and people seem so

    Threatening...

Now my anger and fear has a new meaning
As my power grows stronger w/ those who care
 It's finally time to stop the viloence
 Time for us to take back the night
Bushes seem so...Threatening
Shadows seem so..Threatening
People seem so...Threatening

  Night time is so threatening.

Do you know what it's like
To walk down the street at night?

Do you know what it's like to feel the threat?
A threat that fills the streets as the sun goes down?

    It's just so...threatening.
-SPITBOY

Ways to reduce your exposure

— A knee-length skirt is a
safe bet.

Keep in
mind that men can be fragile creatures
when it comes to medical situations:
They aren't as accustomed as you are to
trotting into a doctor's office to have their
nether regions poked and prodded.

37

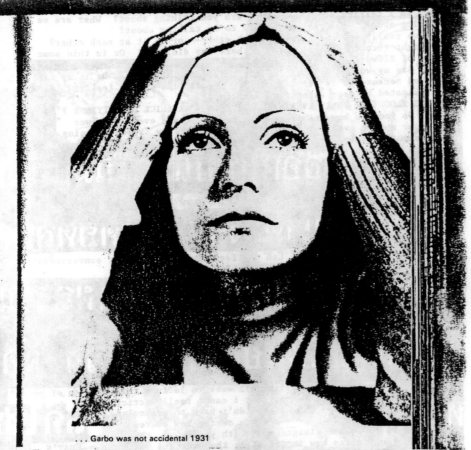

... Garbo was not accidental 1931

She was a waitress. I thought I was in love with her. Nights I drank
root beer floats and watched her like a flamingo take orders and
deliver food. She would ask him what the fuck did he think he was
doing smoking cigars in the non-smoking section. Each night he asked
for a table in the non-smoking section because it was her section
and he smoked-cloves, cigars, banana peels-he smoked and blew smoke
rings at her butt when she turned her back after asking him what the
fuck did he think he was doing. He ate pie. He ate steak and eggs and
wiped drool from his mouth. She became a frustrated waitress and no
longer looked at me when she took my order.
  Then he threw a pipe at her pretty face and babbled, ranted about
his right to smoke in the non-smoking section as long as there were
people in the smoking section who weren't smoking. He babbled and brown
drool formed on his lips. He tore the fake plants from the fake dirt
from the planters that seperated the two sections.
  A truck driver pulled him up by the shirt, asked him who the fuck did
he think he was hurting a woman ain't no real man that'll hurt a woman.
  The frustrated waitress cried, rushing to the restroom. The tired
elderly manager along with the truck driver threw the ranting man out
and he shook his fists for he, too, was frustrated and he too was in
love with the waitress. I paid for my root beer float and left into
the night. I picked up the pipe from the floor before I stepped out,
stuffed it down in my purse. It smelled of vanilla and warmth.
  I walked home to my room of similar fragrances, passing bus stops, litter,
free newspaper stands, trying to remember the color of the waitress's
eyes.
     -Annie Lalania.

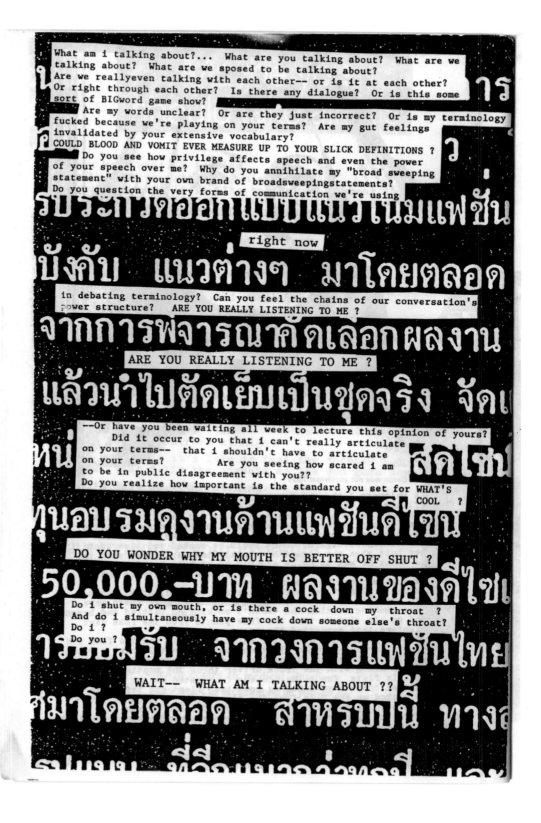

What am i talking about?... What are you talking about? What are we talking about? What are we sposed to be talking about? Are we reallyeven talking with each other-- or is it at each other? Or right through each other? Is there any dialogue? Or is this some sort of BIGword game show?

Are my words unclear? Or are they just incorrect? Or is my terminology fucked because we're playing on your terms? Are my gut feelings invalidated by your extensive vocabulary? COULD BLOOD AND VOMIT EVER MEASURE UP TO YOUR SLICK DEFINITIONS ? Do you see how privilege affects speech and even the power of your speech over me? Why do you annihilate my "broad sweeping statement" with your own brand of broadsweepingstatements? Do you question the very forms of communication we're using

รับระกวดออกแบบแนวเนิมแฟชั่น

right now

บังคับ แนวต่างๆ มาโดยตลอด

in debating terminology? Can you feel the chains of our conversation's power structure? ARE YOU REALLY LISTENING TO ME ?

จากการพจารณาคัดเลือกผลงาน

ARE YOU REALLY LISTENING TO ME ?

แล้วนำไปตัดเย็บเป็นชุดจริง จัดแ

--Or have you been waiting all week to lecture this opinion of yours? Did it occur to you that i can't really articulate on your terms-- that i shouldn't have to articulate on your terms? Are you seeing how scared i am to be in public disagreement with you?? Do you realize how important is the standard you set for WHAT'S COOL ?

ทุนอบรมดูงานด้านแฟชันดีไซน์

DO YOU WONDER WHY MY MOUTH IS BETTER OFF SHUT ?

50,000.—บาท ผลงานของดีไซเ

Do i shut my own mouth, or is there a cock down my throat ? And do i simultaneously have my cock down someone else's throat? Do i ? Do you ?

รับ จากวงการแฟชันไทย

WAIT-- WHAT AM I TALKING ABOUT ??

มาโดยตลอด สาหรบปน ทางล

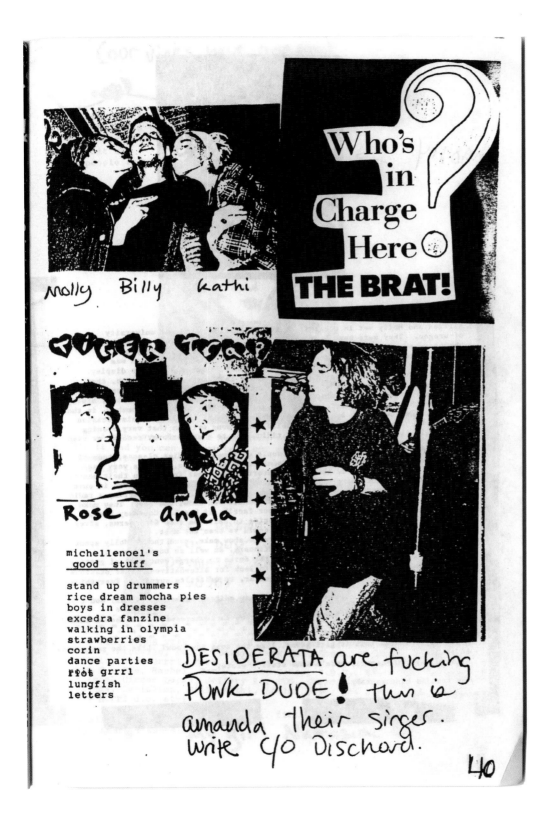

molly Billy kathi

Who's in Charge Here?
THE BRAT!

Rose angela

michellenoel's
good stuff

stand up drummers
rice dream mocha pies
boys in dresses
excedra fanzine
walking in olympia
strawberries
corin
dance parties
riot grrrl
lungfish
letters

DESIOERATA are fucking PUNK DUDE! this is amanda their singer. write c/o Dischord.

40

91

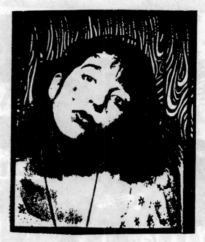

Molly →

Allison and Molly met in the fall of 1989 in the dorms of the university of oregon. They were next door neighbours. Allison first saw molly when she heard someone screaming from the hall phone: "but,... i love you!". Molly was trying to save her heart long distance style, but Allison was nonetheless understandably startled and somewhat frightened by this display. 3 months later agreeing that the dorms were a lame and unhealthy scene, they decide to move in together after the christmas break. The night before Molly went home for chrismas vacation, they both made the hang in the bathroom, hiding out from their respective roomates, dubbing tapes to take home. Somehow, in the process, they decide to be a band called bratmobile. Details on this decision are pretty hazy, although the bratmobile theme song written that very evening remains in Allison's lyric book, too ridiculous to ever perform, record, or even practice.

...so around spring quarter after a couple of women's studies classes, tons of lame punk shows in eugene, some cool punk shows in olympia, and one very essential copy of Jigsaw No. 2, these girls start to get that feeling in their heart; that somethings not quite right the amount of girls they see involved in punk and the world in general, and talk begins in some circles about starting a radio station on campus. Allison and Molly want their own show, and bad. They make a demo tape, it goes: "girl rock...in your face!", it has L7, Courtney Love, Salt -n- Pepa, and Patsy Cline. They decide to call the show Girl Germs, after the song Allison wrote in the fall. It could've been the most.

...But pot smoke and lamoes does not a radio show make, even though Molly spent most of the summer making flyers and stationary, as well as buying tons of records with girls on 'em to play. But the dorks in charge wont hear of getting their asses in gear, so the girls begin to look for alternatives, other stations, ohter formats. They both try to learn guitar, to write, to survive. Everything is hard you know.

...Around october Tobi (cool friend and Jigsaw editor), asks molly :"why don't you do a fanzine?" Hmmmm.

...Molly says to Allison:"hey, this radio scene is nowheresville. Maybe we should do a fanzine."

Allison says:"O.K."

Molly says:"we can call it girl germs, like the song you know? Like the radio show in print."

Allison says:"O.K. cool, here's some stuff I wrote."

The rest is history baby.

41

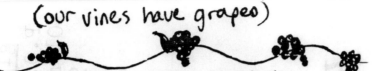

(our vines have grapes)

technical info for girls who want to start a fanzine:
a)have something to write about. (i'm not sure if this is even essential)
b)lay it out in a format you like.
c)print it up.
d)get people to read it.

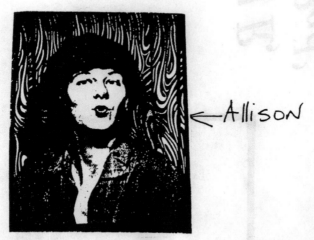

←Allison

...and if you have specific questions write us and we'll tell you how
we did it and you can either take our suggestions, or throw them out
the window; but you know it's mostly a case of trial and error 'cuz
mucho trial + mucho error can = mucho fun.

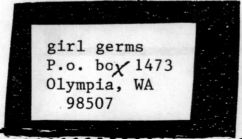

girl germs
P.o. box 1473
Olympia, WA
98507

MASS GIRL GERMS WITH NO RETURNS TO: Tabatha, Kathleen, Kim, Melissa,
Ne-sk8, Michelle, Julie, Daisy, Margaret, Donna, Tiffany, Jenny,
Kristin, Riot Grrrl, Mark, Juliana, Fugazi, Erin, Chia Pet, Don,
Mark E., Tae, Rachel, Torry, Jonny Cohen, N.O.U., Slim, 5th Column,
Rebecca, Circus Lupus, Jeffery K., DUG, Sharon, Becky, Jen S., Anna,
Lai-Nga, Christina, Bill, Kathi, Lo-lo, Hope, and revolution (summer)
riot grrrl d.c. style NOW!

Plus also tons 'o love to Dana (g.g. fiction editor), Jane, Karen,
Erika, Laura, + tasha. My girl Natasia ♡   42

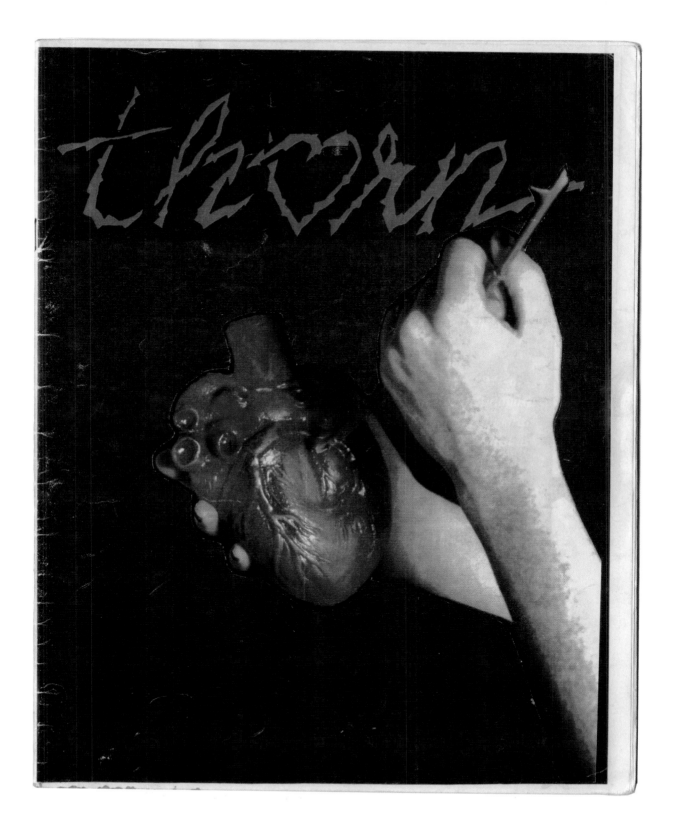

THORN 2 (EXCERPT)

One night I dreamed Jon and I were at a long, thin diner in the desert. We sat side by side in a booth talking about our work, what's important to us. There was a couple of men sitting in the booth in front of us and I could see the man with his back to us, wearing a white t-shirt, was leaning his head back to eavesdrop. After awhile he turned around and with a big smile said, "I've been listening to you and I like what you have to say. I want you to have this." It was a picture of him standing on the hood of his car on a cliff in the desert, krazykat-like mesas in the background. He was looking right into the camera, shading his eyes from the hot sun, and on the back of the photo was writing, a quote from David Wojnarowicz. Straight outta <u>Close to the Knives.</u> The man in the diner **was** David and he slid in the empty seat across from Jon and I and I took his hand in both of mine and said, "I'm so glad to meet you. You're a hero." and Jon smiling with his face red said not to say that. I woke up with such an immediacy/truth of this dream, sure I'd meet him.

Increased mortality teaches me nothing.

and now he's dead. Immortalized through the nostalgic rustlings of the pages of his books. Makes my breath stop with rage that the reason for this hyperrewinds back to a basic root of genocide from hate of gays. People who stand smugly still in their power to do anything about the terror of AIDS because they are sickened by a sexuality not their own. Angered by the fact that AIDS forces them to confront sexuality of pleasure, an existence outside of the silent aqueaking of bedsprings made to creak by the passing of semen to egg. Man to woman, Adam to Eve.

Sexuality defined in images gives me comfort in a hostile world.

When I was a sixteen year old punk rock virgin in Anchorage Alaska, I was riding bus 45 to downtown, and as we passed a row of 50's type clapboard houses(some of my favorite buildings in this eighties boom town), I saw something which gave me a stir down there, between my legs.The clouds were low, and the light was a silver yellow of storms and it was windy. In an instant that we passed the last house, a muscular man with dirty-blonde hair, in jeans and a white tshirt turned the corner heading into the house. He was walking against the wind which plastered his tshirt against his muscly stomach. He had broad shoulders. Left with me a twinge in my pelvis, a desire to know that man with my hands.

At 23, I recall this image as reference to dusty American highways, rundown gas stations and 15cent bottles of cocacola held in the hand of a chevy driving white boy from Grants. A cardboard Levi's ad, which in a creepier moment now surfaces a pair of rough worn hands fumbling at the crotch of his jeans, then callouses against your skin, holding you back against a seat, a wall, a bed, with one hand, while the other rips your shirt and over your breasts. Rush of fury to your panties then thrust grunt as you remain their cursing him softly under your breath alone in helplessness.

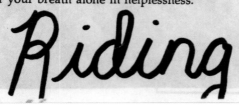

Riding

K. Kelly

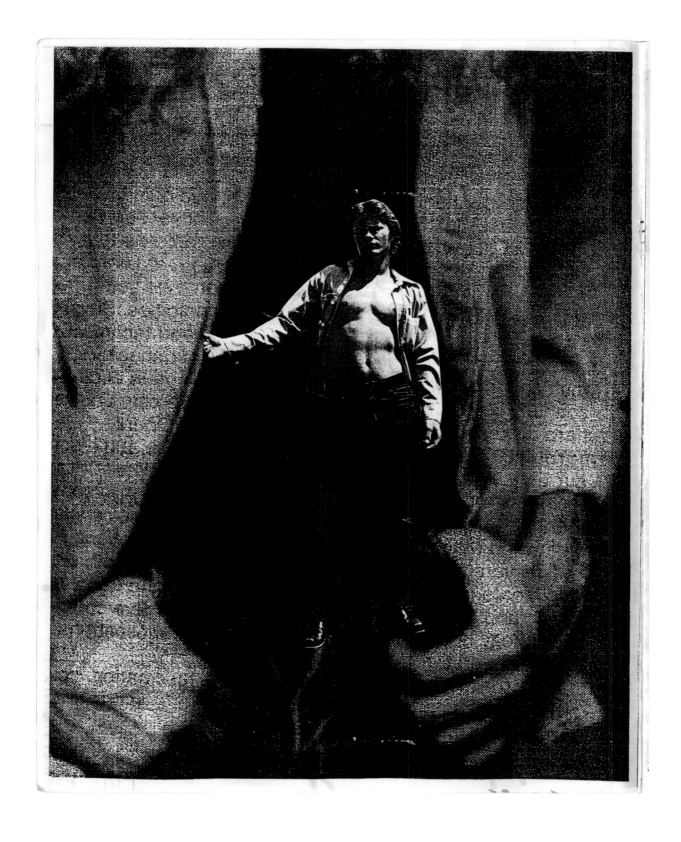

THORN 2 (EXCERPT)

BUT when I found and read <u>Close to the Knives</u>, this sixteen-year-old found image of body, of desire, suddenly spiralled into a taut muscle of power, reclaiming that seen man as an object of desire from the vantage point of a man. Fantasized about desiring that man, man to man. It felt at home, this idea to read the book like this. It seemed more plausible, more safe to imagine touching him as a him. It might seem crazy, but this is what I love about David's writing, his work--it's so not my experience, but described so beautifully it translated a three second glimpse from ago into cock suck photo of now that turns me on. I imagine myself sitting behind him in the car, yukkin' it up, or ranting about the fucked system, then pulling over at a reststop to watch through a hole in the bathroom as he sucks off some flannel shirt trucker, both of their arms strained, tight muscles and me coming with them. Beautiful, intense eyes.

I'm beginning to believe that one of the last frontiers left for radical gesture is the imagination.

And the rage. Somehow it's connected to my despair at David's death since his character filled me to a just before overflowing brim cup of him with his AIDS rage. Becomes me. The situation becomes me and I shelve his written words/experiences into the swell of my heart. Frantic Fury. Wrap myself deeper in a coat of wrath, which i pump out in fuck. Say it do it until your body becomes it in one ready leap, teeth bared claws out at the throats of those who would lead us to believe that desire and pleasure are unimportant, secondary to eating, shitting, surviving.

The only sense I can make out of the nonsense of David Wojnarowicz' death is the power of the words needed to write your body.

What he showed me.

I really wanted to be his friend.

He was so beatiful.

Sew your lips like he to **sow** the pain of the truth of the hate you'll find for what you believe in, who you are.

Rest easy now.

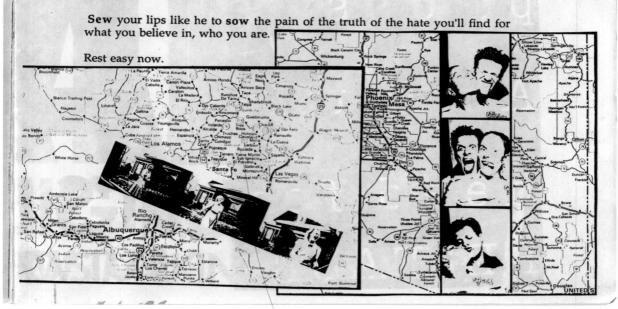

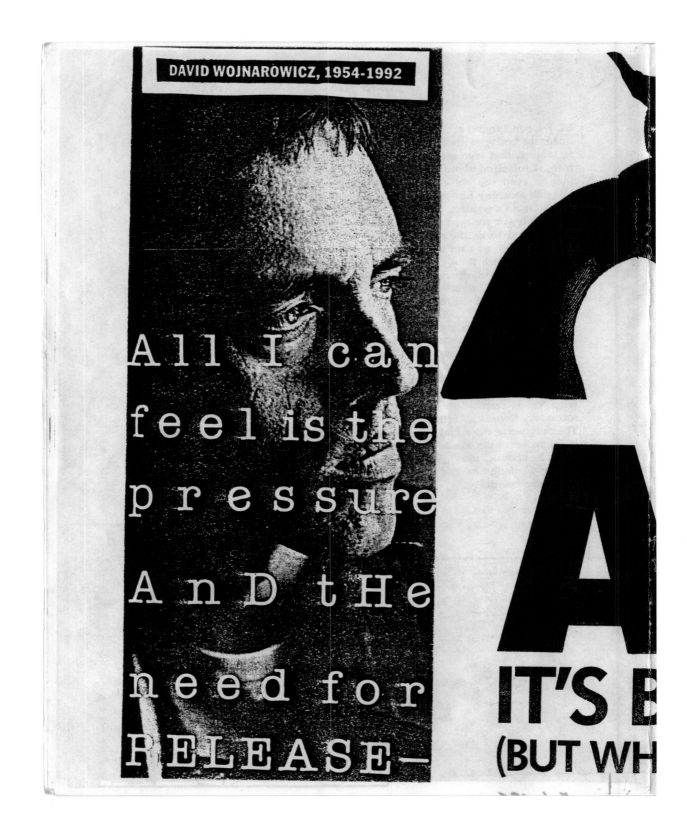

DAVID WOJNAROWICZ, 1954-1992

All I can feel is the pressure AnD tHe need for RELEASE—

A IT'S B (BUT WH

THORN 2 (EXCERPT)

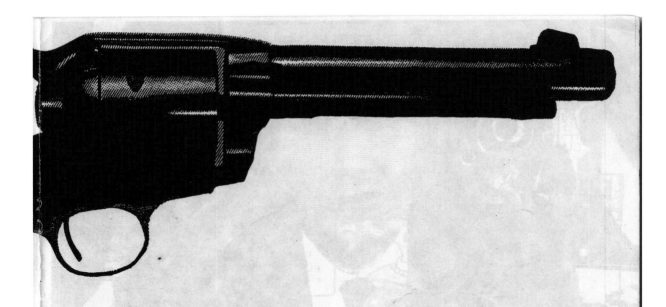

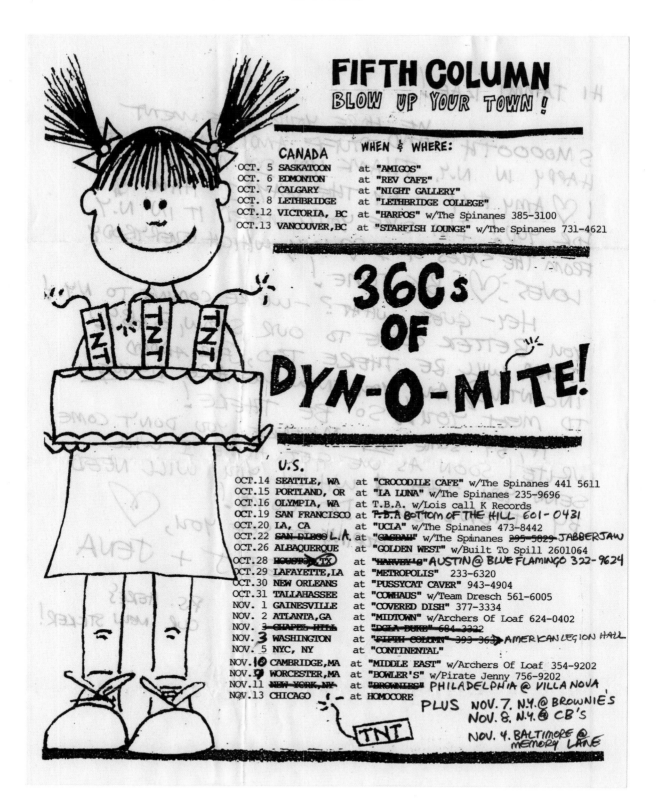

FIFTH COLUMN
BLOW UP YOUR TOWN!

WHEN & WHERE:

CANADA
OCT. 5	SASKATOON	at "AMIGOS"	
OCT. 6	EDMONTON	at "REV CAFE"	
OCT. 7	CALGARY	at "NIGHT GALLERY"	
OCT. 8	LETHBRIDGE	at "LETHBRIDGE COLLEGE"	
OCT.12	VICTORIA, BC	at "HARPOS" w/The Spinanes	385-3100
OCT.13	VANCOUVER, BC	at "STARFISH LOUNGE" w/The Spinanes	731-4621

36Cs OF DYN-O-MITE!

U.S.
OCT.14	SEATTLE, WA	at "CROCODILE CAFE" w/The Spinanes	441 5611
OCT.15	PORTLAND, OR	at "LA LUNA" w/The Spinanes	235-9696
OCT.16	OLYMPIA, WA	at T.B.A. w/Lois call K Records	
OCT.19	SAN FRANCISCO	at ~~T.B.A~~ BOTTOM OF THE HILL	601-0431
OCT.20	LA, CA	at "UCLA" w/The Spinanes	473-8442
OCT.22	~~SAN DIEGO~~ L.A.	at "~~CASBAH~~ JABBERJAW" w/The Spinanes ~~295-5029~~	
OCT.26	ALBAQUERQUE	at "GOLDEN WEST" w/Built To Spill	2601064
OCT.28	~~HOUSTON, TX~~ AUSTIN @ BLUE FLAMINGO	at "~~HARVEY'S~~	322-9624
OCT.29	LAFAYETTE, LA	at "METROPOLIS"	233-6320
OCT.30	NEW ORLEANS	at "PUSSYCAT CAVER"	943-4904
OCT.31	TALLAHASSEE	at "COWHAUS" w/Team Dresch	561-6005
NOV. 1	GAINESVILLE	at "COVERED DISH"	377-3334
NOV. 2	ATLANTA, GA	at "MIDTOWN" w/Archers Of Loaf	624-0402
NOV. 3	~~CHAPEL HILL~~	at "~~DG-A DUKE~~" ~~684-3322~~	
NOV. 3	WASHINGTON	at "~~FIFTH COLUMN~~ AMERICAN LEGION HALL" ~~393-363~~	
NOV. 5	NYC, NY	at "CONTINENTAL"	
NOV.10	CAMBRIDGE, MA	at "MIDDLE EAST" w/Archers Of Loaf	354-9202
NOV. 9	WORCESTER, MA	at "BOWLER'S" w/Pirate Jenny	756-9202
NOV.11	~~NEW YORK, NY~~ PHILADELPHIA @ VILLA NOVA	at "~~BROWNIES~~"	
NOV.13	CHICAGO	at HOMOCORE	

PLUS NOV. 7. N.Y. @ BROWNIE'S
NOV. 8. N.Y. @ CB'S

NOV. 4. BALTIMORE @ MEMORY LANE

FLYER

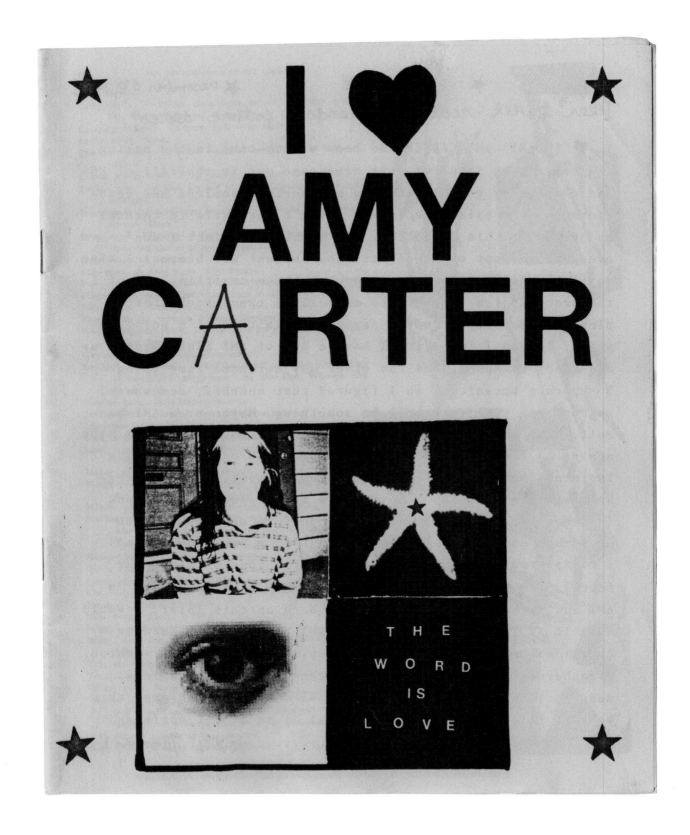

I ❤ AMY CARTER

THE
WORD
IS
LOVE

I (HEART) AMY CARTER 1

Dear sweet readers, friends + future dates,

I ♥ (HEART) AMY CARTER has been a long time in the making.
The very first issue of this zine came out in the Fall of 86'
and despite my good intensions and serious desires and devo-
tions to it's existence, I just haven't been able to channel
my juices in this direction. As a matter of fact I don't
even have a copy of the first (now ancient and historic) zine.
So if by chance there's any one out there coverting one of
the precious few (there were only 25 of them made) pretty
please do send me a copy. Anyways, this time it's going to
stick, I mean I feel like I have a lot of AMY STUFF stored up
and ready to share. And the other day her name came up on
3 seperate occasions, so I figured that somehow, somewhere,
someone was trying to tell me something. Maybe even AMY herself. Also there are two other reasons for starting this zine
again: 1) I recently moved to southern CAL and I'm feeling
isolated, bored, lonely, and wanting to meet rad dorky egg-
head kinda girls...2) I moved here for graduate school and
I need a solid procrastination project to provide me with
an escape, and excuse to not constantly be feeling like all
I do is create fodder for the art world (one of my bigger
fears). And of course the most important of all reasons is
AMY and my commitment to AMYness. More on this later. I would
love it if you would send me any AMY STUFF, and I mean anything; sightings, stories, memories, drawings, comix, photos,
paraphernalia, ANYTHING........also if you want you could
send me info on your favorite AMY TYPE PERSON — whoever this
may be. In general I just love mail. I am a self confessed
mail junkie. So until next time.........★ XO *Tammy Rae*

world.

Camp - verb. To mimic, consciously, or not, the other sex; to be obvious. Adjective - **Campy;** noun - **Camp.**

Carrying on - verb. To camp; to have an affair.

Come - noun. Semen.

Coo - interjection. Derisive signal of recognition of homosexuality.

Crown jewels - noun. Drag jewelry, large and ostentatious.

Cruise - verb. To look for sex in public places; to flirt with strangers.

Daisy chain - noun. Group intercourse. The one on the end is named "Daisy."

Drag - noun. Clothing of the opposite sex. Masquerade party involving clothes of the opposite sex.

Dyke - noun. A Lesbian.

Fag - noun. A male homo. Also **Faggot.**

Fairy - noun. A male homo, particularly one addicted to fellatio.

Finger artist - noun. Lesbian addicted to manual methods.

Fish - noun. A heterosexual addicted to cunnilingus or fellatio.

Flute - verb. To perform fellatio. Derogatory noun - **Fluter.**

Fruit - derogatory noun. Normal term for a homo. Also **Phony, Nance, Pansy.**

Gay - adjective and noun. Homosexual.

Get her! - interjection. (Also "**Get him!**" and "**Get you!**") Sign of recognition of gayness. See also **Coo, Whoops,** and **Swish.**

Hustler - noun. Male homo prostitute.

Jam - adjective. Normal. Noun - A normal person.

Les. - noun. A Lesbian.

Look in the mirror - verb. Female masturbation.

Luke - noun. Corruption of leukorrhea. Feminine precoital fluid.

Maizie - noun. Name for anybody gay.

Marge - noun. The very feminine passive dyke. Adjective - Feminine.

Mintie - noun. The very masculine aggressive dyke.

Mother - noun. One who has "brought out" another. Particularly male. Also **Queen mother, Mother Superior, Mother Hollyhock,** recognized fag leaders.

Mustard Pot - derogatory noun. A passive brownie. Also **Punk.**

Queen - noun. Male homo.

Queer - adjective. Jam for homo.

Rim - verb. Combination of oral and anal eroticism.

Sew - verb. Male masturbation.

Shim - noun. (rare). A dyke.

Swing - verb. Perform fellatio.

Swish - interjection, as **Coo,** etc. Noun - An obvious male homo. Adjective - Feminine.

Teagarden - noun. Restroom.

Trade - noun. A passive, non-reciprocal member of intercourse.

Velvets - noun. Swish male clothing or drag.

Whoops - interjection. (Pronounced with a rising inflection and as if it were spelled "Wool!") verb. To signal recognition audibly with **Whoops, Coo, Swish,** or **Get you.** One can whoops another or be whoopsed.

Wolf - noun. An active aggressive pederast.

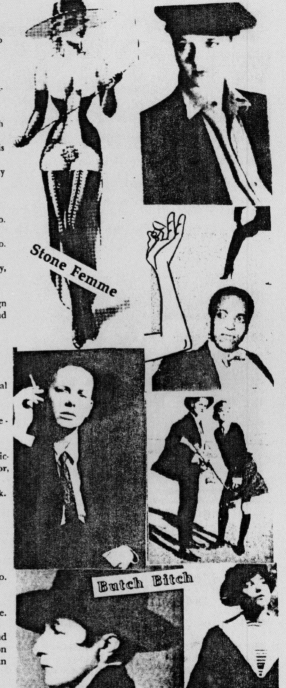

Stone Femme

Butch Bitch

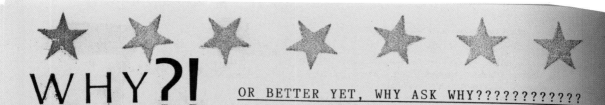

WHY?!

My interest/obsession/crush/wanna-be complex with AMY CARTER started on my 12th birthday, that was the day Jimmy Carter was sworn into office (Jan. 27th, 1977 to be exact).Well I don't quite know how it happened but something clicked, it was like I had found my new best friend only she didn't know I existed. I quess I had an instant crush on her only the crush had more to do with wanting to be her. Plus she was totally geeky and wore glasses and braids and was an only child. I wrote her letters, I'm not sure how many, I only got one response though and it was a form letter. I saved photos of her and talked about her like the other girls talked about The Bay City Rollers, Marie Osmond, Leif Garret and Micheal Jackson. When your a kid you tend to get really emotionally tied up in these kind of obsessions, they're an escape. The reality of it is that kids have   nowhere to run so they often times run away to these safe peaceful people and places inside their heads. Because if someone's fucking with you and you have no means of physical escape you resort to mental +/or emotional escape. Shit this is getting serious, anyways it simply boils down to the fact that I think AMY is this sort of icon cuz she turned out to be a politically active geeky girl artist who makes paintings about race and gender and herself. And yeah, I did want her to be queer, but I guess she's not and that's all I'm gonna say for now, I'll elaborate more on this next time. I do not want to be affiliated with John Hinkley and yes, I probably do have a secret service file.

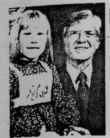

Ex-President's rebel daughter
LOOK AT AMY CARTER NOW

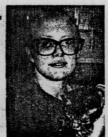

Amy's explanation of her love of painting at the presentation: "It fills the holes in me and gives me back my body parts."

Her paintings also show that she hasn't completely forgotten her life in the limelight. One portrays a group of women passing cake at a tea party—and the White House is the centerpiece in the work.

Another painting, titled Barbara, is a dark portrayal of one of her friends who suffered from a mental illness.

Women, black and white, are a recurring theme in Amy's work—and one of the reasons she chose Brown was because it had a strong women's studies program.

According to one critic, her art is "subtle, yet the colors are vivid and the lines flow. There is also strong symbolism."

"Amy's paintings have an eerie quality about them, sort of like a dream," says K.C. Warren, a public relations official at MCA.

The impish, pigtailed, freckle-faced, little girl with the big glasses who lived in the White House between 1977 and 1981, grew into quite a rebel.

Several years ago she shocked her mom Rosalynn by dyeing her blond hair and eyebrows jet black.

"Why, with her white skin, she looks like a witch," said the former First Lady of her daughter's unusual fashion statement. "It looks as if she put black shoe polish on her head."

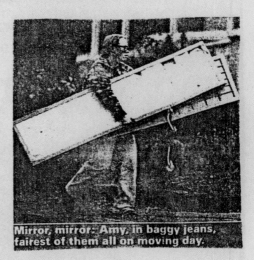

Mirror, mirror: Amy, in baggy jeans, fairest of them all on moving day.

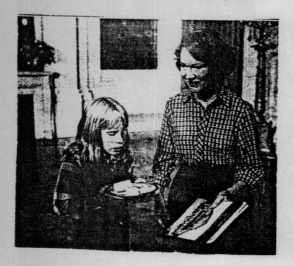

Last year, political activist Amy, who majored in painting at the Tennessee art school, made headlines when she zipped herself up in a body bag and posed for photographers at an anti-Gulf War demonstration in Memphis. But now she says she's determined to stay out of the limelight. "I am a very private person and I want to remain private," Amy tells STAR.

"The reason I don't list my name in the phone book is because I want to be left alone. That should tell everyone I don't want to be contacted."

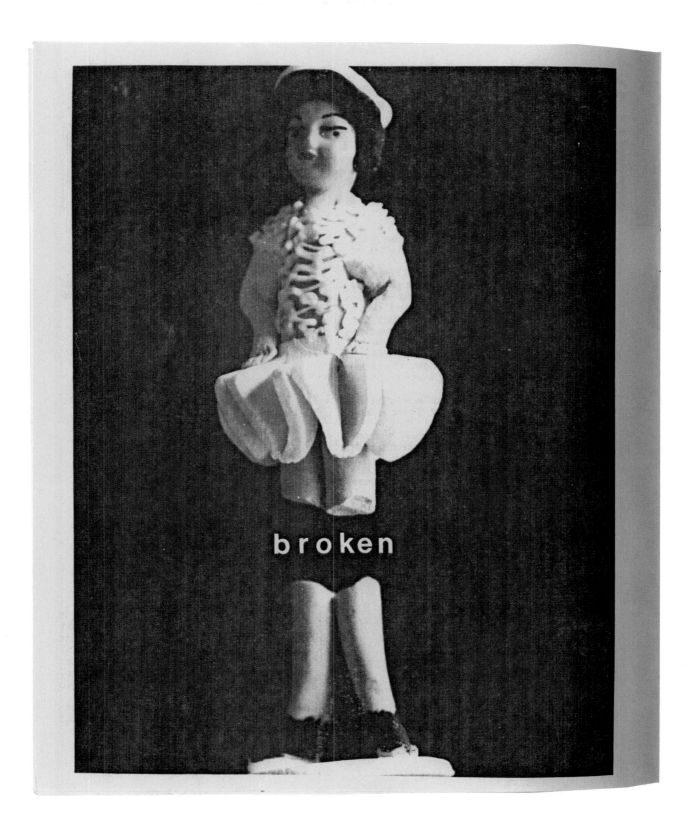

I did not desire her, I wanted
to be her. Not because she was
desire but because she was not
me.

People would mistake us
for sisters.

So much is unsaid and we look
to the floor for secret
passages.

I like her, I don't know about him.

Perhaps you consider yourself
an oracle.

I knew her before I met her.

He said I should go back
to being a girl.

In my head is the constant realization
of the impossibility of our romance.

It's a disturbing comfort.

I shall never get you put
together entirely.

'Empty Nest' star Kristy McNichol in trial marriage — with a woman!

By DOUG and SAMMIE MAYS

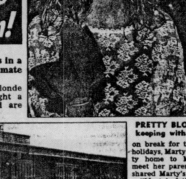

PRETTY BLONDE Martha Allen has set up housekeeping with "Empty Nest" star Kristy McNichol.

"Empty Nest" star Kristy McNichol is in a trial marriage with her longtime datemate Marty — who's a girl!

The 29-year-old actress and pretty blonde Martha "Marty" Allen, 28, recently bought a suburban ranch-style house together and are acting like a married couple, say insiders.

Kristy and Marty are enjoying fixing up their comfy little brown and white home on a quiet street in the San Fernando Valley, revealed a close friend of the couple.

"When they're home, they love snuggling up in front of a warm fire or going for walks in their neighborhood. They spend all their free time together.

"It's obvious Kristy and Marty are in love. They're always hugging and kissing."

Marty has even taken Kristy back to her home in Mississippi to meet her parents — and the girls, who've been dating for 14 months, are talking about getting "married" in a private gay ceremony, according to close sources.

Kristy's girlfriend often visits her on the set. And though producers were furious when they first learned about the relationship last year, now the execs and all of Kristy's coworkers are

Whoa! We're saddled with 65 million horses

Here's the result of the latest "gallop" poll: There are an astounding 65.3 million horses worldwide.

Mongolia, where horses are still used for agriculture, boasts the highest ratio of horses to humans — six steeds for every person.

Although there are 10.72 million horses in the U.S., there's less than one of the hoofers for every 20 people, according to data published in the newsletter of Cornell University College of Veterinary Medicine.

RANCH-STYLE suburban home where Kristy and Marty are living. Marty's black Volkswagen Cabriolet is in the garage.

welcoming Marty with open arms — making the star's joy complete.

"Kristy and Marty couldn't be happier, and everyone is involved with the show is breathing easier," said a series insider. "Now Marty comes to the 'Empty Nest' set regularly and everyone, including star Richard Mulligan, gives her a hello hug.

"Kristy and Marty are treated as if they're a couple of newlyweds."

Said a close source: "Kristy and Marty like to putter around the house on the weekends. Kristy especially likes to tend her garden. They live a very low-key life together.

"They're like any other suburban couple . . . except they're both women!"

In the mornings Kristy waters the plants and then goes off to the set. Shortly after she leaves, Marty heads off to nearby Encino where she works as an insurance agent.

At night Kristy parks her white convertible Mustang next to Marty's black convertible Volkswagen Cabriolet in the garage.

'They're like any other suburban couple . . . except they're women!'

Marty's parents don't object at all to her live-in relationship with Kristy, confided a close friend of the couple.

"When 'Empty Nest' went on break for the Christmas holidays, Marty brought Kristy home to Mississippi to meet her parents. The girls shared Marty's old room.

"Marty's father, a doctor, even took them on a tour of the hospital where he works. He says he and his wife feel like Kristy is part of their family."

Marty, who briefly worked as an actress using the name Martha Allen Miles, had previously lived in a rented apartment. But since she and Kristy were spending so much time together, they decided to buy a house, say sources.

Kristy has put her Los Angeles home up for sale for $975,000.

Though she's happy now, getting others to accept her the way she is hasn't been easy in the past, the insider noted. "For years, her liaisons with other women, including Liberace's niece Ina and a fashion model, have been reported in the press."

As The ENQUIRER revealed last June, network executives were up in arms when they learned Kristy was openly escorting Marty to public events. They felt the gay association could hurt the show's popularity.

" 'Empty Nest' is a show that's big with families and senior citizens," said the insider.

"And after all, Kristy grew up as one of America's little sweethearts playing Buddy on the late '70s drama series 'Family.' "

But recently Kristy boldly confronted producers and flatly said, "Accept me for what I am," revealed the insider.

"She told them, 'Marty is a big part of my life now, and I hope you all understand that. We love each other. Please treat us like you would any other couple.' "

The star's candor won over producers, and they opened their hearts to her and Marty — as did all the cast and crew."

Now the girls are talking about having a lesbian "marriage," the close source disclosed.

"They're considering having a small ceremony for close friends and family to mark their union as a couple. But so far it's only in the talking stages."

Kristy told a pal: "I love coming to work now. I've got the best of both worlds — a role on one of television's best sitcoms and my true love waiting for me when I come home."

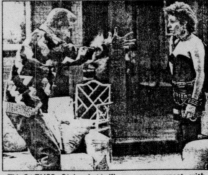

TV FATHER Richard Mulligan seems upset with Kristy in this scene from the show, but in real life he's accepted her lover Marty with open arms.

Strange town where men aren't wanted

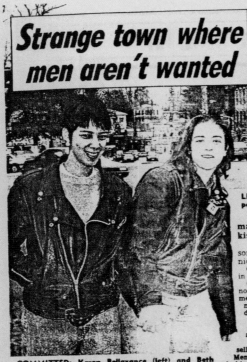

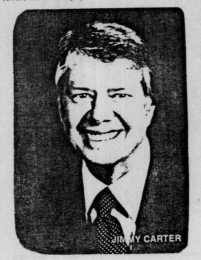

COMMITTED: Karen Bellavance (left) and Beth Grace recently announced their "engagement" in the town's local newspaper.

LESBIANVILLE, U.S.A. — that's what they're calling Northampton, Mass., population 30,000. Some 10,000 gay women live in the area.

Welcome to Lesbianville, U.S.A. — a bizarre town where so many women love women you can even find them cuddling and kissing on Main Street!

The place is listed on maps as Northampton, Mass., but here are just some of the reasons why it got its nickname:

● Some 10,000 gay women live in the town or nearby.

● The newspaper publishes announcements of same-sex engagements and "commitment" ceremonies on the same page as weddings.

● A popular lingerie shop hosts an annual lesbian night.

● One book shop sells "Just Say No to Men" buttons. It also has a lesbian fiction section and a sign telling men to browse elsewhere.

● In bars and restaurants, women hold hands across cozy tables and dance cheek-to-cheek.

● A monthly newspaper lists events such as a lesbian town meeting, plus get-togethers for older lesbians and "Parents and Friends of Lesbians and Gays."

● About half the town's 246 businesses are owned by women, although not all are lesbians.

● There's a yearly Lesbian Home Show — where men are NOT welcome.

● Even the graffiti is gay! On a railroad overpass near

10,000 cuddling, kissing lesbians call it home sweet home

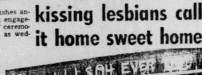

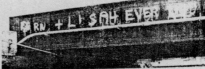

GAY OL' TIME: Even the graffiti is homosexual. On this railroad overpass, two ladies declare their devotion like love-struck teens.

the center of town someone painted: "Fern & Lisa 4-ever."

Northampton (population 30,000) attracts gay women as permanent residents because many stay after graduating from five local colleges, including two all-female schools — Smith and Mount Holyoke.

"I've heard Northampton called Lesbianville and I

think it's kind of nice," said Beth Grace, whose "engagement" to fellow gay Karen Bellavance was recently announced in the town's Daily Hampshire Gazette.

"I feel lucky to live here and to have found a place where I can feel safe. It seems like the town is very accepting of people, no matter who they are and how they want to live."

But not everyone is so happy.

"I don't want to be a watchdog in people's bedrooms, but this type of behavior is not acceptable," declared Pastor Paul Gustine of the Bible Baptist Church.

And local resident Ernie Perkins insisted:

"I know people have the right to live any way they want, but I wish they'd take their sick life-style to San Francisco and leave our town alone!"

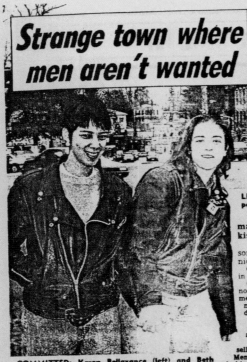

JIMMY CARTER

"DADDY-O"

"Dykes
with
guns,
that'll
scare 'em."
Dorothy
Allison

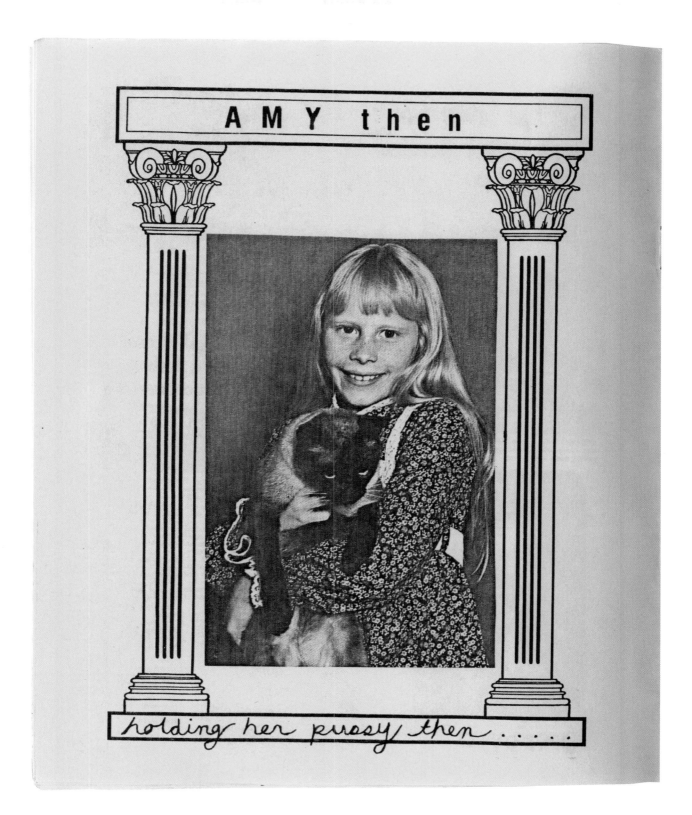

AMY then

holding her pussy then .....

AMY now

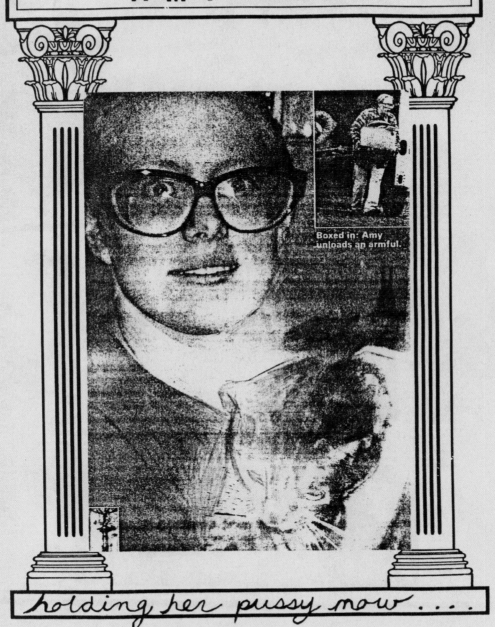

Boxed in: Amy
unloads an armful.

holding her pussy now....

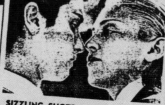

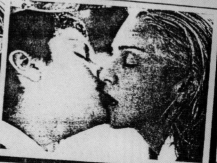

SIZZLING SHOTS — taken by Steven Meisel for Madonna's new X-rated book "Sex" — show Madonna kissing Bernhard's ex-pal Ingrid Casaras. The photos incensed the "Roseanne" star.

Furious "Roseanne" star Sandra Bernhard has accused Madonna of stealing her lesbian lover and putting erotic photos of the woman in her new "Sex" book to humiliate the comedienne!

That's the shocking secret behind the sensational X-rated book which has sold more than 250,000 copies around the U.S. at $50 each.

To add insult to injury, there are several photos of Madonna kissing Bernhard's ex-pal Ingrid Casaras in "Sex," but there isn't a single photo of Sandra — even though she and Madonna had been bosom buddies for years.

The comedienne was so hurt by this one two punch, she called in to radio personality Howard Stern's show last month just before "Sex" was released and she slammed Madonna for stealing her pal.

Madonna "is a jerk," fumed Bernhard on the air. "She's been so evil with me . . . I mean a friend is supposed to be your friend, not your lover's friend."

Stern added: "A real friend wouldn't steal your girlfriend."

"Yeah," declared Bernhard, who plays Tom Arnold's wife on "Roseanne." "There's loyalty between girlfriends . . . real girlfriends."

At the center of this catfight is 25-year-old Ingrid, a dark-haired beauty who appears in the controversial book dressed as a young man being kissed on the lips by Madonna in male drag. "The book is a public slap in Sandra's face," said a friend of Bernhard. "Madonna is flaunting photos of Ingrid and her in the book and Sandra feels it's aimed at her."

Although Madonna states at the beginning of "Sex" that the book is a fantasy and none of it is true, she does include X-rated letters in it about lesbian sex with an Ingrid. And she thanks Ingrid Casaras in the book's acknowledgment.

"I've got Ingrid in the book and that's made Sandra crazy," Madonna told a pal.

"Sandra's just bitching because she's out of

Material Girl used erotic photos of my gal pal to humiliate me, actress fumes

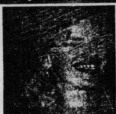

SMILING SANDRA (left) gets a nibble on the neck from lesbian singer k.d. lang. Right, Madonna and Ingrid go jogging with a personal trainer.

lighted in keeping people guessing about their relationship.

They hinted at being lesbian lovers on the David Letterman show and even fondled themselves and ground their bodies together while singing "I Got You Babe" at a New York benefit in 1989.

But their friendship began to unravel at a party Madonna

my life — and good riddance."

Bernhard, 37, and Madonna, 34, were once a big part of each other's lives. They became friends in the late 1980s and de-

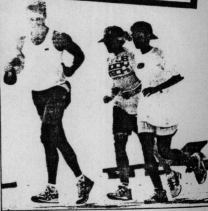

threw last New Year's Eve when Sandra introduced Madonna to her friend, Ingrid. "It

was a kinky all-girl party that Madonna hosted topless," revealed a close source. "And when Madonna set eyes on Ingrid, she knew she had to have her for herself.

"Although Ingrid went home with Sandra, Madonna called her the next day, suggesting she and Ingrid get together. Within weeks she persuaded Ingrid to dump Sandra.

"They've been together ever since.

"When Ingrid is in New York, she stays over at Madonna's apartment. And when they're out together they kiss on the lips and camp it up."

The pair put on a wild show at a party for lesbian singer

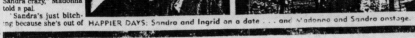

HAPPIER DAYS: Sandra and Ingrid on a date . . . and Madonna and Sandra onstage.

NATIONAL ENQUIRER

I (HEART) AMY CARTER 1

lesbian lover

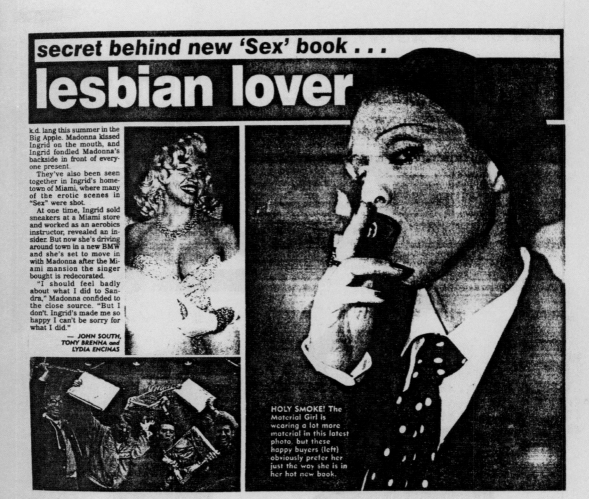

k.d. lang this summer in the Big Apple. Madonna kissed Ingrid on the mouth, and Ingrid fondled Madonna's backside in front of everyone present.

They've also been seen together in Ingrid's hometown of Miami, where many of the erotic scenes in "Sex" were shot.

At one time, Ingrid sold sneakers at a Miami store and worked as an aerobics instructor, revealed an insider. But now she's driving around town in a new BMW and she's set to move in with Madonna after the Miami mansion the singer bought is redecorated.

"I should feel badly about what I did to Sandra," Madonna confided to the close source. "But I don't. Ingrid's made me so happy I can't be sorry for what I did."

— JOHN SOUTH, TONY BRENNA and LYDIA ENCINAS

HOLY SMOKE! The Material Girl is wearing a lot more material in this latest photo, but these happy buyers (left) obviously prefer her just the way she is in her hot new book.

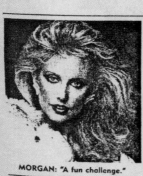

Jilted Sandra finds a new lover on her show — she'll have an affair with Morgan Fairchild!

Sandra Bernhard lost one lesbian lover to Madonna, but she's getting another one on her TV show — Bernhard's character on "Roseanne" will have a lesbian affair with a woman portrayed by Morgan Fairchild!

Bernhard plays Nancy, the wife of Roseanne's real-life hubby Tom Arnold, who left the show last season.

With Tom's character gone, Nancy decides to come out of the closet and shocks her TV pals by announcing her romance with Fairchild.

"I really loved the idea of guesting on the show in any role," Fairchild told a friend. "But playing a lesbian on TV's No. 1 show makes it not just a challenge — but fun as well.

"I'd love it if my character becomes a regular. What actress wouldn't want to be a part of that wonderful cast?"

Morgan won't play the first gay character on the show though. Martin Mull portrayed a homosexual man last season.

Fairchild, 42, is best known for her many TV movies and a starring role on "Flamingo Road."

Her featured episode, entitled "Ladies Choice," airs on ABC November 10.

MORGAN: "A fun challenge."

NATIONAL ENQUIRER

37

113

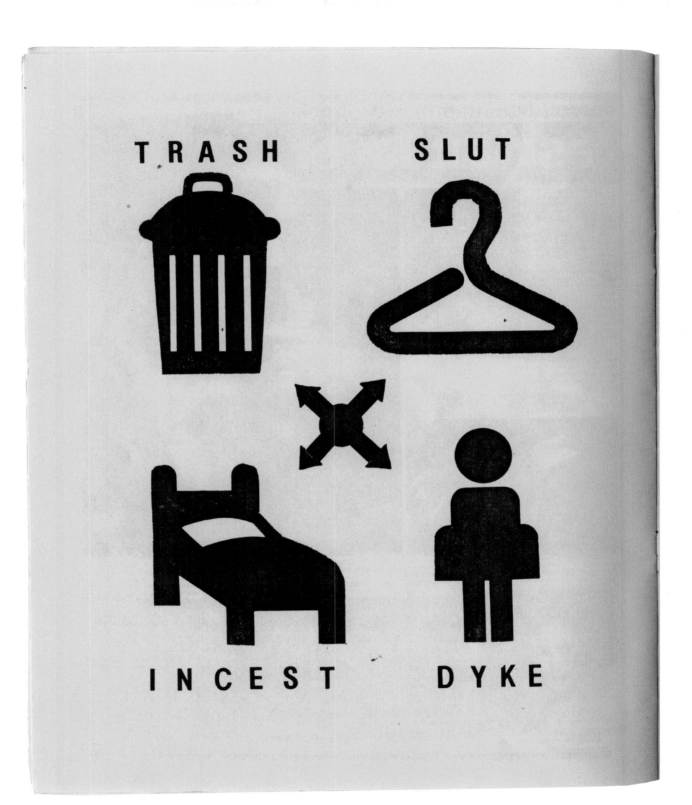

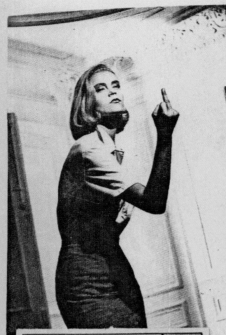

Typical Week and a Half

Mon. Fantasized fucking a woman with a penis and not letting her use her penis on me. No sex today.

Tues. Dressed in jockey shorts and a long white dress. Looked for a woman or a man dressed as a woman.

Wed. Made love to a man with a vagina while I fantasized that I was dressed as a man making love to a woman.

Thurs. Got fucked by a man and loved it. No fantasy.

Fri. Got eaten by a woman and loved it. No fantasy.

Sat. Played with myself. Fantasized that I was a woman playing with herself.

Sun. A man, pretending to be a woman, let me eat him. I fantasized that he was a woman pretending to be a man.

Mon. While being fucked by a man, I pretended I was fucking him. One of us came.

Tues. A woman made love to me. After, she told me that she was a man and hated queers. She never undressed.

Wed. Went looking for a man to fuck me, but changed my mind and went home with someone dressed in pants.

Thurs. Two people picked me up. One had a penis; the other never undressed. I was satisfied by both.

Fri. Filled out a sex questionnaire.

Anonymous

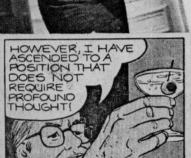

HOWEVER, I HAVE ASCENDED TO A POSITION THAT DOES NOT REQUIRE PROFOUND THOUGHT!

IF ANYONE HAS INFORMATION OF ANY KIND ON AILEEN WUORNOS (infamous lesbian "serial killer") or JONI LEIGH PENN (she locked herself in Sharon Gless' house with a gun) PLEASE SHARE WITH ME WHATEVER YOU"VE GOT BECAUSE I NEED IT FOR A PROJECT I'M DOING. O.K. THANKS

my friend Terri Lemieux sent me this many years ago. XO XO to her.

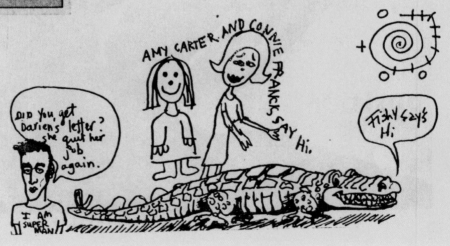

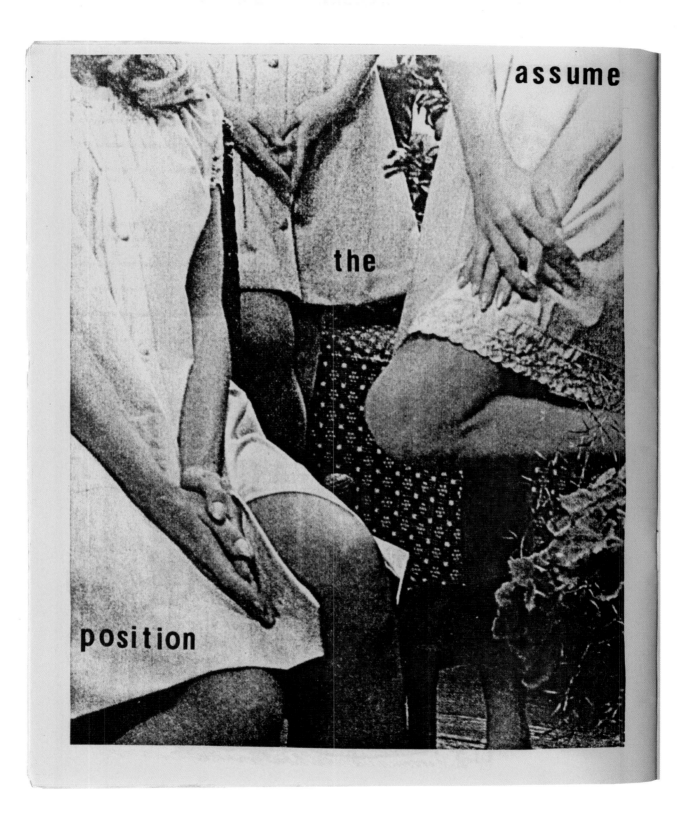

assume

the

position

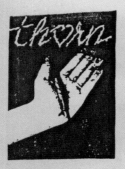 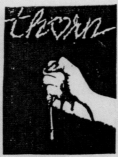

Whether it's articles, music, comix, images or a combination of all of these things, Thorn is about uniting voices and echoing anger and resistance as a positive force for public/personal change.

Send $3.50 (postpaid) to:
Thorn
371 Church #1
San Francisco, CA
94114

(she's back ON the saddle)

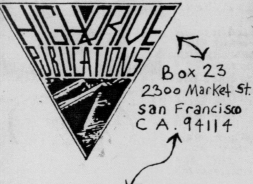

special love and thanks for those who helped me make it through the past year; NANCY, KELLY, SARAH, COSTAS, JON, and HEIDI...XOXOXOXOXOXOXOXOXOXOX

xxxxxxxxxxxxxxxxxxxxxxxxxxxxxxxxxxxxxxxxxxxxxxxxxxxxxxxxxxxxxxx
xxxxxxxxxxxxxxxxxxxxxxxxxxxxxxxxxxxxxxxxxxxxxxxxxxxxxxxxxxxxxxx
HIGH DRIVE PUBLICATIONS is a loose conglomeration of creative minds dedicated to spending all of their time and money to bringing you the most exciting in printed word and image. You can get copies of ANTABUSE, REPORT FROM THE STAR WARS GENERATION, and MY SPOKANE. All of these publication/zines are worth checking out, so do. Write to them for more info. THORN and I ♥ AMY CARTER are also HIGH DRIVE PUBLICATIONS. And we're all friends, isn't that cute. xxxxxxxxxxxxxxxxxxxxxxxxxxxxxxxxxxxx
xxxxxxxxxxxxxxxxxxxxxxxxxxxxxxxxxxxxxxxxxxxxxxxxxxxxxxxxxxxxxxx
xxxxxxxxxxxxxxxxxxxxxxxxxxxxxxxxxxxxxxxxxxxxxxxxxxxxxxxxxxxxxxx

Box 23
2300 Market St.
San Francisco
CA. 94114

117

When rebels dress alike, all conform

Dear Miss Manners: I am a young artist. To fill in the gaps, I've worked as a fashion model and I've come to enjoy wearing beautiful clothes, most of which I make myself.

I was raised in a family which believes that gracious manners are meant to put everyone at ease. But when I get dressed up, I wonder if anyone will take me seriously as an artist.

Judith Martin

All the young artists I know show up at formal affairs wearing torn paint-splattered jeans. It's the badge of a "real" artist. Of course, the idea is to be a revolutionary, and artists have been doing it for a long time.

Do you think it is too shocking of me to dress in beautiful, fashionable clothes and use the manners I've been taught? It sounds funny to ask, but I'm serious.

Gentle reader: What Miss Manners finds shocking is the rigid conventionality of the revolutionaries you describe. Why they do not more often rebel against having to wear a drab uniform, in dour conformity with their peers, she cannot imagine.

But, alas, Miss Manners has come to realize that people who most vehemently champion the right to dress as they wish or, in the current term, in what they feel comfortable with, are the first to attack those of us who feel comfortable dressing conventionally. They have been after Miss Manners and her little white gloves for years.

She would therefore encourage you to seize your freedom by embracing propriety. Let us not hear any more nonsense about artists only being real when they have the superficial proof of wearing studio work clothes. She reminds you that the great painters of history were only too delighted to apply their visual sense to their own persons.

As for your manners, of course you should use them. If rudeness were an indication of artistry, this would be the Renaissance.

---

what's a guy to do? — Lock Jawed, Nebraska

Dear Lock Jawed: Ladies know that using a rough word or so at work gives them the power big shot guys have — and top psychologists back this up. Don't be so prissy.

I'm in love with a guy — and a gal

Dear Dotti: I met this very good-looking boy and I go to where he hangs out whenever I can. Then my sister saw him with another guy — not just another guy, you know, but a gay guy.

I was going to tell him off, but he hugged me and kissed me and told me he hadn't told me he was bisexual because he didn't think I would accept it.

Well, the average person probably wouldn't accept it, but I am also attracted to the same sex, although I've never been with a girl.

I told him this and he introduced me to his cousin who's bisexual, too. She's very nice looking and 16, my age.

The problem is that I like them both. Should I drop one or the other, or see them both? — Every Which Way, California

Dear Every Which Way: Does your mother know you're out, little girl? You need to be smacked across the

---

bottom and kept at home until you learn guys are for gals and vice versa.

Confidential

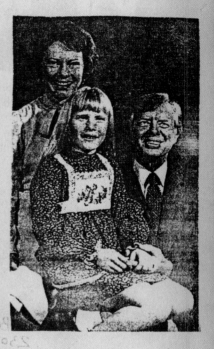

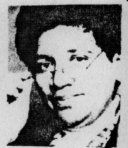

DREW BARRYMORE romances 21-year-old actor Corky Nemec (above) in real life, but she shares her first hot screen kiss with a girl. Drew, 17, kisses teen sitcom star SARA GILBERT in the movie, *Poison Ivy.* "I took Sara's face in my hands and started licking her lips," says Drew. "Suddenly, she opened her mouth and I stuck my tongue in—a full-tongue major kiss."

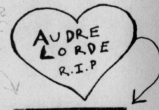

AUDRE LORDE R.I.P

o.k. here's my most recent sob story. my friend kathleen told me that the band fifth column was sure to hit the west coast during their late fall tour of the states. so, needless to say i've been waiting with one eye on the look out. you see i've been a big fan for years, yes years. and also i heard that donna dresch was touring with them, not only is donna THE dorky foxy queer bait rock-n-roll mamma, she is also THE only other utterly devoted AMY CARTER fan/lover/wannabe that i have ever met. so i was hoping to touch base with her and maybe solicit AMY material from her. anyways i went to s.f. for thanksgiving and my first night there i gave my friends the "you've gotta go see fifth column" speech. they were all like, yeah, yeah whatever you say, the next morning another friend informed me that he had gone to see fifth column the previous night, and of course that they rocked and that it was babesville. don't you just hate when this kinda stuff happens. my life seems exceptionally prone to these kinda missed moments. and of course by the time I returned to l.a. they had already played here. ohhhhhh welll1....hey donna if this zine finds it's way to you please get in touch with me cuz i would like to do a phone interview with you for the next issue. there are bigger sob stories at stake here though...like the deaths JO SPENCE (photographer) AUDRE LORDE (writer)/DAVID WOJNAROWICZ (artist)/PAUL, DAVE, and ROBERT (all friends of varying degrees and of great importance to me). Issues of wellness and illness have been a big part of the lives of my friends and i'm feeling rather sad/angry about it today. maybe it has a little to do with the olympia like climate that has suddenly swept over southern CAL, it's the first damp grey sky i've experienced since moving here. so, boo-fuckin-hoo.

If you would like copies of this issue or future issues of I ♥ AMY CARTER please send $2.00 per issue, and a couple of stamps if you've got them. and please do send contributions and love letters.

A B C
D E F

BEFORE

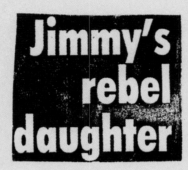

A B C
D E F

AFTER

I ♥ AMY
CARTER

c/o Tammy Rae
512 Rose Ave.
LONG BEACH, CA. 90802

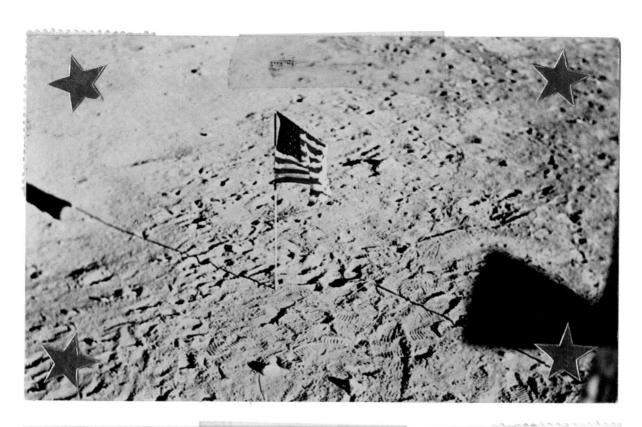

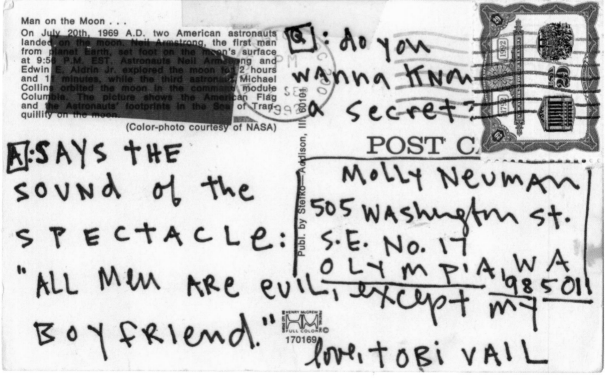

Man on the Moon . . .
On July 20th, 1969 A.D. two American astronauts
landed on the moon. Neil Armstrong, the first man
from planet Earth, set foot on the moon's surface
at 9:56 P.M. EST. Astronauts Neil Armstrong and
Edwin E. Aldrin Jr. explored the moon for 2 hours
and 11 minutes, while the third astronaut Michael
Collins orbited the moon in the command module
Columbia. The picture shows the American Flag
and the Astronauts' footprints in the Sea of Tranquillity on the moon.

(Color-photo courtesy of NASA)

@: do you wanna know a secret?

A: SAYS the sound of the SPECTACLE: "ALL MEN ARE EVIL, except BOYFRIEND." my

POST C

Molly NEUMAN
505 Washington st.
S.E. No. 17
OLYMPIA, WA
98501

love, TOBI VAIL

POSTCARD

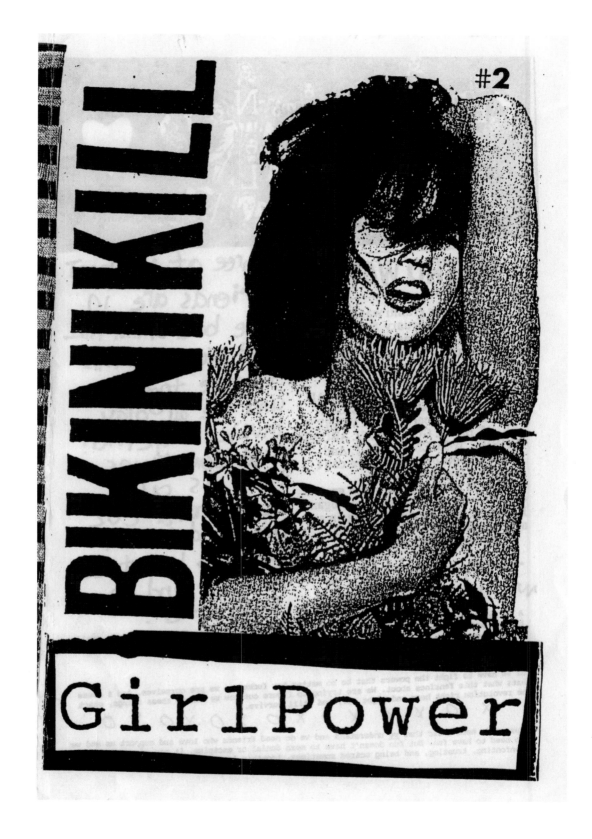

BIKINI KILL 2 (EXCERPT)

METRO WATCH

The anti-war graffiti was terrible in January and February. So now that the war's over? Don't ask.

On the rise downtown is graffiti most charitably described as anti-male. Some use blunter language.

The most quoted slogan is: DEAD MEN DON'T RAPE. UMBILICAL NOOSE is another. Others: WOMEN FIGHT BACK. GOD IS GAY. ABORT CHRIST. WOMEN REVOLT. And there are lots more, many we can't print in a family newspaper.

For that matter, some of the graffiti doesn't even make sense. One slogan Hutchings says he runs into again and again is: BIKINI KILL. Bikini kill?

Curiouser and curiouser.

Three of my best friends are in the band BIKINI KILL and we made this fanzine together. and we all play music together. And sometimes this is all very hard cuz this world doesn't teach us how to be truly cool to each other and so we have to teach each other.

A belief in instant revolution is just what THE POWERS THAT BE want. That way we won't realize that WE ARE THE REVOLUTION. It'll look so hard and instant and far off, someday, someday, that we won't even try to enact it right now.

Cuz we have to fight the powers that be no matter how fucked up we are ourselves. And i guess thats what this fanzines about. We are trying to figure out how we can do these things, enact the revolution right here and right now, and still survive.

X O X O X O X O X O X O X O

Cuz we do need music that __we__ understand and we do need friends who love and support us and we do need to have fun. But fun doesn't have to mean denial or escapism, it can mean struggling, confonting, trusting, and being scared sometimes, together instead of always alone.

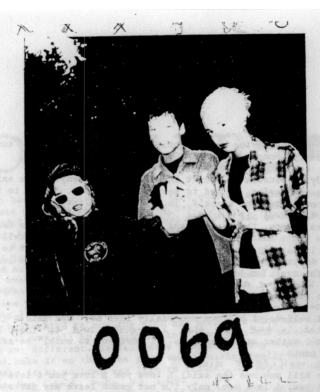

0069

Tabatha says death to all fuckhead
fanzine editors who dare to dis the Brat-
mobile/Bikini Kill/RGSN/Girl Day/Inter-
national Pop Underground Revolution Summer
1991 Riot Grrrl Style Now even!!! To so
completely miss the whole point of everything, yeah well I'm sure he's a "nice guy"
and "harmless" anyways, and besides, I hear
he's had a "rough" life---yeah, so have most
sexist fuckheads and I feel so badly for them,
NOT. But what I'm even more distressed about
is that he is a total square, irreconilably
so, and that it is squares like this that
seem to have the say so about the current
state of "punk rock" and the like: FUCK THE
FLIPSIDE FANZINE GUY, and I don't wanna hate
the kids which is just to say what to do what
to do? about NONREVOLUTIONARIES misrepresenting
the underground to hundreds of potential
cool kids, we're gonna have to fight, well
alright!!! um...it's just unforgivable really,

BIKINI KILL 2 (EXCERPT)

right in the middle of so many punk roc
dreams come true. I'm so sure.(I'm so s
means what the fuck)

Ok and well the Bikini Kill have
been out and about, having teenage kick
all through the night and all around th
world, looking for New! and meeting eve
body and let me just say there is so mu
and as far as the eye can see this Revo
tion Girl Style Now thing is happening
real--"destroying the police and turnin(
coal into diamonds" says our friend the
shmada and it's all accross the nation
with the Nation--on tour-oh yeah, and tl
young idea, dc/olympia! from coast to
coast with spies in morocco(sending our
bass player cool packages and fucked up
indecipherable marriage proposals) and
contacts and the like in virtually ever]
major u.s. city and all the cool towns
in between: the time is now for quittinç
school and breaking the rules cuz, as wa
evidenced in a big way throughout the
entire summer and especially and the I.F
convention, the undeniable genius of thi
generation has surfaced and it's all
about ACTION, no time to decide what's

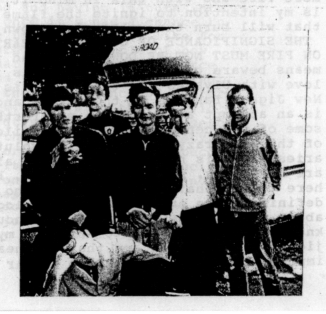

right what's right what's right, gotta
write and everyday its hanging out with
all the cool kids in my neighborhood and
especially with Kathi Wilcox, girl of
style, see cuz we are currently split-
ting the smallest of apartments here
in the Martin(Olympia's one and only
nighttime hot spot) on account of that
we are on the verge of another tour
with the N.O.U. kids and then we are
going to D.C. for an indefinite amount
of time, so yeah, it is true, the slumber
party bunk bed scene, Bikini Kill style
now, is full fledged and me and Kathi
are making pacts and writing on the
walls, running down halls and every night
before we go to sleep we faithfully

repeat the mantra "lets go lets go yeah
yeah yeah"(this, courtesy of S. GAMBOA)
and begin our day with the proverbial
MOD jump and 10 push ups each until our
departure.
     True Love Will Never Die and this
I really do believe, despite bitter cries
of treason from those closest to my own
heart, and alienation becomes fuel for
more fire and with this in mind it
is my intention to ignite the flame
that will burn the walls right down:
 THE SIGNIFICANCE OF OUR YOUNG HEARTS
ON FIRE MUST NOT BE DOWNPLAYED and this
means beware of the girl who falls in
love with Ulysses and that there is a
New Jigsaw fanzine in the making and it
is an attempt at trying to set forth
some of the central existential dilemmas
of the boy crazy modern girl revolution-
aries(which is not to assume that all
are boy crazy, most certainly not, but I'm
here to say that there are some who most
definitely are and we are not apologetic
about this in the least) so you should
know that I am trying to sort out my
jigsaw fanzine mail and that its nearly
impossible because I'm about a year behind

BIKINI KILL 2 (EXCERPT)

so if you wrote me before and I never wrote
you back you should write again and say
so and I'll try and do better this time,
in fact, what with the new riot grrrl press
scene that's about to start up(see this
fanzine somewhere on another page for
more information on this scene phenomenon)
maybe I'll even get all four issues back
in print, yeah so write me a letter at
the address listed for Riot Grrrl in dc...
and hopefully the number five will be
available soon, although I have my doubts
about this, to tell the truth because
I have been writing letters into infinity
and thinking about all these feminist
theory questions to do with punk rock &

don't feel as if I am making any progress
in sorting any of this out and maybe its
gonna take forever to even formulate the
questions that I want an answer to and
that kind of sucks because I feel as if
things are stagnating which is why its
so important to ask some of those questions
here in the Bikini Kill fanzine number 2,
but before you go on to read the rest of
it...have you noticed that there is this
weird phenomenon that happens to do with
naming something and having it turn into
something else once it's had a chance to
assimilate into understanding---like for
instance hardcore is an example of how
an aesthetic that was originally fierce
and powerful and in the vein of fucking
shit up became the the essence of conformity in punk rock, what with the generic
drum beat/song structure/vocal tricksetc.
not ot mention the rigidity of the style
code of nonconformity and this all becomes
a total end in itself, apart from inciting
any kind of strong revolutionary agenda
that could be happening--or another
example has to do with jokes; things that
start out as a joke become a total end
part of everyday life-like how making

fun of the way someone talks can totally become a real way to talk or even to communicate something entirely separate from it's origin--or the thing of in jokes where it goes on and on and on and nobody remembers where it came from or why but they keep referring to it and it ends up being some kind of weird ritualistic assertation of a group identity that has very little to do with the actual situation from which it stemmed...well anyways, I think that this sort of phenomenon could happen in our fanzines too, self-referencing to the point of absurdity which may or may not be significant--personally it is my total entertainment scene which I think is entire valid, politically even--but also, a more serious concern is perhaps at stake here and that is that in this environment it is too easy for our doctrines to turn into dogma and RGSN recitations rather than meaningful interactions is what may- be becomes the political terrain: new standards arise when our whole thing was to shatter the old and replace them with action..again with reference to something our good friend the shmada said said to me one day, we must not let the precedents we set our selves distract us from the very things that drove us to set those precedents in the first place and it is with this in mind that I encourage girls everywhere to set forth their own revolutionary agendas from their own place in the world, in relation to thier own scenes or whatever, rather than to simply think about ours

THis is about making new meanings of what it is to be cool that make real sense to you to do with who you are and what you want in revolution...embrace subjectivity as the only reality there is...context is everything...an idea of aesthtics as subjecthic truth, more on this next time...action.

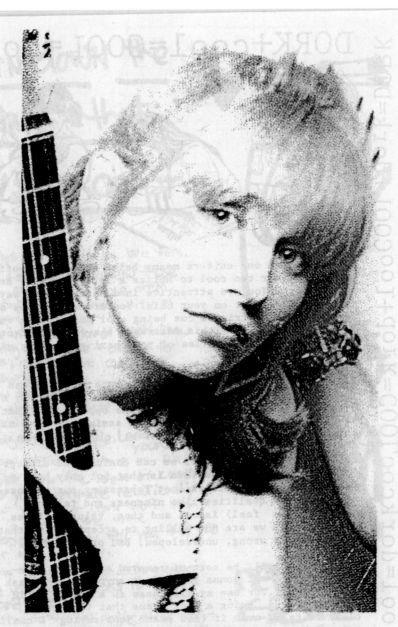

Paula Pierce, lead singer and guitar
player of the all-girl L.A. based
band the Pandoras died of a heart
attack last month. She was so cool.
I used to listen to the Pandoras in
9th grade. She changed my life and
Billy was in love with her. R.I.P.
                              --Tobi

LAME LAME

Why're we always explaining ourselves and our
projects to boys? I'm serious. I have wasted
more time and emotional energy doing this
than i even wanna admit. And see, i have
come to the conclusion that we are banging
our heads against a big wall. We are trying
to find that magic word that will change
their minds, make them see. we are trying
to fit thru the doors of a clubhouse that
s smelly and gross inside anyways...we
only want in cuz we've been taught to want
in...we change ourselves to fit, alter what
we say, how we say it, just hoping, hoping
they will change their rules...and all the
while the clubhouses we could be building
re going unbuilt and us girls are knocking
one by one, on a door that will never ever
open.   we are just keeping ourselves trapped in these nice little boundaries
/having these cohesive arguments with boys where we try to explain to them that sexism
s real and that we are aware of when its being acted out around us. If he didn't know
anything at all about plumbing and pipes, i doubt he'd go up to a plumber and start
talking all this shit about how he knows how to fix a sink better than her/him. So why
the hell is he acting like he knows what it's like to grow up female, and why am i ans-
ering to him? I mean, you can't dialogue with someone who is kicking you to the ground,
o why are you/i/we explaining all this stuff to these boys who really aren't interested
n learning and only wanna "win" an argument? And why are we constructing our arguments
n this dumb right/wrong, you've gotta be "plausible", back it up with facts, there's
nly two ways to be, don't contradict yourself, "prove it to me", level???

t is not our responsibility to explain
ow boys/men are being sexist anymore than
t is our responsibility to "prevent our-
elves" from getting raped. It is their
esponsibility Not to Rape Us and it is
their responsibility Not to Be Sexist.
me, a big part of feminism (or whatever you wanna the rejection of the equation,
rl=dumb) is the simple assertion that us girls are important. Our bodiesheartsminds
e important enough that we will defend them, protect them, ourselves. We don't have
live lives that are filled up with events that are really just sentimentalized versions
abuse. We don't wanna live that way and we don't have to. So why are we taking abuse
the form of these conversations with boys and/or men? Why are we always making these
mb excuses for them, like, "Oh, but he's got a good heart underneath it all", "He's
st really young", or (my personal favorite) "But he really is a nice guy."

BIKINI KILL 2 (EXCERPT)

SO VERY LAME

an illustration of a too often repeated pattern ↓

A GUY DOES/SAYS/MAKES SOMETHING SEXIST

"Hey Baby."

A guy you live with buys an album by a dumb cockrock band that has a picture of naked bludgeoned women on the front of it. He leaves it lying on the living room floor.

A woman is slapped.

YOU TELL HIM IT'S SEXIST

"Leave me alone."

You tell him that the record cover pisses you off and that you don't wanna have to look at it.

She puts her hands up to avoid another slap.

THERE IS A LACK OF RECOGNITION BY SPECTATOTORS THAT ANYTHING IS HAPPENING

People on the street just walk on by.

This is just a friendly disagreement and has nothing to do w/him maintaining his male privelage. She realizes no one will intervene.

YOUR ARGUEMENT IS INVALIDATED

"I was just trying to be friendly."

He tells you to lighten up. Don't take things so seriasly. They only meant the cover as a joke. ha ha

She is slapped again.

YOU RESIST ALL SEXIST CLAIMS AND EXERT SELF AS IMPORTANT AND VALID

"Get the Fuck away from me!"

You tell him he's being a jerk and that if you think it's sexist then it is.

She fights back.

YOU ARE TOLD OR MADE TO FEEL LIKE IT IS YOUR PROBLEM

"What's your problem bitch are you crazy?"

He tells you that you are causing the problem by making such a big deal over a little thing or he says you are the sexist cuz you are being sexist to him.

She is kicked in the face.

Well, if he's such a "nice guy", why does he expect you to NOT ONLY bear the brunt of sexist stuff like harassment, belittlement, and the valid fear of rapemurder BUT ALSO be prepared to have a calm, fact filled discussion with him about something that is more than just a "subject" to you? It is the struggle we engage in everyday by virtue of breathing, everytime we assert our right to exist. Sexism is not a list or something we can prove, it is not a dot on a line and can not be located on a graph or colored in on a chart. It is mapped on the lines of our skin and etched in the deepest reasoni ngs of our hearts. Purple Blue Black, thuds that are like death in the middle of the night. OF COURSE I'M GONNA BE EMOTIONAL WHEN I AM FORCED TO DESCRIBE THE BARS ON THE CAGE THAT I FUCKIN LIVE IN. It is time we stopt describing the bars and time to fucking make our move. We are bustin outta this joint.

But i know it is not so easy. Cuz we live in a world where we are compelled to explain ourselves to men AND we've got to deal with that while at the same time we are trying to create spaces where we are able to breath and we do fit in without trying and belong, without explanation. This is especially hard cuz we have internalized sexism to such an extent that it's not just an issue of us explaining to "them" (as if there is a unified "them") but also an issue of us explaining ourselves to ourselves and to each other. And while i think it is high fucking time that we stop explaining ourselves , i think it's important that we are able to recognize certain criticisms for what they are: Lame attempts, by people who're threatened by what the girl revolution brings, to discount and discourage us. Doing this is sort of like untangling ourselves from a big invisible sticker bush.

The same way that rapists and street harassers don't usually come right out and say, "Okay, I'm gonna rape/harrass you now." Most men/boys (even the "good ones") don't come right out and say that they are against girls having/redefining power. Thus, in order for them to maintain the unequal power distribution of male over female, without looking like assholes (He agrees with you, he just thinks you are going about IT all wrong) they must find more subtle ways of discounting and discouraging you.

1. YOU TAKE THINGS TOO SERIOUSLY. YOU ARE PARANOID.

1 in 3 of us are gonna get raped in our lifetimes...the threat of rape permeates every centimeter of our bodies and influences where we are able to live, work, walk and what we feel safe saying. Women comprise the majority of people who live in poverty. Women don't make as much money or get the same benefits from work that men do. We also have to deal with sexual harrassment, an experience so commonplace, most of us don't even notice it anymore or have desensitized to cuz we know it'll probably never stop and is almost to be expected anyways. And so many of us are single moms too, and our dumb boyfriends and ex-husbands don't pay any child support and say that $100 a month is just too much.   facts. Facts. Facts????
You want facts, you want it in writing? facts aren't as real as watching your bestfrined cry or seeing a woman who lives in her car, carrying a coat around in the middle of the summer.
Women die. Women die of diseases that never get studied cuz no one gives a shit if we have to get our tits chopped off or are laying in our own blood screaming. AND AND AND the NIH (The National Institute of Health that is supposed to be studying diseases but is really spending poor peoples tax money to torture and mutilate animals in repetitive and non-conclusive tests) uses mostly male bodies and cells to study AIDS and cancer on cuz these men like to act like male and female bodies are the same when it's convenient for them BUT US GIRLS KNOW that its a completely different story when they see us on the street. "Nice tits. Nice legs, Nice ass."
And us girls are constantly being told in a million ways that we are shit and that the way we are is somehow wrong and our bodies are dirty and we should hide the fact that we have periods and shit and fart and bleed, bleeed, bleed....we should hide the fact that we have desire at all, don't let anyone know that we are not content ("smile baby") to be mindless machines programmed to serve Boy wants and needs and desires.
AND and AND WE are not the ones who're deciding who the "great" artists or writers or philosophers or musicians are either. That's fucking right, We are totally excluded from the REALM OF THE MASTERS (except those few female tokens who accept fascism in return for their entrance into the white boy toyland) and we have not even existed as artists, etc...as far as "history" is concerned.
We are totally discouraged from learning how to play instruments of fix things because in school it is "suggested" that we take Home Ec (instead of Shop) and Chorus (instead of Band) and then we get treated like we are dumb cuz we can't play Stairway to Heaven on the first try or fix our own cars.
But see, a lot of us don't even have our own cars, meaning we have to walk places....and this is horrifying cuz everyone in the world thinks they can judge us like we are in a walking talking Beauty Contest always. they always wanna comment on you, what HE thinks, what HE sees....it makes you never wanna go out and i guess that's the point. Stare Stare Stare at me, at the show, on the street, on the bus, when you pull your dumb red camaro next to my car at the light, at the AA meeting, in the classroom, the board meeting,The Peeping Tom stares in the window of your own house.
   But i guess that is not enough cuz our girlsouls are very strong so they have to keep trying to crush them.
We are force fed anti-female propaganda via our exclusion and misrepresent-ation within: Films & videos, texts, novels, discussions, oral histories, music, Tv, newspapers, college boards, classrooms, advertising, etc....We walk into video stores (many of us with our friends who can afford a Tv and VCR) only to see female bodies scantily clad, slashed, gashed, mutilated OR at the very least, clinging to some dumb looking guy, on the covers of nearly every single video.

133

There is no free childcare in this dumb ass country and almost all health insurance (for those of us who have it) doesn't cover anything to do with reproduction or sexually transmitted diseases. (Its your fault your female) AND even though we are almost the exclusive victims of male crimes like rape, incest and domestic violence WE are also the ones who are trained to make good victims (those highheels look so nice....YOU HAVE GOT TO BE POLITE GIRL) and NOT trained how to defend ourselves via our exclusion from contact sports and self defense in school.
AND we are constantly reminded that we had better not speak out about any of thisstuff or SOMETHING BAD IS GONNA HAPPEN TO US...from The Little Red riding Hood story we learn as kids to the 14 women gunned down in Montreal, the message is clear: IF YOU STRAY FROM THE PATH OF SILENCE THE WOLF IS GONNA EAT YOU UP. Or if your a college student, maybe he'll just line you and your girlfriends up against a wall and shoot you.

I guess if i was running around telling people that the sky was falling i could understand them thinking i was being paranoid. But in a world where 4000 women a year are being murdered by the men "who love them" (heart heart heart) I don't think talking about the situation of women and girls is an "over reaction." How in the hell can someone take the severe psychic/emotional/sexual/physical abuse of over half the world, "too seriously?"

2. # YOU ARE EXCLUSIONARY AND ALIENATING TO MEN.

Well excuse me, have i hit a nerve?
I guess its hard for people who have been continually fucking excluded form everything to make their main priority BEING ACCESSIBLE to the very people who perpetuate and profit from their exclusion. Duh.
Men/boys need to open their eyes and realize that their is a severe lack of work in every media and field, made from a female perspective (not that their is one, singular, female perspective) and that it is really important that we start making things that make sense to US and to our friends.
And sure, what we make is gonna be really clouded up with its own shit, sexism, in many cases, translates to self hatred and girl competitions for male approval....and thats gonna show up in our work...as is racism, classism, speciesism, heterosexism, ageism, etc....BUT if we don't at least start trying to FUCK WITH THE POWERS THAT BE (outside and inside ourselves) then we are never gonna make it to the world we are struggling so desparately to envision and create.
We have been excluded for fucking ever sa far as i'm concerned. Our voices, no matter how loud or impassioned, are still only muffled whispers as compared to the burly straight white male ones that bellow their stories and opinions into even the smallest crevice of our lives. For men to claim exclusion is totally ridiculous and insulting.
Sure, men and boys who're challenging the fact that their gender roles are sucing them dry of real life and denying them access to our sincerest forms of respect...these men are excluded, like girls/women, from most of what the mainstream and supposeofly "counter" culture has to offer them....but these men also recognize our work/experiments as VALID, being our Brothers in Struggle, why would they feel excluded??????
TO THE MEN WHO DO FEEL EXCLUDED/alienated by the grrrl revolution brings:
If you are not firmly commited to finding a way out of the pit of capitalism and all other "isms", if you are not ready to put the neccesary work in, to posit yourself in history and recognize your privelages.....then maybe you feel so excluded because, as one who profits from the lie and denies it, you are excluded from true life and the revolution........TAKE RESP- ONSIBILTY, DUDE.....go high five your neanderthal brothers on it.........
NO ONE EXCLUDED YOU, you X'd yourself.

BIKINI KILL 2 (EXCERPT)

3. To "GO BEYOND" SEXISM.

This is the same logic that lets people say, "A woman can't be raped unless she wants to be" OR "I would never allow someone to rape me." As if those of us who've been raped, secretly wanted it, or HAD A CHOICE. As if some of us totally "get off" on being harrassed or belittled or denied access to the stuff we need like jobs, etc.....as if, some of us enjoy sexism, cuz we "get off" on talking about it (its so fun afterall) or are so bored that we make this shit up.

A couple of months ago i asked my Mom how the threat of rape affected her life and she said "It Doesn't." And so i said, "Well, what about when you are, like, walking around at night by yourself?" And she replied "I would never do that." [my mother doesn't know what its like to walk down a street when its dark. My mom can't go out and look at the stars]

And Yes, women do have the ability to create environments for them/ourselves where we don't SEE or FEEL sexism as much as we could, but that does not mean that it doesn't exist. The very fact that we avoid certain situations in the first place should tell us how profoundly sexism affects our lives.

And Yes, creating situations (within our bands, our scenes, our fanzines) where we are ACTIVELY DENYING SEXISM just by refusing to accept it or let it stop us.....and plowing "Straight on Thru" it, is really really important. BUT by acting like girls/women who are criticquing sexism in different ways than this, are, somehow, NOT ALLOWING THEMSELVES to "go beyond" sexism, we are obscuring the very real financial, emotional, racial, educational and cultural differences that separate us. And these differences have evrything to do with what projects we are going to choose and how safe we feel about actualizing them.

Does this make sense? See, a girl who got hit by or emotionally abused by her dad whenever she said something that "upset him", might not be able to confront the sexist shit in her own life as firmly as other girls can. Or like a Woman of Color who doesn't have the same mobility, as far as jobs go, as most whitegirls do, might be a little more leary about plowing right over a sexist boss or co-worker. Maybe she will write about her experiences instead, as a way to get some power and feel in control again. And the last thing she needs is someone telling her"Why don't you just confront the person instead of always writing about it?"

This "Women could transcend sexism if they wanted to" stuff, sounds supiciously like something a whitebusinesssuitguy might say. "Blacks are laxy, thats why they don't have jobs. Thay should just pull themselves up by their bootstraps." Well, that's easy for HIM to say.

what is especially maddening about the underlaying assumption that some of us CHOOSE to be affected by sexism (we like it, it gives meaning to our boring uneventful lives) is that it so often puts big rifts between us. This is where the whole "humanist" argument, comes in.

She says: "I consider myself more a Human Being than a Woman."

Its as if those of us who are openly aware of fucked up gender constructs are just "hung up" on the fact that we are female. Its like how Freud (the fucker) said that clitoral orgasms are just this immature stage girls pass thru before getting to the real mature business of heterosexual, vaginal orgasms. HE acted like us concentrating on ourselves was immature and just preparation for the real task of fucking with boys....AND it's the same shit i hear in this certain argument.....it's okay that you're afeminist as long as you acknowledge that you are stuck in the past and just going thru a "phase" that will eventually become the bigger and better, more male inclusive stance of popular humanism.

LOOK! We need to trust each other. We need to trust that each woman and girl is doing what she needs to do. (Even if it seems really lame) Judgements are what the straightwhitecapitalistworld makes ON US, to ignore and silence and put us down. We don't have to play into it though, WE CAN RESPECT EACH OTHERS STRATEGIES EVEN THOUGH WE MIGHT NOT AGREE.

I mean, even if it is possible to transcend sexist bullshit (if only for a few minutes at a time or within our own imaginations) we cannot turn our backs on the girls/women who don't feel 'transcendence' as a viable option in their own lives.

We need each other. Discouraging words. Belittling other girls in front of boys, laughing looks...Have No Place Here. Dialogue Does.
                    Let's make girl love real,okay???

4. YOU ARE NOT <u>REALLY</u> A FEMINIST BECAUSE....

We live in a completely fucked up society with fucked up rules, and then when we assert the fact that we know it's fucked up and want to change the rules (or destroy them all together) We are, again, handed a whole new set of rules. What it is to be a Real Feminist.

The boys wanna tell us what a real feminist is. The girls wanna tell each other what a real feminist is.

As if we can somehow separate ourselves from the stupid society we live in, and be these perfect feminist entities, in and amongst ourselves.

Dualities. It's a man's world and THUS a feminist is the opposite of that. I, for one, have no interest in defining myself as the opposite of anything, I have been unjustly defined, the opposite of male (active, strong) for my whole life.I don't wanna define myself at all. What do i need a staid and pure identity for anyways!

My ideas are gonna change, my lifestyles gonna change - why can't i say i'm a feminist without having it measured against some unchanging thing? How can i be a POlitically Correct type feminist when i have to survive in a world that doesn't even acknowledge struggle as real in any way? How can i be a PC feminist (whatever this means) when i have to eat, stay emotionally alive via my connections to other people and get my needs, somehow, met?

I AM A WALKING TALKING CONTRADICTION BECAUSE I LIVE IN A WORLD THAT TELLS ME I DON'T EXIST AND I REFUSE TO BELIEVE THIS. Inside, i know i exist and am important in my own ways but what i see outside does not match up to how i feel inside AND it gets really weird because i have to struggle to keep my insides (my soulheartbrain) believing that i am good in the midst of all the lies i get told about myself. YOUR LOGIC IS KILLING ME BECAUSE THE ONLY WAY I CAN EXIST IS THRU CONTRADICTION.

And when He/She says that i am not a real feminist because i used to be a stripper, i reply, "Well, motherfucker, this world doesn't make any sense. But i <u>do</u> exist. Deal with it. Deal with my existence."

Cuz my history is more complex than feminist/non-feminist. And my ideas are more pluralistic and complex than just being PRO or ANTI on any given issue. This world is not a place where only two distinctive realities exist. Call it Yin/Yang, Right/Wrong, Male/Female, Feminist/Homemaker....I don't care what you call it. This is the 90's, give it up.

Dualities support hierarchies----which is what sexism, racism, heterosexsim, specieism, classism, etc..are all based on and supported by.

If anyone tells you/me that we are not Really Feminists then they have already missed the point (there is no point ha.ha.ha.) that we don't need anyone telling us what we are or aren't. that we are not playing by white straightboy heirarchicallogicRules or ideas of LinearPowerControl----

WE ARE what we think we are, what we feel we are whenwe wake up evryday:
We are FeministSlutWhoreVirginsPsychoTrampHystericalMachoMotherProstitutes
WithHeartsofGoldTearingDownViolentHateFuckPornographyandthenMasturbatingto
PhotosofOurselvesSittingReadingABookAloneNextToABoyWEfuckBUTwhoWEdon'tREALLY
likeFALLINGinLOVEwithOURbestGIRLFRIENDStakingOFFourCLOTHESandPUTTINGthemBACK
onBEINGquietYELLINGsoLOUDpushingTHEwallsALLdownTILLtheyAREsweatingANDbleeding
FEMMEbutchsONmotorscotterHARLEYScarryingGUNSandBULLEThoIstersFULLofLIPSTICK
HYPOCROBRATSthatchooseChooseCHOOSEnotTOruleORmakeRULES,okay?

I am a feminist cuz i know that the soul of every girl matters.

5. YOU'RE JUST BORED. YOU ARE INVENTING THE PROBLEM BY TALKING ABOUT IT SO MUCH.

BIKINI KILL 2 (EXCERPT)

#1 A lot of really cool punk rock was invebnted cuz the kids were rebelling against (you guessed it) BOREDOM.

#2 If talking about sexism is <u>making</u> sexism exist- I guess we should close down all the rape relief centers, cuz obviously, <u>they</u> are creating rape.Smart.

#3 A lot of times boys would expect me to give t= hem head when we're having sex but then they'd never recipocate, you know, by going down on me. And this sucks cuz i really like getting oral sex done on me and for years i tried to E.S.P. this message to boys i fucked, but they never got it. There was this whole deal, like, you can't talk about sex cuz it'll ruin it. So then i thought, ruin it? Ruin it for who? By not saying anything i'm not getting what i want AND if me saying "I like it when you lick my pussy" is gonna RUIN sex for them, then obviously, HE doesn't give a shit about me getting pleasure and why would i be having sex with a jerk like that anyways. SO now i tell boys and girls what i want and then i know whats going on with them and they with me. Why would i stop talking about =x=x=m=x what my needs are, in bed or outta bed? Talking about things doesn't make things worse, only better, i've found.

#4 The Boredoms are a really great band from Japan, check them out.

6. YOU ARE JUST TRYING TO BE POLITICAL.

And you, are just trying to be a motherfucker and shut me up. WELL, it's not gonna work, cuz, Number One, what is so bad about being political? And Number two, when you say "trying to be" that implies that i am <u>not really</u> AND who makes you the judge of what is Real and what is Not? And, Number Three, EVERYTHING IS POLITICAL.
Okay, so there is this one person who makes this painting of these pretty flowers and then theres this other person who is female and makes a painting of a big cunt with blood flowing all out of it and at the bottom the words are etched in scratcy blood letters "i am prostitute and proud of it."
Now when these paintings get hung up next to each other everyone says that the girl who made the cunt painting is "just trying to be political" and they want to know what she thinks shes doing and who the hell she thinks she is ANd the problem is that this girl is in the bathroom crying because this image was tied up in her soul and even though she was scared, she put it out anyways and then everyones all saying how beautiful the guy's dumb flower painting is and giving her dirty looks. WHEN SHE LOOKS AT THE PAINTING OF THE FLOWERS SHE IS REMINDED THAT A LOT OF PEOPLE JUST DON'T CARE THAT WOMEN DIE because she knows that the flower painting is just as "political" as her cunt is, she knows this cuz, hard as it maybe for some people to understand, SHE IS OFFENDED BY APATHY.
    See, a lot of us who are into revolution have to tolerate boringDenial laden images and music and words out loud, all the time. BUT as soon as we make anything that is in anyway connected to anything real, as soon as we make something that actually makes some sort of sense besides "nice" sense, "pretty" sense Or "hang above your couch" sense, WE are called "political". I guess if your into the existing system and don't give a fuck about the fact that a lot of people are getting seriously fucked with in this world, if you find yourself reinforcing the status quo as a matter of habit, then YOU are considered apolitical and everyone whose a threat to you is, oh no, no, please not that word, political. I guess what you are doing is normal because people smile at you, well, YOUR NORMAL IS NOT OUR NORMAL MR.FLOWER PAINTER, there are so many things to do, you are wasting our time.
    How can we not lash out at the anti-change faction??? Its a matter of our survival. How can we pretend we don't live in a society that completely tolerates terrorism, such as rape as a "necccesary evil" in order to keep wwomen aoppressed and afraid and make things stay the same. How can we pretend that we haven't watched our mothers stiffle themselves before they say something that might not fit into Dad's Grand Scheme? How often have we clenched our fists after being harrassed on the street and known that their is nothing we can do and that it will never ever stop? MY LIFE <u>IS</u> POLITICAL. To be a person who is unsatisfied and willing to organize around that disatisfaction, is to be political. To be a girl who knows the word SLUT is a pile of fucking shit, is to be political. To be a kid who cuts school cuz it seems so disconnecte· and stupid and unreal as compared to REAL LIFE, is to be political.
The revolution is about resistence and imagining a world where resistence is a constant part of life yet largely unneccesary because THERE IS ROOM FOR EVERYONE ...this is the way that the band i'm in and the girl who made the flower painting are political. Apathy is just another political choice. So, in essence, saying i'm political is redundant, since everything is political in one or another, and besides you really can't judge me cuz you don't really know me and no one who did would say something so mean cuz i am a really nice person. And And And also....NEXT.

WHAT YOU ARE DOING IS

SEXIST TOWARDS MEN.

Our culture is based on the idea that there are only two ways to be (in
 any given situation) IN CONTROL or OUT CONTROL, THE FUCKED or THE FUCKER,
a person WHO KNOWS WHO THEY ARE or someone in process of AN IDENTITY CRISIS.
Our society trains us to be so anti-confrontational cuz we think this means
one person (usually the CONFRONTER)is "right" and the other (CONTRONTED)
must be "wrong". We are afraid of arguing cuz we see everything in terms
of WINNING/LOSING instead of in terms of understanding each other.
    This is where the idea of reverse sexism came from. men get threatened
by feminists cuz they think we are accusing them of being "wrong" instead
of trying to help them understand how WE feel about things and see our points
of veiws on things. We want them to empathasize with us so that they can
change those behaviors of theirs that are hurting us. We need to move beyond
this archaic concentration on blame and move on, towards change.
    it seems in most conversations about sexism, men wanna immediately take
the focus off of how sexism affects women and put it onto how feminism affects
them. And once again, men are placed in the middle of the action, as the
central characters, his needs come first, you know? So, esssentially, the
cry of "reverse sexism" is just another form of sexism. He's making a judgement, he thinks we do everything to affect, offend, push his buttons, never
for our own sakes. We are obviously screaming, he thinks, to hurt his ears,
and not because, we are, genuinely, in serious pain.
    If a guy starts saying you are reverse sexist, he is obviously threatened
by what you are doing. he's threatened cuz he thinks theres only two ways
to be, powerful or powerless. He assumes you asserting your right to exper-
ment, fuck around, have fun and scream when you gotta, is an attempt to
take power away from him. he assumes you wanna "switch places" with him.
he knows you get treated like shit, he knows he gets advantages from your
supposed feelings of inferiority (it makes him feel like a big man) he's
fearing REVENGE, girlfriend. His fear of "reverse sexism" is basically an
admitation, on his part, that he knows you get treated like shit and he does
not want to switch places with you.

Power+Prejudice=Oppression

it is not possible for oppressed people to turn around and "oppress" cuz
we don't have the power, economic power, weapon power, confidence power,
media power.And yes we are mad...we have damn good reasons to be mad. But
why do so many people assume that people who have lived thru this shit want
to turn around and "do it" to them? I mean. is this guilty concious stuff,
or what?
    The assumption that because someone is Pro-girl means that they are anti-
male is stupid, insulting and LAME. Why is the emphasize always put on how
a feminist feels about men and not on how she feels about herself and other
women. We talk about men all the time and the fucking second we start talking
about ourselves, it gets turned around on us, and again, we are talking about
men.
    And also, while i'm at it....instead of telling me my anger is a sign of
my reverse sexism, why not inquire into the larger system which forces us
to protect ourselves and thus, be leery of men??? Why not ask WHY DO THEY
OPPRESS US instead of always asking WHY DO WE RESIST. Of couse we will resist,
and of course we are pissed off. Duh.

DON'T WORRY BE HAPPY!!!!!!

Hey little angel, why the long face?
Don't take it so serious, lighten up, you should smile more often, thats
right, it'll make you feel better.

You want no reminder that i am sad. that i have damn good reasons to be sad
pissed off scared. My girlfriend is crying cuz you left her for someone
who had a tighter ass, no stretchmarks, was quiet, aquiescent, agreeable.

Don't tell me to be happy motherfucker.

I saw a tee shirt today at the store. It came in large and extra large sizes. There were ten of them, hanging there, dark black with white letters. I imagined some girl's boyfriend coming home in one. SHUT UP BITCH written across each one.

Don't _tell_ me to be happy motherfucker.

I listen to _you_ all the time. _Your_ worries and _your_ troubles are the stuff that is like breathing. The stuff so often repeating that it sounds lick a ticking clock or a real live heart. Yet i'm the one who is told i talk to much.

Axl Rose is on MTV. The image is like this: Guns-n-Roses are performing an acoustic set for a gradeschool assembly. Axl is singing these words, "I used to love her, but I had to kill her. I had to put her six feet under." The kids are laughing. Little girls are sitting on the floor at his feet, laughing.

I am making such a big deal outta nothing. I'm sorry. Sorry. Sorry, I'm so sorry.

You never state how you feel and say maybe if i was more like you i would just deal with things "inside" more often, and "by myself". But see, being silent to you means safety, to me it means being gagged.

"Smile princess."

Why do you always ask me why i'm not smiling, you don't really wanna know.

I WANNA KNOW WHY ITS IN YOUR BEST INTEREST THAT I ACT LIKE EVERYTHING IS OKAY.   ITS NOT, ITS NOT OKAY. I AM NOT OKAY.

I guess its not enough that i accept the evil sexist dumb commodity bullshit that eats up my true life and threatens to engulf me in fear and drain me of all hope....you want me to TAKE IT WITH A SMILE too.

No.

9. BUT I KNOW A GIRL WHO LIED
ABOUT BEING RAPED....

This is also called 'Passing the exception to the Rule off as The Rule.' Mainstream movies (propaganda) are really good at this one. Take the movie, FATAL ATTRACTION, for example. Okay, so like, 99.9% of all abusers/ harrasssers in heterosexual relationships are male and then this movie comes out where this woman is running around totally scaring this man and wrecking his whole white and married and middle class thing. And like EVERYONE nad their fuckin dog goes to see this movie and i am very very upset cuz i know it is an evil force in the world and that men are just gonna use it as more fuel. You know, if we don't keep those crazy lying bitches down, look atall the havoc they'll cause.
     The Dangerous Woman. We are so evil, oh yea. Well who are the real rapists, child molesters, serial killers and general bullies in our society anyways? Who are the real people in power???

They take the total freak abberation and play it on every channel, Donahue has a special on women who beat up their husbands, cuz there has just gotta be a reason why women are oppressed, cuz guilty concious' have to go somewhere, cuz men to make themselves afraid of us enough to justify their violence AND there stupid ways of thinking (evil lying women, you just can't trust 'em) cuz without this propaganda it would be harder to not SEE whats really going on.

So, yes, some women have had to 'lie' about rape to save their own asses....like when it was illegal (hangable) to have sex with a Black man and when an interracail affar got caught women would be put in the position of either saying it was rape or getting killed or like, sometimes white men would USE women to get Black guys lynched and FORCE them to tell lies under threats to their own safety. And all this sucks so totally bad BUT these are the exceptions.

A woman or a girl might also 'lie', not about THE FACT that she was raped but about who did it cuz it might be safer to say a stranger did it (the courts understand rape as an abbberation where a big scary evil guy comes limping from the darkness to "take" a damsel, okay?) than to tell the truth that it was DAD or uncle henry or joe bob captain of the footbal team, or the whole footbal team including the coach or the rich doctor who everyone loves and respects and no one can imagine doing such a thing. (Evil lying whore bitch)

So, yea, when you quote these exceptons to me as raesons why "Maybe i'm going a little overboard with this whole rape thing, afterall women are really bad and fucked up too", ALLS I HAVE TO SAY TO YOU IS that WOMEN DON'T LIE ABOUT GETTING RAPED, WE DON'T CALL CRISIS LINES CUZ ITS FUN AND WE DON'T GET OUR JOLLIES BY BEING HUMILATED BY THE COURT SYSTEM OR SCARY MUSTACHE CCPS WHO WANNA MAKE US FEEL LIKE HELPLESS LITTLE VIRGIN GIRLS OR DESRVING WHORES .... The only reason you would go talking about an exception as if it is the rule is cuz you will look for any thing, anything, anything to support your misogyny and justify YOUR fear/hatred of me and the other girls.
YOUR FEAR, not mine.

 COMPLAIN, COMPLAIN, COMPLAIN.....

 AT LEAST YOU DON'T HAVE IT AS BAD AS
a)women used to
b)people of color
c)women in other countries

I had this job for like 4 years at this LIBeral typy college and when i voiced some anger about getting treated like a lackey all the time and not shown any kind of respect or appreciation, ever....i was told, 'Well in the REAL world you'd be treated much worse, so you should be thankful to even get treated this good."
And i was like "God thanks for totally not even listening to me."
Cuz all i was saying was "look you all are hurting my feelings and making me feel bad when i'm at work" and no one could address that, they just defended themselves and ignored what i was really saying.

Its like i am trying to make my life better by sticking up for myself and it gets turned into this thing like, you are being completely self serving, and, at least you don't have a spinal cord injury, at least your not a Black Lesbian in a wheelchair, at least you even have a job.

Its like people think of oppression as a test you can either pass or fail. Okay, you get one point for being poor, one more for being female, but oh no, you score a negative one for being white and able bodied

BIKINI KILL 2 (EXCERPT)

and.........I'm sorry but it just doesn't work that way. I mean, addi
nice when your counting your fingers or toes but not when your trying
to talk about what it feels like to be hungry or lied to or treated
like shit or beat up. If organizing around my own issues is somehow
wrong cuz there are other people who are in situations that are even
more life damaging then me, then i am wrong.

.Cuz, see, i talk/write about girlstuff so much cuz i am a whitegirl
and i am not really into trying to speak for other people or species
although i am becoming a better and better listener. I mean, me writin
about this stuff in this zine doesn't mean i think girl oppression is
any more important or pressing than racial or species or sexual oppres
Its just that i need to organize around what i know and support others
to do the same cuz i can't speak for everyone but i do see all this
shit as connected.

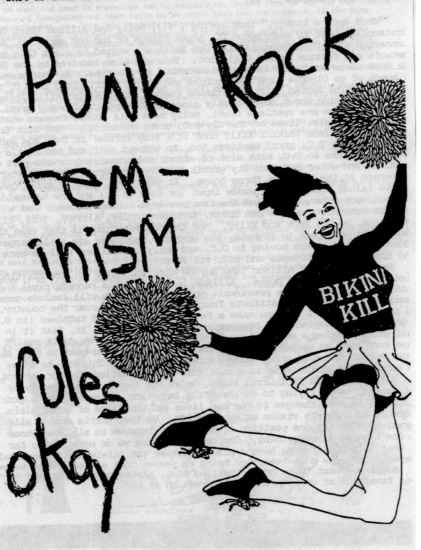

PUNK ROCK
Fem-
inism
rules
okay

riot grrrl

RIOT GRRRL... Believe in me!

"Once upon a time..." last spring ('91), Molly and Allison (Girl Germs, Bratmobile) went to Washington DC, shook things up and got shook up, and connected with this radsoulsister Jen Smith who wanted to start this girl network and fanzine called Girl Riot. (This was also inspired by the Cinco de Mayo riots occurring in her neighborhood at the time.) So that summer a bunch of us Olympia kids (Bratmobile and Bikini Kill) lived in D.C. to make something happen with our friends there. Tobi (Bikini Kill, Jigsaw) had been talking about doing weekly zines in the spirit of angry grrrl zine-scene, and then one restless night, Molly made this little fanzine stating events in the girl lives of the Oly-D.C. scene connection-- and Riot Grrrl was born. Kathleen (Bikini Kill) took it a step further in that she wanted to have weekly D.C. grrrl meetings too, to connect with and see what's up with the grrrls in D.C. With alot of effort and organizing on the part of Kathleen and other D.C. and Oly grrrls, weekly Riot Grrrl meetings started happening at the Positive Force house. It was great, like 20 girls came and we talked about female scene input (or lack of it) and how we could support each other, etc. And the fanzines kept coming out each week with certain contributors like Jen Smith, Kathleen, Molly, Allison, Tobi, Tiffany, Christina, Ne Sk8 Rock and Billy. And the coolest thing is that even though many of us went back to Olympia, the meetings and zines are still happening. (Soon Bikini Kill are moving to D.C. and Molly and Allison will be back and forth between Olympia and D.C. til forever.)

Now Kathleen and Allison (and anyone else who wants to) are starting Riot Grrrl records and press. Allison is gonna do the records/tapes and Kathleen is gonna do the press/mail order stuff, which will include grrrl fanzines. We want to distribute fanzines by girls all over the country. So if you're a girl and you make a fanzine, you can send Kathleen (in D.C.) a good _flat_ unstapled copy of your zine so she can xerox it, list it in the mail order catalogue and mail it to whoever orders it. We don't really have much cash so we can't pay you for your zine, but we plan to give each contributor copies of other girls' zines. Cool deal. This can be a way to support and participate in a cool girl network nationwide (or interntl?)

With this whole Riot Grrrl thing, we're not trying to make money or get famous; we're trying to do something important, to network with grrrls all over, to make changes in our own lives and the lives of other girls. There is no concrete vision or expectation. We Riot Grrrls aren't aligning ourselves with any one position or consensus, because in all likelyhood we don't agree on everything. One concrete thing we do agree on so far is that it's cool/fun to have a place where we can safely and supportively confront, express ourselves, and bring up issues that are important to us.

So if you want to be on the mailing list, please send a postcard (or your fanzine flat copy) with your address on it to:

> RIOT GRRRL
> c/o The Embassy
> 3217 19th St. NW
> Washington DC 20010

BIKINI KILL 2 (EXCERPT)

Riot Grrrl is.......

BECAUSE us girls crave records and books and fanzines that speak to US, that WE feel included in and can understand in our own ways.

BECAUSE we wanna make it easier for girls to see/hear each other's work so that we can share strategies and criticize-applaud each other.

BECAUSE we must take over the means of production in order to create our own meanings.

BECAUSE viewing our work as being connected to our girlfriends-politics-real lives is essentia if we are gonna figure out how what we are doing impacts, reflects, perpetuates, or DISRUPTS the status quo.

BECAUSE we recognize fantasies of Instant Macho Gun Revolution as impractical lies meant to keep us simply dreaming instead of becoming our dreams AND THUS seek to create revolution in our own lives every single day by envisioning and creating alternatives to the bullshit christian capitalist way of doing things.

BECAUSE we want and need to encourage and be encouraged, in the face of all our own insecuriti in the face of beergutboyrock that tells us we can't play our instruments, in the face of "authorities" who say our bands/'zines/etc are the worst in the U.S. and who attribute any validation/success of our work to girl bandwagon hype.

BECAUSE we don't wanna assimulate to someone else's (Boy) standards of what is or isn't "good" music or punk rock or "good" writing AND THUS need to create forums where we can recreate, destroy and define our own visions.

BECAUSE we are unwilling to falter under claims that we are reactionary "reverse sexists" and not the truepunkrocksoulcrusaders that WE KNOW we really are.

BECAUSE we know that life is much more than physical survival and are patently aware that the punk rock "you can do anything" idea is crucail to the coming angry grrrl rock revolution which seeks to save the psychic and cultural lives of girls and women everywhere, according to their own terms, not ours.

BECAUSE we are interested in creating non-heirarchical ways of being AND making music, friends, and scenes based on communication+understanding, instead of competition+good/bad categorizations.

BECAUSE doing/reading/seeing/hearing cool things that validate and challenge us can help us gain the strength and sense of community that we need in order to figure out how bullshit like racism, able-bodieism, ageism, speciesism, classism, thinism, sexism, anti-semitism and heterosexism figures in our own lives.

BECAUSE we see fostering and supporting girl scenes and girl artists of all kinds as intregal to this process.

BECAUSE we hate capitalism in all its forms and see our main goal as sharing information and staying alive, instead of making profits or being cool according to traditional standards.

BECAUSE we are angry at a society that tells us Girl=Dumb, Girl=Bad, Girl=Weak

BECAUSE we are unwilling to let our real and valid anger be diffused and/or turned against us via the internalization of sexism as witnessed in girl/girl jealousies and self defeating girltype behaviors.

BECAUSE self defeating behaviors (like fucking boys without condoms, drinking to excess, ignoring truesoul girlfriends, belittling ourselves and other girls, etc...) would not be so easy if we lived in communities where we felt loved and wanted and valued.

BECAUSE i believe with my holeheartmindbody that girls constitute a revolutionary soul force that can, and will, change the world for real.

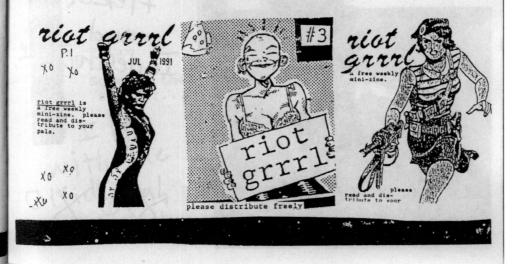

riot grrrl
P.1
XO   XO
JUL 1991

riot grrrl is a free weekly mini-zine. please read and dis- tribute to your pals.

XO   XO

XO   XO

#3

riot grrrl

please distribute freely

riot grrrl
a free weekly mini-zine.

please read and dis- tribute to your

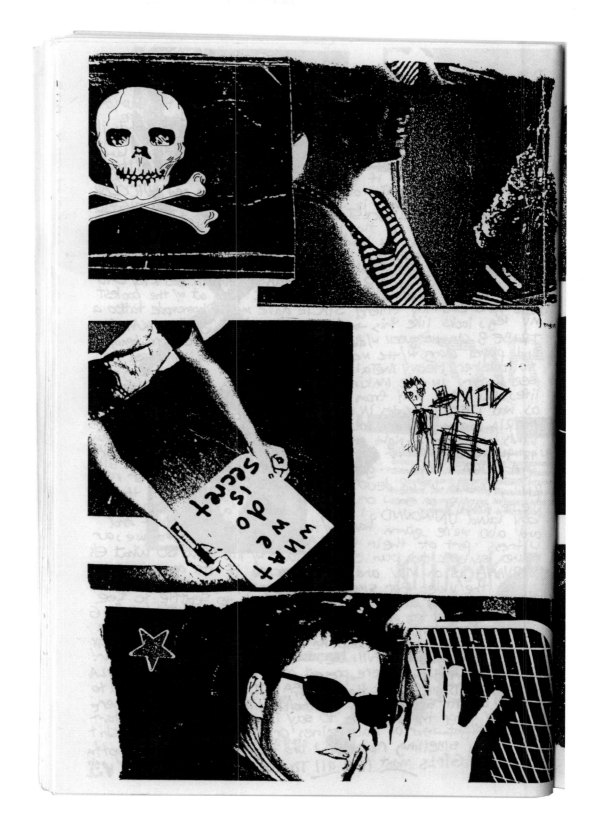

BIKINI KILL 2 (EXCERPT)

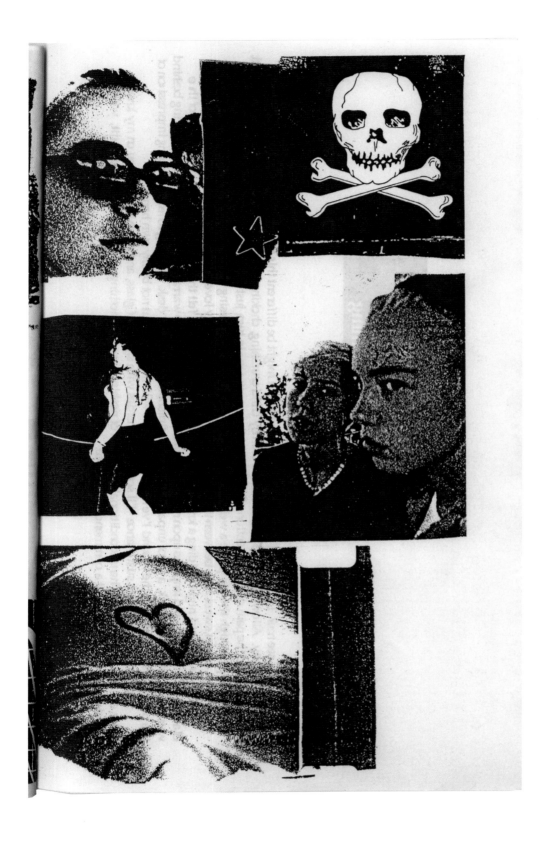

LYRICS

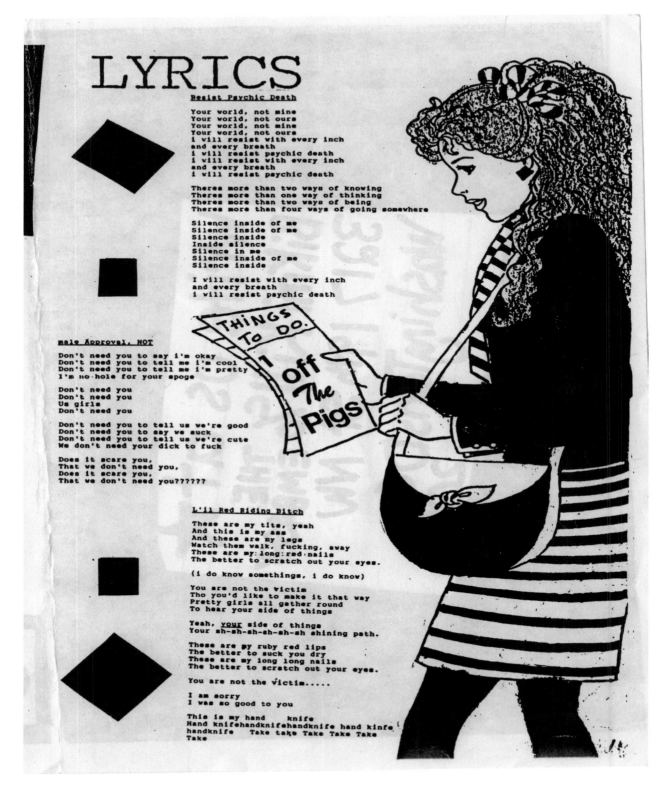

Resist Psychic Death

Your world, not mine
Your world, not ours
Your world, not mine
Your world, not ours
i will resist with every inch
and every breath
i will resist psychic death
i will resist with every inch
and every breath
i will resist psychic death

Theres more than two ways of knowing
Theres more than one way of thinking
Theres more than two ways of being
Theres more than four ways of going somewhere

Silence inside of me
Silence inside of me
Silence inside
Inside silence
Silence in me
Silence inside of me
Silence inside

I will resist with every inch
and every breath
i will resist psychic death

male Approval, NOT

Don't need you to say i'm okay
Don't need you to tell me i'm cool
Don't need you to tell me i'm pretty
I'm no hole for your spoge

Don't need you
Don't need you
Us girls
Don't need you

Don't need you to tell us we're good
Don't need you to say we suck
Don't need you to tell us we're cute
We don't need your dick to fuck

Does it scare you,
That we don't need you,
Does it scare you,
That we don't need you??????

L'il Red Riding Bitch

These are my tits, yeah
And this is my ass
And these are my legs
Watch them walk, fucking, away
These are my long red nails
The better to scratch out your eyes.

(i do know somethings, i do know)

You are not the victim
Tho you'd like to make it that way
Pretty girls all gather round
To hear your side of things

Yeah, your side of things
Your sh-sh-sh-sh-sh-sh shining path.

These are my ruby red lips
The better to suck you dry
These are my long long nails
The better to scratch out your eyes.

You are not the victim.....

I am sorry
I was so good to you

This is my hand   knife
Hand knifehandknifehandknife hand kinfe
handknife   Take take Take Take Take
Take

BIKINI KILL 2 (EXCERPT)

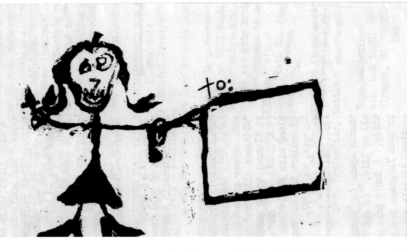

heavens to betsy
p.o. box 7842
olympia, wa 98507

july 4, 1993

hello there this is Corin and you might think it is really lame to be getting a newsletter but we have so much mail we cannot deal. we would have our personal secretary write you a note on our letterhead (ha ha) but instead we spend our time working shitty jobs and being tired and worrying about money and sometimes maybe once a week getting together and actually doing this band thing which is TRULY living. if we don't try and create something better than the shitty jobs or the corporatewhitesupremacist sexistUSA around us then we have nothing but it. THAT is why creating thinking dialogue rock band is life to me. i can't sing and be numb. i can do most other things numb 'cause i have to but not singing creating. so to all the girls out there singing creating and FUCKING SHIT UP -gogogo! the letters we have gotten have been inspirational to me. sometimes when we get paid so little (like $5 for a show) for our work and have so little time and equipment to work with it really makes me want to quit. getting a letter from a girl in whose life we make a small difference makes my day. thank you....

.....so now for the news part of the newsletter....

H2B +BRAT SUMMER TOUR PART TWO XOXOXOXOXOXOXOXOXOXOXOXOXOXOXOX!
          July 7 Portland, OR XX-ray cafe
          July 8 Olympia, WA Capitol Theatre
          July 9 Bellingham, WA
yep, these are our shows. we love to rock you.

***********other things going on with us***************
   THESE MONSTERS ARE REAL.... 7" on Kill Rock Stars
                               four songs three bucks
                               we are very proud of this
                               record and we sell it cheap!
   you can order it from: Kill Rock Stars!
                          120 NE State St. #418
                          Olympia, WA 98501

   we have a song on the Yoyo Julep Compilation (number 2) it's called "she's the one" (our song that is) other bands include Lync, Bratmobile, Tattle Tale, Slant 6 Tiger Trap and Adickdid...
   you can write....   Yoyo Recordings
                            p.o. box 10081
                            Olympia, WA 98502
                                         USA

*****************more projects*********************

WE HAVE T--shirts!!!! yeah, t-shirts and they have the cool design on the front of this newsletter only the sign from the gun says heavens to betsy. they are way cool. so you can order one for $5 dollars or if you have a favorite shirt you want it silkscreened on then you can send us that and $2.50. make checks out to: Corin Tucker. our address: p.o. box 7842 Olympia Wa 98507

something else i (Corin) have made is a film. it's called... "a riot grrrl tells her own story" it's seven minutes long super-8 and audio transferred to video. the film is me talking about riot grrrl, corporate media and racism. you can order it and watch it with your girlfriends, talk about it and tell me what you think. send $5 dollars and a VHS video tape to Corin Tucker p.o. box 7842. 2-8 weeks delivery

&&&&&next weekend we are recording . hopefully we will have a full-length LP sometime. we'll let you know!

++++++++++++other things to check out+++++++++++++++++

riot grrrl press is soon coming out with a nationwide catalogue of girl fanzines. really amazing. you can write: Erika Reinstein and May Summer p.o. box 1375 Arlington, VA
                                                        22210

...numb to nothing is a record label that uses dumpster--dived (doved?) recycled tapes. the tape is a compilation to benefit the Washington Freedom Coalition, which is fightin anti--queer groups like the OCA and the CAW, conservative "citizens alliance" that are queer-hating. The Oca had made it illegal to be gay in Springfield, OR and Wilsonville, OR. FUCK THEM!!!!!! h2b has an AWESOME live song on this tape along with MANY OTHER RAD BANDS too many to mention. send $5 dollars to: Dan Hanson and Izaac Brock. p.o. box 7454 Olympia, Wa 98507.

****

thanks again for your letter. i have written fan letters all my life. to get one from a rad girl is a beautiful thing. i don't have any secret revolutionary doctrine or code language for you. i do think we should try and continue to talk to each other. and to question the bullshit, the racism, the sexism the corporations around us and expecially inside us.
                    xoxoxoxoxoxo, Corin

slut.

Things you can do:

*Talk to your friends about what they think a "slut" is.
*Think about how you feel about this stuff.
*Remember that bad comments hurt as much or more than getting hit or kicked. Bruises hurt, so do words.

✦ ✦ ✦ ✦ ✦

Lots of girls get bad reputations.

*By sticking together and saying we don't like being called names and shit, we can change things. We can help each other out, if we are willing to take the risk.

Usually SLUT is a put down meaning that a girl has sex, likes sex, or has sex with lots of different people.
It is also a very easy way to hurt a girls feelings.

?

—Why are people afraid that a girl would "like" sex?
—Why is it anyones business who a girl sleeps with anyways?

WHY AREN'T BOYS CALLED SLUTS?

I am writing this because I was one of "those girls" (a slut) in high school. I remember living in fear of someone saying "that word" around me, always fearing it, afraid it could be just around the corner.
I got my bad reputation because I told this guy I didn't like him and he wanted to look cool in front of his friends so he told everyone he fucked me and that I was this total sleaze who liked all this weird shit and would "do it" with anyone, etc... REGARDLESS, who gave him the power to MAKE or BREAK my reputation?

BEFORE YOU USE THE WORD SLUT Think

about a time when someone spread a rumor about you, insulted your body or hurt your feelings. If you're really mad at a girl you could write her a note or tell her IN person.That is a lot more courageous than stabbing her in the back anyways. Destroying her reputation just feeds into the same system that gives other people the RIGHT to JUDGE you UNFAIRLY.

FLYER

For more information or to talk to a counselor call safeplace #754-6300

WE ALL HAVE DIFFERENT THINGS WE THINK ABOUT AND NEED TO DEAL WITH.
THE PROBLEM IS THAT THERE ARE SOME THINGS THAT PEOPLE DON'T SEEM TO
WANT TO HEAR ABOUT. THEY ACT LIKE IF A GIRL TALKS ABOUT CERTAIN THINGS,
SHE"S NOT BEING "POLITE". WE WANT TO START A GROUP WHERE GIRLS CAN SAY
WHAT EVER THEY WANT. IT WILL BE FREE TO GO TO AND WE'LL PROVIDE BUS $$$
IF ANYONE NEEDS IT. THERE WILL BE WOMEN THERE WHO ARE TRAINED AS
COUNSELORS AND KNOW STUFF ABOUT RAPE, EMOTINAL/PHYSICAL VIOLENCE, DECISION
MAKING METHODS ETC....THE WOMEN WILL BE THERE TO HELP GET THINGS GOING
AT FIRST, BUT THE IDEA IS THAT, ULTIMATELY, THE GIRLS IN THE GROUP WILL
MAKE IT THEIR OWN THING. PLEASE COME TO SEE IF YOU'D BE INTERESTED IN
HELPING THE GROUP FORM, BRING YOUR IDEAS AND OTHER GIRLS WHO MIGHT WANT
TO COME. THANKS

flip me ➜

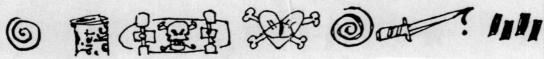

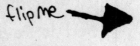

MAY 15th

at The Oly. Comm. Center

222 Columbia St.

3-5pm

Room 202

(Next to the downtown fire station)

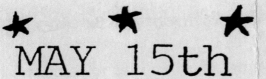

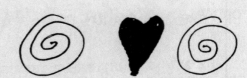

Girl Talk

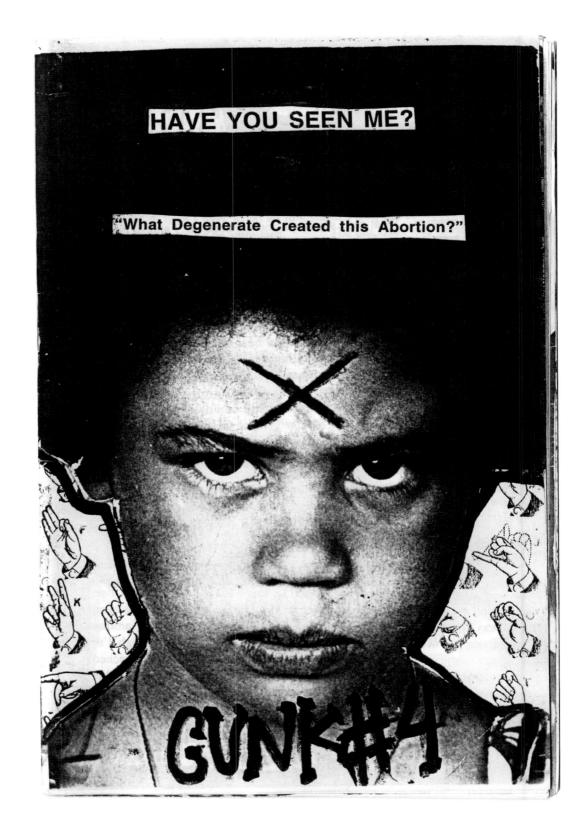

GUNK 4 (EXCERPT)

Gunk is Junk

Aaaaaaah!!! it's GUNK.... finally once again in your grubby little hands. So it's taken me a hella long time to put this issue out, seems like a century... What can i say the laziness kicked in. I almost decided that I wasn't gonna do this anymore and i joined breifly with the masses and be came a slacker. But, here am up in your face again coming from the stinky filthy depths of suburbia... I've sorta come to the harsh realities that being a 'zinester aint all it's cracked up to be... it gets really annoying and almost haunting especially when I keep getting letters from people requesting 'zines issues that I no longer have. But nonethelit is also totally rewarding, because I get to hear all these good ideas and communicate with all these totally interesting sorts of people who are doing and seeing all kinds of great stuff. I guess alot people inspire me regardless if they know it or not. These people have given me that extra kick in the booty that has kept me working on this issue. If you have been a faithful GUNK reader you will notice GUNK has changed alot since the first issue, which looked like it was put together in about 15 minutes. I love that issue, it cracks me up completely. I was so excited about doing a 'zine that I kinda forget that it also has to be intelligible. But o' well Progression has been on my mind lately and I'm trying to really progress with things I'm doing, so I don't grow bored and dissatified... which for me is totally all tooo common.

As you may be able to tell by this issue the genuine feel I've been getting as I've been compiling stuff to put into this isssue has been very weird. Alot of unmatched puzzle pieces have been floating aroung inside my skull and I'm starting to put them together even though I'm sure some of them are mismatched but I've learned that mismatched puzzle pieces are really essential. Maybe you don't understand that comparision... what I'm saying is that it's alright to be a completely at odds with yourself sometimes... it works for me atleast.

(SSh! that's me on the front cover when I was about 8 or 9) I desperatly wanted to be in the Jackson Five

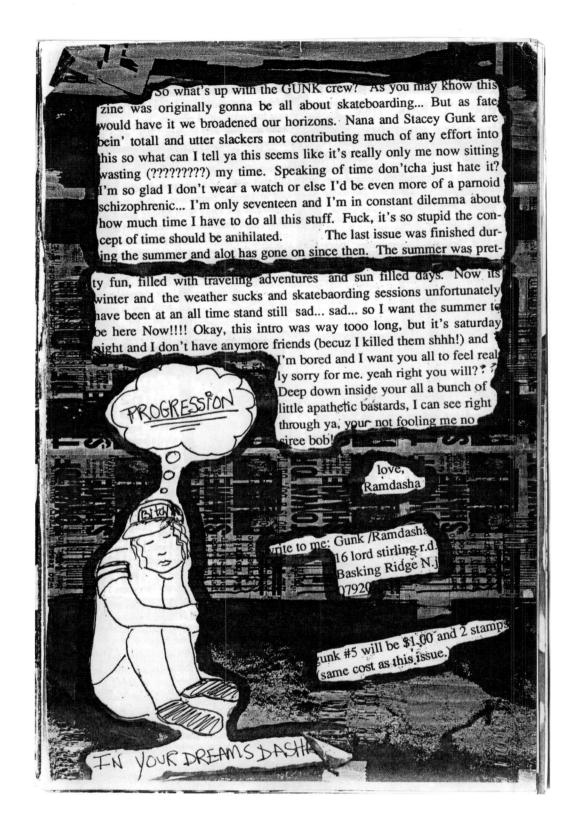

So what's up with the GUNK crew? As you may know this zine was originally gonna be all about skateboarding... But as fate would have it we broadened our horizons. Nana and Stacey Gunk are bein' totall and utter slackers not contributing much of any effort into this so what can I tell ya this seems like it's really only me now sitting wasting (????????) my time. Speaking of time don'tcha just hate it? I'm so glad I don't wear a watch or else I'd be even more of a parnoid schizophrenic... I'm only seventeen and I'm in constant dilemma about how much time I have to do all this stuff. Fuck, it's so stupid the concept of time should be anihilated. The last issue was finished during the summer and alot has gone on since then. The summer was pretty fun, filled with traveling adventures and sun filled days. Now its winter and the weather sucks and skatebaording sessions unfortunately have been at an all time stand still sad... sad... so I want the summer to be here Now!!!! Okay, this intro was way tooo long, but it's saturday night and I don't have anymore friends (becuz I killed them shhh!) and I'm bored and I want you all to feel really sorry for me. yeah right you will? Deep down inside your all a bunch of little apathetic bastards, I can see right through ya, your not fooling me no siree bob!

PROGRESSION

love,
Ramdasha

write to me: Gunk /Ramdasha
16 lord stirling r.d.
Basking Ridge N.j.
07920

Gunk #5 will be $1.00 and 2 stamps same cost as this issue.

IN YOUR DREAMS DASHA

GUNK 4 (EXCERPT

I'm laughing so hard it doesn't look like I'm laughing anymore...

I'm humming really loud along with a couple othere thosand people, I'm trying to drown out the sound of myself and everyone else.

I laugh sometimes when things aren't very funny, it's a nervous laughter because I sometimes don't know what else to do. When situations escalate to a point where I've lost control, I laugh. But lately, I've stopped laughing and I'm starting to get a grip on things.

I used to laugh at this whole white bread punk rock scene, but now i'm not laughing as much as I'm getting more annoyed. I swear every punk show I go to I'm usually the only person of color in the joint and nobody seems to even question this or even seem to mind. I think my friend Beth was telling m that somebody said that punx were the "white niggers". What exactly does this mean? I guess it means that punx, like African Americans often reflect what alot of people don't want to see. They don't want to see the result of their opressive society. Punx are revolting against a society that has repressed personal expression, which has intern resulted in the way of alot of them (us???)

ress and act etc... Whereas in the case of African Americans their (our????) opression has resulted in poverty, lack of education, and low self-images. But, what this concept of "white nigger" fails to realize is that white punx couldn't possibly come close to the stigma that is attached and associated with African Americans. White kids in general regardless if they are punk or not can get away with having green mohawks and pierced lips 'cause no matter how much they deviated from the norms of society their whitenss always shows through. For instance, I'll go out somewhere with my friends who all look equally as wierd as me, but say we get hassled by the cops for skating or something. That cop is going to remeber my face alot clearet than say one of my white girlfriends. I can just hear him now..."Yeah there was this black girl w/pink hair and two other girls"

Another true to life exampl would be when I used to be friends with this boy and he kinda got a crush on me. He was a white boy and his mom was ultra consevative. She didn't mind so much that I was friends w/him, but as soon as she found out that he wanted to be more than friedns she immediately said: "I don't want you hanging around with that BLACK* girl. (note that she didn't say I don't want you hanging around that green-haired-shaved-head-too many holes-in-her-ear girls ... she said BLACK* girl) You see, she could handle the way I looked, but she drew the line

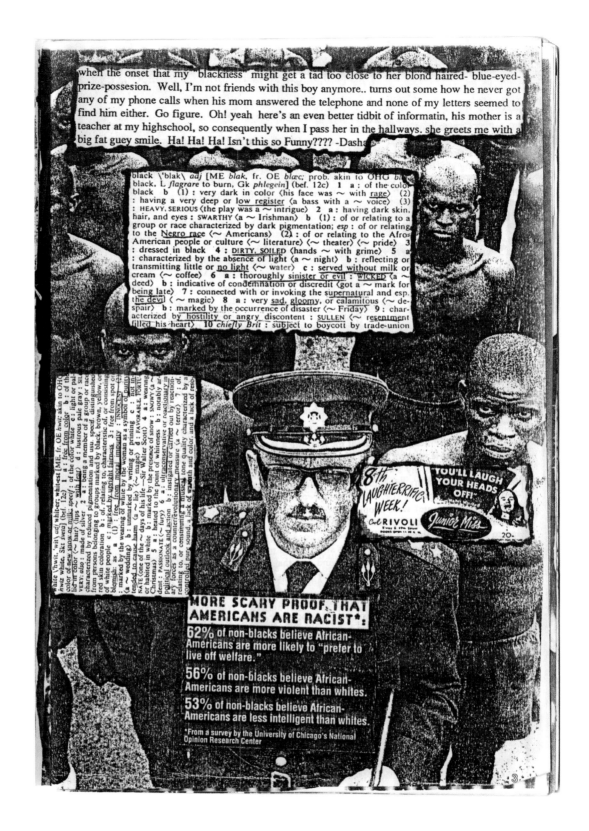

when the onset that my "blackness" might get a tad too close to her blond haired- blue-eyed-prize-possesion. Well, I'm not friends with this boy anymore.. turns out some how he never got any of my phone calls when his mom answered the telephone and none of my letters seemed to find him either. Go figure. Oh! yeah here's an even better tidbit of informatin, his mother is a teacher at my highschool, so consequently when I pass her in the hallways. she greets me with a big fat guey smile. Ha! Ha! Ha! Isn't this so Funny???? -Dasha

black \'blak\ adj [ME blak, fr. OE blæc; prob. akin to OHG bl... black, L flagrare to burn, Gk phlegein] (bef. 12c) 1 a : of the color black b (1) : very dark in color ⟨his face was ~ with rage⟩ (2) : having a very deep or low register ⟨a bass with a ~ voice⟩ (3) : HEAVY, SERIOUS ⟨the play was a ~ intrigue⟩ 2 a : having dark skin, hair, and eyes : SWARTHY ⟨a ~ Irishman⟩ b (1) : of or relating to a group or race characterized by dark pigmentation; esp : of or relating to the Negro race ⟨~ Americans⟩ (2) : of or relating to the Afro-American people or culture ⟨~ literature⟩ ⟨~ theater⟩ ⟨~ pride⟩ 3 : dressed in black 4 : DIRTY, SOILED ⟨hands ~ with grime⟩ 5 a : characterized by the absence of light ⟨a ~ night⟩ b : reflecting or transmitting little or no light ⟨~ water⟩ c : served without milk or cream ⟨~ coffee⟩ 6 a : thoroughly sinister or evil : WICKED ⟨a ~ deed⟩ b : indicative of condemnation or discredit ⟨got a ~ mark for being late⟩ 7 : connected with or invoking the supernatural and esp. the devil ⟨~ magic⟩ 8 a : very sad, gloomy, or calamitous ⟨~ despair⟩ b : marked by the occurrence of disaster ⟨~ Friday⟩ 9 : characterized by hostility or angry discontent : SULLEN ⟨~ resentment filled his heart⟩ 10 chiefly Brit : subject to boycott by trade-union

8th LAUGHTERRIFIC WEEK!
at RIVOLI

"YOU'LL LAUGH YOUR HEADS OFF!"
Junior Miss
20¢

MORE SCARY PROOF THAT AMERICANS ARE RACIST*:

62% of non-blacks believe African-Americans are more likely to "prefer to live off welfare."

56% of non-blacks believe African-Americans are more violent than whites.

53% of non-blacks believe African-Americans are less intelligent than whites.

*From a survey by the University of Chicago's National Opinion Research Center

GUNK 4 (EXCERPT)

Riot Grrrl Convention Summer 92

Day #1

So I had heard about this happening for awhile, but I sorta forgot about it until MRR ran the add, it showed that the convention was coming up real soon. At the time I was in Tucson, Arizona being really bored and lonely 'cuz I have no friends there... I called up Stacer Gunk, she recently had been kicked out of her of house, so she was staying in Philly w/ her mom. I told her about the convention and she and I concurred that it would be probabaly b a fun thing to go to. Considering my summer had been very unproductive and it was looking like it was gonna be staying that way, I decided to shell out the cash and take a freaking plane to D.C. Stacer took a train. I had called the positive force house a couple days earlier to hook up a place for us to stay. They got us person who was so kind to let us stay with them and eat their food. When I arrived in D.C. I had to take the Metro, which is like a sort of subway system to this place in Maryland which is right out side of D.C. When I got there the girl Sarah who I was going to stay with came and picked me up along with Stacey who I was very excited to see. When Stacey and I got to Sarah's house we jammed with her 'cuz she plays drums (rad!) then later on.. we went to this big park thing in D.C. where all these awful live bands were playing and nobody was listening to them. This place gave me the creeps it was basically this huge punk rawk hang-out where all these punk-ers hung out and socialized. Maybe it was all the *dumb* jocko tough guy punkers and skins who bothered me so. I think Stacey and I both agreed that place was really lame. When we first got there some ass-hole tough guy threw something at Stacey and I. There were tons of dorky little skinheads and tough guy punk rawk studs, luckily though Stacey had our boards with us so we were not completedly dying of boredom. We scoped out the place and found a nice big patch of cement that had some low stairs near it. Stacey did the most awesome manual across the length of it, I was impressed. I managed to pop some nice oillies but that was all. After awhile of skating I took a break and decided to "people watch" for awhile. I started to notice something very strange brewing... all these punx & skinheads started swarm-ing together in a sort of tight huddle. I noticed in the middle of this crowd was some guy who obvioulsy was in deep shit. There was some big argument going on and the crowd of dummies kept getting bigger and closer to wear Stacer and I were. When I first realized what was about to happen, I started to tell Stacey that it looks like we better skiddaddle, but even before the words came out of my mouth the swarm of say 30 or 40 started headed toward us kickin' the shit out of this guy who was running away in our direction. Stacer and I wanted to steer clear of this atrocity but there was no where to go except to jump over this very high wall and have the possobility of maybe breaking a few bones. But there was no time to think, Stacer and I hurled our boards over the wall and jumped on over. When finally out of the way we saw this poor fellow get his head slammed into the pavement where we had just been standing. Alas we escaped with only a few minor scrapes and scratches. Not one of the best welcoming parties I have had. Thoughts of "So this is D.C. the way cool scene capital Right??" filled my head. Duh!

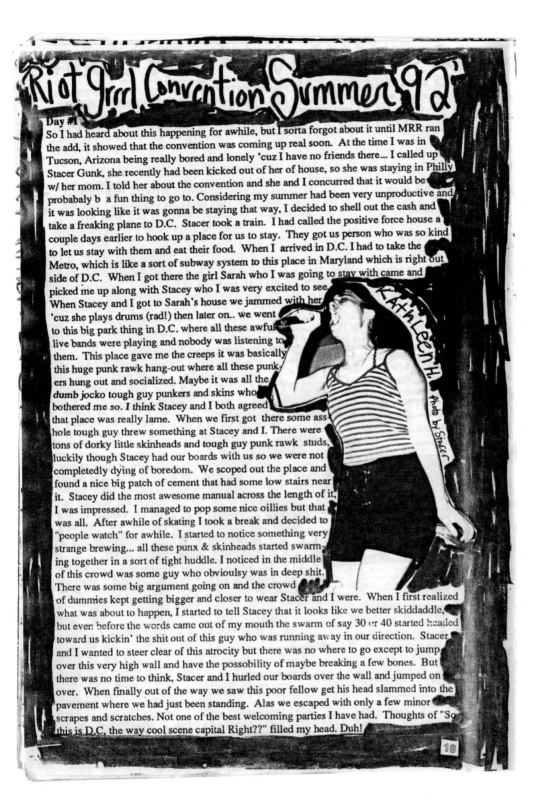

KATHLEEN H.
photo by Stacer

18

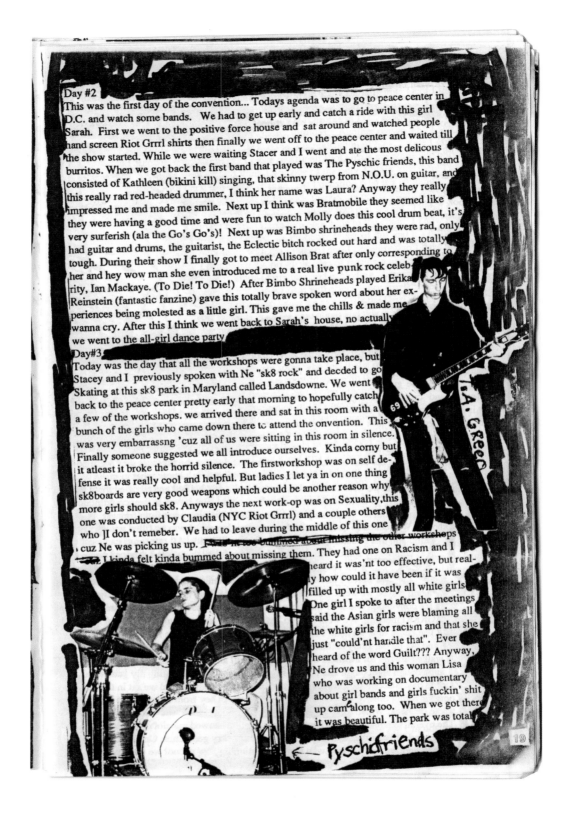

Day #2

This was the first day of the convention... Todays agenda was to go to peace center in D.C. and watch some bands. We had to get up early and catch a ride with this girl Sarah. First we went to the positive force house and sat around and watched people hand screen Riot Grrrl shirts then finally we went off to the peace center and waited till the show started. While we were waiting Stacer and I went and ate the most delicous burritos. When we got back the first band that played was The Pyschic friends, this band consisted of Kathleen (bikini kill) singing, that skinny twerp from N.O.U. on guitar, and this really rad red-headed drummer, I think her name was Laura? Anyway they really impressed me and made me smile. Next up I think was Bratmobile they seemed like they were having a good time and were fun to watch Molly does this cool drum beat, it's very surferish (ala the Go's Go's)! Next up was Bimbo shrineheads they were rad, only had guitar and drums, the guitarist, the Eclectic bitch rocked out hard and was totally tough. During their show I finally got to meet Allison Brat after only corresponding to her and hey wow man she even introduced me to a real live punk rock celeb-rity, Ian Mackaye. (To Die! To Die!) After Bimbo Shrineheads played Erika Reinstein (fantastic fanzine) gave this totally brave spoken word about her ex-periences being molested as a little girl. This gave me the chills & made me wanna cry. After this I think we went back to Sarah's house, no actually we went to the all-girl dance party

Day#3

Today was the day that all the workshops were gonna take place, but Stacey and I previously spoken with Ne "sk8 rock" and decded to go Skating at this sk8 park in Maryland called Landsdowne. We went back to the peace center pretty early that morning to hopefully catch a few of the workshops. we arrived there and sat in this room with a bunch of the girls who came down there to attend the onvention. This was very embarrassng 'cuz all of us were sitting in this room in silence. Finally someone suggested we all introduce ourselves. Kinda corny but it atleast it broke the horrid silence. The firstworkshop was on self de-fense it was really cool and helpful. But ladies I let ya in on one thing sk8boards are very good weapons which could be another reason why more girls should sk8. Anyways the next work-op was on Sexuality,this one was conducted by Claudia (NYC Riot Grrrl) and a couple others who JI don't remeber. We had to leave during the middle of this one cuz Ne was picking us up. I was too bummed about missing the other workshops I kinda felt kinda bummed about missing them. They had one on Racism and I heard it wasn't too effective, but real-ly how could it have been if it was filled up with mostly all white girls. One girl I spoke to after the meetings said the Asian girls were blaming all the white girls for racism and that she just "could'nt handle that". Ever heard of the word Guilt??? Anyway, Ne drove us and this woman Lisa who was working on documentary about girl bands and girls fuckin' shit up cam along too. When we got there it was beautiful. The park was total

Pyschicfriends

19

the time there wasn't many people there to get in our way. I was having a good time until I took a terrible spill on my sk8board and slightly spraind my wrist. Aw shucks, I was through for the day.

When we got back to D.C. we went to this park called Dupont Circle where there was gonna be this outside show, With a bunch bands and a couple spoken word pieces. It was a beautiful day! A bunch of people had asked if Gunk was gonna play at this show, but considering we had no instruments and no drummer it didn't look to good. But Stacer and I managed to borrow a guitar and bass and instantly Gunk became a Duo. We knew we were gonna play awful considering we hadn't practice in months, hell who gives a shit it's only punk rock. Meanwhile, a bunch of bands played All the bands were made up of girls and they had so much energy and were just really good. This band Cheesecake played and they looked so cool the singer had this tiny little voice when she spoke but when she started singing it was like a huge semi-truck. One of the other highlights was this band Slant 6, they had hella catchy songs and had this rad stand up drummer. I cannot describe the feeling I had watching all of these women up there, I felt really proud. When some guy says to me you only like a particular band 'cuz they have girls in it, well part of this is true, because they're has been this terrible void, and that void is the lack of women participation. When I see them up there it's like yeah now I know what's been missing and why I was so bored before.

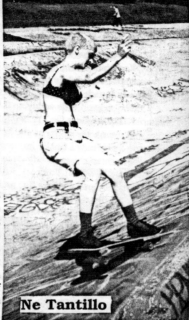

Ne Tantillo

These girls might not be the best musicians but just wait and see at the rate that they were going there is no stoppping us. I noticed a few boys there that just didn't know what to make of all this becuas we were there and in control and it just baffled and terrified them completely. In there heads this couldn't be right... But it was & they could'nt do anything about it. When we played it was in my opinion one of our funnest shows. We sucked so bad, My singing was a nightmare. I was so filled with adrenalin that I couldn't control my voice or my hands. All our songs came off as completely spastic and disjointed, but the funny thing was I think a few people recognized that there was something there. I mean we weren't just standing up there screaming and makin' noise. Then again maybe we were. But it was just Fun! Fun! Fun! This was the last day of the convention and after the show Stacer and I were too tired to go to the Riot GRRRl meeting. We went back to Sarah's house and went to sleep, I think. The entire time we hadn't showered, on the last day there we took a shower and put on our filthy clothes and left Sarah's an took the Metro back to D.C. We walked around for awhile. I out of my good will and guilty conscience scraped up some dough and bought this homeless guy a burrito, thus fullfilling my good deed for th day. Stacer took the Metro back to the Airport with me and we sat in the airport for a long time. We met this really foxy southern boy from Atlanta who never wrote me back. Whah!

The overall experience of the Riot Grrrl convention showed me alot of different things and I'm sorry to say most of them were not very good ones. On the first day we got there we met this boy who kept suggestioning how uncool we were because

we hadn't heard of these dumb D.C. bands. He went on to babble about how D.C. was the scene of all scenes and that we were really missing out. Duh! I found out later after this ultra cool guy saw us play at the outside show, he couldn't beleive how punk we were. Duh! Duh! Basically alot people in D.C. annoyed me with thier scene antics and they're "way cool man" atitudes. Another reason why I was kinda unhappy about the whole D.C thing was realization of how.... dare I say "white bread" everyone was. I mean mostly all Riot Grrrls are white and only a few asians were there. I think I was one of the only 3 black kids there I mean Riot Grrrl calls for a change, but I question who it's including. Another thing was that most of the girls there were pretty aware and tough so why did we need to be continually told that we are. I mean it's important but it's kinda like preaching to the choir. I know alot of the "Riot Grrrls" are probably aware of this and it's difficult to come up with the solutions and I certainly don't have them all. But basically the whole idea of putting a name on this move ment is kinda of limiting and excluding. I mean the liberation of women is not just for us it will effect every single aspect of this fucking planet so when we say o' it's the Grrrl movement, it sug gest that this is all we care about and this is all we stand for and we only want what we want Me! me! me! is all I hear. This sounds kinda snotty but I see Riot Grrrl growing very closed to a very chosen few i.e white middle class punk girls. It's like it's some secret soci ety, but then again there are some who feel that a secret society is what we need. I constantly don't feel comfortable with this cuz I know so many girls that need to hear this shit, but weren't there cuz they would feel intimi dated 'cuz they don't look punk or they never heard of Bikini Kill. Was this the point? I think Riot Grrrl is filled with positive stuff and as a group I think it give girls a sense of solidarity and self worth to girls in need. But still when you have all your beliefs in one bucket and you say this is all I'm about and I won't change my mind 'cuz I'm a Riot Grrrl and they do this and that and this is how we are suppose to be.... Your digging yourself a serious hole and it's called stagnation. Fuck! I'm not all negative about Riot Grrrl cuz there were so many aspects of this whole con vention that were so fuckin rad! Like I was filled with joy to see all these young dyke girls kissing and holding and hands and feeling   no shame. Also I almost forget on one of the nights there was this all-night, all-   girl dance party. Not many people showed up but it was cool anyway.   And we got see these great women go! go! dancers. Kathleen Hanna   was an epecially cool dancerto watch. It was a great experience for   two dorky surburban girls from Basking Ridge if only I parents could   have been there it would have been beautiful. Another thing that really was   great about D.C. was that practically ev-ery girl we met three either   sk8ed or played in a band. Seemed like every girl played the   drums. I'm really glad I went 'cuz I fi-nally got to meet a   lot of my pen pals and also meet alot of other rad   people. And it was also the first time Stacer &   I played a how where some id-iot guy did   not   scream out "there a   bunch of dykes!" or   the ever so popular   "they're not a   real band!".
                        I'm not to tally dis

Allison (Bratmobile)

Erin Smith (Bratmobile)

GUNK 4 (EXCERPT)

Amerikkan Gurl

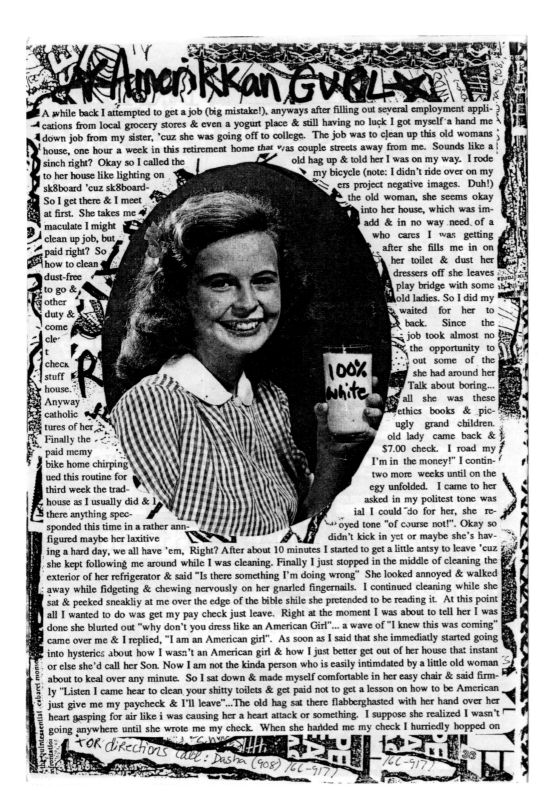

A while back I attempted to get a job (big mistake!), anyways after filling out several employment applications from local grocery stores & even a yogurt place & still having no luck I got myself a hand me down job from my sister, 'cuz she was going off to college. The job was to clean up this old womans house, one hour a week in this retirement home that was couple streets away from me. Sounds like a sinch right? Okay so I called the old hag up & told her I was on my way. I rode to her house like lighting on my bicycle (note: I didn't ride over on my sk8board 'cuz sk8board- ers project negative images. Duh!) So I get there & I meet the old woman, she seems okay at first. She takes me into her house, which was im- maculate I might add & in no way need of a clean up job, but who cares I was getting paid right? So after she fills me in on how to clean her toilet & dust her dust-free dressers off she leaves to go & play bridge with some other old ladies. So I did my duty & waited for her to come back. Since the cle job took almost no t the opportunity to check out some of the stuff she had around her house. Talk about boring... Anyway all she was these catholic ethics books & pic- tures of her ugly grand children. Finally the old lady came back & paid memy $7.00 check. I road my bike home chirping I'm in the money!" I contin- ued this routine for two more weeks until on the third week the trad- egy unfolded. I came to her house as I usually did & I asked in my politest tone was there anything spec- ial I could do for her, she re- sponded this time in a rather ann- oyed tone "of course not!". Okay so figured maybe her laxitive didn't kick in yet or maybe she's hav- ing a hard day, we all have 'em, Right? After about 10 minutes I started to get a little antsy to leave 'cuz she kept following me around while I was cleaning. Finally I just stopped in the middle of cleaning the exterior of her refrigerator & said "Is there something I'm doing wrong" She looked annoyed & walked away while fidgeting & chewing nervously on her gnarled fingernails. I continued cleaning while she sat & peeked sneakliy at me over the edge of the bible shile she pretended to be reading it. At this point all I wanted to do was get my pay check just leave. Right at the moment I was about to tell her I was done she blurted out "why don't you dress like an American Girl"... a wave of "I knew this was coming" came over me & I replied, "I am an American girl". As soon as I said that she immediatly started going into hysterics about how I wasn't an American girl & how I just better get out of her house that instant or else she'd call her Son. Now I am not the kinda person who is easily intimdated by a little old woman about to keal over any minute. So I sat down & made myself comfortable in her easy chair & said firm- ly "Listen I came hear to clean your shitty toilets & get paid not to get a lesson on how to be American just give me my paycheck & I'll leave"...The old hag sat there flabberghasted with her hand over her heart gasping for air like i was causing her a heart attack or something. I suppose she realized I wasn't going anywhere until she wrote me my check. When she handed me my check I hurriedly hopped on

FOR directions call: Dasha (908) 166-9171

166-9171

38

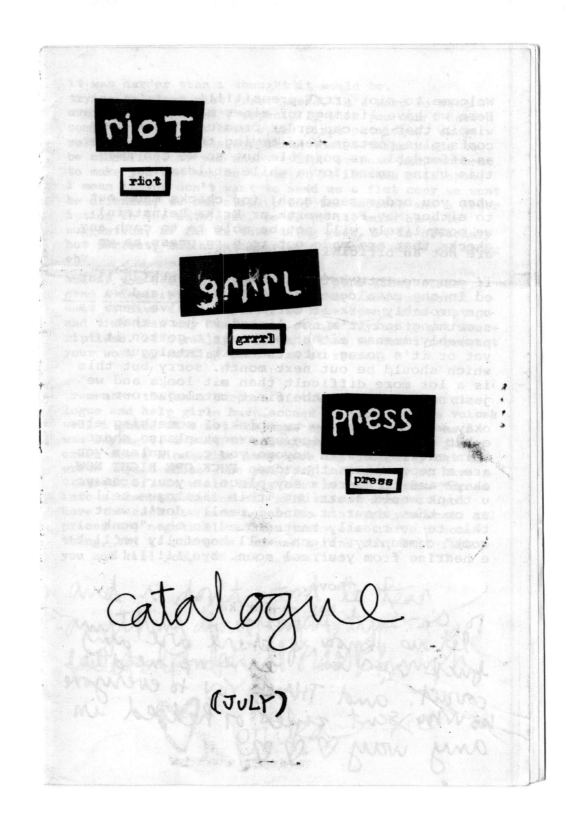

riot

grrrl

press

catalogue

(JULY)

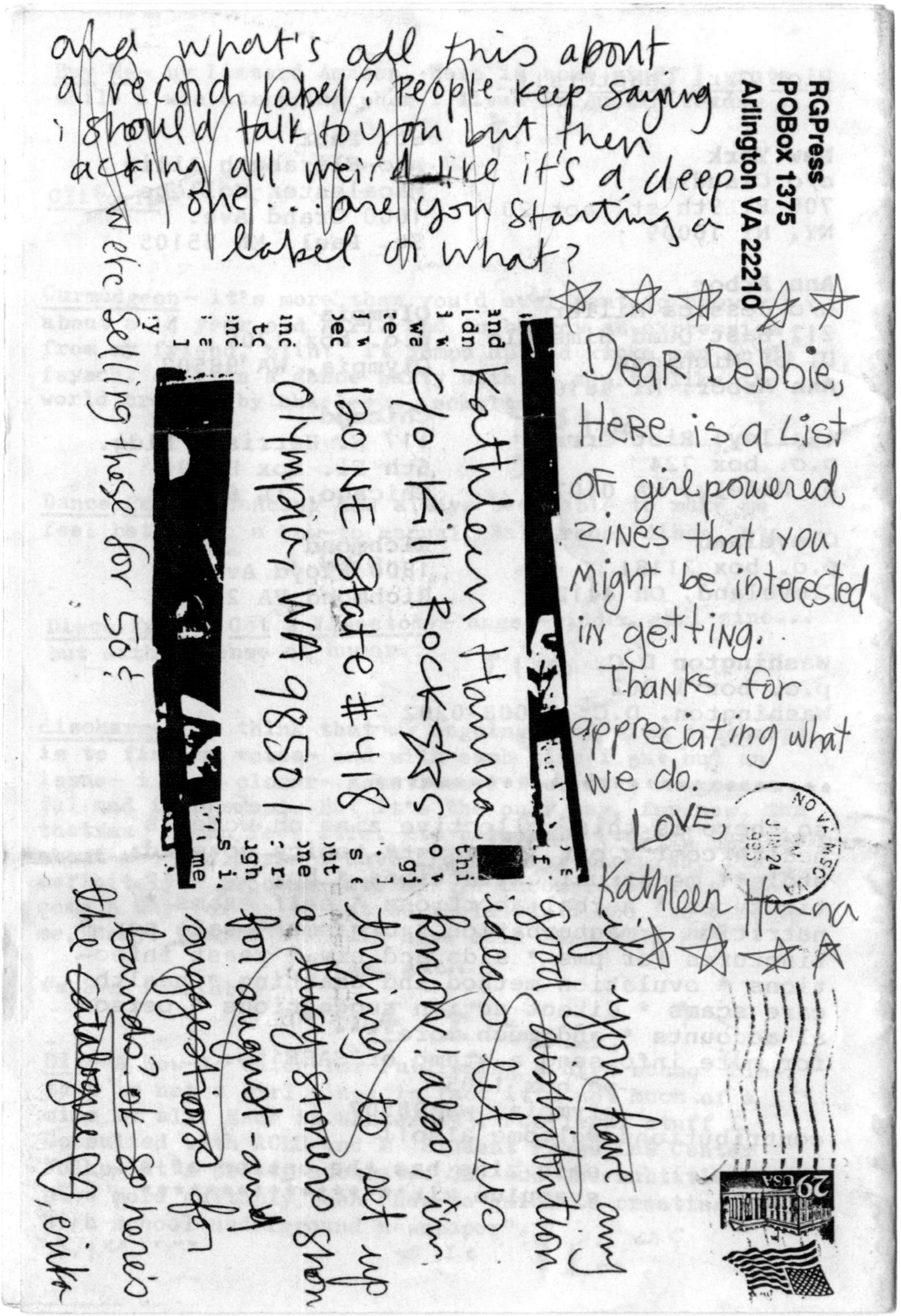

and what's all this about a record label? People keep saying i should talk to you but then acting all weird like it's a deep one... are you starting a label or what?

we're selling these for 50¢

RGPress
POBox 1375
Arlington VA 22210

☆ ☆ ☆ ☆ ☆

Dear Debbie,
Here is a List of girl powered zines that you might be interested in getting.
Thanks for appreciating what we do.
LOVE,
Kathleen Hanna

☆ ☆ ☆ ☆ ☆

Kathleen Hanna
c/o Kill Rock ☆ ☆ 's
120 NE State # 418
Olympia, WA 98501

good distribution ideas if we you have any know! also i'm trying to set up a bucy storing shon for august- and suggestions for bands? ok so here's the catalogue ♥, erika

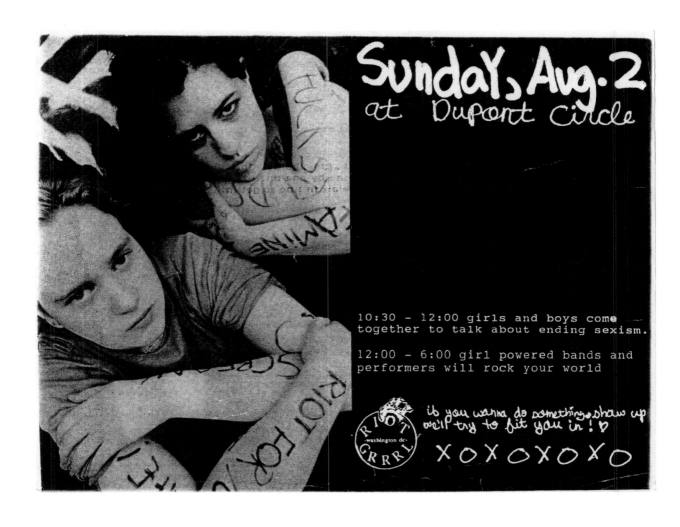

FLYER

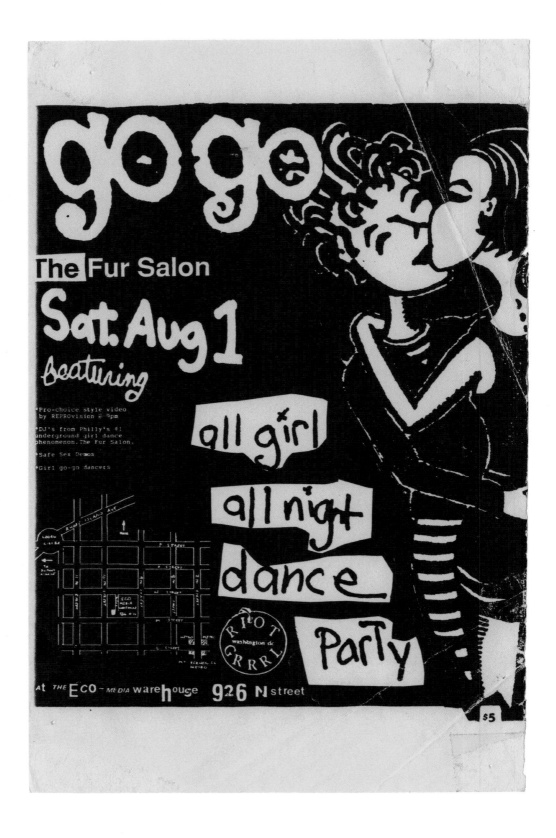

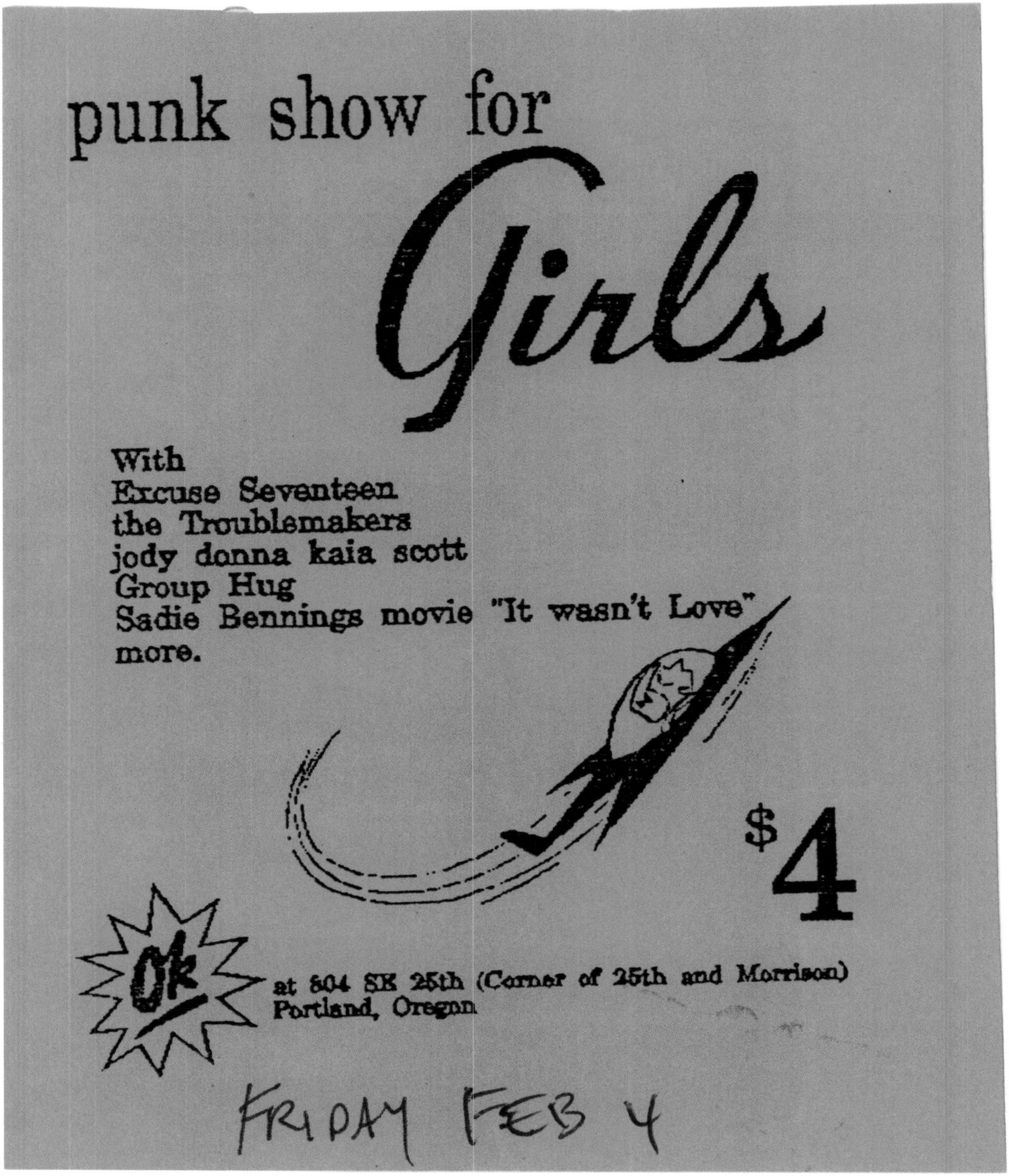

punk show for

Girls

With
Excuse Seventeen
the Troublemakers
jody donna kaia scott
Group Hug
Sadie Bennings movie "It wasn't Love"
more.

$4

OK

at 504 SE 25th (Corner of 25th and Morrison)
Portland, Oregon

FRIDAY FEB 4

FLYER

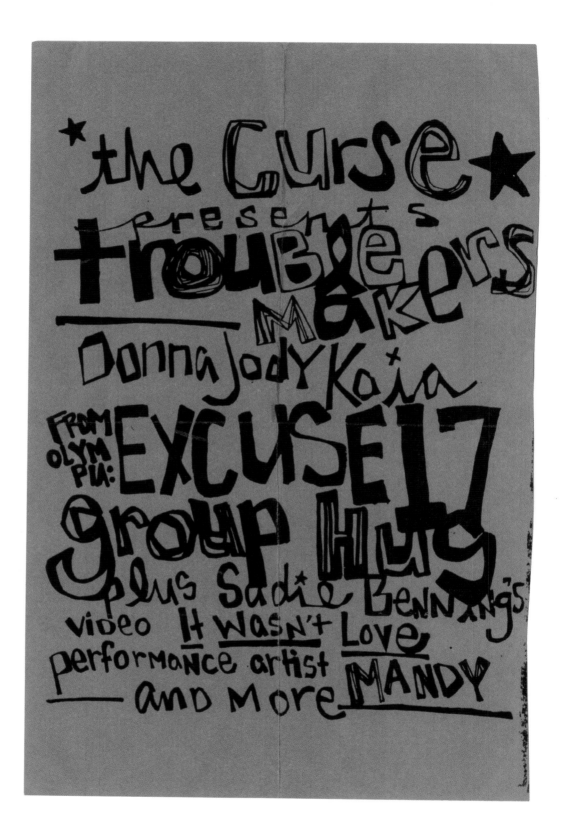

the Curse
presents
+troublers
makers
Donna Jody Kaia
from Olympia: EXCUSE 17
group Hug
plus Sadie Benning's
video It Wasn't Love
performance artist
— and more MANDY

FLYER

★ Riot Grrrl ★ Convention

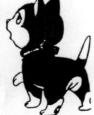

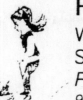

This summer in L.A on

July 29th at The Jabberjaw, 30th at the Pomona Veterans Hall, and 31st at The Jabberjaw.

Several Wonderful bands

Performing plus : Spoken Word,

Workshops, Fanzines, Literature, Stickers, Booths, ect..........

For more info call: Sam (818) 242-9304 or write: 1321 Greenbriar Rd. Glendale, Ca. 91207

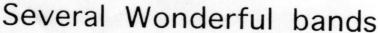

Tickets for the 30th on sale <u>now</u> for $5. Bands performing are:The Free to Fight tour which is Lois, 151, Phranc, & self defense lessons, and also Nikki McClure, Lucid Nation, Sue P. Fox, Bubby Girl, Erin, the Fanatics, Girl Jesus, and much more...........
<u>Write to us for tickets A.S.A.P. Or buy them at</u> <u>No Life Records on 7209 Santa Monica Blvd. a</u> <u>few blocks west of La Brea.</u> (if you are coming from out of state and need a place to stay call:Chelsea (213) 669-8537)

Riot grrrl Orange County

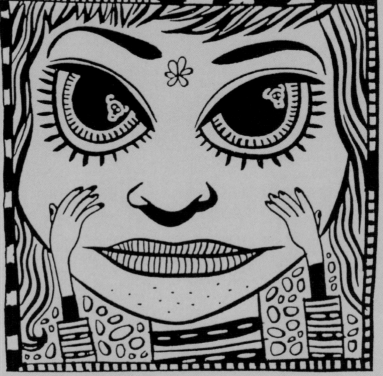

if You Live in Orange County or The
South Bay areas and Want a girl
Revolution, Come Join us in **Riot
grrrl Orange County** ♥ We'd Love to
Meet you!!
xx
Write us at: P.O. BOX 5533
OR CALL   IRVINE, Ca. 92716-5533
310.4388790 PLease SenD A STAMP...
We're Poor!

WhAt IS RiOT GRRRl?

riot grrrl
is :...

BECAUSE we will never meet the hierarchical BOY standards of talented, or cool, or smart. They are created to keep us out, and if we ever meet them they will change, or we will become tokens.

BECAUSE I need laughter and I need girl love. We need to build lines of communication so we can be more open and accessible to each other.

BECAUSE we are being divided by our labels and philosophies, and we need to accept and support each other as girls; acknowledging our different approaches to life and accepting all of them as valid.

BECAUSE in every form of media I see us/myself slapped, decapitated, laughed at, objectified, raped, trivialized, pushed, ignored, stereo- typed, kicked, scorned, molested, silenced, invalidated, knifed, shot, chocked, and killed

BECAUSE I see the connectedness of all forms of oppression and I believe we need to fight them with this awareness.

BECAUSE a safe space needs to be created for girls where we can open our eyes and reach out to each other without being threatened by this sexist society and our day to day bullshit.

BECAUSE we need to acknowledge that our blood is being spilt; that right now a girl is being raped or battered and it might be me or you or your mom or the girl you sat next to on the bus last Tuesday, and she might be dead by the time you finish reading this. I am not making this up.

BECAUSE I can't smile when my girlfriends are dying inside. We are dying inside and we never even touch each other; we are supposed to hate each other.

BECAUSE I am still fucked up, I am still deal- ing with internalized racism, sexism, classism homophobia, etc., and I don't want to do it alone. BECAUSE we need to talk to each other. Commun ication/inclusion is key. We will never know if we don't break the code of silence.

BECAUSE we girls want to create mediums that speak to US. We are tired of boy band after boy band, boy zine after boy zine, boy punk after boy punk after boy.

BECAUSE I am tired of these things happening to me; I'm not a fuck toy. I'm not a punching bag, I'm not a joke.

No we are not paranoid.
No we are not manhaters.
No we are not worrying too much.
No we are not taking it too seriously.

BECAUSE every time we pick up a pen, or an instrument, or get anything done, we are creating the revolution. We ARE the revolution

riot

start a Fuckin HELP ME

Riot Grrrl
P.O. Box 5533
Irvine, CA. 92716-5533
PLEASE SEND A STAMP
(FOR easy reply)

FOR MORE INFO:

BIKINI KILL TOUR

9/11--morgantown,west virginia.fuzzy:(304)296-1669.
(608 elm street)
9/12--daytoon,ohio.frank:(513)278-2801.also ken gross...
(Brookwood Hall)
9/13--cincinnati,ohio.mark shaffer:(513)681-8358.
9/14--indianapolis,indiana.steve:(317)848-5883.
(also shane/kyle/toni--317-920-8529)
9/15--off
9/16--chicago,illinois.casey:
(czar bar...call us at jeremy's:(312)243-0818.)
9/17--off.
9/18madison,wisconson.robin davis:(608)256-0678.
(madison punk resistence,basement location)
9/19--minneapolis,minnesota.shmurtck,shmrstck:(612)333-0340.
(loft/party show starting at midnight,also try jay:612377-8467 or
jessica from hit it or quit it:(612)374-5616...her band and godhead silo are both playing)
9/20--st.paul,minnesota.john pucci:612 647-1561--aces.
(speedboat gallery with godhead silo and smut)
9/21--fargo,north dakota.mike kunka's mom:(701)239-4105.
(teen dance club with godhead silo)
9/22--either rapid city or sioux falls,call kunka for info...
9/23--omaha,nebraska.tim moss:402-346-8843.
9/24--lincoln,nebraska.dave rabie:(402)474-3543 or475-3524.
9/25--lawerence,kansas.jeff fortier:(913)749-7475.
(the outhouse)
9/26--oklahoma city,oklahoma.toby lawerence:(405)528-8124.
9/27--either dallas,ft.worth or denton texas...call kelly keys
during the day at direct hit for information:(214)826-5222.
9/28--austin,texas.rick:(512)478-3060 or 472-4757.
(the cavity)
9/29--off.
9/30--tuscon,arizona.steve eye:(602)884-0874...also try sara:
602-881-7462...DowntownPerformanceCenter.
10/1--phoenix,arizona.greg sage:(602)968-6955.
10/2--yuma,arizona.???greg sage...
10/3--san diego,california.crisanta:(619)755-1897.
(show at some cafe other than che with heroin:(619)476-0909)
10/4--los angeles,california.gary:(818)899-6598,(213)732-3463.
(jabber jaw with pussy willow and oiler)
10/5--pomona,california.john:(714)629-3747.
(munchies with heroin)
10/6--santa barbara,california.rene:(805)964-6591.
(anaconda with red ants and mudwimmin)
10/7--los angeles,california.gabbie strong:hm-310-397-6912,
wk-444-6669,sh-825-1958...UCLA with shudder to think.
10/8--LA.ROCK FOR CHOICE. with firehose and the muffs.
10/9--san francisco,california.little mike:(415)648-6826.
(klub kommotion,partial benefit for filth fanzine with mdc and
maybe tiger trap on borrowed equipment and films and spaghetti
and mike proclaimed punk rock kareokee...for real.)
10/10--GILMAN STREET,CA.mike stand:(510)678-9656.we're playing
with pansy division and tribe 8 and pre marital sex and someone
else I forgot...
10/11--SF.EPICENTER.w/honey's band...gordon:(415)431-2725.or matt.

FLYER

169

1.MOsHING Tips

While enjoying the lovely sounds of tXXXthe Bikini KIll
please remeber.Things go best when the boys mosh in back!
The Kills strongly encourage   girls/ladies/women to dance up
front. x
       Ultimately,its up to the audience how this goes.

2.For security reasons, Bikini Kill would like to maintain as
much control over the stage during our set, as possible. If you xx
have an announcement to make please tell whoever is working the
zine table ...they will try and arrange it with the bands and xixx
figure out a gooddtime for XXMXIX it happen.
If there is a problem during the show that you and/or yr friends
can't/won't/or don't wanna deal with (like someone's fucking with
you) again,please tell whoevers working the zine table and they'll
tell the show organizers so that something WILL be done.
IF THERE IS AN EMERGENCY please don't hesitate to notify the band
on stage, we ask, however, that people reserve this tactic for xxx
emergencies only since its really hard for people on stage to
know whats going on in the audience at all times and so having
"the band" stop to deal with truble can often only make things
more confused and HEATED...

3.If you would like to DIALOGUE with the Bikini Kill...we're
gonna hopefully do a radio show on KAOS 89.3 FM soon where you can
call and ask questions, make criticisms, discuss things,get more
info,etc...we'll make fliers about this.........

The reason we made this flier is cuz we've had to deal with a lot
of violence at our shows and are trying to fxdeal with this better
It takes everyone, not just the people on stage to make for a cool
show.   thanks for coming.

I hate danger

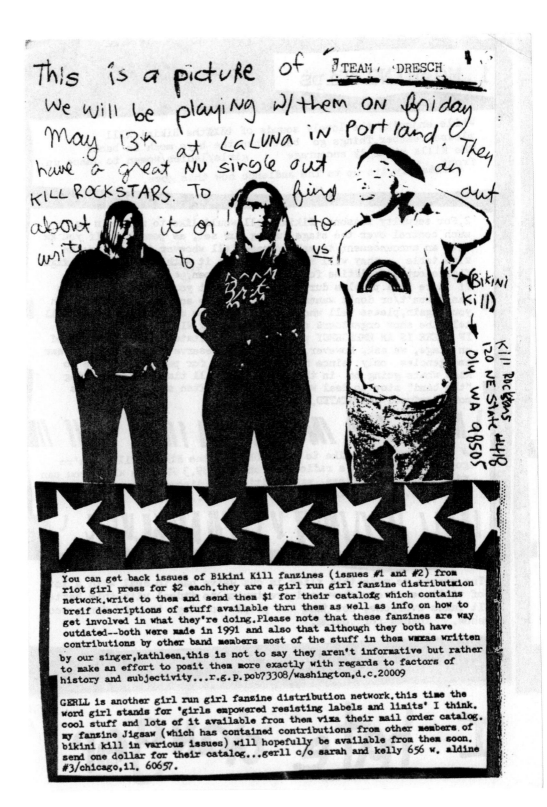

This is a picture of [TEAM DRESCH]

We will be playing w/them on friday May 13th at LaLUNA in Portland. They have a great NU single out an KILL ROCKSTARS. To find out about it on to write to

vs

→ (Bikini Kill)

Kill Rockstars #418
120 NE State
Oly WA 98505

You can get back issues of Bikini Kill fanzines (issues #1 and #2) from riot girl press for $2 each.they are a girl run girl fanzine distribution network.write to them and send them $1 for their catalog which contains breif descriptions of stuff available thru them as well as info on how to get involved in what they're doing.Please note that these fanzines are way outdated--both were made in 1991 and also that although they both have contributions by other band members most of the stuff in them wwzas written by our singer,kathleen.this is not to say they aren't informative but rather to make an effort to posit them more exactly with regards to factors of history and subjectivity...r.g.p.pob73308/washington,d.c.20009

GERLL is another girl run girl fanzine distribution network.this time the word girl stands for 'girls empowered resisting labels and limits' I think. cool stuff and lots of it available from them vixa their mail order catalog. my fanzine Jigsaw (which has contained contributions from other members of bikini kill in various issues) will hopefully be available from them soon. send one dollar for their catalog...gerll c/o sarah and kelly 656 w. aldine #3/chicago,il. 60657.

HUGGY BEAR + BiKiNi KiLL
U.K TOUR 1993

Also StaRRiNg
Witchy POO
X O X O...

WHY??????

Because I am a female performer who has been verbally/ and physically assaulted while being on stage and its really scary when men are taking up the first few rows, to me, I mean.

And also: A lot of times several girls/women will have trouble with the same guy or group of guys BUT cuz the girls dont know each other and are scattered about, we can't warn each other about said jerks presence OR protect each other effectively. If we are in a big gang we are less isolated from each other and more likely to start <u>talking</u> and <u>dancing</u> together and having some FUN

I mean if yr a guy could you just realise for a minute that us girls have no way of knowing if you are a "good boy" or a "bad boy" (as if these distinctions REALLY exist)

And, like, it is not cool or "punk rock" in anyways for guys to smash into us or rub against us while we are trying to watch a show. You know? I am sick of going to shows where I feel completely unwelcomed and banished to the back cuz I just get grossed out by moshing, harrassment, etc.....

IT IS **NOT** SUBVERSIVE TO ACT LIKE YR UNCLE

And also, I really wanna look at female faces while I perform. I want HER to know that she is included in this show, that what we are doing is for her to CRITISIZE/LAUGH AT/ BE INSPIRED BY/HATE/WHATEVER.... Her opinion is more important to me than some guy from Melody Maker and so I (along with my friends) are gonna make the one for real effort to let her know this.

Because this is our fucking show: the GIRLS the QUEERS, the WIMPS, the OUTCASTS......
And the kids who wanna act like their PARENTS are the ones who arent welcome. DIG.

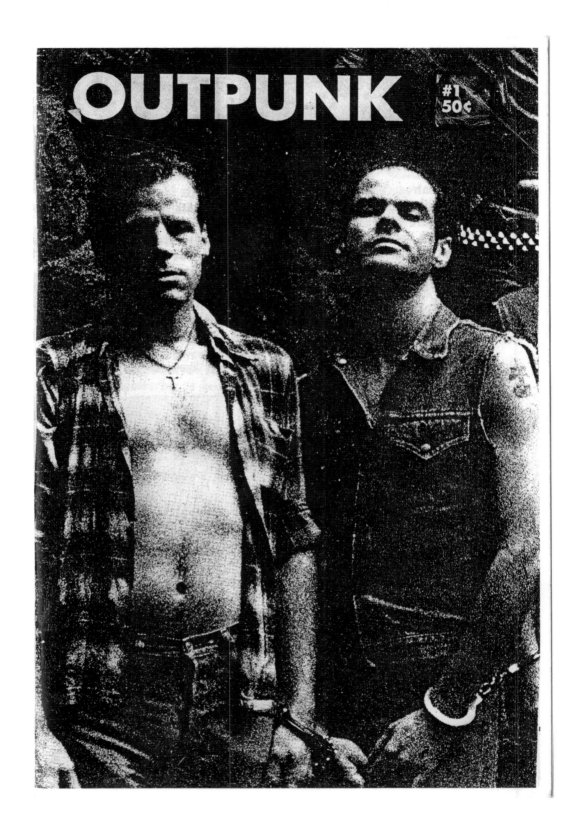

OUTPUNK 1 (EXCERPT)

His scrotum was tender and swollen to twice the size of a grapefruit.

$1.00 postpaid, world

P. O. BOX 170501
SAN FRANCISCO, CA
94117 U.S.A.

This is an introduction to a zine that changes too fast for me to keep up with. Look at it as a newsletter of sorts, with some other shit thrown in here and there. I guess lots of zines use this space to outline the identity you're supposed to assume if you want to join "the scene". Well, this thing may be opinionated and possibly alienating, but as long as you're being honest and sincere, I won't hold anything against you. Other than that, in order to be in my club, you must :
-worship the Smiths and Shudder to Think
-date people twice your age
-own a CD player
And, think of yourself as the punkest person you know. If you don't measure up, you lose. So sorry!

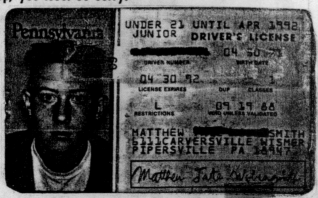

COVER: Chris D. of the Flesheaters (on rt.) looking very gay. But I'm not implying anything, now.

Everything herein was written by Matt unless credited otherwise. Dykes - we want your opinions and contributions for future issues- please?

20256
TO THE PARENTS OF
MATRESSA SMITH

SAN FRANCISCO CA
94117

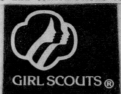

GIRL SCOUTS®

Feedback is encouraged, but personal replies may be out of the question.

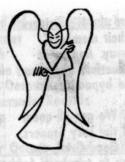

Satan can disguise himself. (2 Co 11.14)

Why Are There So Many Queers In Punk Rock ???

Shit, I don't know, but there are tons. A lot more than I will tell you. And so many more that I just don't know about. So big deal, you're thinking. What does someone's private sexuality mean to anyone else? It means a fuck of a lot, OK? There are a few of us on the front lines who take the heat for everyone, without role models for us to follow and to be empowered (such a great word) by. Yes, dammit, it is empowering to know that someone you respect and admire is queer, too. It makes us feel that much less alone, and the possibilities for a better world that much more plausible.

I'm just going to ramble on without much order; no doubt I'll forget a few on the way. It's a commonly known fact that Darby Crash of the Germs was queer, and that it probably had a lot to do with his suicide. If he was out and learned to deal with it, he would have inspired lots of punk queers later. Like Gary Floyd of the Dicks (now in Sister Double Happiness), or Biscuit of the Big Boys. Or perhaps all three members of Hüsker Dü (Grant Hart, Bob Mould, and the other guy- I hope I'm right on this). And Karen, an out lesbian in the Arizona HC band Conflict. I'm in no way complete - I have a personal list that just keeps growing and growing. Every conversation on the topic just brings up more and more. I would never name anyone who wasn't already completely out and confident in themselves. But there are so many, right now, who are just beginning to come to terms with thier sexuality, that we have only witnessed the very tip of the iceberg. In about a year, there will be an explosion. In five years, the punk rock scene will become the underground queer youth support network. The climate is ready, the seeds have been sown, and all factors indicate that something very big is on the horizon. Bet on it.

OUTPUNK 1 (EXCERPT)

THE RECORD LABEL

is what this zine is about. Hopefully, withthis mag I can make my goals clearer, and it's not like they're that complicated to begin with. They are:

 a. To provide images, role models, information, support, and strength to isolated queer kids who need it.
 b. To give queer kids the tools to cope with and/or change their environments.
 c. to give queer kids options that I never had!

All of this is fueled with no small amount of anger, but even though I am overcome with anger, it is <u>not</u> misplaced aggression. I'm staring my enemies in the face and I know who/what they are. If anyone reading this currently attends high school, drop me a line and maybe I can send you a stack of these for maximum effect. This is most definitely a youth struggle, as we are all but forgotten in this world, except when it comes to using us or fucking us. Sure, you like our pretty bodies, but not enough to include us in your world or take us seriously. So now, I'm getting flooded with mail, and the hype surrounding this stuff is getting bigger. I have a certain reporter who's been calling me and leaving messages trying to get the scoop on what I'm doing. He used to work for the largest gay mag in the country, and even <u>he</u> knew about this stupid zine long before it was out, even though I've only told a few friends. This really scares me, cause I'm a small-town kid and I'm shy, and not used to the attention, and I have tried to remain as low-key as possible to avoid all of the idol-worship and self-promotion that I see all around me. I would do this anonymously, but I have to take credit for my actions. I'm trying to show people that you can speak up, and be out, and you don't have to hide. If that helps anyone, then I'm glad. As a 21-year-old <u>kid</u>, I have been neglected by the community that I'm supposed to be a part of, and abused by the rest. It only makes sense to ignore these institutions like they did to me. So don't look for this stuff in the *Advocate* (unless they can pay me lots of $$$, but get real, now). I keep thinking about how people "slide into the mainstream without doing anything to change the bigotry", and now I know why things still suck so bad after all these years of fighting for "liberation". Sigh.

OK, here's the scoop on the Blatz/Tribe 8 split 7" on Lickout Records. By now, it should be available. There were a few problems, and I'm sick of explaining it again and again, so here's the final word. The 7" was completed months ago, while Tribe 8 was touring in Europe. Upon returning, they freaked out to find a record cover that did <u>not</u> represent them. They disagreed heavily with the cover concept, and were seriously misquoted. It was agreed that the old covers would be scrapped, and new ones made. However, many got out there, no thanks to certain distributors who sold them despite our protest, just to make a quick buck. Everything has been straightened out now, and the new covers are even better than the old ones, if I do say so myself. Any further explanation, ask the bands, cuz I'm tired. Oh yeah, and the 7" rules!!!

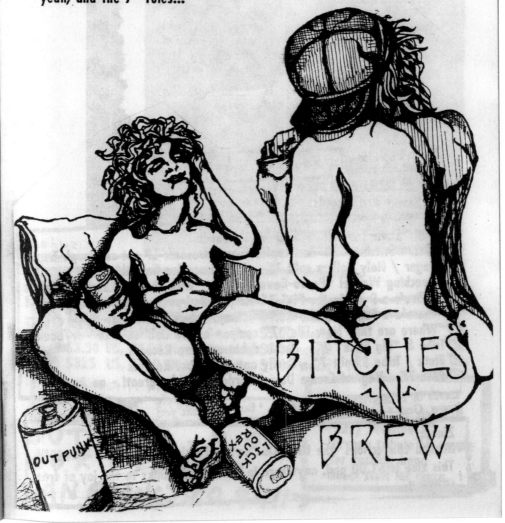

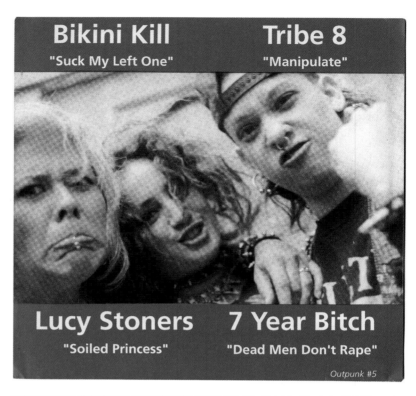

Bikini Kill
"Suck My Left One"

Tribe 8
"Manipulate"

Lucy Stoners
"Soiled Princess"

7 Year Bitch
"Dead Men Don't Rape"

Outpunk #5

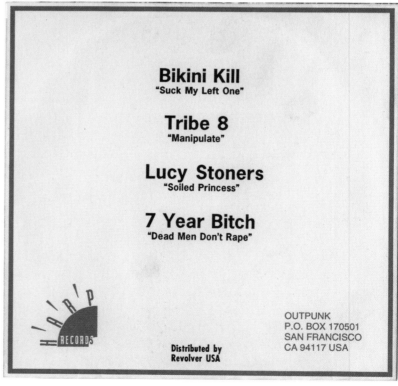

Bikini Kill
"Suck My Left One"

Tribe 8
"Manipulate"

Lucy Stoners
"Soiled Princess"

7 Year Bitch
"Dead Men Don't Rape"

HARP RECORDS

Distributed by
Revolver USA

OUTPUNK
P.O. BOX 170501
SAN FRANCISCO
CA 94117 USA

RECORD COVER

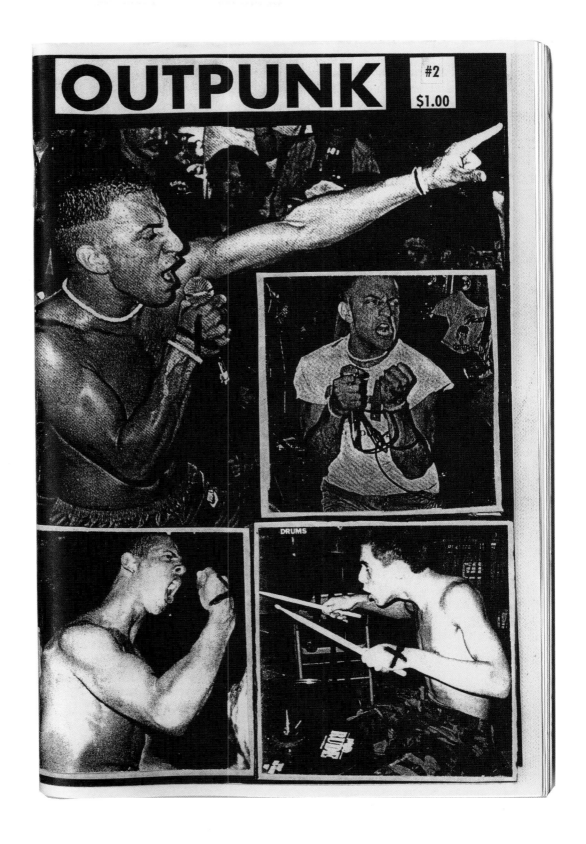

OUTPUNK 2 (EXCERPT)

-There's this weird phenomenon that I've noticed recently. If I'm hanging out with a bunch of women, and there's another guy present, there's often this strange kind of tension. It's like he either condescends me or ignores me completely. It's not as if I really care, but this dumb competition crap is so silly. Stop the J-word, jealousy, from ruining boy love! (please everyone, have a sense of humor now)

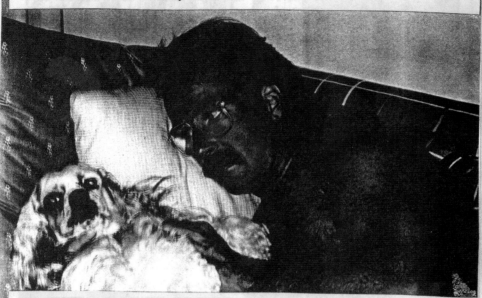

-It can really suck trying to date queer in the punk scene. Most guys I date are completely non-punk, and conversation can be difficult. On one hand, it's cool, because it forces you to meet new people, and to try to relate stuff that you're involved in on a bigger scale. But there are also times when I feel like such a misfit, and would die just to be involved with someone who was into the same stuff as me. Unfortunately, your choices of dates in the punk scene are like choices A, B, and C, and that's hardly a choice at all. And then there's always choice D, but chances are, D is totally gorgeous, and completely not interested in you. Figures.

-And on a related note, it seems like the only punks that flirt with me these days are the hetero ones! Actually, any guy who would have sex with me is far from straight, but it can be so annoying for all these blatant heterosexuals to be constantly hitting on me. Well, OK, not <u>constantly</u>, but enough to make me fairly uncomfortable. If they're just coming out, fine, that's understandable. But the underhanded and belittling way in which they flirt with me is just so disgusting. I wonder if that's how they pick up girls. There's no way that shit will fly with me. Just fucking say what you want - don't fuck with my head. You could get lucky - or not.

-I totally believe in sexual openness and freedom. I like sex a lot, although it's definitely overrated in some ways. There's a line in this movie "Hippy Porn" that says "sex is overrated, shitting is underrated". Genius or what? What I would like to see is a freedom <u>from</u> sex. There's so much emphasis on having sex in this society. You're made to believe that there's something wrong with you if you don't have an active sex life. Truth is, not everyone likes sex, or can have sex, or can find people to have sex with. I went through hell growing up because I couldn't prove my promiscuity or impress my peers with how much I got laid. Yuck! It was so difficult - I hated it! So I hate to see people being pressured into having sex ("you just need to get laid", as if that will solve all of your problems). As my friend Kim put it, "I masturbate to come, I fuck cause I'm lonely".

-I am so sick of all this anti-Riot Grrl hysteria. People are making such a big deal out of it, like they're so threatened by it. They develop these strange perceptions, as if Riot Grrl is taking over punk and soon the castration squads will be sent in. Not that we couldn't use a few castrations here and there, but get serious everyone. People keep insisting that RG is somehow "separatist" and "sexist to men". First off, what is so wrong with being separatist? Why do you suppose people would behave that way in the first place (duh)? And this "reverse sexism" bullshit is such a load of crap! Sounds like people are so scared of the fact that others are aware of their sexism that they have to invent a scenario that makes <u>them</u> the victim. Untill I see men being treated with the same hatred and oppression as women, I refuse to believe that men are capable of suffering sexism. Seems like every time a women stands up for herself, people get threatened. Riot Grrl tells it like it is, so deal with it.

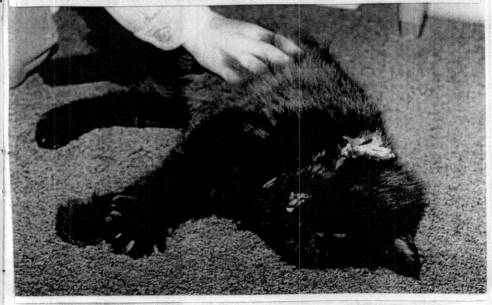

OUTPUNK 2 (EXCERPT)

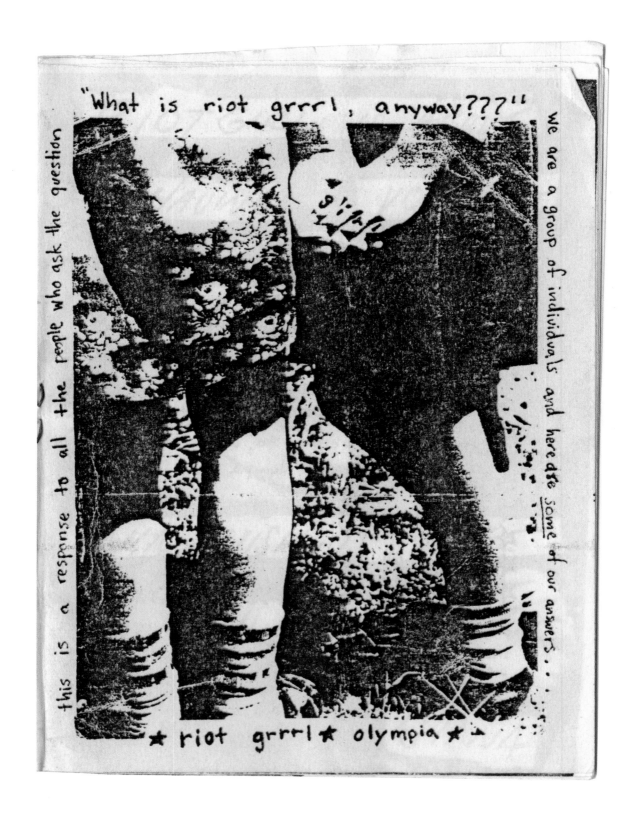

"What is riot grrrl, anyway???"

we are a group of individuals and here are some of our answers...

this is a response to all the people who ask the question

★ riot grrrl ★ olympia ★

WHAT IS A RIOT GRRRL, ANYWAY? (EXCERPT)

Riot Grrrl is so many things and has so much potential. we are a support & open & covert action group for any and all girls and womyn. we are coming together in full force because we know the world treats us like littlegirlsdumbsluts stupidwhoresuglybitchesoldmaidshelplesscreature PROPERTY. and we know what we really are. (sometimes). yes we do work to understand our links and differences. we are a collective of individuals. we don't have a favorite color. we are living our lives through feeling. our life experiencees have taught us different strategies and we are accepting all of our struggles and strategies as real and valid. i have heard a lot of people say a lot about Riot Grrrl being exclusive. here are some thing i have NOT heard those same people say: — the way i/we speak is exclusive ("hey guys, yeah man" etc.) — the way i/we write is exclusive — straight edge is exclusive — punk rock is exclusive — my coolclub friends & i are exclusive. — ETC. this american society is centered around, by and for richstraightwhitemales. (duh).

being male is usually enough. so, DON'T talk to ME about exclusion. i wish i was at a point where i could say it is amusing to me that i never heard a word about exclusion until there was something going on that is not about rich — straight white males. but i'm not. i can't. it bums me. boys, what we do is NOT about you or your needs/desires/wants. Riot Grrrl is not kissing your ass. Riot Grrrl is because i was scared walking here tonight because a collective that is by, for, & about girls & womyn is an absolute necessity, because of how beautiful and alive and free i can feel in a girl environment that is non-competitive and supportive and engaging. Riot Grrrl is because we need to tear it all apart to put ourselves back together again, for real this time.

love,
angelique ♡

Riot Grrrl is a girl gang with secret
plans to destroy Olympia. you don't
have to know me to be in a gang with
me. some people think riot grrls are
white grrrls with cool glasses and cool
shoes. but it's not about fashion or
a dress code or a look cuz i don't have
it. but i am a tuff grrl, sometimes.
maybe you could come to a meeting and
i would meet you and you would say i
don't want to walk home by myself. so
i would walk with you and we would be
a gang cuz we are fighting all the time
on the streets for our lives so walking
together we are a kickass girlgang yea!
this one night at a riot grrrl meeting
some girls started talking about all
these rapes that started happening at
the college here. we got so mad at the
total way the school and the media
ignore sexual abuse and harrasment. and
how shitty it is to live in fear. so
we made up a secret plan and carried
it out that night. we laughed and held
hands and ran around in the dark and
we were the ones you should be looking
out for. in a girl gang i am the nite
and i feel i can't be raped and i feel
so fuckin' free.

WHAT IS A RIOT GRRRL, ANYWAY? (EXCERPT)

i have only been to one Riot Grrrl meeting, but it was the first time in my life i have had a discussion with a large group of people i didn't know, which didn't involve men trying to force their opinions on me, or laughing at my opinions, or worst of all, not caring about my opinions but laughing at the way i look or the way i sit or my style of dress.

the meeting wasn't terribly personal and it didn't cover any intense or frightening issues, but there was this sense of acceptance which is rarely experienced in the real world. people listened to what other people had to say and they didn't interrupt, or yell and scream, or try to inhibit anyone else in any way.

contrary to popular belief, there was no man-bashing involved at all. the only time men were mentioned at all was when a couple of girls said that they tended to hang out with mostly men and they enjoyed the opportunity to experience an all-female environment.

the only bashing i experienced occurred after the meeting when i told various friends about my enlightening first encounter with Riot Grrrl. The prejudice which was unleashed upon me before i could even explain was unbelievable. the responses ranged from "did you do any man-hating for me?" to "those fuckin' freaks?" this kind of unfounded hatred simply perpetuates itself and i find it very sad that even the minute portion of the population which professes to be "alternative" and open-minded is just as ignorant as the rest of the world.

i don't think that the whole world should agree on everything, or even that all of olympia should, because that would probably get very boring. but a little more listening and tolerance and a little less shouting could only improve the world.

Molly Z.

Thus far, I've only been to one Riot Grrrl meeting, so I can't really tell you any history of it, or how it functions, or even what it does, because I don't really know all of that. Instead, I'll tell you why I decided to go the meeting, and what I thought of it.

I consider myself a feminist. Almost militantly so. I'm in an all-girl band, and I think it's really important that girls have a chance to express themselves in our male-dominated society. I agree with almost everything I've heard from Riot Grrrl, but up until a couple of weeks ago, I was afraid to become involved because it seemed so "cliquish," and I was afraid that if I had differing opinions, I would not fit in. Then one day I was riding the bus with a girl who happens to be involved in Riot Grrrl, and I was telling her about a paper on Feminism that I was writing for my English class. She asked if I'd ever considered going to Riot Grrrl meetings. I kind of cringed and said "Well, yah. . . but I'm afraid to," and I told her why. To my surprise, she said that she had thought the same things until she started going to meetings, and found that Riot Grrrls were really accepting and very cool. So I thought about it, and talked some of my friends into going with me to a meeting.

The day that we decided to go was a very emotional day for me, (I got in a super-huge fight with my dad) and I was considering not going, because I didn't know if I could deal with it if it didn't turn out well. My friend talked me into it. When we first got there, I felt really uncomfortable because I didn't really know anybody. My friends and I stood in a little clump and didn't talk to anybody else. But by the end of the meeting, I was so happy that I thought I was going to cry. (This probably had something to do with the amount of crying I'd already done that day—I was crying at the slightest provocation, and I don't usually do that. But really, the meeting made me very happy.) It reminded me of the all-girl slumber parties that my friends and I have been

WHAT IS A RIOT GRRRL, ANYWAY? (EXCERPT)

having for the past two years. I've realized that most of the time (not always, but almost always) I feel much more comfortable and unthreatened around girls than around boys. It's not that I don't like boys, it's just that they're *different*, and there are just some things that they can't relate to. Unfortunately, an all-girl atmosphere is pretty rare.

The meeting wasn't all that personal--we mainly just talked about business things. (At the end of the meeting, everyone agreed that they would like future meetings to be more personal.) But it was business discussed in a different way than I'm used to. There was no hierarchy, no "rules", no condescension, and no boys. All of this, plus, we were united for a Feminist cause! I intend to keep going to Riot Grrrl meetings, because I really think that this is the kind of interaction and purpose that girls really need.

Nomy

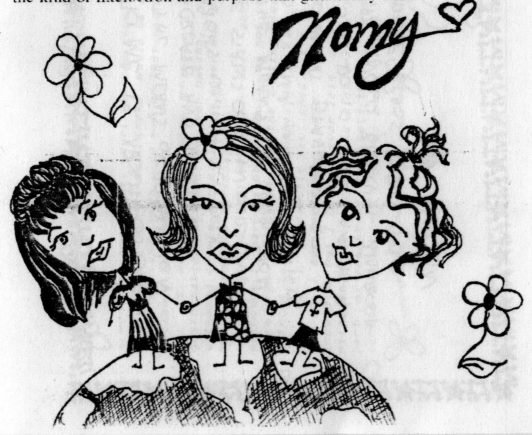

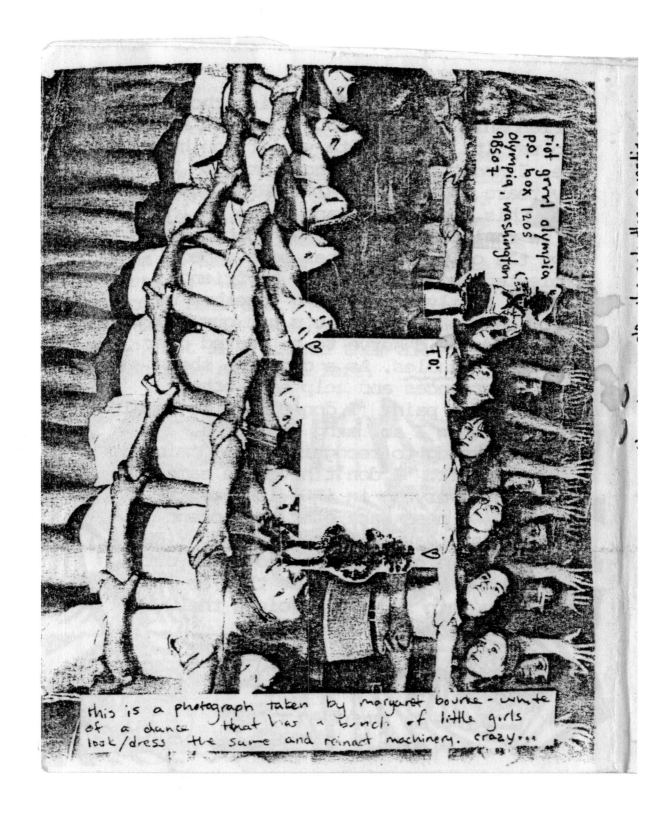

this is a photograph taken by margaret bourke-white of a dance that has a bunch of little girls look/dress the same and reinact machinery. crazy...

riot grrrl olympia
p.o. box 1205
olympia, washington (
98507

TO:

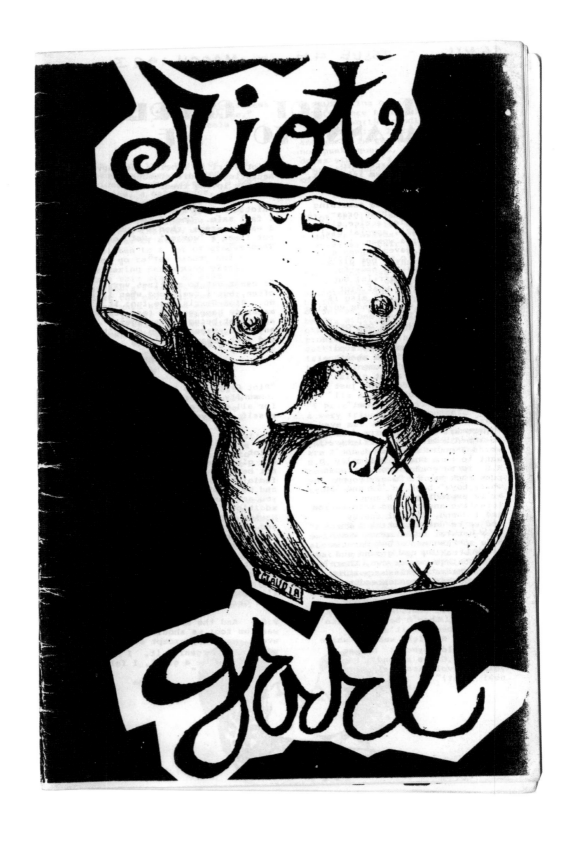

RIOT GRRRL NYC 5 (EXCERPT)

WHAT RIOT GRRRL MEANS TO ME

"Putting the punk back into feminism, and feminism into punk."
--Liberty

"Riot Grrrl is turning something negative into something great. At work, I'm called a nice girl, what a smart girl, special girl. Not a person or a woman, just a girl, when I haven't been a girl for years. O.K. but girls can be dangerous and powerful. So call us girls (grrrls) but watch out. That's what Riot Grrrl means to me. It also is a gathering of women minds working for us and our issues and interests. A support network."
--Polly O'

"Riot Grrrl is about how cool it is to be a girl and about how hard it is to be one sometimes. It's about girls with punk rock ideas who just don't want to put up with all of society's crap anymore."

"There are a lot of nice fancy mass media kind of descriptive words I could use, but I don't want to be a bore. Basically R.G. is to young women now what punk rock was to "angry young white boys" back in '79 and '80. We're exploding with anger (creative anger!) and inspiration and I dunno, lots of energy. And we're united, which I think is a natural trait among women, more so than men. But because we're breaking new ground and doing things on our own, there's a huge media backlash, putting us down, being condescending and acting as if we're "rejected cheerleaders" who are cutesy and a little ooh...angry! Look out! Yes, they'd better fuckin' look out because it's not a goddamned straight wealthy white men's world anymore! Not as long as R.G. is around! Fuck yeah. Revolution girl style now! (Ugh!)"
--Alex Progress

"Riot Grrrl is closing the gap. Accepting the differences and finally loving them."

"Riot Grrrl is a place where I feel safe. Once I thought I was a person, then I found out I was a 'woman.' Not here. Thanks."
--S.

"I can't get to meetings very often, but I feel good when I do. Riot Grrrls have fun; it makes me happier and less scared about not being a teen-ager anymore. Here the fun doesn't end just because you're a grown up."
--MEB

"Riot Grrrl is a network, a community, an exploration outward for all of us as women and within myself, as, yes, a woman."
--Sarah L.

"Riot Grrrl is about not being the girlfriend of the band and not being the daughter of the feminist, and all that stuff, and being whatever it is that you are, and not being the addition. Empowerment, I guess. Having fun and making friends and meeting lots of women who are my peers and whom I respect, and well, I think they're cool. I'm sick of boys anyway and I went to a grrrl college and there's boys everywhere and that's all any body thinks about so I'll get my separatist fix here. Riot Grrrls are so RAD.

P.S.- And the Riot Grrrl show was fun too; we should have one every weekend, except some body else could organize it. I didn't even feel like a grrrl, I felt like a person."
--Emma

VOICE February 23, 1993

Grrrlfriend

In Charles Aaron's review of Bikini Kill ["A Riot of the Mind," February 2], he states: "Of course, like the 'riot grrrl movement' itself . . . [Kathleen] Hanna's imagined, loud-and-clear moment exists only in the minds of a handful of boho progeny with access to copy machines and feminist reading lists."

Before you can verbalize you have to be able to shout. There are no leaders in Riot Grrrl, only committed, passionate individuals, many of whom are devoted to helping women come out of depression and mental anguish induced by sexual, physical, and verbal abuse. I endured all the above. I thought I was insane until women like Kathleen Hanna stayed up long nights with me

talking me out of suicidal thoughts. Now I have friends in every major city in the U.S. who are active in Riot Grrrl groups. That's real to me.
Claudia von Vacano
Manhattan

VOICE March 9, 1993

Jeerleader

The Year of the Woman, my ass. Deborah Frost's horrifyingly hateful and self-hating attack on Riot Grrrl ["Bondage Up Yours," Pazz & Jop critics' poll, March 2] was more painful and bewildering than the time my father got drunk and felt me up on my Sweet 16. At least I understood my father. I cannot understand Ms. Frost's destructive glee. Oh, look, some young women are encouraging other young women to read Audre Lorde—they must be "an amorphous blob of . . . cheerleader rejects and unhappy amateur musicians [who] started coagulating near Seattle." And if the "revolution translate[s] into little beyond a rape-free zone," I would dance in the rape-free streets. As it stands, I'm through with your sour, vindictive, conservative wolf-in-progressive-sheep's-clothing newspaper. The *Voice*'s response to Black History Month is to pull down Alex Haley, and your response to young women is to ridicule one of this generation's first autonomous self-help groups. FUCK OFF.
G.F.
Manhattan

FIGHT THE RIOT GRRRL BACKLASH!

in the MEDIA, the boy's club called the "punk" or "alternative" scene, schools, etc.

-A.L.

Who Is Choking and Dying? by KAKE

O.K. - I've got a bone to pick with Sassy magazine.
Yes, I admit it's a personal grievance, I have had
times of low confidence where I felt the only
way to insure my happiness was to starve and
vomit and try to become one of the females
inside a fashion magazine. That's where the
trouble begins with Sassy, their format of
visuals is the same as all other magazines with
a female audience - thin, VERY attractive models
AND the "Lose weight so boys will like you" ad-
vertisement in the back.

My roomate disagrees with my disgust towards
Sassy, she argues that they write good articles
about incest survivors, rape, witchcraft, how
to make clothes, etc... Alright - all well and
good, except the articles are the substance of
bubble gum icecream with the cherry being "cute
band alert." Yes - too stupid to even MENTION,
"cute band alert" degrades any woman who takes her
music seriously , except me because I judge a
band by their looks and fashion by their lyrics
and music.

Perhaps I am in a dream world with my desire
to have articles and pictures of the average
girl growing up in cheap discount clothes amidst
her piles of souvenirs, collectibles, memories,
dreams and books that she always carries close
to her imagined too large/too small chest.

But that's why Riot Grrrl exists - so all that
our grandmothers, mothers, sisters, aunts, friends
and selves have fought and suffered through will
not be compacted into easily digested bullshit
bits of information. I just hope that as individuals females will start and continue to follow
their inner soul to create a world where - well -
whatever wonderful we want can happen.

"Riot Grrrl is subversive
activity. I came to make new
friends and to find a type of
activism that would have tangible
results for me. This is working
to promote expression in a
community of cooperative young
women."

--Sandra

"At first when I heard about
Riot Grrrl I thought it was
something really great that I
couldn't be a part of. When
I finally decided to go to a
meeting I really felt like not
only could I be a part of R.G.,
but I could get involved in
something that could really affect
me and other people."

--Zoe

"There are so many ways to
criticize feminism and everything
else that women work on together--
Riot Grrrl is the first thing
I've found that totally says
'fuck you' to all the excuses--
it's way more emotional, which
to me is real."

--Joanna

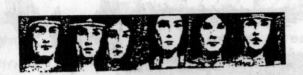

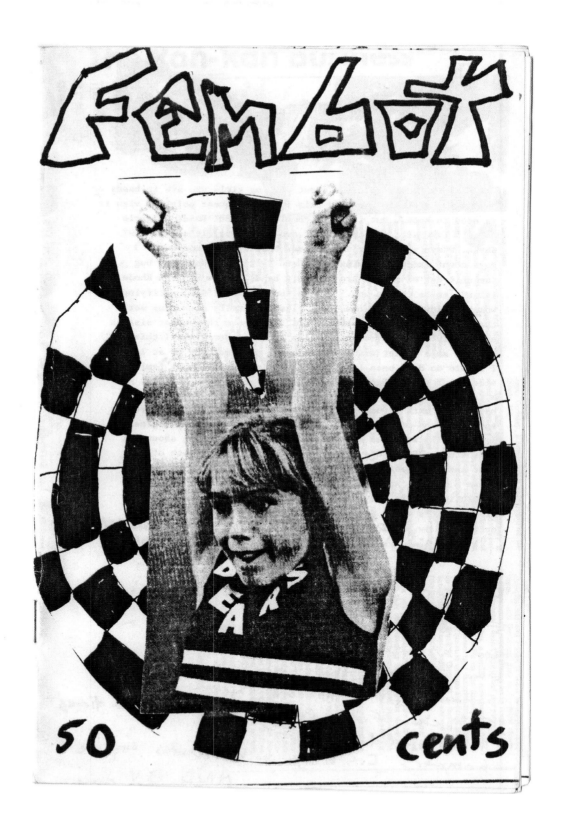

FEMBOT 1 (EXCERPT)

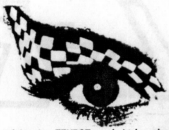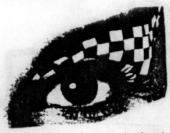

Hi this is FEMBOT and it's about digging girls who are in bands or bands with girls in them and this is from a queer point of view if ya need to know. But it's not completely about bands of girls cause I like alot of other stuff too but mostly it's gurls ok? Chyks, Wymyn yeah cool. Even bands that are one woman and 3 guys count except Throwing Muses and Talking Heads, they bug the shit out of me and are the only bands I know of from Rhode Island, maybe that's why. Please don't think I'm objectifying women or anything, I kinda feel like I identify with them more than I do guys singing, that's all, even more than other sissies especially Morrissey who's a dildo anyway. Sometimes I think maybe I am a closet transgender person or something or at least I should do drag once in awhile to be in touch with my feminine side but I haven't gotten around to it. Even though I just got a free groovy dress - maxi. I had a dream once where I was having sex with a woman as a man with a penis then I had breasts and was a she-male then I was a complete woman with a vagina and I was really startled and puzzled so I got wondering about all this stuff. But I dig being a guy and having sex with other guys and that wasn't in the dream at all but it was just a dream - right? Anyway I just want to say I support the revolution of girl style now maybe you don't want my support or think it's weird after you read this but that's for you to decide. Oops I didn't write much about ~~punk rock~~ this time but next time I will - I SWEAR!

FEMBOT is sponsored by: Summer's Eve
"I'm dreaming of summer,
cool breezes fresh air
When I want that feeling
Summer's Eve takes me there
That clean Fresh feeling keeps the good times
on my mind
Summer's Eve brings back freshness anytime"
AND BY...

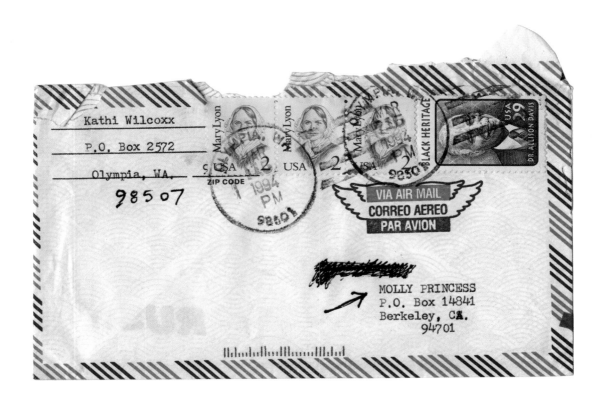

Kathi Wilcoxx
P.O. Box 2572
Olympia, WA.
98507

VIA AIR MAIL
CORREO AEREO
PAR AVION

MOLLY PRINCESS
P.O. Box 14841
Berkeley, CA.
94701

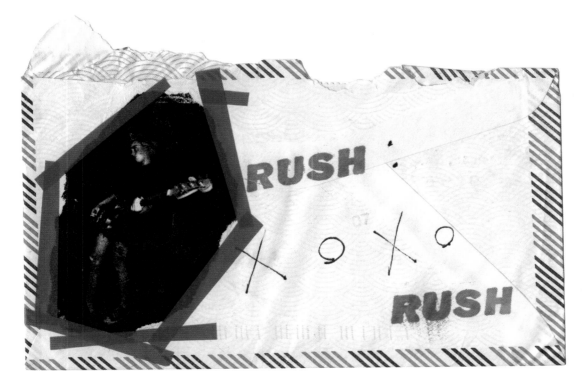

RUSH

XOXO

RUSH

ENVELOPE

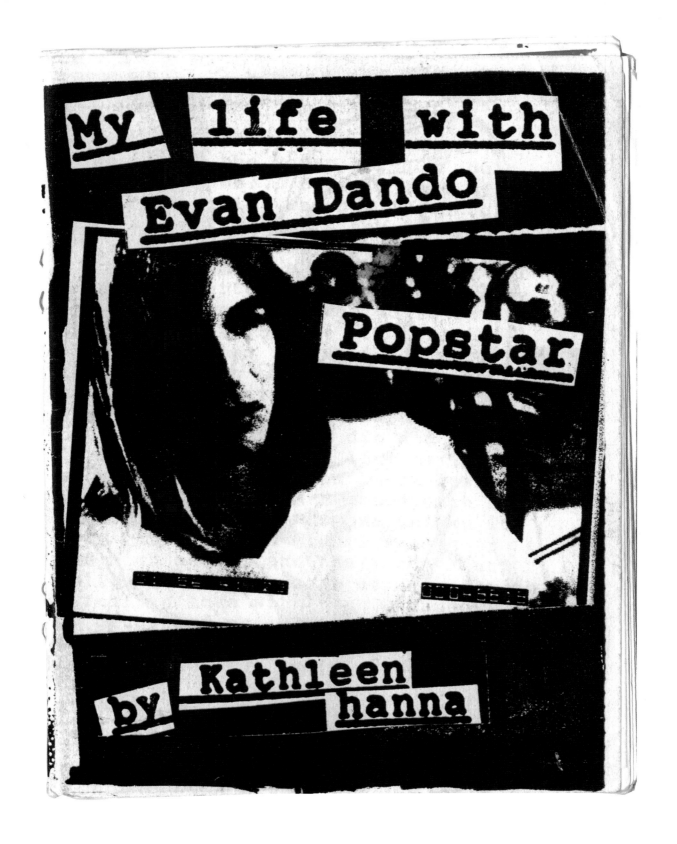

My life with Evan Dando

Evan Dando

Popstar

by Kathleen hanna

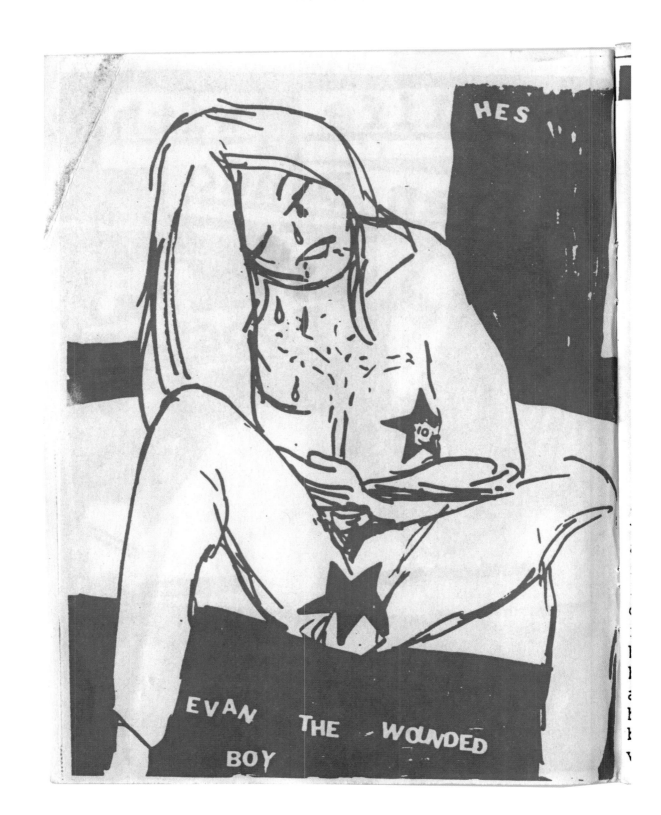

MY LIFE WITH EVAN DANDO, POPSTAR

I fell in love with Evan because it seemed like the worst thing i could do at the time. I fell in love with Evan because it was totally uncool and pathetic which is how i felt inside. I fell in love with Evan because the band i am in started getting all this weird attention and i felt like he was the only one who would understand. I fell in love with Evan because sometimes i wish i was a boy and that the worst thing that ever happened to me was having too many girls like me. I fell in love with Evan because i wanted him to die and thought if i could get him to love me i would show him what a broken heart really was. I fell in love with Evan because he is a total slut and everyone thinks its very cute, unlike when i was in jr hi and high school and the word "slut" followed me everywhere at arms length. I fell in love with Evan because i don't do drugs and so i need other destructive pasttimes. I fell in love with Evan because i can't deal with real boys barely at all and yet am wildly attracted attracted their flat chests and strait hips (sometimes) and Evan is my perfect boyfriend because i am allowed to invent him all by myself.

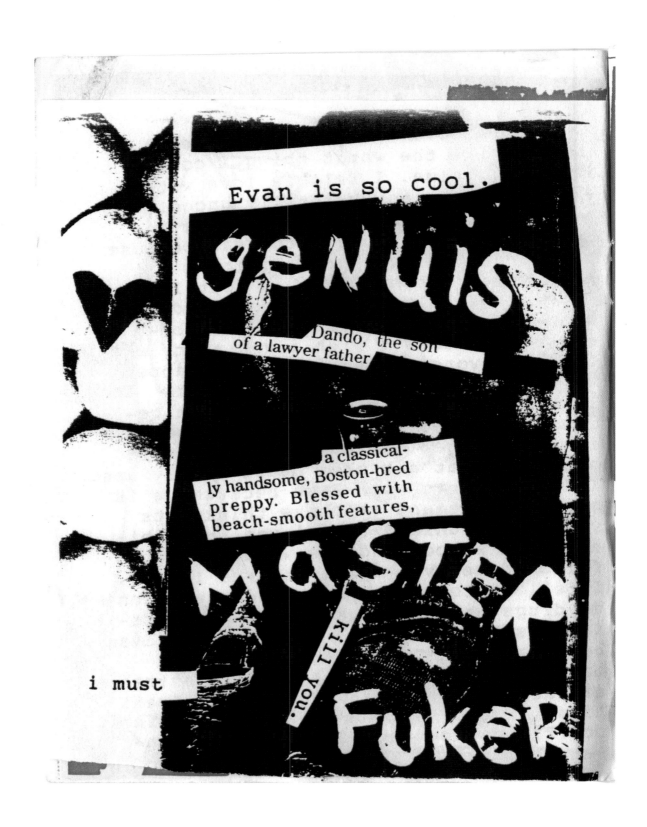

Evan is so cool.

genuis

Dando, the son of a lawyer father

a classical-ly handsome, Boston-bred preppy. Blessed with beach-smooth features,

MASTER

kill you.

i must

FukeR

cuz he's a rock-
star and yr not.

specail,
yeah,oh yeah.

Hey, Evan, how are you doing?
ED: I'm doing really well, man.

Being white and male doesn't hurt

(vrooom, vroom)

This is biological determinism.

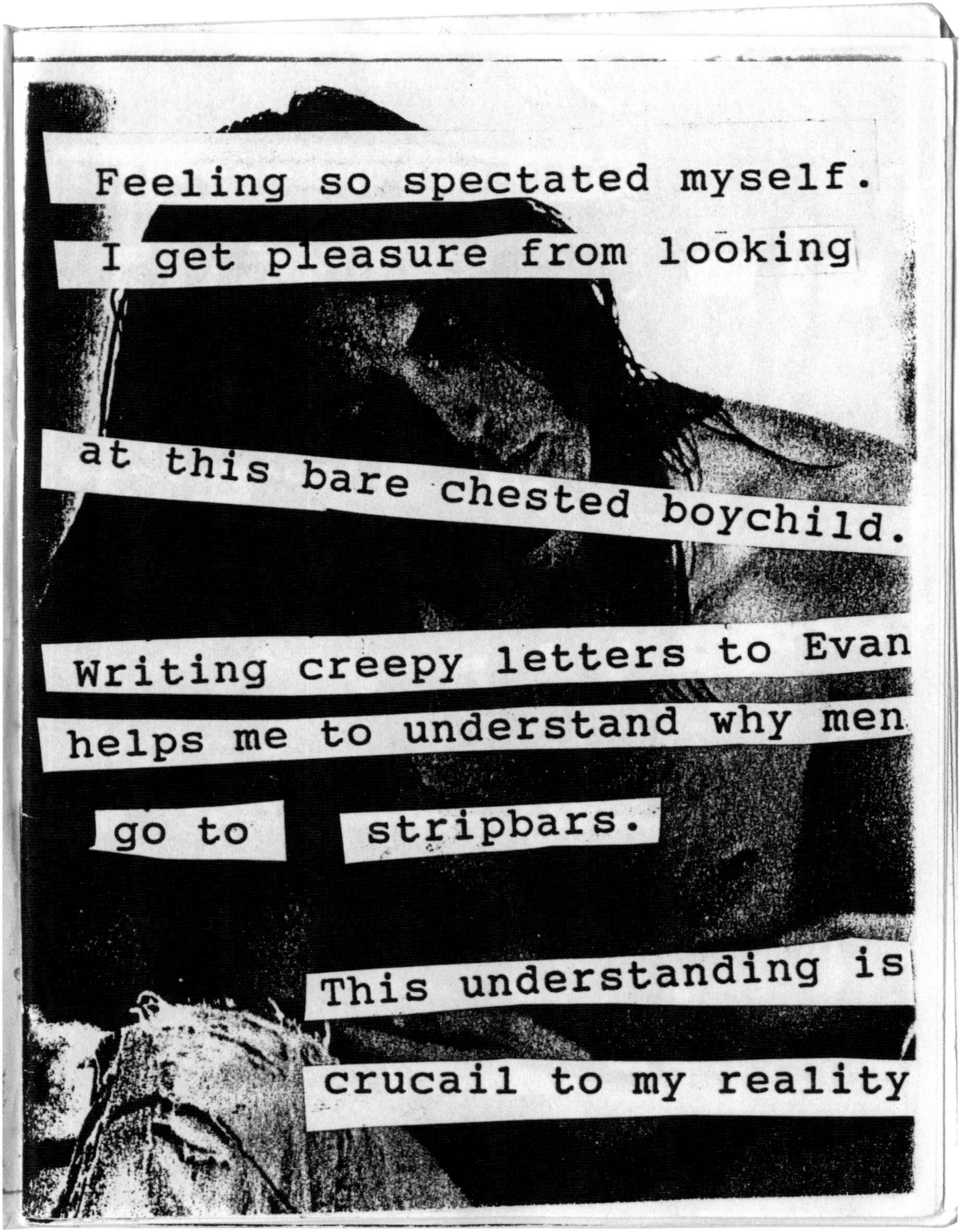

Feeling so spectated myself.
I get pleasure from looking

at this bare chested boychild.

Writing creepy letters to Evan
helps me to understand why men
go to   stripbars.

This understanding is

crucail to my reality

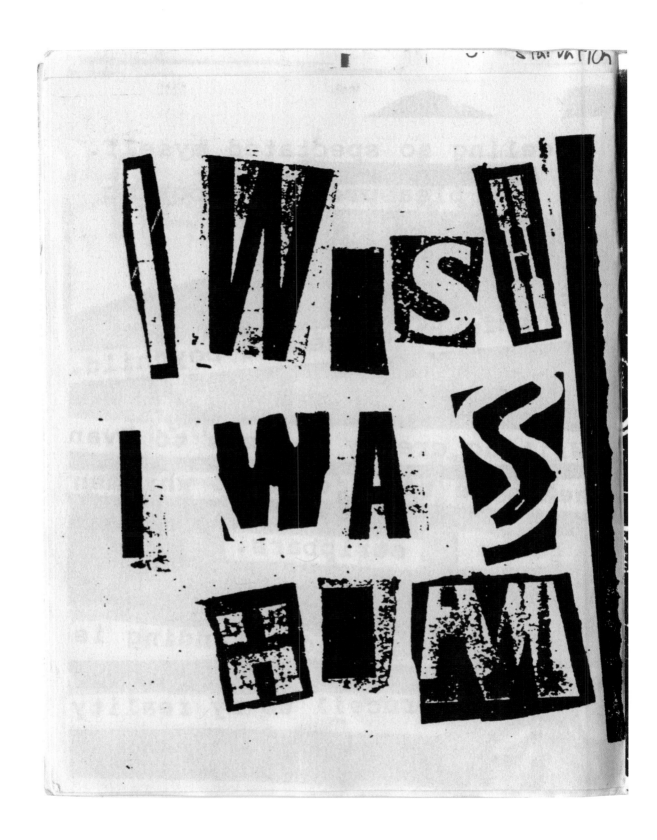

I WISH I WAS HIM

MY LIFE WITH EVAN DANDO, POPSTAR

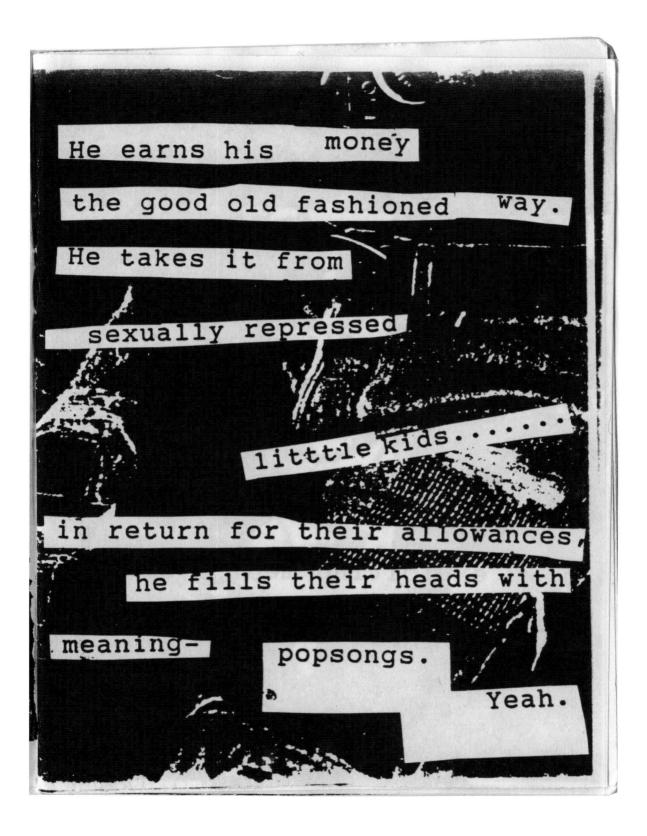

He earns his money
the good old fashioned way.
He takes it from
sexually repressed
litttle kids.........
in return for their allowances,
he fills their heads with
meaning-
popsongs.
Yeah.

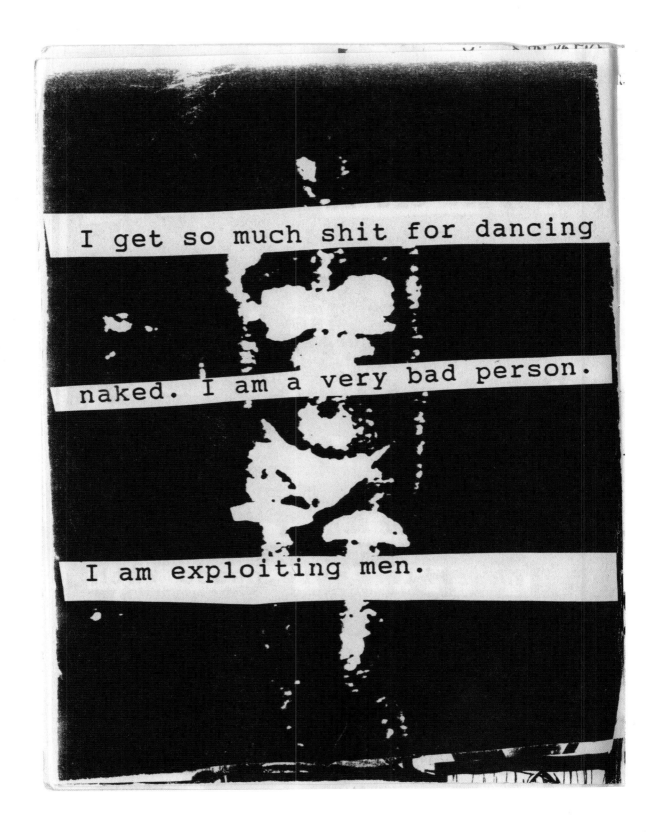

I get so much shit for dancing

naked. I am a very bad person.

I am exploiting men.

MY LIFE WITH EVAN DANDO, POPSTAR

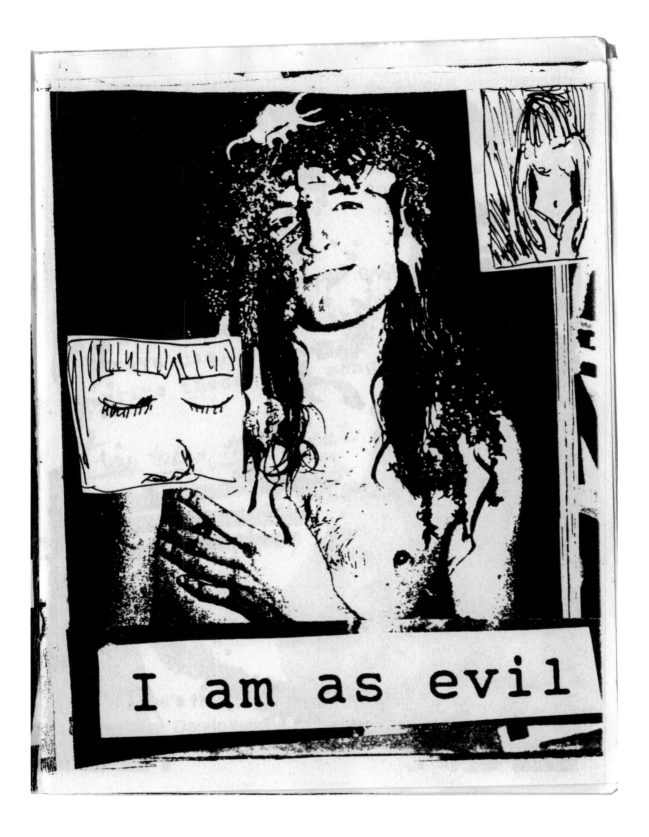

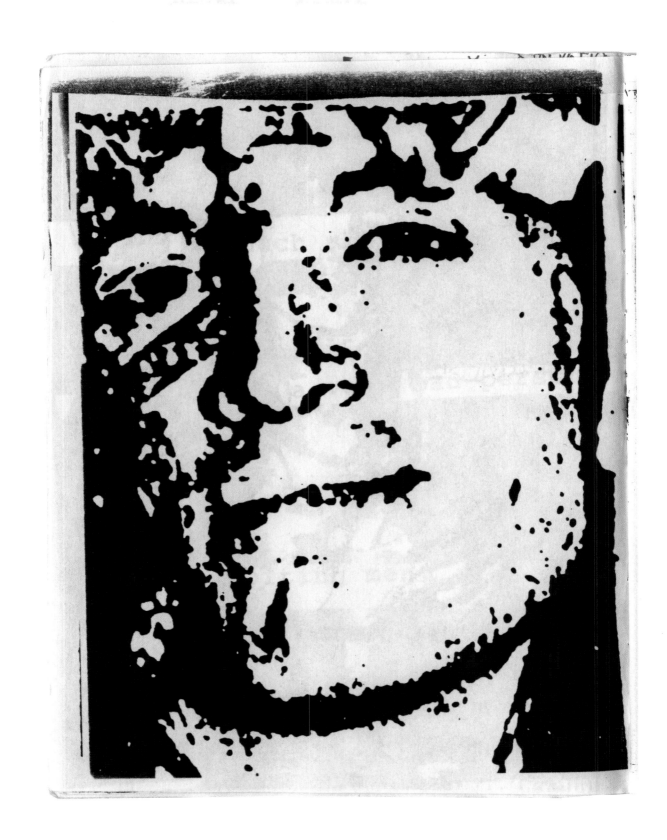

MY LIFE WITH EVAN DANDO, POPSTAR

Evan writes songs about stuff
and someone decides they are
good songs and that everyone
should like them. No one tells
me why they are good songs.
Just that they are.

Neutrality ~~wears~~ WEARS a happy smiling face.

It must be magic that Evan
always has, and always will
write these good songs.

Evan takes the treats

He is specail

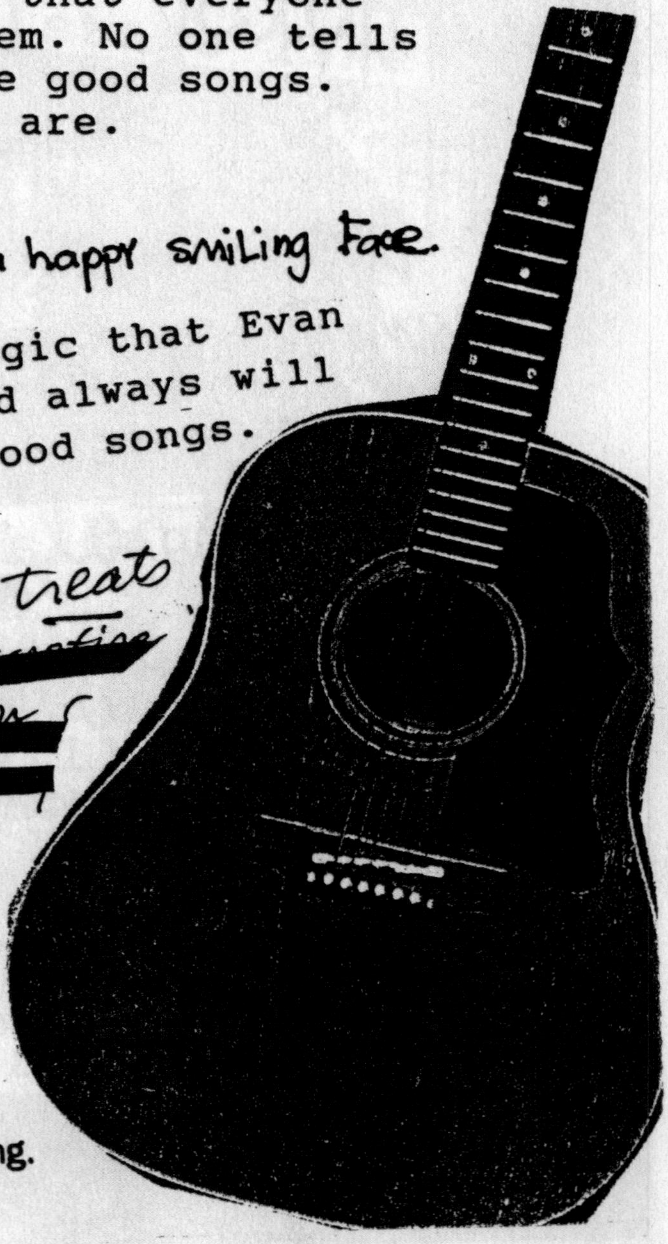

Who's this?
It's Evan Dando talking.

Confuse "truth"
with fiction
~~~~~ attempt to
de-centralize the
manufacturing of
"truth".

use language as a weapon.

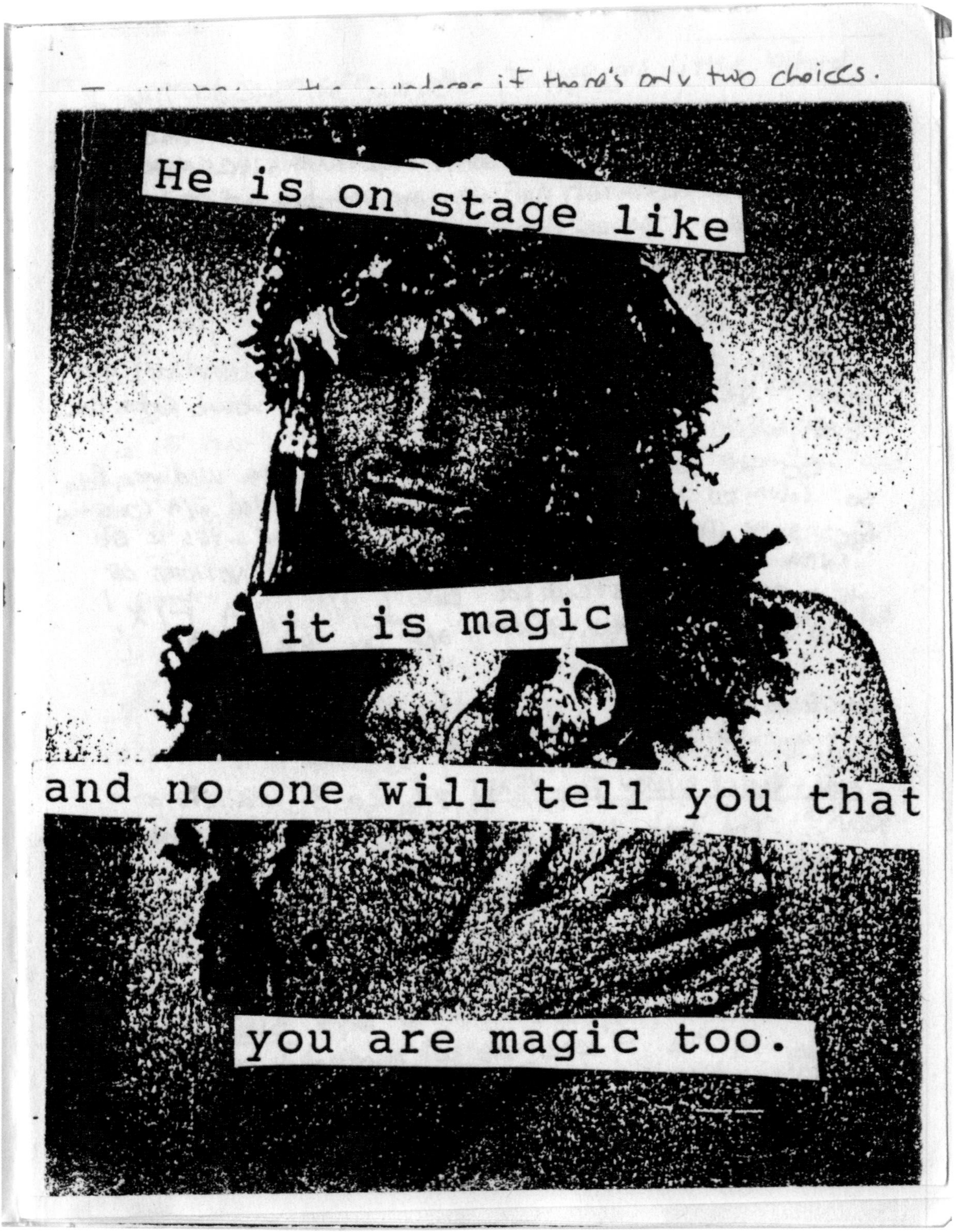
if there's only two choices.
He is on stage like
it is magic
and no one will tell you that
you are magic too.

Dear Evan Dando - I have decided to make you my life. This is because as a marginalized person i MUST HAVE A ROLE MODEL [identity politics + control question here] AND this ROLE MODEL has got to be ME and not YOU. YOU are an insipid pop star who believes in ideas of transcendence in art OR ELSE you are a tortured artist whose work is becoming assembly line monotony, you hate yrself and need someone to save you. (ME will RESCUE YOU)

I am screaming yr name, yr dick size, MY love all over town. "It's a long way to the top if you wanna Rock n Roll". Evan, baby.

So the deal is i feel powerful taming the wild man. Bein so colonized myself (heart brain gutcunt) i am filled w/a long-ing for some controlled. Being exploited/distorted — YES I DO WANNA CHANGE THINGS - I WANNA CHALLENGE NOTIONS OF HEIRARCHY MY POWER + CONTROL. But, I NEED A FIX!
I feel like I am sliding off of the earth.

Dear Evan.
I am what is not supposed to be- a female stalker.
ANN + NANCY WILSON FROM HEART got 2 or 3 stalkers a year.... And Joan from Jett gets crazy people following her too. I NO WANT THIS TO HAPPEN TO ME. (did i mention i am a punk ★?) MY pitchure was in NEWSWEEK magazine, i have a bikini on and my FULL NAME is followed by the words "feminist" "stripper" and "incest victim". I am going to the store to buy a shirt that says KILL ME on it.

They say the 14 women who got murdered in Montreal were just getting punished for being feminist (hating men) ONLY I KNOW they got kilt for breathing. For existing. PLEASE remember this. PLEASE Remember this.

I will become the murderer if there's only two choices. I am mass murdering all rockstars in my head. I like to kill pretty boys by fucking them and then rolling over like nothing happened. They wanna hold me and pretend we are in Love only i will not engage in any Lying Behavior w/them. "You were just a fuck" i say. My barefeet like the kitchen door and the sand of the popstar finding his shoes. Goodbye.

I have to remember that tHE MAN (who shall remain nmeless cuz He doesn't matter anyway, fucker) kilt THEM NOT cuz of ANYTHING they did but cuz HE felt outta control and needed some way to feel IN CONTROL.

This is what i am doing only i am justified. Besides i'm only murdering in my head.

I hate pretty boys cuz they get all the goodparts of bEING female (clothes, jewelry, hair, slutpower) ONLY none of the bad ones (rape, murder, poverty) I hate Evan Dando cuz he's so much prettier than me. Because I hate him my cunt is uncontrollably wet.

Marc Lepine, the guy who killed the 14 women in Montreal (I am always going back on my word) is cloned. He is geniric "CRAZY GUY". I love isolated crazy guy killer theories cuz it makes it seem so easy. Ted Bundy's dead, and so, ALL MY PROBLEMS'RE NOW OVER. ha. ha. ha.

I am a punk star who is a slutty feminist bitch and we are going to play the big rock show in Los Angeles that the money goes to keep abortion legal. OF course,

Isolated crazy Marc Lepine guy goes to this show. He is in love/hate with me and he has a gun. I look like i have good muscles in my legs. Evan, who doesn't know me yet, is eyeing the muscles in my legs.

I am singing songs about an elusive society that is fucking me over into an expensive microphone. I am doing the lowest common denominator thing or I am singing to a bunch of rich people who i hate.

I am convinced the rich people will slowly starve me to death if they think I am talking serious shit on them and/or having fun.

Marc Lepine is a retard. (Not like being retarded is wrong or bad... i am guilty... i am guilty) He has no friends and no one likes him but he is not cool. He's into the rugged individualist thing. He hates women OR allows his self hate to manifest itself as, that word, misogyny. He's got his hands on the trigger of some gun.

Evan looks just like this one boy who tore my guts out and displayed me as a public humiliation. He should be happy i have chosen him to stalk. He askt for it by looking like he does. Like the "beautiful" victim who finds fame in death (yeah, right) he wants to be my victim.

You think i am crazy and you can just fuck yrself cuz just coz i am wordplay Reversing i am all true + personal and you can't imagine this is art and not autobiography.

Evan has long hair like a girl. The synapses in his brain are dirty from drugs. He searches thru a bag that only has a shirt in it for the other thing (cigarettes) even though they are laying right next to him. This kind of stupidity

Is supposed to be cute. I want to slap his Little behind As a punishment only he is sitting on it. cute. cute. Cute.

Marc Lepine is ~~always~~ so uncool that he doesn't even know how boring i am. You don't stop a Revolution by killing bank tellars you know.

So, Evan is a hot babe, i'll admit to this. Hot like a 13 year old virgin. He knows nothing. I am wondering on the size of his cock. I ♥ Tall Boys. Tall boys, oh yeah. Evans got eyes that squint in the sun when he talks about Surfing.   Grass.

I know why Valerie Solanas shot Warhol and not the President — cuz everyone knows politicians're corrupt BUT warhol was trying to act like he was questioning notions of fine art (transcendance=biological determinism) thru the admiration of mechanical Reproduction [the destruction of the master artist via exclusive] ONLY Warhol was FOR REAL exploiting certain people (workers) AND certain Revolutionary conceptions IN ORDER TO Buy himself two thousand dollar "Mammy" "black" cookie jars.

Valerie Solanas ~~shot~~ shot Warhol to stop cooptation and also to be funny.

On the magazine HE (reminder to me) reclines, the picture is like he just fucked you and then he's rolling over to ask you if you wanna smoke another joint with him, "or what", he says, "or what". ~~striked out line~~

Marc Lepine raises the gun above his head. No one hears it go off except the people standing right next to him. Who may or may not have SEEN the gun. Evan is in the front row stareing at me when the bullet shoots straight thru my head.

Marc Lepine is trying to escape the building. He's actually being smart by trying to look natural. Everyone is running or trying to run for the door.

No one who SAW the gun will stop Marc Lepine for fear of getting shot.

Evan is lying over me.

"I don't even know you"

~~You remind me of my ex-boyfriend~~

"I love you and don't want you to die"

~~I wish we could fuck only I am bleeding~~

The version in the papers has Evan's hippy hair all caked in blood as he peers into the ambulance.

```
I am in a band ( a musical expressive group) where we are three
women and one boy                                        And in
this band

                            we are routinely spit on and/or beat up.
The question from the interveiw guy goes :
1. "Why do you hate all men?"
2. "Why are you a stripper/whore for your job?"
3. "Who the fuck do you think you are anyways?"
4. "Tell me what yr Daddy did to you in graphic detail, now."
5. "Maybe i would rape you and beat you up if i had the chance only
I am positing myself as a neutral reporter just now at this moment."

The question that is never asked or maybe even thought has to do with
the fact that there are movies about girls getting murdered being
played out all over my body PLUS i have been told to my face that i
am a worthless human cunt who deserves to die and so why would i be
anything but completely afraid???? Why would i wanna sit in the room
with the journalist man ????AND why would i be thinking about Evan
Dando at all????
```

My fear of death is pushed behind my desire to fuck Evan Dando.

romantically

A NOTE ON THE NATURE OF HISTORY OR HISTORICAL REMEMBERING:

Valerie Solanas and Jacques Cousteau died in the same week. Jacques, being Rich, died a rich man's death. Valerie, however, died of starvation on the street as a bag lady. Since they both died in the same week everyone got confused.

ThereFoRE, I was told that Jacques Cousteau died of starvation on the street in some big city. Valerie Solanas was not even mentioned.

Everything is completely arbitrary.

Evan Dando is staring at me off of the cover of a Magazine. HE is better at being a woman than I am. He doesn't have to deal with the shit that I do, either. I wanna see if he still feels as happy about being a bare chested woman in front of everyone after i shove a coke bottle up his ass. I wanna know HOW MUCH he wants to be a woman.

I hate Evan for taking the treats that I can not take because i am a MARTYR whore who cannot except pleasure when i am too afraid of RAZORS to feel my own cunt.

I WILL NOT LET JACQUES COUSTEAU TAKE CREPIT FOR VALERIE SOLANAS' DECREPID DEATH.

I will not let Evan Dando be sexier than me.

Your,
Kathleen

I am as evil

as any rapist

stripbar customer,

which doesn't mean

i am any less

pissed off

than i was before

MY LIFE WITH EVAN DANDO, POPSTAR

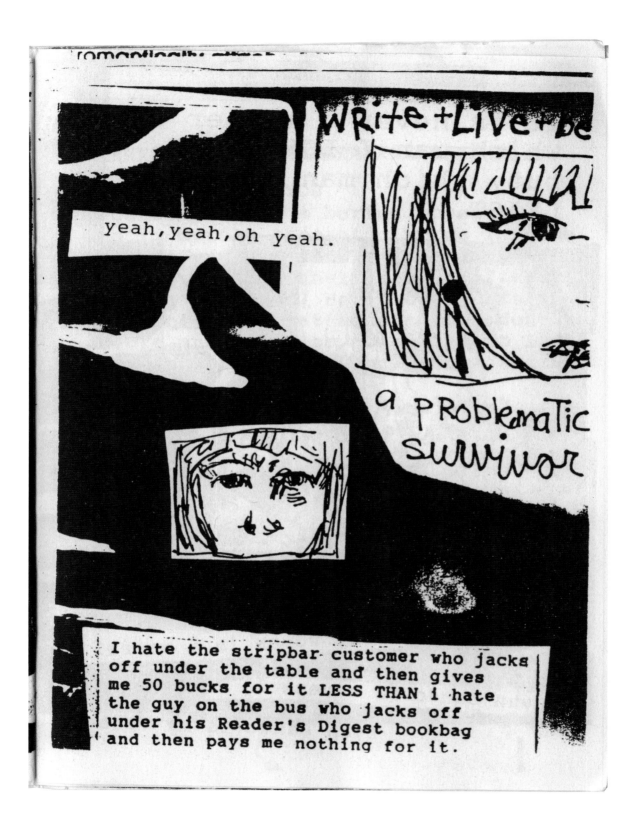

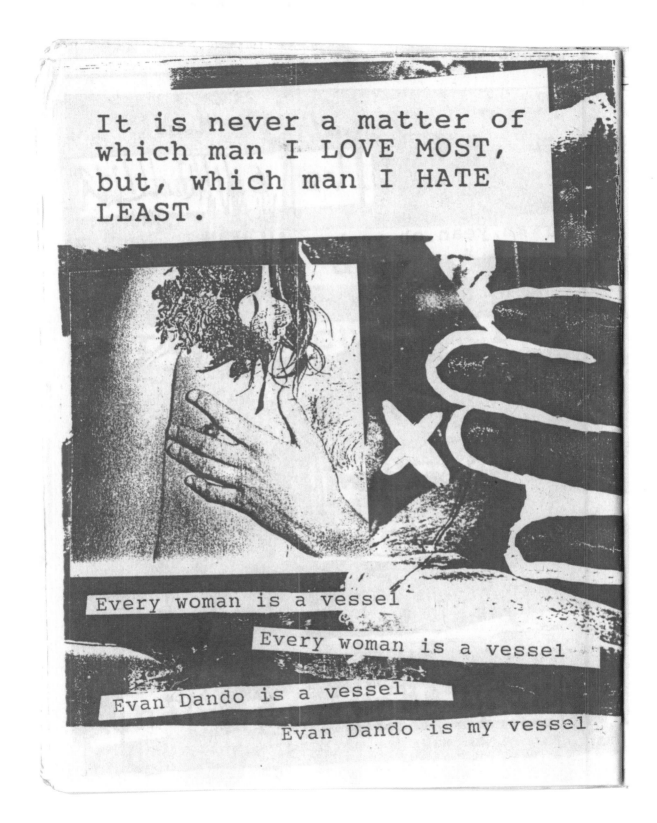

It is never a matter of which man I LOVE MOST, but, which man I HATE LEAST.

Every woman is a vessel

Every woman is a vessel

Evan Dando is a vessel

Evan Dando is my vessel

MY LIFE WITH EVAN DANDO, POPSTAR

XxXXXxXxXXXXXXXXXXXXXXxXXXXXXXXXXXXXXXXXXxXxX

I HAVE CHOOSEN YOU
because you are a boring popstar
who is merely repeating words in time.
Because you are feeding the machine
(unlike Tanya Donnely who is,afterall,
feeding the tree) Because you are
doing nothing that hasn't been done
before and yet i am compelled to love
you, and/or want to fuck you

Part of the man's master plan is that
we will not only WORSHIP FALSE IDOLS
but also he will prop cardboard cut-
outs up in front of himself in order
that we will be distracted from our
real enemies. AFTER the cardboard cutout
Is FILLed with holes from our guns.....

"Da-na-na-na-na-na-na-na."

I'm like a walking karaoke torture machine. [laughs]

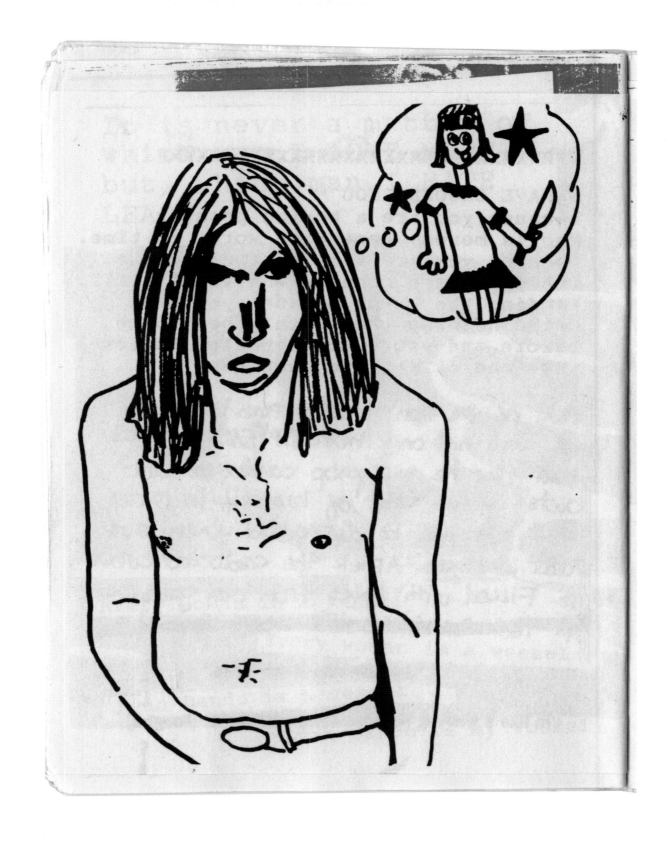

MY LIFE WITH EVAN DANDO, POPSTAR

Becasue my skin is wet with the scent
of murder only i am afraid of jail
and don't wanna kill my real friends

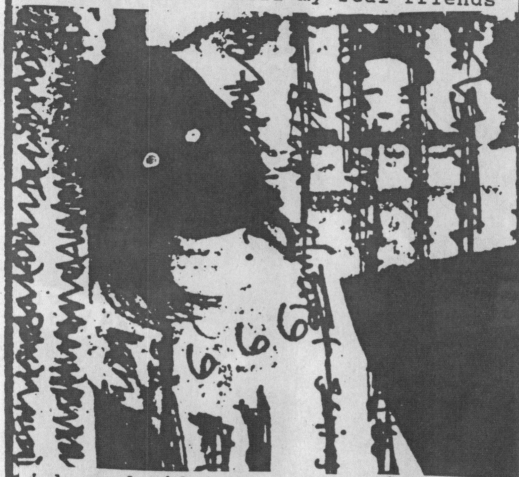

i have decided to do the only sane
thing: Direct all negative energy
towards you (telepathic hate hate)
AND begin to murder with words.

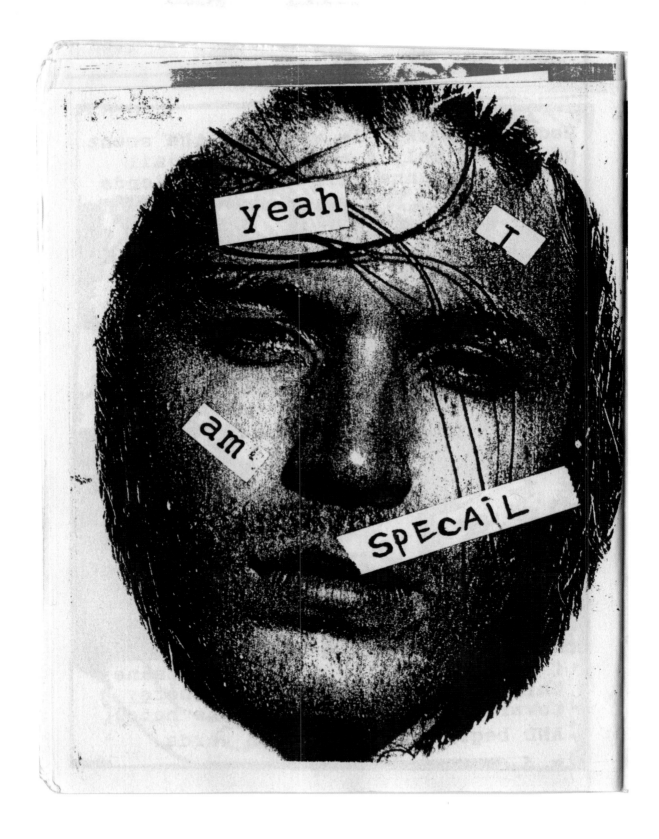

MY LIFE WITH EVAN DANDO, POPSTAR

let the Lemonheads help you to live in a chronic state of forgeTfullness......

A couple of years ago, I started thinking, I would love to make people happy with m music. That would be the best thing.

Yeah. You can afford to be NEUTRAL, MaN.

(white ,male,psuedo liberal, promelgating the myth of the transcendant artist)

The silent subtext always reads. We all have the same access to everything

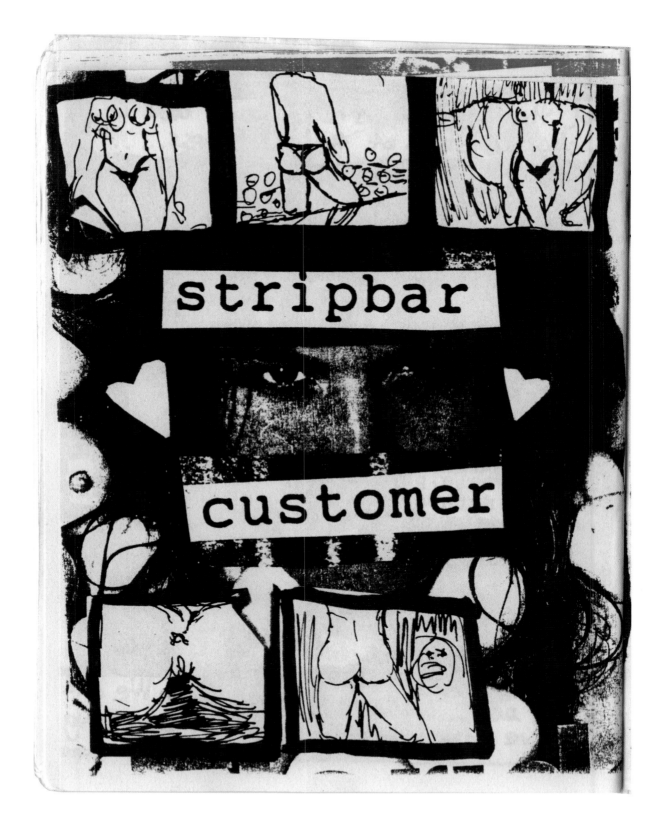

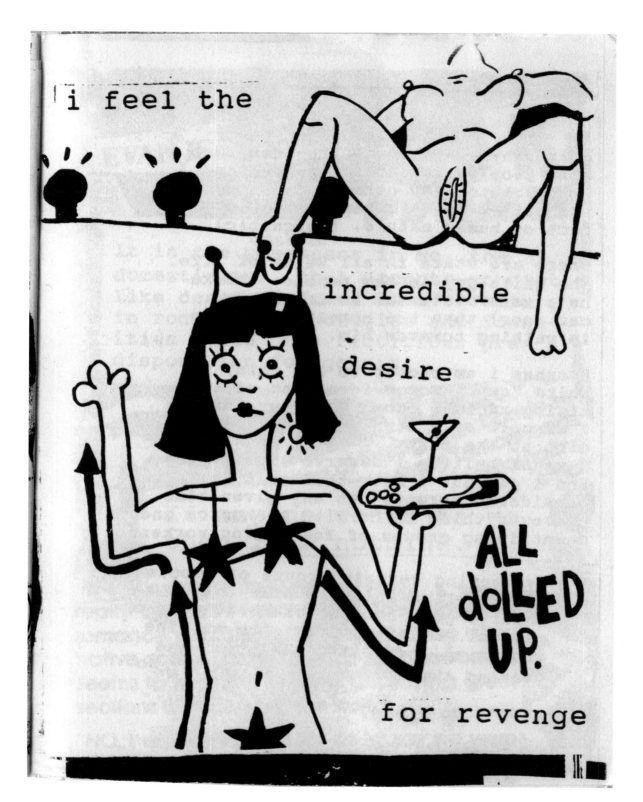

Heirarchy is based on the idea that
some people are naturally inclined
to be on top and others to be on
the bottom. this is an immutable
fact of human nature. (sarcastic)

There are stars in all walks of life.
The white guy in the porshe · thinks
he's more a star(as he locks his
car door) than the homeless guy who
is walking towards him.

Because i am closer to the thin,
white, small nosed idea that advertising racists shove down our throats
I am more of a star than the big
girl at the party
I wanna believe i deserve the attention i get but i know that what is
considered "pretty" at any given time
has everything to do with economics and
maintaining groups of low paying workers

By keeping certain groups of people
feeling like shit and like they don't
deserve good housing or healthcare or
respect or sexy points, the machine
churns on, benefitting elites, and
tearing the arms off of anyone who

won't go along.

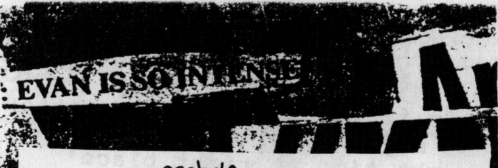

EVAN IS SO INTENSE

It is the ~~oppressor~~ asshole in me, the domesticator, that accepts concepts like deserved fame. That revels in rockstar mythologies and identities based on a ficticious predisposition for genuis.

...idea of dating Evan Dando to ...every Lemonheads ...calculating a hair

If anyone could be me, then i am nothing.

really shouldn't ignore Juliana's supposed romance with fellow bombshell of the alternative scene Evan Dando, who nowadays seems to very much enjoy displaying great sections of his logic to the world.

"NO, I wouldn't go so far as to say we were romantically attac

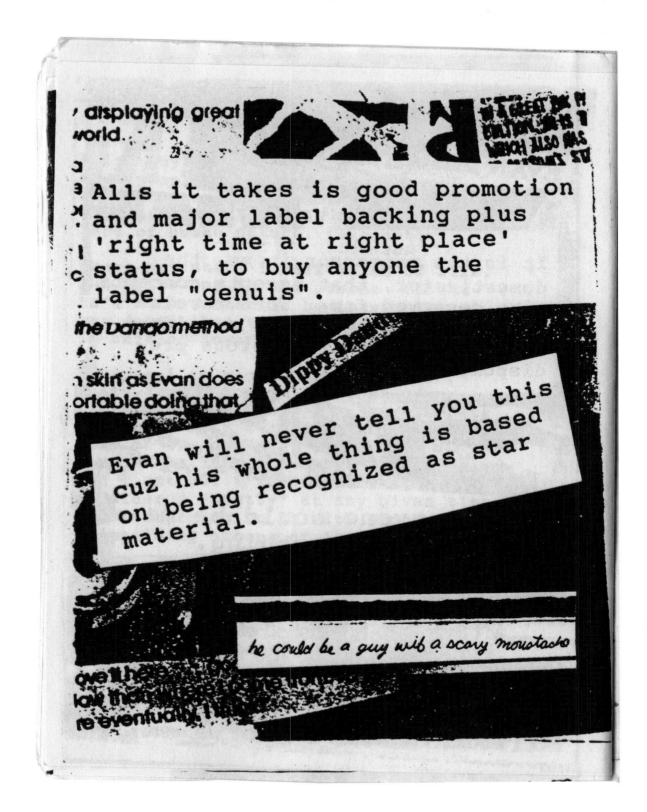

displaying great
world...

Alls it takes is good promotion
and major label backing plus
'right time at right place'
status, to buy anyone the
label "genuis".

the Dando method

skin as Evan does
ortable doing that

DIPPY DANDO

Evan will never tell you this
cuz his whole thing is based
on being recognized as star
material.

he could be a guy with a scary moustache

There is a part of me that buys this logic

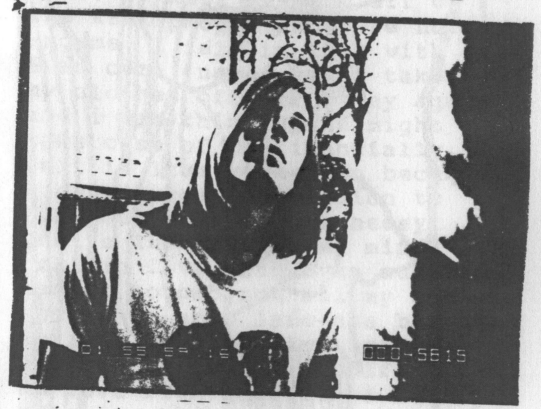

He will die old and alone. Hated. With no friends maybe a wife that hates him

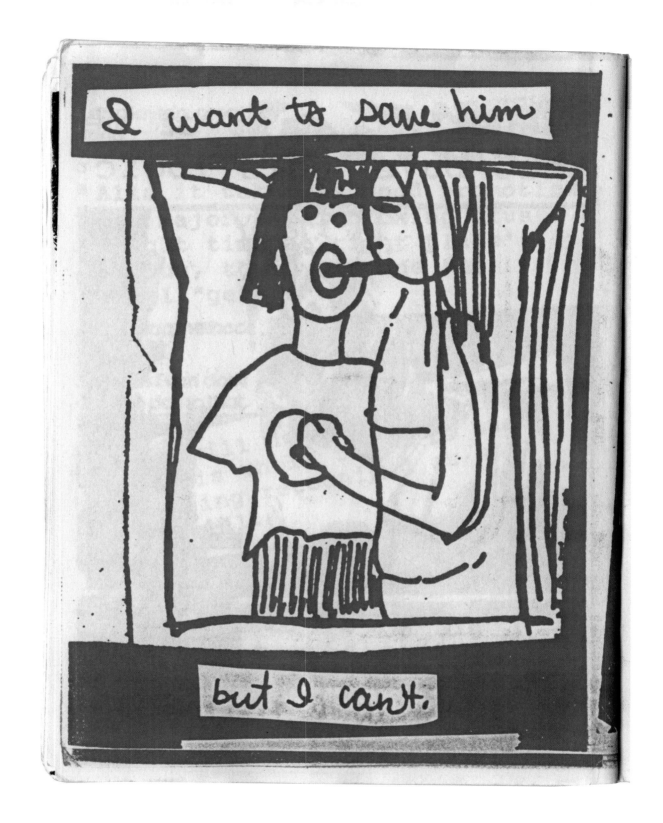

MY LIFE WITH EVAN DANDO, POPSTAR

I fell in love with Evan because it kept my mind off of the REAL people who were hurting me. I fell in love with Evan cuz i never wanna take my clothes off for money again and i was thinking he might take care of me financially. I fell in love with Evan because i gave myself permission to find out what gross cheesy smells lurk inside my mind. I fell in love with Evan cuz its easier to project all my coolness onto some lame-ass boy than to risk being called selfish or vain by loving myself. I fell in love with Evan cuz i am guessing that he has a big dick. I fell in love with Evan cuz he just happened to be there on the day i went completely insane.

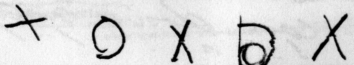

kathleen plus Evan forever.

8.Write stories that complicate the idea of "the other". Portray
the so-called "marginals" as central, uglybeautiful ,and complex.

9.Attempt to confuse the line that separates truth from fiction and,
therefore, decentralize the manufacturing of truth/authenticity.

10.Challenge obsessive "product" making by publishing both prepared
and unprepared work (journal pages and letters) Allow both "the
finished" and the "unfinished" to occupy the same space successfully

11.Write whatever you want because writing is sexy and terrorists
deserve art.

13.~~Expect to be paid for yr writing~~

13.Choose who will have access to yr work based on issues of safety
and need, as opposed to clever marketing strategies..

Admit to yr subjectivity.

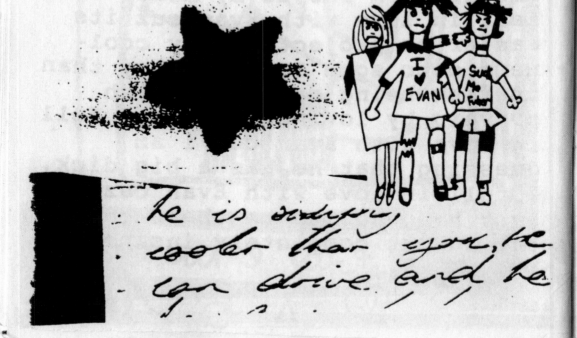

He is older, cooler than you, he
can drive and he

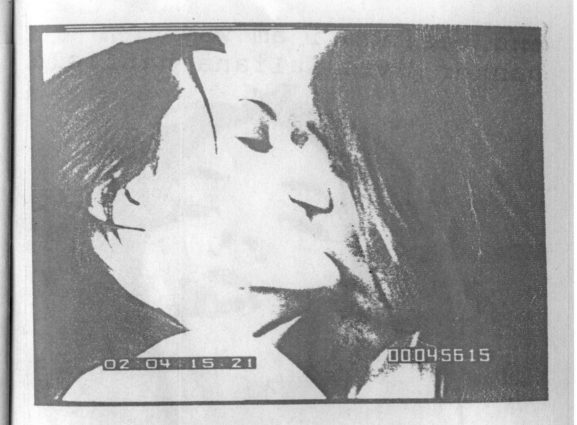

02:04:15:21 00045615

1. Write about all the bad people who have power and why i hate
them. (but i do not believe in good/bad anymore)

2. Write a letter to a person who has exploited me and ~~explain why
they are fuckers. (but then i am just supporting a myth that~~
~~their action is even important at all and deciding what direction~~
~~form~~ my resistance might take, ie, reactionary instead of actionary)

3. Write a letter to a person who has abused me only it doesn't make
sense in terms of traditional logic. Don't even send it.

4. Write something about killing people i hate that makes me feel
powerful.

5. Write about fucking.

-- ~~akes someone who lacks power (myself) look real~~

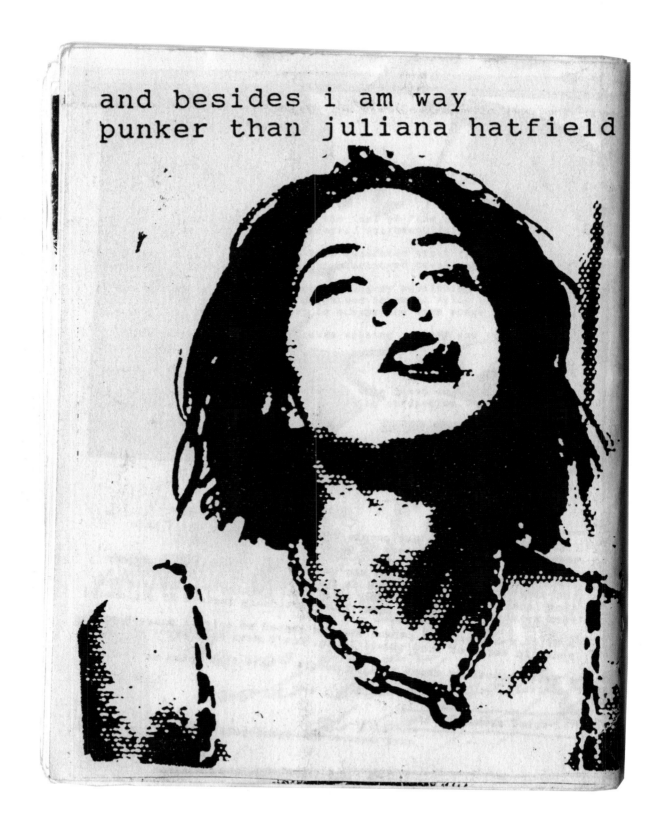

and besides i am way
punker than juliana hatfield

MY LIFE WITH EVAN DANDO, POPSTAR

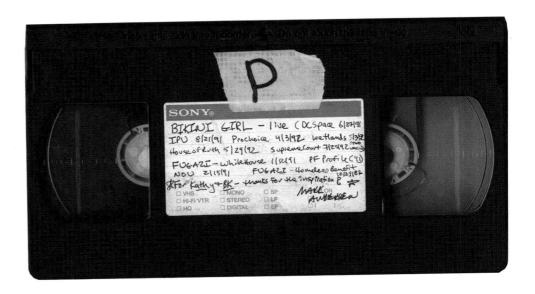

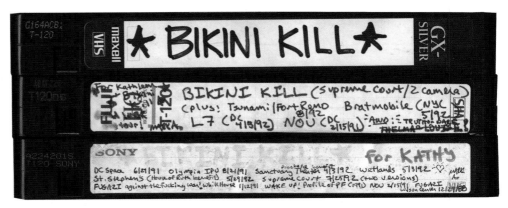

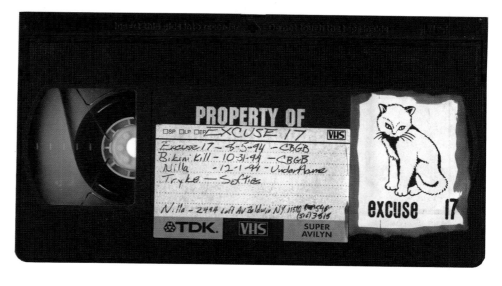

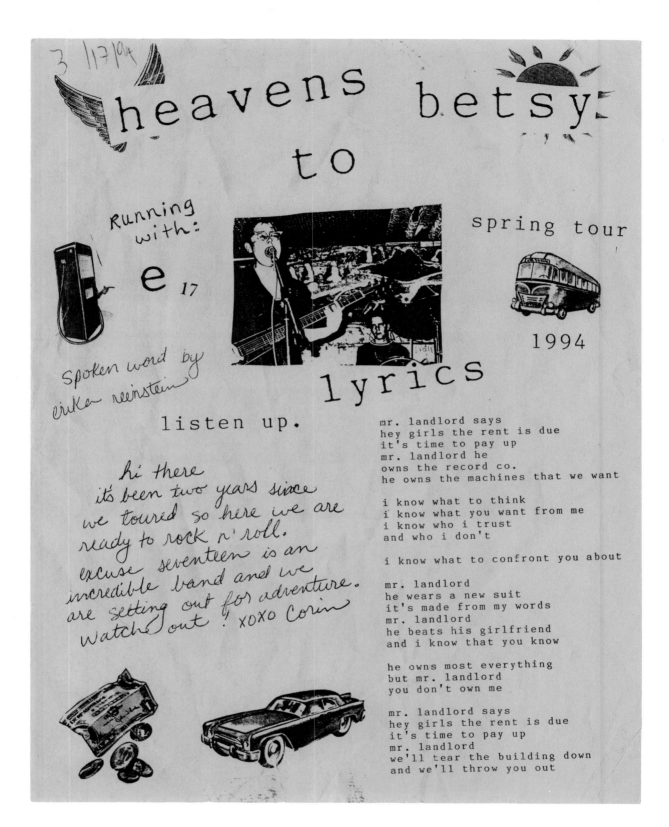

heavens to betsy

spring tour 1994

Running with:

e 17

Spoken word by
erika reinstein

lyrics

listen up.

hi there
it's been two years since
we toured so here we are
ready to rock n' roll.
excuse seventeen is an
incredible band and we
are setting out for adventure.
Watch out! XOXO Corin

mr. landlord says
hey girls the rent is due
it's time to pay up
mr. landlord he
owns the record co.
he owns the machines that we want

i know what to think
i know what you want from me
i know who i trust
and who i don't

i know what to confront you about

mr. landlord
he wears a new suit
it's made from my words
mr. landlord
he beats his girlfriend
and i know that you know

he owns most everything
but mr. landlord
you don't own me

mr. landlord says
hey girls the rent is due
it's time to pay up
mr. landlord
we'll tear the building down
and we'll throw you out

FLYER

240

it is so frustrating to be girls in a puke rock band and to
keep banging our heads against the walls of the
"alternative" scene. what is so alternative? everything in
punk and alternative scenes is still owned by white men and
so many of the same racist and sexist structures still
exist. is it really alternative to use a racist
objectifying national geographic picture as a joke on your
"way cool" punk record? i feel like a dialogue does not exist
for people to talk or deal with anything. i mean, i think
some people in the punk rock community really would like to
talk to each other but the way in which to do it is really
complicated.
discussions in Olympia did happen in Oly riot grrrl. riot
grrrl in Olympia doesn't happen anymore for so many reasons.
riot grrrl Oly had a lot of the same problems
going on as many white middle class feminist movements have
always had. we often centered on white middle class sexism

and white middle class girls and therefore excluded women of
color and white working class women's issues from our
discussions. i think our discussions about racism and white
privilege were important but we had a long way to go. and
also, the bombardment of media attention on riot grrrl made
everybody crazy and took away our control of so many things.
our image was sold and sold and sold until we didn't even
know what we looked like anymore. these things are very
difficult and there was so much tension and it was like we
all broke up. the thing that sucks is that although i
recognize that there was a lot of racism and fucked up
things going on in riot grrrl, there is now no organized way
for women and girls to talk to each other in Olympia. and
although this might be good in some ways, i feel like girls
hardly get to talk to each other anymore.
     so i guess this is a challenge to girls, women, men who
don't talk very much to look at the ways in which we live
and work. i would really like to see a girl-run collective
where women produce there own records, shows, discussions,
artwork, everything... i want to work on building a
community that is not male-controlled, that deals with
racism and sexism and where people are not too afraid of not
being cool to talk about the work they produce. i want the
resources right now right now right now. don't settle for
anything less.

you can write to us at:
heavens to betsy
P.O. Box 7842
Olympia, WA 98507

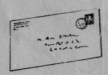

And no I don't believe
that cool is the answer
but style isn't the

opposite either at all

Do you believe
There's anything beyond
mom + dad reality
I wanna know

I believe in the
radical possibilities
inherent in
pleasure

Is it so hard to feel okay
Is being happy
What I'm afraid of?

~~If it feels safe~~ Being in control
was denied to me
~~But now~~ I don't wanna
die from ~~a~~ being a control freak

Just cuz i can have it
Doesn't wish it away
I'm not the opposite of what i hate

Because my world
is so full of rape
does that mean that sex
is n't okay

Since the man eats
should we starve ourselves
Since he uses his strength
to knock me down
Should I neglect my health?

No   No   No No No   No No

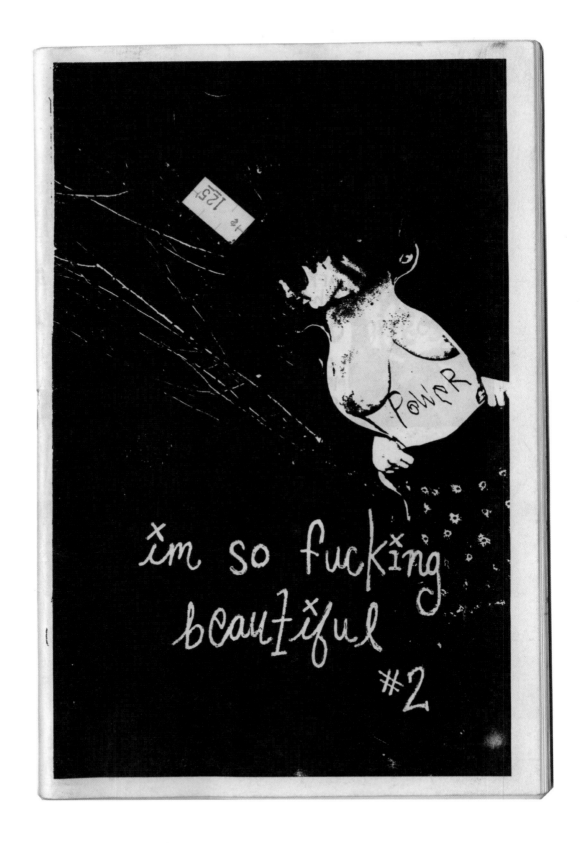

I'M SO FUCKING BEAUTIFUL 2 (EXCERPT)

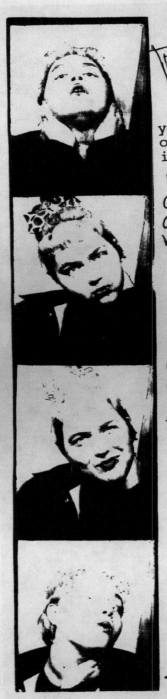

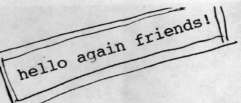

you are about to read issue #2 of i'm so fucking beautiful! i am nomy and i am nervous.

I am nervous cuz I'm in competition with myself. I'm afraid I won't live up to what I've done before.

that's why it's taken me almost a year to come out with a second issue.

okay, if you haven't read ISFB#1 then you really should, cuz I'm not gonna explain everything all over again in here. Send me 35¢ + 1 stamp & I'll send it to you.

that brings me to a subject that seems to have caused a lot of confusion: my address. i have people writing to me at three different addresses. so i'm gonna clear it up once and for all. you can write me at this address until june, when i'll be moving:

4221 indian pipe lp. nw
tesc p107
olympia, wa 98505

← aren't i cute?

I'M SO FUCKING BEAUTIFUL 2 (EXCERPT)

this is my parents' address, which you can write to me at forever and always, and i'll be sure to get it. (it just may take a little longer.)

1505 nw groves ave
olympia, wa 98502

REMEMBER: FAT OPPRESSION IS A FORM OF INSTITUTIONALIZED OPPRESSION

a quick list of rules

for you to keep in mind:

1. fat is not ugly
2. fat people do not lack control
3. fat people do not need to lose weight
4. we do not make "fat jokes"
5. fat is punk rock yee haw!
6. you do not call yourself "fat" if you're not. learn the difference.
7. diets are 20 times more unhealthy than being fat
8. i am not ashamed of my body
9. i am susceptible to pain. don't try to hurt me.
10. if you consider me a threat, if you fear me now, then just wait. the fat grrrl revolution has begun.

(the REST IS all questions...)

FAT GRRRL = Punk Fukin' REbEL

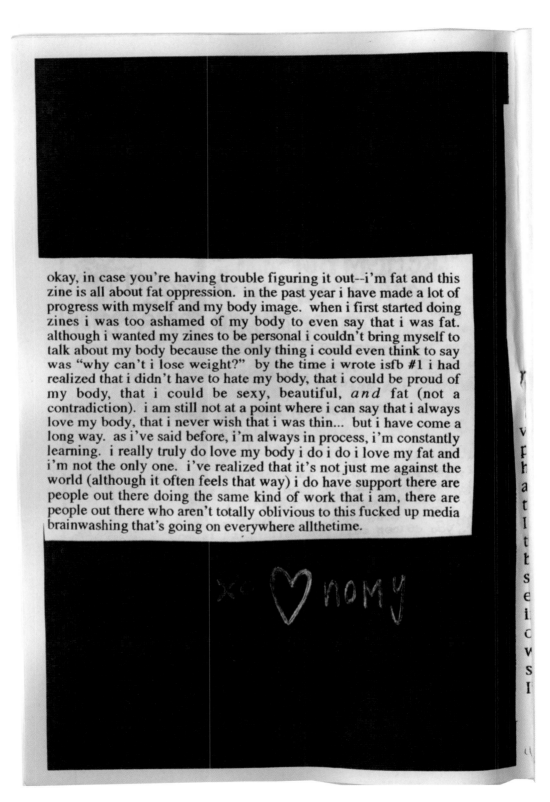

okay, in case you're having trouble figuring it out--i'm fat and this zine is all about fat oppression. in the past year i have made a lot of progress with myself and my body image. when i first started doing zines i was too ashamed of my body to even say that i was fat. although i wanted my zines to be personal i couldn't bring myself to talk about my body because the only thing i could even think to say was "why can't i lose weight?" by the time i wrote isfb #1 i had realized that i didn't have to hate my body, that i could be proud of my body, that i could be sexy, beautiful, *and* fat (not a contradiction). i am still not at a point where i can say that i always love my body, that i never wish that i was thin... but i have come a long way. as i've said before, i'm always in process, i'm constantly learning. i really truly do love my body i do i do i love my fat and i'm not the only one. i've realized that it's not just me against the world (although it often feels that way) i do have support there are people out there doing the same kind of work that i am, there are people out there who aren't totally oblivious to this fucked up media brainwashing that's going on everywhere allthetime.

xo ♡ nomy

I'M SO FUCKING BEAUTIFUL 2 (EXCERPT)

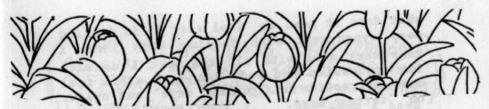

i've been feeling...um...sexy lately. i'm not exactly sure why, but these are the reasons i've been able to come up with:

1) i have this neat purple sweatshirt that i wear a lot, and for some reason i always feel attractive when i wear it-- even though i don't usually think that i <u>look</u> particulary stunning in it. funny how that works.

2) i've been doing a lot of naked-in-front-of-the-mirror assessments lately, and i'm getting more and more comfortable with my body.

3) a while ago i was at a party where we all took turns saying who in the room we had been attracted to at some time. all of the boys said they had been attracted to me at some point, which i really wasn't expecting. (well actually every boy there had been attracted to every girl there. surprising?) it sounds silly, but it was kinda a nice ego-booster.

4) okay, this reason is really sick. i haven't had much money lately, so i've been really low on food. consequently, i'm hungry almost all of the time.

feeling hungry makes me feel sexy.

this is the kind of thing that i thought i was beyond, but apparently it's still affecting me. it's not something that i usually even recognize, i mean it's totally subconscious. i have been **conditioned to believe** that when i'm hungry i'm well on my way to being thin, which of course means *more attractive*.

what does it mean to "feel sexy"? is feeling sexy synonymous with feeling *thin*? cuz i know that even with all the work i do with fat oppression and body image, i still feel more attractive on "thinner days" and uglier on "fatter days." i know that i'm never gonna be thin, and i don't WANT to be thin (usually), but i still have this thing like "well maybe if i were just a little bit smaller then not only would i just be able to accept my body, i'd be able to really really love it!" and no matter how much i say that fat

is totally awesome and that we should revel in our fatness, i don't think i'd want to be any fatter than i am now. so what if i <u>do</u> get fatter? what if i gain 50 pounds in the next year or so? will i then like my body less? will it then be less okay for me to embrace myself and my fatness?

and this is so fucked up, cuz it means that i'm still operating under this hierarchy of thinness. like i'm more able to accept being fat than someone who's fatter than me, and girls who aren't as fat as me are a little more revolutionAy or something cuz fat oppression has not had the same stifling effects on them as on me. (so <u>their</u> work is more <u>effective</u>, right?)

> and SeLF-eSTeeM is aLWays INVeRSeLy PROPORTIONaL TO BODY SIZe, ISN'T IT?

and by the way, exactly what counts as being fat? i've had girls write to me and say "i'm 5'3" and i weigh 145 pounds, so i know exactly where you're coming from." and i read this and think *this person has no idea where i'm coming from. this person does not know what it's like to be fat. how dare she undermine my struggle?!?*

(are you 5'3" 145 lb. GIRLS FEELING
RELIEVED now cuz I said you're not
FAT? DON'T FEEL RELIEVED. Thin ≠ COMPLIMENT
FAT ≠ INSULT. but then i have
to wonder, isn't there something fucked
up in the fact that even girls who i
see as being thin still think that they
are fat? isn't there something fucked
up in the fact that these girls <u>can</u>
relate to what i'm saying? because the
truth is that i know of maybe 5 girls who do
not feel fat. compare this with the fact
that i know maybe five girls who actually <u>are</u>
fat. but then, that's fat according to my
definition--and what the hell is my
definition? does "fat" mean "bigger than or
the same size as me"? because that's totally
fucked up. that's me putting myself right at
the cut-off line for fatness, therefore
making myself right on the verge of being

thin. which i know is not true. i
don't feel good about deciding who has the
right to define themselves as fat. the
fat grrrl revolution does
not belong to me. but at the same
time, i don't think that it's fair for people
who aren't fat to say that they are. this
is something that happens a lot, and all it
does is reinforce the idea that fat is this
horrible thing that we all must dread and fight
against, cuz it's ready to swallow us whole at
any moment. in other words, your mistaken
identity adds to my oppression.

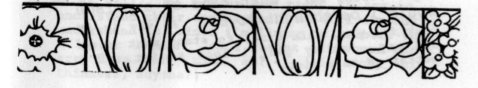

"and i do believe you are me.
yes i do believe you are me.
whoever you may be..."

FaT gIRL look ME in The eye
I see you and we don't have To
ReSenT each oTHeR's RecogniTion.
when I smile aT you
aRe you haTing ME FoR The FacT ThaT
I'M acknowLeDging ouR BonD?
aRe you haTing The FacT ThaT
you & I have a common expeRience?
and MayBe you'Re on a DieT
So you'Re on youR way To
DiSaSSociaTing youRSelF FRoM Me.
oR MayBe you USeD To Be Thin
and you can'T accepT youR
new-FounD FLesh.
That's noT The
Real you," IS IT? xo

I'M SO FUCKING BEAUTIFUL 2 (EXCERPT)

no

no we can't look each other
in the eye
cuz that would mean acknowledging
something far worse than
each other's validity.
that would mean acknowledging
our own bodies.

yes I am fat.

yes you are fat.

but I'm rude to recognize that.
fat girl, we can be sisters.
as soon as we stop resisting
each other
we can START resisting
this thing that keeps us

apart

xo   xo

in a recent interview with me in mrr about isfb#1, they said that my zine was about a "seemingly superfluous subject." (they then went on to say that my zine convinced them that it wasn't. this isn't an attack on carrie from mrr.) the idea that fat oppression was a "superfluous subject" kind of surprised me. i'd never thought of it in that way before, and it got me wondering if maybe other people think it is superfluous. (read: no big deal compared to other forms of oppression.) like maybe it's not important enough or political enough to dedicate an entire zine to. so now i feel i have to justify it or something.

okay, first of all, just the fact that we all deal with body image problems, we all have fucked up ideas associated with fat, makes it important enough. i don't know of anyone who can't relate to this.

secondly, i think it's important that people realize that fat is definitely a political issue. fat oppression is an institutionalized form of oppression, just as racism, sexism, classism, homophobia, able-bodyism, ageism, etc. are deeply rooted in, and in fact create the foundation of, Capitalist Amerika. our minds are totally colonized with lies about fat. (sound familiar?) i recently read the beauty myth and reread shadow on a tightrope, so i have a lot of facts fresh in my mind.

for one thing, like all other forms of oppression, fat-hating is not just a personal choice made by an individual. "i don't have a problem with other people being fat, i just don't like it on myself--it's a personal thing," is bullshit. capitalism needs people to hate fat in order to sustain itself. without fat-hate, the $33,000,000,000 a year diet industry would collapse. despite substantial medical evidence that fat is not caused by overeating and that only 1-10% of all fat people who go on reducing diets will be capable of keeping off the weight, we are still told to "keep on trying." (of course this medical information is largely kept secret, because who knows what revolution might occur if people knew the truth? we wouldn't want that, would we?) every year or so, the government issues

I'M SO FUCKING BEAUTIFUL 2 (EXCERPT)

"new findings" on obesity--facts that are meant to "prove" that fat people are much more unhealthy and have shorter life expectancies than thin people. however, these reports fail to mention that these studies are conducted on people who have most likely been dieting for most of their lives. is it any news to you that people who endure long-term starvation are going to be unhealthy? also, these studies do not take into account the physical toll of living in constant oppression. in an essay titled "the fat illusion" (from shadow on a tightrope), vivian f. mayer points out that "the handful of studies existing on non-persecuted fat people suggests that they are quite healthy, whereas studies of persecuted groups other than fat people, such as black people, show these groups to suffer from many of the diseases 'characteristic' of fat people." and regarding the shorter life expectancy of fat people--these statistics include early deaths of fat people due to dieting and reduction surgery. (an estimated one out of ten people who undergo intestinal bypass die.) so these crimes that are committed against fat people are then thrown back in our faces--"we've killed you, how dare you die!"

the result of fat-hating propaganda is that fat people are told to either lose weight, or keep out of the public eye. **shape up or ship out.** since the odds of losing weight are significantly slanted against us, most fat people tend towards the latter. even if we don't want to, we often are given no choice. fat people are ridiculed for eating in public, and ridiculed for exercising in public. even if a fat person wanted to go swimming in public, they would have a hell of a time finding a swimsuit to fit. in fact, it's difficult for a fat person to find clothes in general, and when they (we) do, they cost considerably more than smaller sizes. the justification for overcharging an oppressed group of people, who are traditionally in a lower economic class in the first place, is that larger sizes cost more to make because they require more material. "that'sbullshit. if they're selling 100 of

this item in sizes under a certain size and five or ten over that size, they could divide the extra cost of material between the 110 people and it would be only a few more cents for everybody. instead, i have to spend five dollars more. it feels punitive... i'm being punished for being fat." (from an interview with judy freespirit, <u>shadow on a tightrope</u>.)

women are often kept out of the job market for being fat. there are many ways that this is done. as would be expected, there are many many cases of women being discriminated against and not given jobs simply because they are fat. sometimes the reason is that "fat people are sick more often." (a lie. duh.) sometimes the reason is some "professional beauty qualification," as in modeling, stripping, etc. but the professional beauty qualification is actually much more widespread than that. being told that you "don't have the right image" is pretty much the same as being told you just aren't pretty enough. then there are even more subtle reasons that fat women are kept out of the work place. okay, since fat women have a harder time getting a job in the first place (and what is available is usually menial low-paying work) they are going to have less money. in order to get a good job you must dress "professionally." women in general may have a difficult time finding professional looking clothing for a reasonable price, but for fat women it is nearly impossible. so it becomes this vicious cycle: fat women need jobs in order to have money, need money in order to buy decent clothing, need decent clothing in order to find a job. and the fatter the woman, the more difficult it's going to be to fulfill any of these requirements. i was unemployed for two years, and although i went to several interviews and know that i was qualified, i didn't get the jobs. part of this may have been because i am fat, part of this may have been because my clothing wasn't professional enough. my parents would always bug me about how i needed to get nicer clothes if i wanted a job, but they weren't supplying me that money. the clothes i have come from thrift stores and free boxes, and it's pretty damn rare that

I'M SO FUCKING BEAUTIFUL 2 (EXCERPT)

i find anything "presentable" in those places. and i think that when i went to interviews i looked pretty conservative--i didn't have any piercings or tattoos at the time, i didn't have really weird hair (it was black), and my clothes were the best that i could do. still i never got the jobs. i now have a job that i got over the phone, and it was just because i have work-study. i have a huge fear of trying to find a job in the real job market.

fat people are also greatly oppressed by the medical industry. i've always dreaded going to the doctor because i knew that i would be weighed. and after the weigh-in i would be told that i was "overweight" (so there's a certain weight that it's not okay to be over...) and that i needed to go on a diet. then of course there are those fabulous medical diets where you starve yourself for the good of your own health. then there is reduction surgery and all of that. then there is the fact that medical research has <u>proven</u> that all these justifications for fat-hating are lies, yet that information is withheld from us. but one of the worst things is that fat people are often even refused medical service. for one thing, fat people are usually unable to find medical insurance that will cover them, because they are "health risks." then, even if they are able to afford going to a doctor, whatever medical problem they have is blamed on their "obesity." my father was once very sick and was told that in order for him to even be diagnosed he had to lose weight because "the things in his blood that could be causing the illness were identical to the things in his blood that were caused by being fat." this is such complete BULLSHIT!!!! even if this <u>was</u> true, which i seriously doubt, medical science does have the technology for figuring out how to diagnose <u>despite</u> this problem. they just don't *bother* to figure it out. i don't remember whether or not i talked to my dad about how stupid this was. if i did i'm sure it didn't make any difference to him. it's incomprehensible to most people that, yes, **doctors lie**. most people in our society will do anything they can to perpetuate the

myths about fat. doctors, being in a position of authority, are a prime resource for keeping fat oppression as a fully functional tool of our abusive society. doctors are so convinced that fat is bad that they will do anything to get people to lose weight, even if it means lying. cuz in the long run those gluttonous slobs will be better off, right? fuck doctors. but in reality, even if my dad had realized that he was being lied to, it wouldn't have done any good because the doctor still wouldn't have diagnosed him unless he lost weight. i once went to the doctor (a woman doctor who i'd been told was really great) because of period problems and was told that she couldn't tell anything from the examination because i was too fat. and once again, even if this is true, there should be resources available so that they _can_ tell.

i think i've made it pretty obvious that sizeism is not just a matter of body-image. fat oppression is literally everywhere. yes, even within our punk-feminist community. one example of this can be found in just about any feminist zine. the assumption that all women have to deal with sexual harassment, have to deal with being told we're sexy, every day, is extremely sizeist. that is _not_ my biggest problem, and i think it's really exclusive of other women to assume that it is. and i hope that you realize that i'm not discounting sexual harassment as an extremely important issue, i just think it's also important to recognize that not all women are considered societally "beautiful," and our experiences are just as valid.

anyway, i feel like this whole piece about fat oppression being institutionalized and political sounds like a fucking college essay or something. i hope that it wasn't too boring for you, but i do think the information is really important so i hope you read the whole thing. and forgive me if i'm not a skillful enough writer to be able to write about "intellectual" things without sounding like a textbook. i'm working on it. ♡nomy

I'M SO FUCKING BEAUTIFUL 2 (EXCERPT)

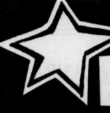

more fun things about fat
(continued from last issue)

1. fat floats, so i don't have to worry as much about drowning!

2. i guess my fat hides my muscles, so boys are just that much more surprised when i beat them at arm wrestling! nanny nanny boo boo.

3. my shoulders are really comfy to lean on.

4. oh, i just want to reiterate just how much fun fat is to suck on. if you haven't tried this, you must! *

5. if yer gonna have a tummy slappin' party, be sure to get some fat people to go so that you get a variety of tones. (fat bellies tend to have a higher pitch, i think.)

and, oh yeah i almost forgot:

6. "two hard bodies don't feel as good." this wonderfully enlightened and liberated insight was given to me by one of my dear readers. so remember boys, when yer lookin' fer good sex, you know who to call! (fuck you.)

*warning: if you don't have enough fat to try this on yourself, be sure to get permission before trying it on someone else.

i've been doing some performing lately and **i always end up talking about fat oppression**. i'm getting sick of it. there are a million other things that i could talk about, but i feel like i have to talk about it or something. i'm afraid that if i'm not talking about it, if i'm not calling it to people's attention constantly, then they'll just sit there and think "she's fat" instead of listening to me. no matter what it's an issue.

when i was thirteen i choreographed this dance to the song "macavity" from cats. i showed it to my dad, and the whole time he just sat there and when i was done he just nodded and when i asked him what he thought he said "oh, it was fine." i felt really shitty about it and i didn't understand why he didn't like it, cuz i'd worked really hard on it and i thought it was really good. later my mom told me that the reason he didn't like it was that i "looked fat" while i was dancing. **i looked fat while i was dancing...** so what i got from that experience was that fat people do not dance, because we don't want to call attention to our fatness. fat people do not perform. we sit in the corner and hope that nobody will notice our bodies, and we can't wait till we lose weight cuz then it'll be **us** up there on the stage. then **we'll** be the sexy performers. then **we'll** have men drooling at our feet. i am a good performer, but i'm not allowed to show that unless i'm thin.

do i have to be especially good in order for my performance to be valid? if i were thin would my performance be more enjoyable for you? if i talk about **sex** are you wondering who in their right minds would have **sex** with me? ...or maybe you're just thinking that you'd never have **sex** with me... when you watch fat people perform, what are you thinking? **what are you thinking?** are you thinking that their weight is an issue that they should address? are you (like me) wondering if they've been "educated" about fat oppression?

XO   XO

see this is something i think about a lot. sometimes i am afraid to perform because i don't want to deal with fat oppression. and what if i'm in a situation where i'm talking to people who are still operating under the assumption that fat is **bad** (as if anyone in our society has really escaped that assumption... yeah, even me)--like if i'm talking to a group of people who aren't "punk" or whatever, who i haven't ever performed for before, do i have to start at the beginning for them or just perform and not give a fuck? cuz

it's really important to me that i be taken seriously. okay but then i feel like even at "punk" shows a lot of people don't get it, like it doesn't really sink in, they're just clapping so they can be fucking v a l i d a t e d or something. like "oh, wow, that white emo boy is so supportive and sensitive. *look at how he's supporting that fat girl."*

(am i wasting my time?)

i don't want to think about it like that cuz i know that there are a lot of people out there doing the same kind of work as me and there are a lot of people out there who support us (yeah even white emo boys) and i don't want to invalidate them or myself.

okay well i wanna talk about exercise, cuz i think that performance and excercise are really connected. there's this whole double standard when it comes to fat people and excerise, cuz it's like "well, no wonder she's fat, she never exercises." but at the same time, people totally make fun of people who exercize. "oh, watch out, i can feel the ground shaking!" ha ha ha. when people exercise, they become showpieces. there is no fucking way that i'm gonna put on a bathing suit and go swimming, put on a pair of shorts and go jogging...

well actually i've just started doing some exercise-- i'm going to the weight room at evergreen every week to lift weights and stuff, cuz i wanna be stronger. but when i do this, there are two fucked-up things that i have to think about. 1) of course i'm afraid that people are gonna be laughing at me cuz i'm a wimp and i'm fat and i get out of

XO   XO

breath and tired after even walking up the stairs. 2) i don't want people to think that i'm exercising to lose weight. i'm not gonna give people that satisfaction. i should make a shirt that says "NO I'M NOT TRYING TO LOSE WEIGHT, AND IF YOU SAY 'BOOM BABBA BOOM' THEN ONCE I GET BIG MUSCLE-Y ARMS I'M GONNA BEAT YOU UP." (my sister rose gave me that idea.) this is off the subject, but when i drink diet sodas i have the same dilemma. i like the taste of diet colas better, **really honestly i do** (probably just cuz that's what i'm used to, my parents being on perma-diets and all),but i hate buying them cuz i know that people will think that i'm on a diet, and besides **i don't want to support the diet industry**.

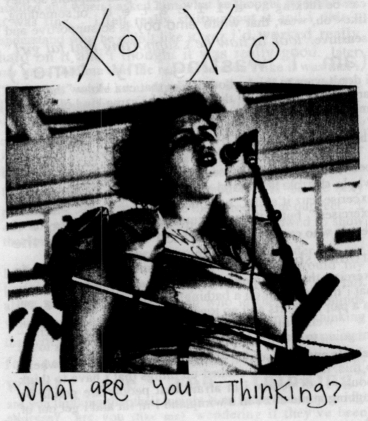

what are you Thinking?

yr $
goes
here

i'm in love with...

You + Me = REVOLUTION XO

nomy lamm
4221 indian pipe lp.
lesc plo7
olympia, wa 98505

there are three reasons why i'm doing this
zine.

1) as a personal outlet and a way to express
myself creatively and get rid of some shit at
the same time.

2) to try to help other people learn to love
their bodies, because a big part of all of
this is how we view ourselves.

3) because fat politics are not just a personal
thing. it's important that we deconstruct
the myths that we are fed from birth regarding
fat vs. beauty, fat vs. health, etc. we
need to not only accept our own bodies, we
need to accept (love) other people's bodies
too.

Interviews with Clit Club Owner (NYC's longest running dyke club) and fellow Pinay mutt-eteer Julie Tolentino, Iraya from Outpunk band Sta-Prest! on girls who pretend to be oppressed to be "cool", all-girl rocker/funkers from Japan - Super Junkey Monkey, and an old interview from the dusty cobwebs of my brain with Front 242 (no estrogen like past interviewees, but they rock my world)!

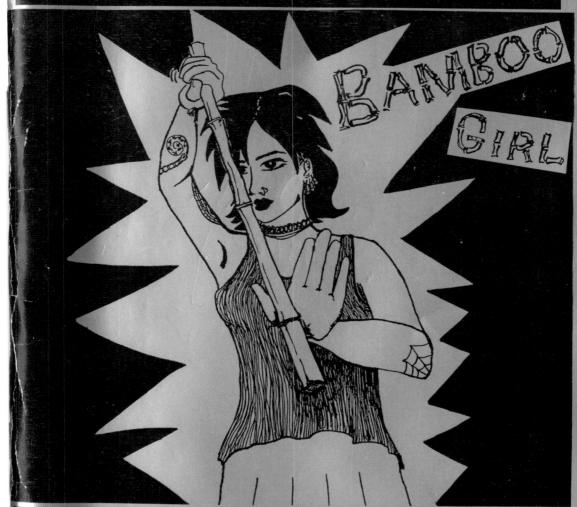

BAMBOO GIRL

Martial Arts to Protect the Fairer (?) and more Attacked Sex / Alibata - Ancient Filipino Script / More Harrassment in Corporate AmeriKKKa / More Info on Great Resources for Chicks of the Shade, More Angst, Ranting & Raving, Weird Filipino shit, music & zine reviews! (And - ooh - sexy special anniversary cover! enjoy it while it lasts buckos...)

1st Anniversary Issue! $2

BAMBOO GIRL 5 (EXCERPT)

MAGANDANG araw!

Welcome to the 1st Anniversary Issue of <u>Bamboo Girl</u>!

I've been asked a coupla times why I bothered to do this zine, so I figured it would be pretty appropriate to explain why in this 1st Anniversary Issue:

Sometime early last year, I became increasingly frustrated with not being able to find any publications that spoke about MY issues, which were mainly ones on being mixed blood (in addition to that of the Filipina kind, I'm Spanish & Irish/Scottish, with some Chinese), what my issues were, what having a voice meant for me, and to dispel the bewilderment at not being able to find anything on the anti-racist/-sexist/-homophobic bend of things. At the time, I was hearing a lot of "Don't do this," "Don't be too loud," "Why don't you try out for a beauty pageant?" (If you're Filipina, you know why that thought makes me wretch), and mostly, "Why don't you try to be more <u>NORMAL</u>?!" Now these aren't things people would outrightly say, but it was evident in the way I was treated, talked to, and interacted with, and especially from the point of view of an Asian mixed chick who likes to wear whatever the fuck and have whatever the fuck like tattoos & piercings (although these 2 aspects are as common as pig beatings by now you'd think people would stop having a cow over it), loud opinions, whatever, on me — let's just say there was a lot going on, and no way to get it out of my system.

I was also emerging out of a place where I was refusing to be victimized anymore, where it was time for me to break out of the mold of thinking in the "safe" ways I was used to (although I had always been trying to break out of it, this has always been a struggle). For instance, there was a lot of left over rage I had towards the racism in the boonies that I grew up in, and seeing too many "people of color" trying to be "white" to fit in, and ending up denying where they came from. Also, there was much physical violence bullshit going on in my house, earlier on towards my ma, but later on, mostly towards me. It shaped what I thought of women, and specifically, of Asian/Filipina women. I didn't want to be weak like my mom, and I wanted to stop my silence, as I was not allowed to open my mouth or show emotion at all, stoic if you will — I didn't know what it meant to defend myself. Being that I was pretty much an emotional time bomb by that time, I eventually exploded and took my anger as high as I could. That got me punching morons I didn't even know, if they were giving me unwanted physical advances, as well as getting into fights with people who even hinted at putting me into a sexist context.

The punk and hardcore music/culture helped a lot with helping me to further form my issues, and also gave me the validation I needed for not being the beautiful petite Asian flower all my friends were — that I was in fact a girl with a lot on her mind, that I knew by such a small age that I was Queer without knowing the word for it, that I was angrier than the rest of my peers, that I was some kind of over achiever, and perhaps thought too much about serious things that always made me look older than I was.

One day, I finally got some kind of a grip; all my random thoughts became more focused, and it hit me like a ton of bricks. After getting help and happy pills to balance out some mental shit, life got better. My close friend, Jewgirl (who does Plotz), finally said one day "If you can't find something to read, why don't you make it?" I was like "Forget it," but obviously, I finally took her suggestion.

So now I'm here owning my space again. <u>Bamboo Girl</u> is like a big FUCK YOU and validation for myself, and other girls, who have found it a bitch to get to the point where they believe they're worth it. And this time, I AM NOT BEING QUIET ABOUT IT! This is my personal experience, but I know I'm not the only one who's had it. This is my chance to slap people back and say, "I'm not your fucking geisha!"

That pretty much says it all.

It's always interesting to hear what readers like the most about the zine. It tends to be things like the "Tagalog for the Novice" and the fucked up Filipino mythology shit. Then it's also the Angst (pretty much everything in the zine), and also the angles on being a fierce Asian and/or fierce girl, whether they be of color or not.

Thanks for all the feedback! After reading my hospital madness in my previous issue, many letter pals shared with me their hospital/medical horror stories, which made me feel not so slapped with bad luck. Maraming salamat! Did you know that people from past relationships who I don't even talk to anymore called me or my parents up (if they didn't know I moved to New York) right after it happened because they had a dream I was calling out to them? Pretty fuckin' freaky...

To update y'all on the <u>Raw Like Sushi: An In-Your-Face Collection on Identity by Young Women of Color</u> anthology thang I'm doing, I've gotten many entries and am now in the mode of compiling all of it. I'll let you know what's next...

<u>WHAT'S HAPPENED IN MY WORLD LATELY:</u>
° I've told you guys about my fucked up corporate job. Because of it, I've actually gotten attitude from "friends" because they think it's a sell-out. My answer: blow me. People who think it's easy to survive NYC need to get a reality check about life and stop living with their parents. Anyways, some shit hit the fan where I was passed up for a promotion because I happen to not have a dick. Sex discrimination from the suits, what a surprise. But this is a warning to all of yunz. I wrote about it in this issue. Now I have a new job & I'm suing the blasted corporation (Yeah. Wish me luck!)

° I am no longer homeless, as I've found a place to live. It's no longer in the city, which is OK, because now my space is bigger and cheaper. Had some fun planting "little treasures," as my shrink calls them, all over my ex-roomie's apartment: Cut up some barbie doll parts and put leg parts, feet, hands, and decapitated heads all over his room and in his clothes, I also left a head floating in the toilet plunger basin. Peppered the place with egg and cheese to give him something to look forward to when he comes back from Spain after the hot summer. Last but not least, I stuck a rubber eyeball and rubber cockroach in his ice cube tray, for when he entertains guests. I hope he appreciates all the trouble I went through for him. The bastard threw me out because of my near-death-sent-to-the-hospital incident — I lost some work days, which meant I lost rent money, so I was late on payment. I told him what happened, and he just said, "Yes, I understand, but I just need someone more financially stable. I need the money." Then I find out that he's not getting a roommate yet and he's going to Spain. Gee, I wish I was THAT poor. Motherfucker. Whatever. Had a little fun going out...

° Julie, from the Clit Club here in NYC (the longest running girl bar/club in NYC), decided to have a Pinay-theme night. Before hand, I asked some questions about dancing there. Before you know it, I'm taking the stage the night of Pinay-ness! I was pretty overdressed for your usual dancer, as I had a t-shirt on, as well as my *malong* (tube of fabric) wrapped around my waist and *tubau* (piece of fabric that is wrapped around the head). Gigi the topless drummer was goin' at it, and I just went with it, using the tribal Filipino dance forms that I knew. My friend Eleanor, who dances with a Filipina Indigenous dance troupe, said I was great and that I had unknowingly gone through all the tribal forms/styles in the Philippines, ranging from the Northern styles, to the Southern. I was stokin'! Later, I donned the leather bondage garb and traipsed on the bar. It was fun!

°I took part in the Mix 96: Gay & Lesbian

BAMBOO GIRL 5 (EXCERPT)

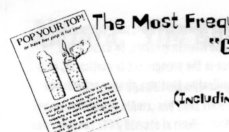

The Most Frequently Asked Questions/Comments "Girls of Color" Are Assaulted With & The Responses
(Including the "Nice n' Usual" Answer vs. the BG Answer)

1. **"Where are you from? REALLY from?"**
"NICE N' USUAL" ANSWER: "Oh, my parents are from ___(put your parents' country(ies) here___, but I was born in the States."
BG ANSWER: "From New York, idiot! Where are YOU from? Besides from under a rock?! ", or if you have light skin: "Zimbabwe.", or if you have dark skin: "Ireland."

2. **"Why is your skin that color?"**
"NICE N' USUAL" ANSWER: "What do you mean? Well, people from where my parents were born are usually this skin tone."
BG ANSWER: "Our peoples' skin always turns this color when we are about to tear apart the bones of foreign devils."

3. **"Why is your nose so flat/big/flared/(nonAnglo)?"**
"NICE N' USUAL" ANSWER: "People come from many different backgrounds, and they each have their own characteristics."
BG ANSWER: "Why is yours so pointy/small/pug/(nonEthnic)?"

4. **"You must be Asian, I can tell because of your eyes."**
"NICE N' USUAL" ANSWER: "You're right.", or "Actually, I'm not."
BG ANSWER: "You must be an assuming asshole, I can tell because of your racist jackoff assumptions."

5. **"Since you're Asian/Black/Ethnic, you must know Martial Arts..."**
"NICE N' USUAL" ANSWER: "Actually, I don't. That's just a popular misconception." or "In fact, I do."
BG ANSWER: "Yeah, I do. Wanna spar?"

6. **"By the way, I really think Connie Chung/Ethnic Flava of the Month is so beautiful."**
"NICE N' USUAL" ANSWER: "Yes, she is." or "Thanks for sharing that with me. That's nice to know."
BG ANSWER: "So what the FUCK does that have to do with me?"

7. **"I heard your kind is really good in bed.."**
"NICE N' USUAL" ANSWER: (laughing nervously) "He he, actually, that is another popular stereotype that is not so positive for Asian women in general, or men for that matter."
BG ANSWER: "Well this chick's pussy's got teeth. Wanna give it a whirl?!"

8. **"Why is your hair so straight/kinky? I thought all people from ___put your ethnic makeup__**

4

country(ies) here____ have kinky/straight hair?"

"NICE N' USUAL" ANSWER: "Au contrare, not all people born in these countries have the same type of hair. Especially if their ethnic makeup is made up of more than one homeland"

BG ANSWER: "Because your forefathers raped my foremothers, which begat — me."

Yes, I agree, some of the BG Answers may be harsh, but they are the responses that are secretly hiding in the back of many a rainbow-colored girl's mind, under all that guilt we were taught to have towards not being the standard "white issue", and plus, they're sure to stop bubbly conversation in its tracks.

So, remember girls! Whenever you are asked stupid racist and/or sexist questions, do stand up for yourself. Have fun with it! Just make sure you don't rip your lovely manicure in the process of gouging their eyes out.

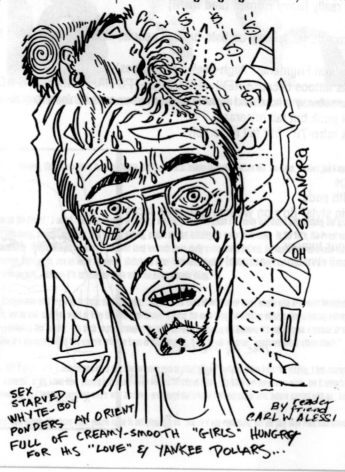

SEX STARVED WHYTE-BOY PONDERS AN ORIENT FULL OF CREAMY-SMOOTH "GIRLS" HUNGRY FOR HIS "LOVE" & YANKEE DOLLARS...

BY reader friend CARL W. ALESSI

MARTIAL ARTS:
HARRASSMENT ON THE STREETs

Yes, I've gotten shit by some men who claim that I take things "too seriously" or that "I think too much" when I get angry about being harrassed in the streets. You know what I say? Damn straight! I mean, I have a lot of male friends who get angry for me or really try to sympathize, but you know what? You don't know it until you're in it. Often I'm advised to "let it go," "try not to be so hard on the ignorant suckers," or "take it easy." Take it easy? YOU want ME to take it easy?!

Let me tell you the kind of things that happen to me EVERY FUCKING DAY when I go to or from work (I used to work in Midtown Manhattan, and now work in Chelsea - the latter has not posed as much a problem for me), or when I hang out with friends (in the Lower East Side). It ranges from the myriads of cat calls, "Oooh, baby, like dem Chinas!", "I wanna put you between two pieces of bread and lick in between!", "Love your legs!", to things that are just irritating, like "Smile" (like women are not allowed to look like they're thinking and are only there to look pleasant?), getting grabbed by the arm by total strangers because they're intrigued with my tattoos "Oh COOL! Did that hurt?", "Hey baby," or the always ambiguous but annoying "MMM, nice..." Or sometimes a guy passes by me at close range and grabs my thigh. I get this <u>every</u> day. Sometimes it's mild, sometimes it's unbearable. Either way, IT SUCKS and after a while, it gets old real quick.

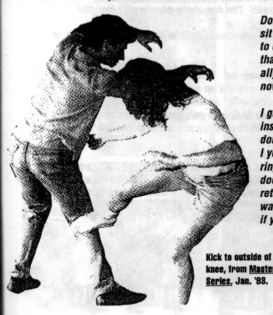

Kick to outside of knee, from <u>Master Series</u>, Jan. '83.

Don't tell me that if you get this every day, you're gonna sit back in your seat on the train comfortably and not try to close your legs together more tightly than usual? Or that you won't get just a little fed up? Or how about actually SPEAKING UP for yourself? That would be a big deal, now, wouldn't it?

I guess you can tell what kind of reaction I would have in instances like these. I DO speak up, I DO tell them that I don't appreciate it, that it's rude to stare, and if I need to, I yell back. One thing my martial arts teacher told me rings true, "If you defend an attack, the person usually doesn't expect it. They just expect you to take it and not retaliate." It's true. You can defend yourself in many ways when you are being harrassed, attacked verbally, or if you even fear for your life:

1.   Tell them that you don't appreciate being stared at, talked to like that, touched like that. I know that sounds corny, but no guy ever expects that you'll use your voice on them, so it usually

59

blows them away (they'll pretend they're cool, but they'll shrink away from you REAL quick.)

2.   Yell. It's always scary to hear a woman yell. You can just go off, or shout "fire!," since unfortunately, "rape!" and "help me!" usually doesn't get you much of a response.

3.   If you're attacked physically, always know that you have OPTIONS: use mace (which is became legal at 12midnight on Halloween in NYC), yell, kick, scream, and it never fails to strike the butt of your palm into their face. Anywhere on the face, a strike stuns them for a little while and can help you escape from a tight grasp. And no matter how big the guy is, he is gonna freak if you jab your straigtened fingers into the throat in one hit.

4.   Another option if you're attacked: sweep their feet from under them using a scooping motion behind the ankles with your feet. Another way to get them on the ground is to whip yourself behind them, grab their shoulders, and push either foot into the back of their knee. Once you get them on the ground, use what women do when they train in Model Mugging: hold the assailant down with one leg, and kick like hell with the other one — on any part of their body you can reach. Scream while you do it. They ain't gonna feel good, that's for sure. Then you can make your escape.

5.   If someone tries to grab your thigh (this is a popular one that happens to me), you can: strike the face, grab the guy's hand and twist it towards the outside using both hands (this KILLS like a mother!), or yell "Get your hand off me FUCKER!" Embarrassing the hell out of them works wonders in public places. They usually start laughing nervously, try to look cool, while looking around to make sure they've protected their rep.

6.   It helps to carry a piece. If you don't have one, or don't feel comfortable with one, always know that you have weapons in everyday things: pens (to the eyes, nose, throat), books (same targets), even knapsacks and heavy things in your pockets. Those chain wallets are great! You can choke people with that shit.

7.   You can always try to educate, although from personal experience, this is not usually an option, as most harassers don't get it or are too stupid to care.

These are just some pointers that may help you feel more empowered. Essentially, the main thing is to keep in mind that you should not let yourself be victimized, and once you speak up and simply tell the person you don't appreciate what they're doing, you'll find out who you're dealing with: an innocently harmless person, educateable asshole, clueless jerkoff, or all out psycho. Everybody has their own personal likes and dislikes when finding out what they're comfortable with in situations like these. But always remember that you don't have to take it, and to SPEAK UP!

THE FOLLOWING ARE FROM AN ISSUE OF <u>INSIDE KUNG FU</u>, MAY 1978. THE GARB IS TOTALLY DATED AND ENTERTAINING (HEY MY DAD USED TO WEAR SHIT LIKE THAT!), AND IT GIVES YOU SOME STARTERS ON THE LAYWOMAN'S APPROACH TO SELF-DEFENSE. (The only fucked up thing is that the perpetrator is Asian attacking a White female. Horror of horrors!)

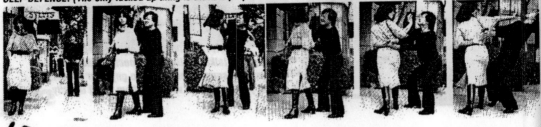

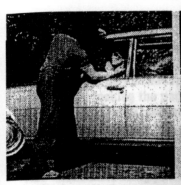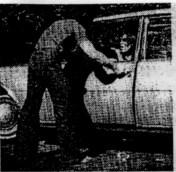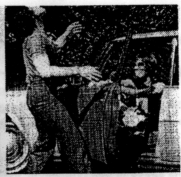

HERE ARE SOME PICTURES FROM A MORE RECENT ARTICLE ON SELF-DEFENSE FOR WOMEN (MASTER SERIES, JANUARY 1993).

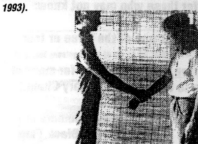

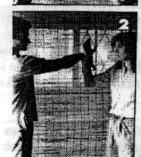

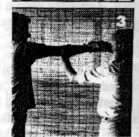

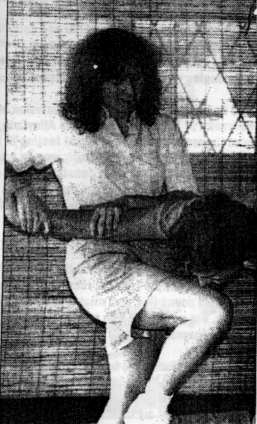

"Ye Olde Question: Who's Punkier Than Thou?"
[Ka-lawang Parte (Part II)

I got many responses to my article of the same name in my last zine, I decided to make a Part II, and include some thoughts by people who wrote.

My Vietnamese friend Paul Tran, formerly of the band NAM, sent me a shit load of stuff from his abode in San Francisco: some tapes, some publications. One of them, <u>Bam</u>, dated Feb. 9, 1990, featured an article "Anti-Heroes: California Punx Past + Present." He underlined various lines, that I think are really important to point out for those who may not know:

" ...[T]he punk explosion of the late '70s and early '80s was one of the three or four most important turning points in rock 'n' roll history...
Spiritually, if not musically, the original punk explosion was responsible for many of today's most challenging rock acts, from the Replacements to the Jesus and Mary Chain."

" Punk also helped pave the way for the inclusion of more female band members in rock. Exene Cervenka of X, Dianne Chai of the AlleyCats, and Kira Roessler of Black Flag were but a few of the women who found equal footing in the punk movement.
'Before punk there really weren't many women, especially young women, who were representing [rock],' observes Penelope Houston, former singer for San Francisco's Avengers. 'There was a sense of being out there without many comrades. But as far as the small community we moved in, people treated me like any other Avenger. There was no sense of sexism or division. You were a punk before you were male or female. Looking back on it, I think punk rock did a lot for women in rock.'"

Shawn Stern, the former singer-guitarist for the LA band Youth Brigade, mentions in the article, "There were certain people who got into hardcore and started imposing their viewpoint on what a band should sound like and what it should look like. I suppose people inevitably start creating roles, but punk rock was supposed to exist to break down the rules." (GOT THAT pseudoass fashionpunks?)

Check out the letter (see "Letters") by Jonny Mayo of the band Li'l Big Head (MD) -- he goes into how he discovered punk, but also states that he acknowledges that he will "not say I'm punker than thou because I was in the scene fairly early and got a black eye and hit with flying jello and peas because of my clothes." As a straight white male, he also talks about how he "can never understand the feelings that minorities have and the abuse that they suffer, nor am I trying to compare my drunken little foray into punk fashion to being a real

62

minority in this country..."

Straight white males, Asian men, and others wrote to tell me their stories and how they see punk and that it's meant something more to them than the little fashion freaks that are "dressing" the part nowadays to be "hip & NOW!" Most, if not all, expressed that punk hasn't been just looking the part, although they recall the ostracizing effect of their clothes that were considered strange at the time; to them, and to me, it's been a whole attitude and going against the grain thing that's supposed to be a constant challenge.

So, I think this brings up some relevant points, and helps me solidify what I said in the last issue about what being punk, or being in the punk community, means to me -- and evidently to many people who actually took part in the bands that played a role in the whole scene.

An actual envelope sent to me by CA reader friend Irene. Cool, huh?

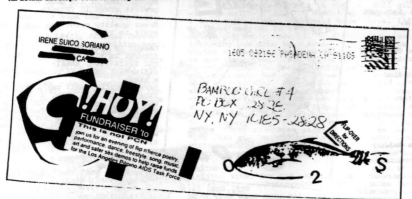

Fucked up Vaseline skin care kit pamphlet copy courtesy of Robynn Takayama@Static

Factoid

Pale is back...pale skin, in vogue during the Victorian era, is back again, but this time for different reasons. Gone are the days when skin color was a status symbol — and only laborers were tanned. Today, as the incidence of skin cancer continues to rise, skin tone is now a matter of healthy living. High powered sunscreens now replace the sun-shielding parasols of days past, but with the same goal in mind — healthy, young-looking, radiant skin.

63

271

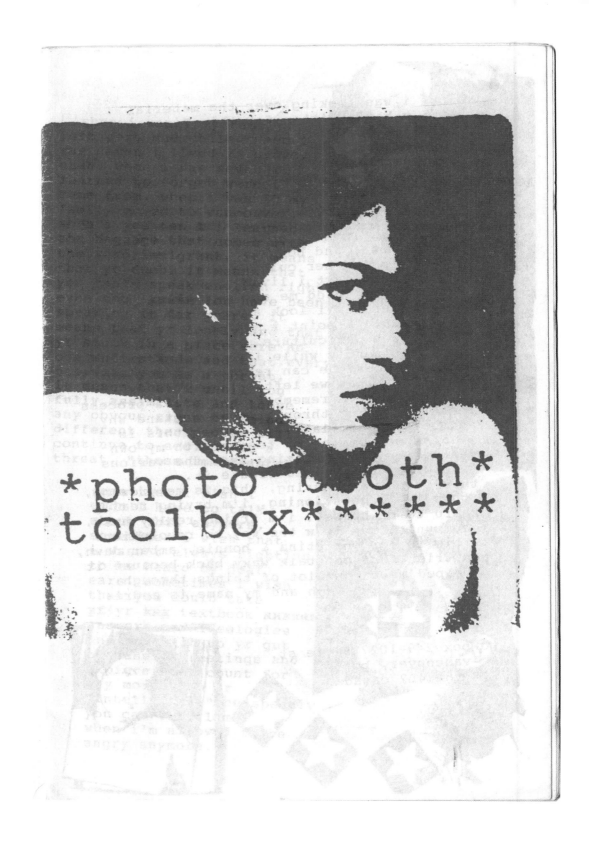

PHOTOBOOTH TOOLBOX 1(EXCERPT)

this past month i decided to call my long
distance grrrl stars and what i found was that
my "scene" is not boound by geographical boundaries
ⅹⅹⅹⅹⅹⅹⅹⅹ my scene is not defined ⅹ by image.
it empowers me that there are other girls working
towards the same goals as i am. that i'm notk ⅹ
trying to change things in vain. i know that
i have people there to support me.especially when
no one here will. lately i've been on this whole
revolutionary trip and it's so easy to think that
i hve this all figured out and that i always know
what i am talking about. it's so easy to forget khⅹ
that i am still learning.
        i'm in the process of s h a r i n g ideas
and am working to be able to change my conditioning
          i'm trying to incomrperate the idea that
communication is the way for revolution into my
life. i'm trying to understand other people'S
perspectives and i'm learnign to be an active
listener.
i'm trying to get past image and this whole
        hierarchy that i've become a part of.
i don't want torestrict my encounters with people
because they don't look the way i think
   a 'revolutioanary' should look like.
I8m learning to uhderstand my past and the decisions
that i made and the end results.
i'm learnign to f go on my gut ⅹinstinct and
   becoming a believer in the idea that everything
happend for a reason.
i'm learnign to love myself and take care of my
health and my body. i'm working on builⅾing
self respect and i'm learning to ask for help.
what i'm especially working hard on is trying
not to alienate people who may not appear to
be my allie but infact are. and i am learning
that people do change , no one ever reallystays
the same. and i'm learning to believe in myself
and realize my talents and my faults.
****

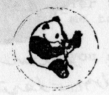

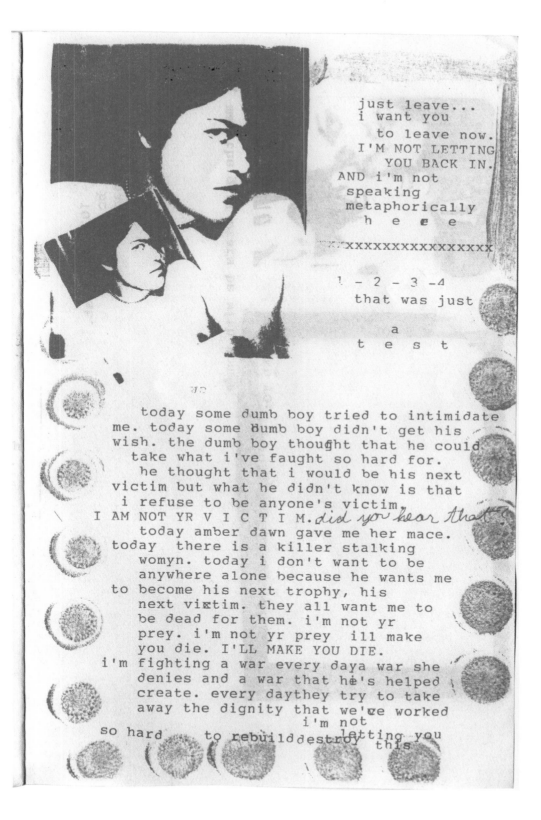

just leave...
i want you
    to leave now.
I'M NOT LETTING
    YOU BACK IN.
AND i'm not
speaking
metaphorically
h e r e

xxxxxxxxxxxxxxxxx

1 - 2 - 3 - 4
that was just
        a
    t e s t

today some dumb boy tried to intimidate
me. today some dumb boy didn't get his
wish. the dumb boy thought that he could
take what i've faught so hard for.
he thought that i would be his next
victim but what he didn't know is that
i refuse to be anyone's victim.
I AM NOT YR V I C T I M. *did you hear that*
today amber dawn gave me her mace.
today there is a killer stalking
womyn. today i don't want to be
anywhere alone because he wants me
to become his next trophy, his
next victim. they all want me to
be dead for them. i'm not yr
prey. i'm not yr prey ill make
you die. I'LL MAKE YOU DIE.
i'm fighting a war every daya war she
denies and a war that he's helped
create. every daythey try to take
away the dignity that we've worked
            i'm not
so hard   to rebuilddestroy letting you
                        this

DORIS #6

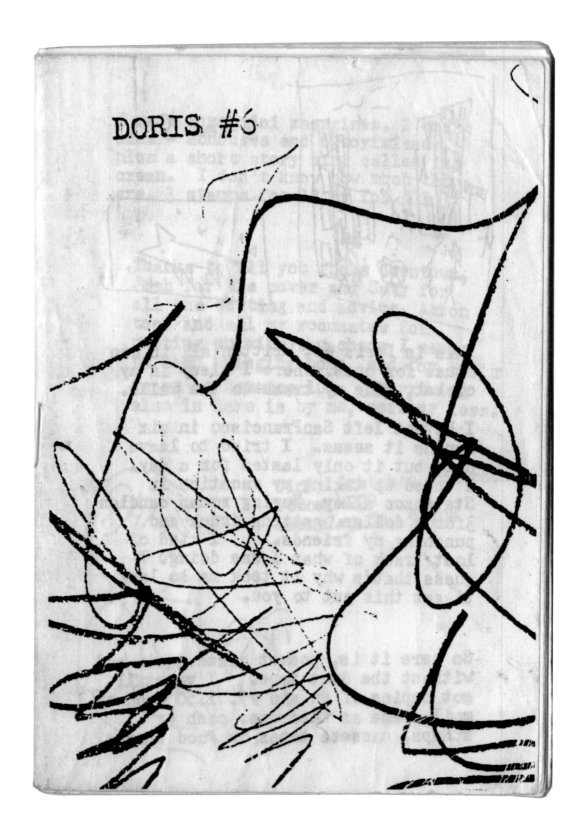

DORIS 6 (EXCERPT)

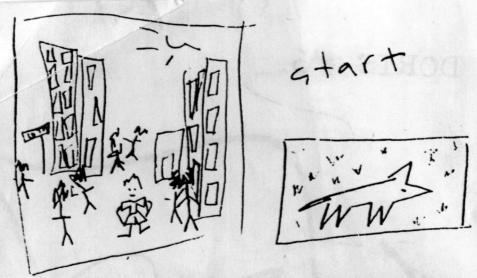

start

This is Doris #6. Written all in one house for once. where I sleep in my closet, glue my trash to the walls.

I havent left SanFrancisco in six months it seems. I tried to leave once but it only lasted for a day. I ended up taking my vacation in Stevenson alley. Buying roman candles 3for a dollar. getting drunk and punching my friends. I kind of lost track of what I was doing. I guess that's why it took me so long to get this out to you.

So here it is, pocket sized again and without the duct tape. I've still got copies of #4 and #5. 1.50 each by mail, same as this one. cash or stamps, cassete tapes or food stamps.

I made some mini magazines. 2 comic
ones - 28houses and 67boyfriends.
plus a short story mini called ice
cream. I don't know how much they
are. 3 stamps-for 1? 4½ for all 3?

Thanks to all you fucks downtown,
Josh for the cover and Caty for
all the editing and advice. Aaron
too. and all my roommates for
putting up with the chaos I seem
to keep bringing home, and for their
imput on Romance 101. Everything
else in here is by me, more or less.

Cindy Gretchen Ovenrack
POBox 4279
Berkeley Ca, 94704

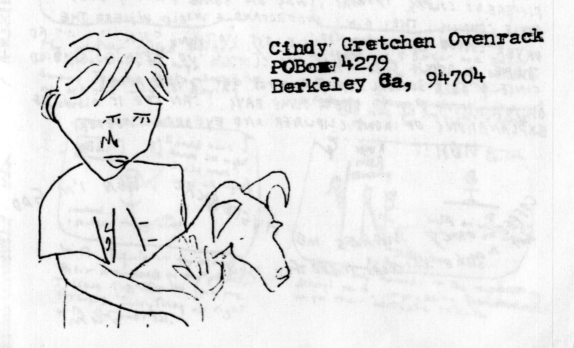

277

bugs

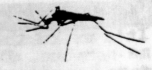

Lately I've been itching to stop
harrassment. I walk the dark side streets
looking for Natashas van to sleep in.
Looking for Colby and his loud little dog.
I stop in intersections and scratch at my
ankles. If someone's walking up, I grimace
and itch my head. If they think I have
bugs, maybe they won't bother me. I know
it's a rediculous idea.

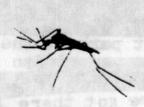 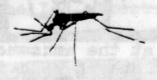 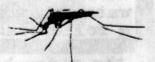

But truth is, I'm use to being bothered
and I take it pretty well these days. I
use to carry a switchblade around with me
and in my head I dared anyone to come near.
I was angry enough already. I wouldnt mind
feeling someone else's blood.

And then with Anna I owned the streets.
People crossed to the other side when they
saw my big dog.

And now, I don't know, I'm not scared
anymore. Maybe that's stupid, but it's
true. The guy outside the hotel says-
How about it baby? and I look at him
weary, simpathetic and shake my head.
It's that 'I know your situation but I'm
not your girl' look. More underatanding,
way more, than I actually feel. It comes
from a life time of learning how to not
aggravate. How to keep tempers down to
keep myself safe. I see both sides when
there should be only one. with one look,
one gesture, I prove myself their equal.

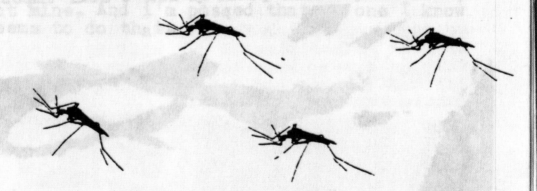

I don't see them as an agressor, don't
see myself ax a victim. And I know that it
it's bullshit, thatmy proof is all wrong.
But that's what I've been doing, when
itching doesn't deter them.

· end ·

Truth is, I'm bitter. Bitter about a lot
of things. Like my friends who live in a
poverty fantasy. The ones who have access
to money and always will. i can see   them
wanting to refuse it. Wanting to learn to
make it on their own. I think that's
important, I guess. And it would be fine
if they didn't talk about being broke.
Down to their last dollar. How are they
gonna make it through the month. When I
know all it would take for them is one
phone call. One trip to the bank.   Or
something like that. And truth is, I don't
understand it. I don't know how they   -
couldn't see that their words are insulting
to someone whose poverty isn't self imposed

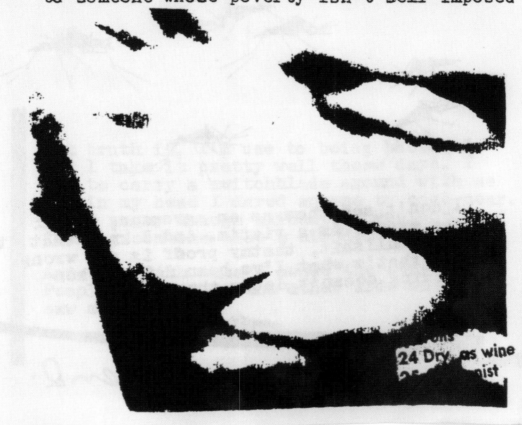

24 Dry, as wine

DORIS 6 (EXCERPT)

I'm bitter about my friends who have left
me behind. I guess I let go easily or not
at all. Once I learned about friendship.
What I wanted and how it could be. Deep and
strong and something that changed you, not
just distraction, another face to help pass
the time. Those days I wouldn't stand for
shalowness. I wanted everything out on the
table. no small talk. I pushed myself hard.
I went overbord, forgot to walk in the woods
go swimming or put my hands in the snow.
But I learned what I wanted and now I have
it. I know how to think into a person and
push them for more. How to get them to grow.
I know how to talk and how to be quiet. I
can see them through their own experiences,
not mine. And i'm passed that no one I know
seems to do that.

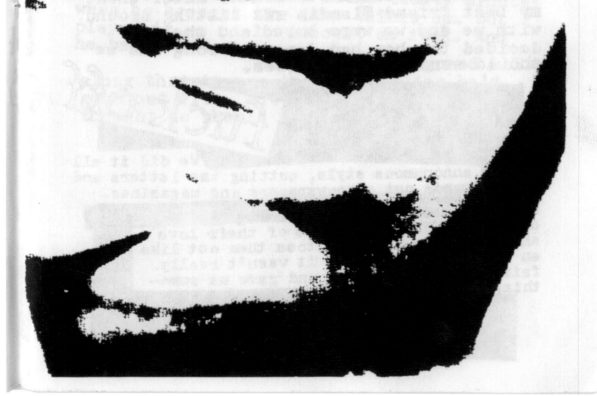

first love

Me and my first boyfriend were getting
kind of sick of eachother. At least we
were getting sick of driving around in
his moms little toyota and looking for
places to park and ..... . fuck.
Neither of us were any good at it. So
when he left to go be counceler at some
summer camp I didn't really care. And
when I heard he'd gotten together with
some other girl, I was pretty relieved.
I didn't even think to be mad or bitter
or anything 'til a few months later when
my best friend Claudia was sitting around.
with me and we were bored and she
decided the boy had done me wrong and we
should send him hate notes.

fuck off

We did it all
annonomous style, cutting the letters and
words out of newspapers and magazines.

Short letters like 'Die Scumbag' and long
ones like 'You rob people of their love
and affection and then toss them out like
an old sponge'. I knew it wasn't really
fair, but it was funny and gave us something to do all day.

Then a few months later me and Claudia
were downtown and missed the last bus
home. The boy was the only person we knew
who lived around there and had a car and
would probably drive us home. So we
sauntered over to his house, regretting
those stupid letters we'd sent. 'he'll
never think it was you' Claudia said, but
I wasn't so sure.

We hadn't been in the house twenty minutes
when he brought the damn things up. But I
played it so cool, inocent as fuck. And
he believed me.
                He said he'd figured all
along that it was this girl Alice he'd
gone out with, but she denied it so he
thought he should ask me.

alice

Then he told me about her. She had this huge hatered toward birds that he always thought was pretty strange, but he never knew how serious it was til this one day he was standing at her locker and she opened the door and all these bird houses and bird feeders came falling out. The whole locker was full of them, hardly any room left for books. And it turned out that every day she walked to school and stole all the birdhouses and birdfeeders out of peoples yards along the way. She'd stash them in her locker and then eventually throw them out.

He told me he'd been scared to run into me in case I was the one who had sent the letters and not alice. cuz he didn't want me to be pissed at him and he'd never meant to do anything wrong. -I said yeah, I was never mad at him at all. And he gave me and Claudia a ride home.

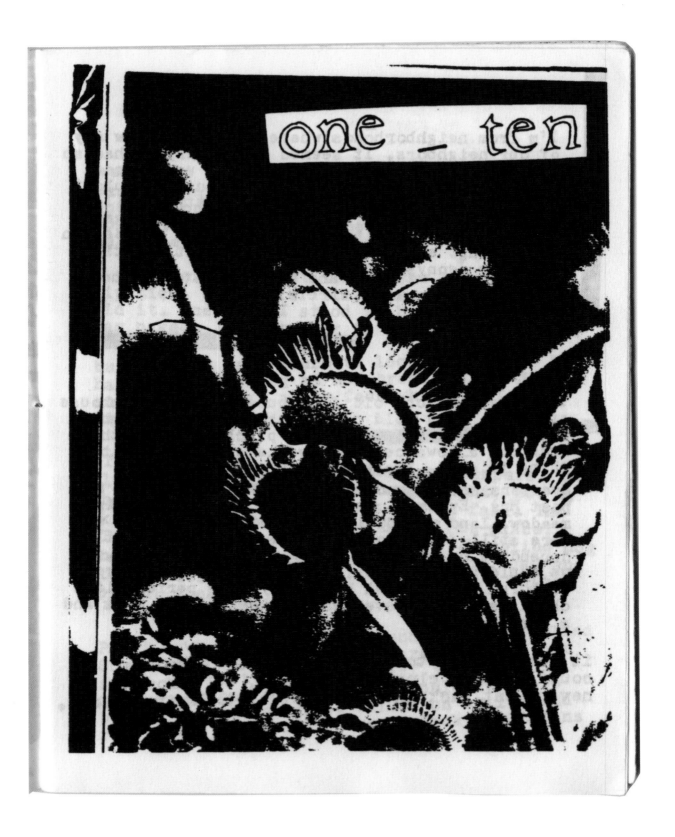

one_ten

downtown

What do you do when your best friend is dead and
your sister is gone and your body is scrapped
out and bleeding from some medical procedure and
the boy you want near you shows up in town but
he is lost too, more crazier than you and you
ride the tunnels together fast under the bay and
him sitting next to you is the only comfort you
have left but he gets off the train at powellst
street station and says I'll come find you
before I leave

which isn't for a week and
you want to yell get back here and stay
but you know that you never wanted to need him
and you never wanted your love to be clutching
and you know that this individualist culture
makes us think we can do it all on our own when
we can't,

no matter how much of a loner you are.
and you have no community to fall back on and no
family to run to and no history to ground you
and your comfort just left you at powell street
station.

DORIS 6 (EXCERPT)

nirvana

Maud had a secret love of Nirvana. Listened
to them only when no one was home. Or when
I was over because I'd never heard of them
so who cares. She'd put it on and sing along
and stop it and say "listen to this. What do
you think it says right there?"

She was dog phobic and when we walked somewhere it always took twice as long 'cause
there were streets with dogs we'd have to
avoid. Once we rounded a corner and there
was the biggest dog in town standing there
not even on a leash. Maud jumped up on my
back and climbed up on my shoulders. She was
small enought and quick enough to be able to
do that. Strong enough to pull herself up.

I hear she's playing drums now and I wonder
if she's still doing the politics that made
us stick together in the first place. The
one time I called her in Tucson she said she
was watching a movie and could she call me
back. It had been a year since I'd talked to
her. I said yeah, sure. but didn't leave her
with my new #. If she even did call she would
have gotten a disconected message.

        That night I punched the walls of my
new house and found out they were stronger
than me.

page

You know what. I've fallen in love with
this kid. I swore I'd never let this
happen to me again. Her name is Page,
she's three years old. I've taught her
to tango. She remembers my name now.
She helps me wash the dishes, blocks my
exit when I try to go. I always say to
people that I hate kids, but the truth
is, that's a total lie. I'm just scared
of how quickly I fall for them. How
much of my life I would give up for
them if I'm not careful.
Page, she is stubborn andhangs on to my
feet. I say 'I'll be back before you
can count to twenty'. she only knows
how to count to ten. When she mumbles I
say 'girl, you gotta be more articulate
and she knows what I mean, she's not
dumb. Sometimes she takes my keys and
pretends she's leaving, she brings back
invisable gifts when she comes home.
She want play airplane with me because
my feet are to dirty. She wants to wat
watch sesame street of winnie the pooh.
Sometimes she falls asleep in the crook
of my arm. I carry her to bed, I tuck
her in.

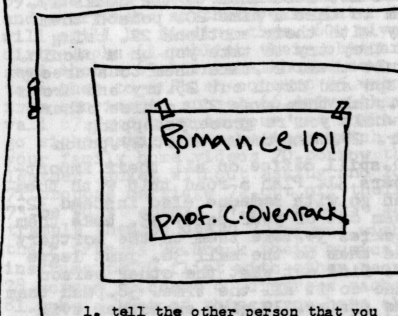

Romance 101

prof. C. Overrack

1. tell the other person that you can't stand them. 2. kick them. 3. make the other person feel like shit. 4. spit 5. have terrible times together. 6. tell the other person that you could care less. 7. crush them with your bare hands 8. steal their bike. 9. give them a dead rat 10. ditch them when they really need you 11. stand eachother up 12. take them to Operation Dumbo Drop 13. Break both their arms and leave them to die in the woods. 14. make a special tape of hate songs 15. talk openly about how annoying they are and how much you hate

them. 16. become their nightmare 17. steal
their bed 18. feed them to the ducks 19.
tel them to take a hike 20. poison them
21. play with their emotions 22. bring
ants if they try to take you on a picnic.
23. insult them. 24.take them to a creepy
health spa and ditch out 25.try and drown
them 26.push them away 27. cruise other
people while you're groceryshopping
together. 28.burn their toast 29.punch
them
      30.spill coffee on all their import-
ant papers 31. Plan a road trip with them
and then go with someone else instead 32.
kick them out of your party 33. bake them
worm cookies 34.take them to the mortuary
35. take them to the mall 36. just leave
them 37. find out what the other person
hates and do it all the time. 38.push them
down the stairs. 39.give eachother evil
glares 40.rip the radiator out of their
car 41. take them fishing and push them
overboard 42. talk about them behind their
back 43. hurt them 44. get them fired from
their job 45. ruin their favorite song for
them 46.destroy everything they ever loved
47. hold them at arms length 48. use eye-
contact to let them know how much they
disgust you. 49. write eachother letters
seething with hate 50. call them late at
night and hang up 51.lie to eachother 52.
givethema black eye 53.make sure their
family hates you 54.trip them 55.makethem
sacrifice everything for you 56.send a
letter bomb 57.have no respect for them

DORIS 6 (EXCERPT)

58.put them on a spaceship to the moon
59.hide hate notes in alltheir clothes
and everywhere so that years later they
will still be finding them. 60. give them
dirty looks 61.publish their obituary 62.
send thorns 63.burn theirhouse down 64.
take them to a Phish concert 65.watch TV
from sunrise to sunset 66.drive them up a
wall 67.feed them to your pet snake 68.
go sightseeing 69. make them watch all
your family home videos 70.borrow their
leather jacket without asking and lose it.
71.propose marriage 72.cut off their ear
73.be worst enemys 74.get a horse and
trample them to death 75.go out with all
their friends 76.break their musical
instruments 77.flirt with other people
78.scream 79.cheat 80.distress eachother
81.make a list of things you hate about
eachother 82.read their diary and discuss

it with your friends 83. steal their
friends 84.put a severed horse head in
their bed 85.only cook things they hate
86.find out what makes them miserable
87. drive eachother insane 88.be uncaring
89.watch them leave 90.die 91.dedicate
the song 'fuck you' to them on ther raido
92.send death threats 93.destroy their life
94.step on their feet 95.play mean jokes on
them 96.think about how much you can't
stand eachother 97. find out what makes the
other person sad and then bring it up all
the time 98.steal their skateboard 99.trade
insults 100.shove icecubes down their pants
101.fuck

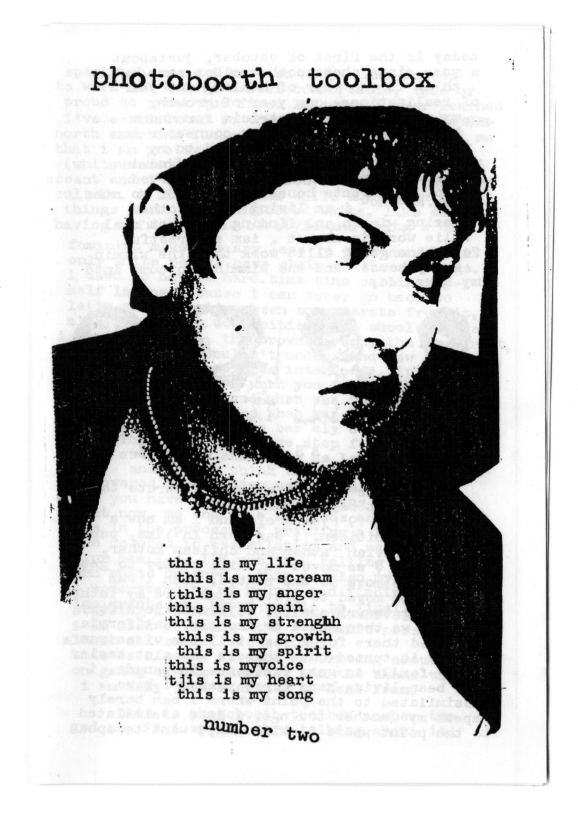

photobooth toolbox

this is my life
 this is my scream
 tthis is my anger
 this is my pain
 'this is my strenghh
  this is my growth
  this is my spirit
 this is myvoice
 tjis is my heart
  this is my song

number two

PHOTOBOOTH TOOLBOX 2 (EXCERPT)

today is the first of october, justabout
a year since photobooth toolbox came out.
   th is is one year of healing one year
of realizations, one year of growth.
   my name is andrea patricia fernandez
   henriquez. my name is my connector to
my heritage to my culture and to my
mother tounge. i am 19 years oldand i
am tasting and feeling freedom. imoved
out of my parents house a couple of mo nths
   ago. and now i am living with 5 other
   amazing wimmin and finding out what real
   allie work is about . iam so greatful
for the ongoing allie work that the wimmin
   in my house and the wimmin who come into
my house do.

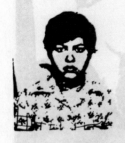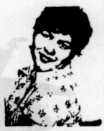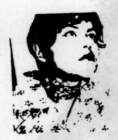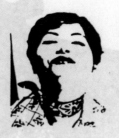

A N G E R   A S   A   T O O L'

   ~~~ this is from a letter i wrote to
   bianca, it says it all.
      "i am 19 years old and i am now a
   canadian citizen. i was born in lima, peru
   to a peruvian father and chilean mother.
   when iwas 7 we moved to chile to try to get
   a visa to move to the states. when i was
   7 1/2 we moved to provo, utah were my father
was going to university. we lived there for
2 years. we then moved to anaheim, california.
and lived there for a year till our visas ran
out and it turned out that it was alot easier
for my family to getv residence in canada. i
have been living here for 9 years. i have
   assimilated to the point where i can barely
   speak my mother tou nge. i have assimilated
to the point where i still don,T want to speak

spanish because i have so many shame issues
to work out before i feel comfortable, safe or
proud to speak the first language i ever learned
i've assimilated to the point where ~~still there~~
north american fuckers have the nerve to tell me
that i am pretty white for an ethnic person
(whitewashed) CUZ YOu know i have a slight
accent and i cand blend pretty well into weastern
culture. i listen to punk WHITE music and do
things that are considered white, like as if
having a fuken sense of style and being a damn
feminist makes me any less la tina. and as if
only white people have claim on these things.
i used to have a hard time time calling myself latina because i can never go back to
latin culture. i've been so seperate from it,
always being in communities and skools where
i was the latina, the brown person, the immigrant,
the person who couldn't understand how the
white/middle class kids interacted. it's hard
maintaing a culture when you feel a shamed &
like and outsider and when the rest of yer
family does too, and when yer parents work
their asses off and are bar ely ever around."
          This zine is a huge step for me. this
is my attempt at skreaming as loud as i can
      and if you think that this can only
be covered in ONE zine well lets just say
that you have better stp reading this zine
right now. me and th e fabulous andrea lee
are in the process of writting a kkick ass
zine devoted to assimilation and racism and
co ur healing. i'M not thru telling on weast-
tern white culture. this is also my attempt
at understanding my wounds and finding other
immigrants and brown people to finally
starting a community that we deserve.
i am sick of being 'the ' nonwhit person in
almost all social situations.
this is also my attempt at writing about my
on going eating disorder and the shame that
i am only just starting to heal from.

          this is photobooth toolbox number two
and no, ﾞ1 i am not thru talking about it.

PHOTOBOOTH TOOLBOX 2 (EXCERPT)

these are the ways that i am healing from
my eating disorder, fat oppression and
19 years of a messed up body image.
* eating in front of people. i fight the self
hate that i feel that stops me from eating in
front of people. realizing that i am not
gross and a "pig" FOR eating when i want to
and that it doesn'T mean that i am "bad" or
that people are going to be grossed out or
judging me for what i am eating.
*buying food. not feeling ashamed for buying
"fatty" foods. again not thinking thatb
 people will judge me and think that isthe
reason she isn't thin"
*realizing that my body is beautiful
         .everycurve and stretch mark is mine
  and is beautiful. my body is normal and
    should be celebrated and not starved and hated
*wearing clothes xthat make me feel attractive
   even if thety are fitted aand show every
   curve. because every curve of me is beautiful
   and sexy. ᵡⁱᵡᵗʰᵉᵘ,ᵗʰᵉᵗ
*eating . even when i have gained weight. just
cuz i have gained weight doesn't mean that i have
 to lose weight or go on a starvation diet.
* knowing my body and whatni need. if i need
 to eat more than usual its prolly for a reason
*kn owing that i don't have to compete with
other peoples weight loss or eating disorders.
*knowing that other peoples eating disorders
 lo affect me and triiger and influence me
*tearing down posters for get thin quick(die
quick) scams
*not supportingthe diet industry anymore
 ie gyms,diet foods, ect
* speaking out against screwed up idead about
 fat and hellth that people try to impose on me
*learning and knowing that fat is no a bad word
and that thin/slim/skinny are not good words either
-*knowing that my abusers and tormentors were
 screwed up and their wordswere just representation
of how screwed upTHEY are/were and that it had
        nothing to do with me

*knowing that i am cute wwwx ashell and that
peopleare/will be attracted to me. knowing i
am worthy of positive attention and crushes
*not believing the media and what it portrays
'real' wimmim and men to be ie bone thin and
  rich
*findingball bodies attractive and beautiful
*standing up to my parents and their skrewed
up oppressive views
*being comfortable with my body
*believing in myself.
*taking care of my body by eating nutnitius food
  and trying to avoid foods that are bad for
  me(ALLERGIES trigger depression and do bad
  mental things to me)
*talking about my herstory with food and eating
  disorders
d *acknowledging my eating disorders and realizing
thxxt who it bennifits (not me; but the diet
industry and those in power)
*LOVING MYSELF

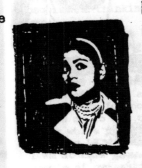 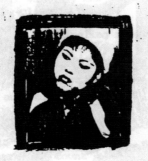 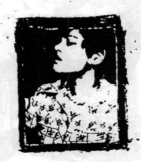

HEALING

PHOTOBOOTH TOOLBOX 2(EXCERPT)

1. Has the band relocated to Portland?

1 . No, the band hangs out primarily in olympia right now, The singer lady (kathleen) recently spent an extended hangover (she doesn't drink this is metaphor of course) in an all woman house called the CUrse. At this house she was taught the true/false meaning of girl love,girl hate and girl revenge, plus desire and ingenue-ity. As a group, however, The Kill like the phrase about the stone that keeps rolling and so no one can kill it first. We live whereever it seems to make sense at the Time.

2. Have you (Kathleen) done anymore spoken word besides the Wordcore 7"?

. Kathleen is currently planning a follow up to her first wordcore seven inch, entitled appropraiately "Kathleen, simply,Kathleen."

3. How long has it been since you've played a show? Why has it been so long? Are you planning a tour? Do you even tour?

The Kills just played Olympia Grange hall and now La luna in Portland . Before that it was ayear and six days, appx. The Kill has been known to tour alot and in terrible vans. Often times they have braved terrible sickness' and snowstorms to do this because the Kill loves the smiling faces of children and the young at heart who enjoy lovely kill styled music. The Kill did not play live for a while because they had better things to do. Like maybe The Frumpies and maybe sleeping late and having terrible affairs with bad people that we should've not ever touched at all cuz all the neighborhood became an uproar. However, after meeting Joan Jett , the Kill was stricken with The "I love to rock and I Rock to Live" disease, at which point we decided that touring is in our imminant future.

4. What do you think of the "success" or "popularity" of your Rebel Girl 7"?

14 Who cares.

5. How did you hook up with Joan Jett? Do you plan on working with her more in the future? Is she cool?

We met Joan at the roller skating rink in Lacey Washington. She had a jacket on that said "Good times" in sparkly letters. Kathleen asked her to couples skate and she said yes. There were no plans made besides not telling our parents we were hanging out with Joan Jett. How can you even ask if she is cool, i mean, she didn't even have to rent skates.

6. Are Frumpies planning anything, a full-length or any live shows?

19

20

21

7. Are you a "riot-grrrl" band? What is a "riot-grrrl"? Do you hate this question?

23   Yes.

8. Are "riot-grrrls" not supposed to talk about the movement/rebellion with the media or the press? yes/no.

25

9. Do you kick out males for aggressive behavior at your shows? maybe.

10. There are rumors that you have charged men different prices at your shows than women. Would you like to respond to this?

28   no.   **11. Do you still do the Bikini Kill zine?**

11. The Bikini Kill zine #1 and #2 are available from Riot Grrrl Press PO BOx 73308, wdc20009. We are planning a BK 3 to deal with/elaborate upon our experiences with and ideas on the media. Besides that Tobi does JIGSAW zine and kathleen does different weird things she sells and/or gives away at shows.

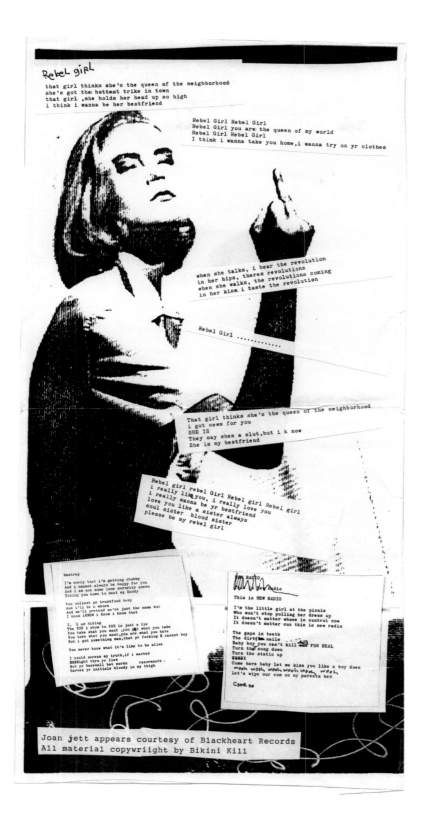

Rebel girl

that girl thinks she's the queen of the neighborhood
she's got the hottest trike in town
that girl ,she holds her head up so high
i think i wanna be her bestfriend

Rebel Girl Rebel Girl
Rebel Girl you are the queen of my world
Rebel Girl Rebel Girl
I think i wanna take you home,i wanna try on yr clothes

when she talks, i hear the revolution
in her hips, theres revolutions
when she walks, the revolutions coming
in her kiss i taste the revolution

Rebel Girl ....

That girl thinks she's the queen of the neighborhood
i got news for you
SHE IS
They say shes a slut,but i k now
She is my bestfriend

Rebel girl rebel Girl Rebel girl Rebel girl
i really like you, i really love you
i really wanna be yr bestfriend
love you like a sister always
soul sister   blood sister
please be my rebel girl

Demirep

I'm sorry that i'm getting chubby
And i cannot always be happy for you
And i am not some lame sorority queen
Taking you home to meet my Daddy

You collect yr trustfund baby
And i'll be a whore
And we'll pretend we're just the same but
I know iKNOW i Know i know that

I, i am hiding
The YOU i show to YOU is just a lie
You take what you want ,you get what you take
You take what you want ,you are what you hate
But i got something man,that yr fucking i cannot buy

You never know what it's like to be alive

I could scream my truth,if i wanted
XXXRight thru yr lies
But yr baseball bat words   razormouth :
Carves yr initials bloody in my thigh

This is NEW RADIO

I'm the little girl at the picnic
Who won't stop pulling her dress up
It doesn't matter whose in control now
It doesn't matter cus this is new radio

The gaps in teeth
The dirty nails
Baby boy you can't kill   FOR REAL
Turn the song down
Turn the static up
GRRRX
Come here baby let me kiss you like a boy does
wooh wooh wooh wooh wooh wooh
let's wipe our cum on my parents bed

come on

Joan jett appears courtesy of Blackheart Records
All material copywright by Bikini Kill

RECORD LINER LYRICS

girlconvention

we're planning a girl convention to create a community of strong and
active girl allies. we want to focus on the destructive behaviours and
ways we fuck each other over. and we will recognize that it is possible
for us to communicate in a rad and sincere way without creating these
destructive dynamics-like competition and jealousy. thru workshops and
discussions we hope to recognize that we can be truly cool with each
other-making it that much easier to be active in our communities. and
all of this will be done in a challenging way- no hiding under safety
blankets and privilege. cos being safe=not having to recognize or
take responsibility for yer/our own privilege and ways you/we oppress
others. it's really vital that we build our community (and community
does not _just_ mean bands/records/music.) community means talking
sincerely with each other, critiquing, telling each other how fuken
rad we are and learning from each other-thru fanzines, voice, music-
and any other mediums we come up with.

this will all take place on **JULY 56&7**

so far we've got workshops dealing with these issues:

self-defense, youth liberation, racism, violence in queer and boygirl relationships,
classism, girl run projects, women's health, privilege and how that affects whether you
are active or inactive, women in collective and radical politics, pro-choice 101,
and others.

other rad events: girl made movies, spoken word, art displays, a skating/dance
party, tables set up by girls to sell t-shirts,records,stickers,whatever. plus
a girl made fanzine table (send us a flat,unstapled,black and white copy and we
will make copies for you). and some _awesome_ bands will be playing.

girl convention
headquarters.

1215 e.spring
box 36
seattle,wa.98122
(206)328 9282

we really need more girls to help us plan
this huge event so please get in touch with us
if you are into helping in any way.
we are also putting together an infozine which
will have everything you need to know-a place
to stay,where to eat, directions, what's gonna
happen at the convention,etc. _please_ let us
know if you have _any_ questions about the
planning, events or whatever. we also desperately
need money (to rent space, pay bands, workshop
people) so please donate money- if you
have extra. contact us.
e-mail nerds write anngirl @
anngirl@seattleu.edu
or write marcy,alicia and rahhel

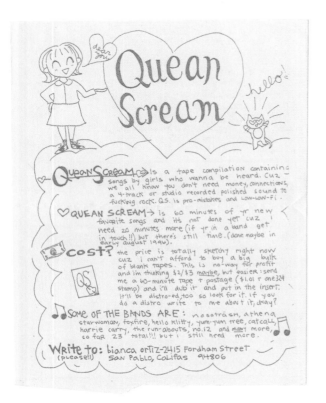

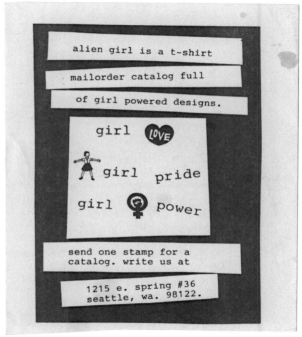

FLYERS

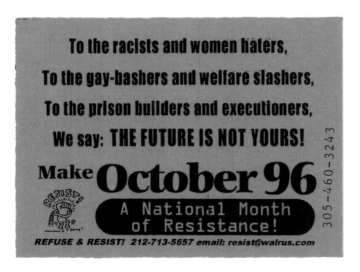

To the racists and women haters,
To the gay-bashers and welfare slashers,
To the prison builders and executioners,
We say: THE FUTURE IS NOT YOURS!

Make **October 96**

A National Month
of Resistance!

305-460-3243

REFUSE & RESIST! 212-713-5657 email: resist@walrus.com

SUPPORT VAGINAL PRIDE

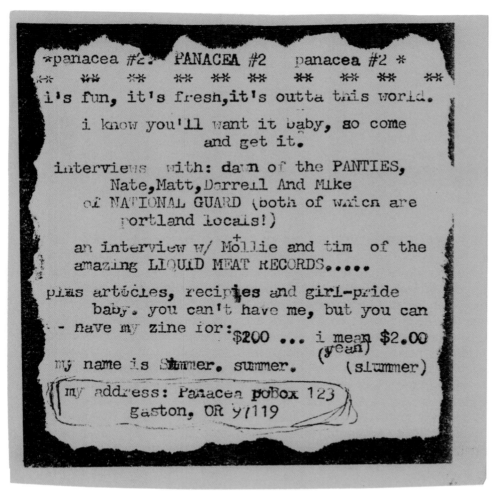

*panacea #2. PANACEA #2   panacea #2 *
** ** ** ** ** ** ** ** ** **
i's fun, it's fresh,it's outta this world.

i know you'll want it baby, so come
and get it.

interviews with: dawn of the PANTIES,
Nate,Matt,Darrell And Mike
of NATIONAL GUARD (both of which are
portland locals!)

an interview w/ Mollie and tim of the
amazing LIQUID MEAT RECORDS.....

plus articles, recipies and girl-pride
baby. you can't have me, but you can
- have my zine for: $200 ... i mean $2.00
(yeah)
my name is Slummer. summer.   (slummer)

my address: Panacea poBox 123
gaston, OR 97119

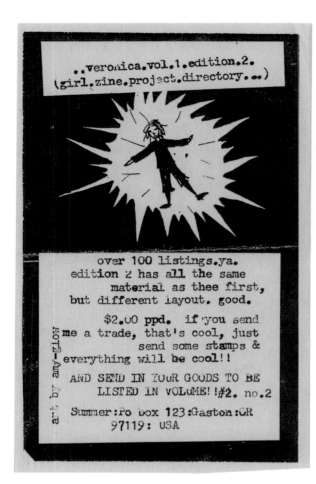

..veronica.vol.1.edition.2.
(girl.zine.project.directory...)

over 100 listings.ya.
edition 2 has all the same
material as thee first,
but different layout. good.

$2.00 ppd. if you send
me a trade, that's cool, just
send some stamps &
everything will be cool!!

AND SEND IN YOUR GOODS TO BE
LISTED IN VOLUME!!#2. no.2

Summer:Po box 123:Gaston:OR
97119: USA

art by amy-glow

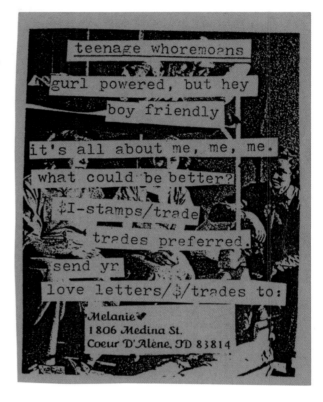

teenage whoremoans

gurl powered, but hey

boy friendly

it's all about me, me, me.

what could be better?

$1-stamps/trade

trades preferred.

send yr

love letters/$/trades to:

Melanie ♥
1806 Medina St.
Coeur D'Alene, ID 83814

BECAUSE SKOOL HAS FUCKED OVER SO MANY OF US. The majority of kids I talk to today say they hate skool, and with good reason too. Help me put together a compilation zine to demonstrate only a *portion* of the absurdity of the public skooling system. **Send me your stories of bullshit skool-imposed punishments.** I need your true stories on times when the system fucked you over, blatantly rejected your side of the story, exercised their dictatorial powers on you. For example, (this is rumored) how this elemantary kid gets *suspended* for wearing fishnets .. or people who have received detentions/suspensions for having zines which discussed 'dirty' things .. or have gotten in trouble for violating dress codes with hair, etc .. or describe teachres who have gone way too out of line in behavior/disciplines methods. You get the idea. Give me the details of your stories! Get pissed off, get others pissed off, and show just how *un*democratic our skool systems REALLY are and have always been. Send stuff by 1997 if possible to: **Menghsin SideTracked / 7534 Farmington Ave. / Kalamazoo, Mi 49009.** [please pass this flyer on or reprint it, and be sure to let yr non-zinester friends know about it too!]

FLYERS

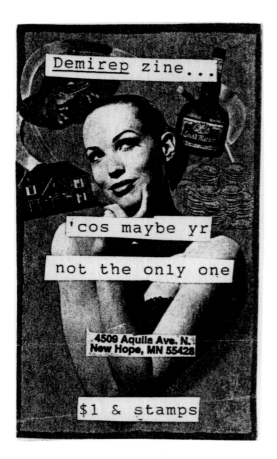

Demirep zine...

'cos maybe yr

not the only one

4509 Aquila Ave. N.
New Hope, MN 55428

$1 & stamps

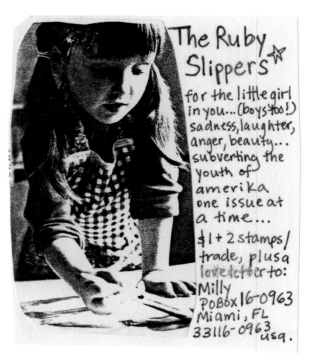

The Ruby
Slippers

for the little girl
in you... (boys too!)
sadness, laughter,
anger, beauty...
subverting the
youth of
amerika
one issue at
a time...
$1 + 2 stamps/
trade, plus a
love letter to:
Milly
POBox 16-0963
Miami, FL
33116-0963
usa.

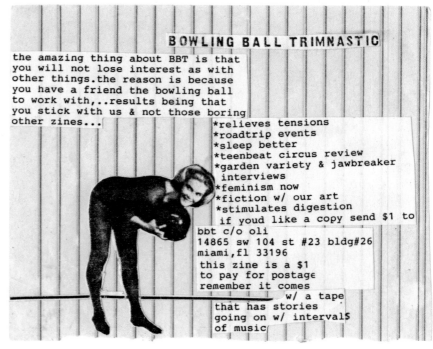

BOWLING BALL TRIMNASTIC

the amazing thing about BBT is that
you will not lose interest as with
other things. the reason is because
you have a friend the bowling ball
to work with,..results being that
you stick with us & not those boring
other zines...

*relieves tensions
*roadtrip events
*sleep better
*teenbeat circus review
*garden variety & jawbreaker
 interviews
*feminism now
*fiction w/ our art
*stimulates digestion
 if youd like a copy send $1 to
bbt c/o oli
14865 sw 104 st #23 bldg#26
miami, fl 33196
this zine is a $1
to pay for postage
remember it comes
          w/ a tape
that has stories
going on w/ intervals
of music

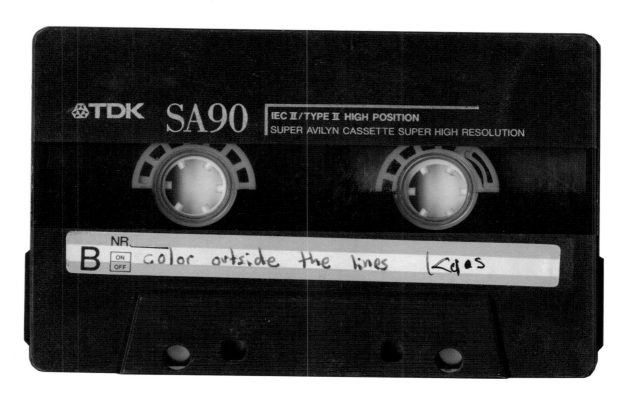

B color outside the lines

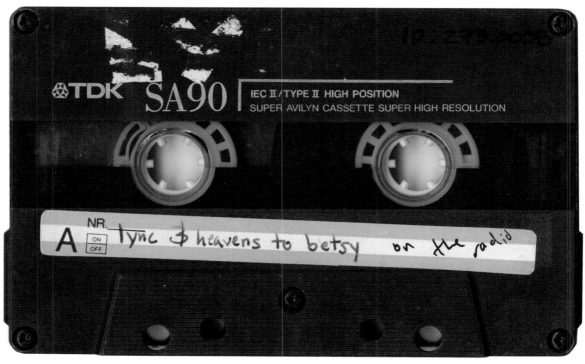

A lync & heavens to betsy on the radio

AUDIOCASSETTE

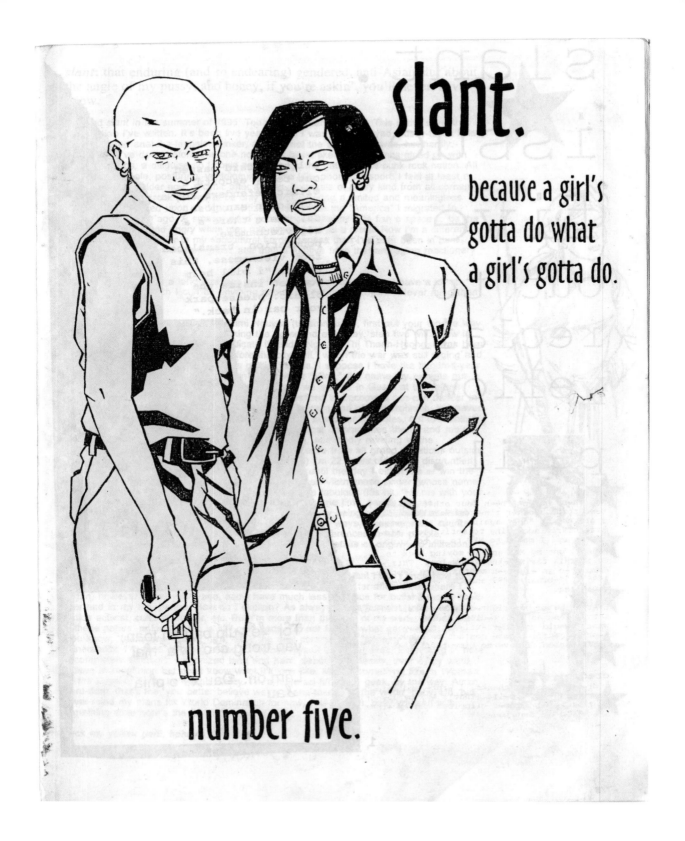

slant.

because a girl's gotta do what a girl's gotta do.

number five.

Revolution don't come easy, honey.

This is where I wanted (to start) to talk about me and riot grrrl. It's really difficult to write easily because it's such a complex relationship I have with it, after all these years struggling with what it means, who it includes and so of course, who it doesn't and my struggle to situate myself as a Vietnamese refugee/US citizen, reading riot grrrl and feeling incredibly alienated. This is only the beginning, I intend to write a mini-zine about my ambivalence and mixed feelings about riot grrrl. These are some pieces I'd written at various times, but I want to make it crystal clear that I totally support riot grrrl as a feminist project, period. I care, therefore I critique. If I don't push, the car doesn't go, right? XOXO *mimi*

February 93: Not every girl is a riot grrrl. Maybe your oppositional grrrl identity is imagined exclusive of "Asian" or "immigrant," those things that would've made a difference to me, those things that ensured my involuntary/voluntary exclusion from a much-fabled "girl unity" in a younger, less articulate (read: alien) incarnation. Fuck: I was never "socialized" like you were, growing up in a Vietnamese refugee family, devastatingly uprooted, divided by wars (civil and neocolonial) and geopolitics, and unfamiliar with/outside of normative whitegirl culture, of any class.

The mythic & organic "sisterhood" that slipped notes written in bubble letters into your backpacks & exchanged furtive kisses in pink bedrooms, I read about in Judy Blume but it was nothing that I knew or aspired to. A small town of working-class and lower middle-class white families meant after-school fights, blood trickling from my younger brother's ear, poverty re-upholstered in yards of cheap discount fabric, blown-up mailboxes for Fourth of July, & hate letters (my mother & I read these and laughed because we were stronger than you) from the same whitegirls who held hands & whispered "girl love" to each other. (And don't you feel sorry for me: the years I spent in relative isolation with my family were more precious to me than any potential third-grade friendship.) And it was the little whitegirls with their nascent blood-sister ties that forced this estrangement from them/you, that compelled my distance from a distinctive "girlhood" that years later still grates, still chafes against my exiled-daughter-fugitive-sister me, because I was different, weird, alien (refugee, accented, yellow): & that ain't girl jealousy, sweetie.

Let's chant it together now: difference & deconstruction, killer of your universal girl love.

So every other grrrl zine definitively announces, "silence is complicit with oppression," or "silence is a middle-class tactic," or (specifically and especially grating) "your silence follows guidelines and values about behavior and manners and passivity that I never could learn to follow. Your silence says nothing to me about who you are, so why should I trust you." (*wrecking ball*) But speech (as the imagined opposite of silence) does not always = truth, okay? I think this is fucking offensive: silence is one way I've *always* resisted and I'm so fucking sick of whitegirls negating --and I mean *actively* refusing to recognize-- the ways in which I resist their/*your* fucking intrusions. Like, these (politeness, quietude) are all distancing strategies that I think have everything to do with my being a refugee/alien (English not being my native language, "America" not being a space nearly comprehensible enough) and Vietnamese (and, duh, being raised a *Buddhist*) in the U.S., completely specific to the ways I learned to cope with invasive questioning or commands. Subaltern histories of colonized peoples document native acts of resistance that confounded Europeans (and obviously continue to do so, at least in riot grrrl): silence was only *one* tactic. *My* silence deliberately says nothing to you about me: *I* don't trust *you*, so why *should* I reveal any part of myself?

"At first I did not speak because of her order; later I found not speaking to be a useful form of resistance. I would stand mute before her, even when being questioned, which added to her rage and frustration." –Kartar Dillion, "The Parrot's Beak," in *Making Waves: An Anthology of Writings By and About Asian American Women*

continues on page 27.

12

SLANT 5 (EXCERPT)

continued from page 12.

I know a *hapa* (half-white, half-Japanese) girl who resisted validating the totally colonizing appropriations of a whitegirl who wanted to be fucking down on the racial tip; she refused to speak to her about it. I understand this: we get tired of explaining the obvious. Why bother, when whitegirl would probably just colonize our experiences as her own, anyway? Whitegirl wrote a song about her, about how she was oppressing whitegirl with her silence. Some (white) girls just don't get it. *Get it?*

"The most problematic of [Euro-American] feminist methodologies are those which are based on the premise of the personal is political....I remember cringing when one of my campus women's center meetings began with the check-in topic, what do you like/dislike about your body? I had no desire to share intimate information with a group of voyeuristic women eager to learn about an exotic Easterner. How could I describe my childhood self-hatred to a roomful of women who bore so much resemblance to the cruel little white girls who once told me that my brown skin was ugly?" -- Sayantani Dasgupta, "Reinventing the Feminist Wheel," *Z Magazine* (September 1994)

In November 1994 I went to the Bikini Kill/Riot Grrrl show at Gilman Street with an agenda. I got up on stage after the second-to-last band and made a speech, fueled by my frustration over recent clinic bombings in California, asking for clinic defense volunteers. (I'd been going out to clinics every Saturday and organizing car pools in the East Bay.) This is what I wrote about that night.

November 1994: Our revolutionary, incendiary slogans stencils across t-shirts and backpacks and we scream them at the top of our lungs on a graffiti-ed stage, and then what--? I saw you dance, joyfully, defiantly, I love it/you, I thought it meant more than it did. I asked you (over two hundred of you) to join me, I asked you in a space where I thought, happily, "How can you not?" I stood on stage after two women sang/screamed: "I'll get an abortion if I want to! Fuck you and your Bible too!" You listened and said your "right-ons" and raised your fists. I felt like I was not alone in my fear, my anger, my outrage. And I tried to move you: I thought I had. And then you avoided eye-contact with me once I came down off that stage, you turned your silk-screened backs to me.

I *am* pissed and I won't pretend it's not you I'm angry at. After you screamed your songs and strutted your bad-ass punk grrrl attitudes and paraded your slogans like so much cheap costume jewelry, I was left standing talking as if underwater or in Vietnamese. I used to think that I was one of you, or that you were one like me; but girl power t-shirts a revolution it doesn't make, honey, and I learned that it *doesn't* make for a revolutionary, either.

I approached you and your friends, raucously decorated in glitter and grrrl slogans and cat stickers, and I though maybe, if I asked you directly, let you *see* the invitation, the need for you to be there with me, how could you not? (I repeat myself in disbelief.) No blood or exchange of souls involved. But instead, and I couldn't believe it (but had to), you looked away in every direction but mine. Your sweater buttons and lunch-box clasps became hypnotic and I could not break the spell of your deliberate disinterest. Not even a simple "no," you muttered something unintelligible under your sweet-candy-girl breathe, if anything at all. Deliciously foul-mouthed, ruby red lips twitching: I was distasteful to you. I waded through a crowd of you that became to me, despite your stars and bright words, hostile. I was alien here.

I left before Bikini Kill took the stage. I don't think I've ever, ever felt quite so betrayed by my so-called punk rock feminist revolutionary soul crusader sisters, et al. To me, it seemed/seems the revolution, girl-style, shrunk/shrinks to fit the size of your zine, the lyric sheet I shove in my pocket when I get out of the car, square my shoulders and face another bleary-morning confrontation with anti-abortion extremists blocking sidewalks and doors and women's lives.

"Some chick says thank you for saying all the things I never do, I say you know the thanks I get is to take all the shit for you." –Ani DiFranco, "Face Up and Sing"

End of Part One.

27

307

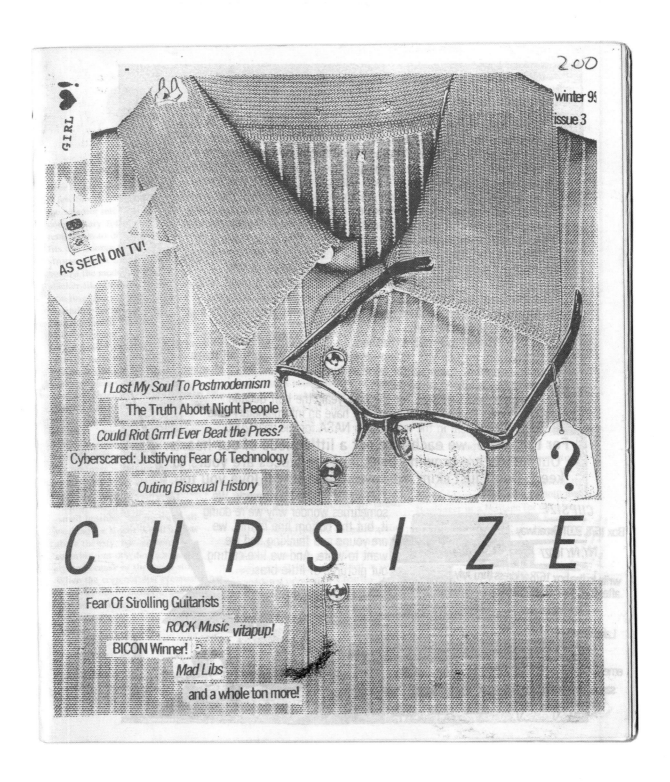

GIRL

AS SEEN ON TV!

winter 99
issue 3

I Lost My Soul To Postmodernism

The Truth About Night People

Could Riot Grrrl Ever Beat the Press?

Cyberscared: Justifying Fear Of Technology

Outing Bisexual History

?

C U P S I Z E

Fear Of Strolling Guitarists

ROCK Music vitapup!

BICON Winner!

Mad Libs

and a whole ton more!

CUPSIZE 3 (EXCERPT)

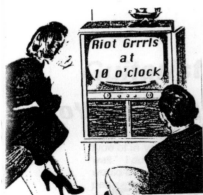

Dealing with any press and/or media can be very difficult--often in their quest to be objective, opposite ends of the spectrum are presented by never the gray area in between--like "All Riot Grrrls are man-haters," and "no, Riot Grrrls are not man-haters." How about the truth, like some Riot Grrrls hate men, some don't?--Kirsten Frickle

Directions: pls read these three quotes and then proceed to 'ext. Don't sit too close to the tv.

the mainstream press tends to distort things and get everything all out of proportion...this is because in mainstream media everything operates with signifiers, stereotypes and summaries. that's how a story is built to get the audience's attention. usually the story is summarized and often sensationalized and also the media likes to use spokespeople or symbols and rg doesn't lend itself well to that.-- Jordana Robinson

the reporters hardly ever seem to understand a few basic things about riot grrrl. like we don't gave a cohesive philosophy or dogma. it seems like even though we try to tell them they just can't seem to grasp the idea of a movement of individuals working together without some kind of map or chart or set of rules. if reporters don't understand that, they understand even less that we are actively and continually trying to eliminate hierarchy when possible. it seems like you could look a reporter in the face and say a thousand times, 'there are no leaders,' and they'll still write 'so-and-so, the president of riot grrrl.'-fantastic fanzine

I asked myself these questions not so long ago: By hiding in the underground, did Riot Grrrl keep itself from becoming a feminist identity for a wider group of girls in America? By persistently avoiding interaction with the mainstream press, did Riot Grrrl preclude the possibility of having a broad cultural impact?

These questions evolved into an end-of-the-semester paper. The research that I did directed me to the answer that as a culturally specific movement, any representation of Riot Grrrl to a mass audience loses a lot more in translation than it gains in the numbers of adherents it might pick up. RG is such an unwieldy subject to write about because it is so rooted in punk and feminist theory (though not necessarily framed in academic language) and most down-home Americans I know are fluent in neither punk nor feminism.

According to the comments from these grrrls, the space limitations and structural dictates of journalistic writing effectively rule out any chance of really communicating what Riot Grrrl is about. They question whether it would be possible for the mainstream media to ever accurately represent Riot Grrrl.

The word limit of a typical feature would prevent the journalist from presenting nuanced understanding of RG. RG's philosophies and modes of operation require pages of explanation. Ten pages of the New York Times Magazine might do it, a two-page feature in TIME wouldn't. The journalistic tendency to quote opposite poles of the spectrum would also prevent a more "authentic" look at RG (as in some RG's hate men, some don't). Since RG refuses a certain set of goals, there is no easy wrap-up of its purpose without distorting RG's intent. And because RG refuses a hierarchical structure, it doesn't make a very easy interview for a regular Jane or Joe reporter. There's no club president so, YOU'LL HAVE TO INTERVIEW EVERYONE. The endgame is that RG encourages grrrls to tell their own stories, write their own zines, make their own music and reject corporate media--the mainstream media would have little interest in selling the movement so well that they would lose subscribers and viewers. For these reasons, it seems that the media would never really do more than titillate the reader and present incomplete assessments of the RG movement.

7

? RIOT GRRRL

It seems fairly obvious that the mainstream media would exploit a story like RG--but what I wondered was whether RG could manipulate the media to its advantage, like the Lesbian Avengers and ACT-UP have done. Because of the unique (anti)philosophy and structure of the RG "movement," there seem to be limited possibilities for engaging in outreach through the channels of mainstream media. RG is simply too anarchic, and because it positions itself in opposition to "Older feminists, seventies, NOW, MS." as one respondent put it, RG is not in a position to learn tactical tricks of media work from more experienced activists.

The result of all the past media hoopla is the birth of a population of hipsters who think that they know something about RG and feel free to make their various judgments, without ever really understanding anything about it. Before I did my research, I would estimate that I had only generalized, caricatured impressions of Riot Grrrl. As I got more and more involved with the project, it became increasingly clear that I had come into the paper with little real understanding of what RG is (or was) about. For example, in my first questionnaire, I spelled grrrl with two r's. That was an immediate tip-off of my outsider status. That might seem initially surprising in light of the fact that I basically fit the RG demographic: a young feminist who goes to RG and RGish events. The "riot grrrl" label has even been applied to this zine. One would expect that I would have some familiarity with RG tenets and lingo. But like almost everyone else who thinks that she or he can make a judgment about RG, everything I ever heard about it was filtered through the lens of the (mostly) mainstream media. THE FACT IS THAT MOST OF US REALLY NEVER KNEW ANYTHING ABOUT IT. Us being those who weren't involved first-hand or didn't have direct access to RG culture. Most people took their SPIN soundbite accounts of Riot Grrrl and ran with them, feeling free to apply the label to any feminist or female rocker. The research I did convinced me that while "the media" is structurally incapable of delivering anything approximate to the truth about RG, they have succeeded in convincing the general gen x public that they know something about it.

It seems unfortunate that one wouldn't really "get" Riot Grrrl without having had first-hand contact with a group, a Riot Grrrl or a RG zine, because there are severe limitations on the people who will be reached through personal, underground means. There are so many girls out there who would benefit from the knowledge that something other than Seventeen and Sassy (RIP) exist. Is Riot Grrrl dead? I don't think you can answer that question, given that RG is so decentralized and has emerged in different communities since groups in DC, NY and Olympia have ceased to exist. I have pretty much concluded that RG isn't equipped to "recruit" through most media with large audiences, but I don't think that because RG is incapable of that kind of work, that all forms of grrrl activism are similarly disabled.

Sarah Dyer's experience is a taste of success. She publishes Action Girl, a newsletter that lists girl zines and resources. Sarah has been contacted by Fox TV, Sassy, Seventeen and has carefully considered the pros and cons of working with the mainstream media. She wrote:

There's only so much preaching to the converted you can do before it gets pointless--we've got to find ways to bring information to people who haven't been exposed to it at all...(in response to 'can you work with the mainstream media without losing your integrity?' Yes. I think so. Consider each decision very carefully. What is my advantage? What is the person's/media's advantage? Who will benefit most? I think it depends on exactly what's being promoted. A resource, a philosophy, a message--those should be mainstream. A zine, a band, an individual, no.

continued on pg 28

8

RIOT GRRRL cont. from p.8

Rejecting offers from the rest, Sarah chose to work with Seventeen. The magazine had received a number of letters from readers asking about zines, and they wanted to expose their readers without plugging one zine. (This is very responsible behavior--according to Sarah, Sassy has reviewed more than one zine without telling the editor, and has consequently spelled the zine's demise by sending unexpected mountains of orders). Seventeen rented a PO Box for the orders for Action Girl and gave Sarah "the most incredibly accurate review I have ever gotten. So much for punk rock." As a result, Sarah has received over 600 orders for Action Girl from girls who would have never had access to underground culture. Sarah's experience proves that it is not entirely possible to engage in a productive dissemination of underground resources and culture. (to read more about it, write away for Kikizine through Action Girl.)

I really admire Sarah's careful consideration of the issues at stake and her commitment to girl activism that incorporates a target group that extends beyond strict "scene" identifications. I think that we should all really think about how we can get through to people who could really benefit from the knowledge that independent girl-produced culture exists. No, we'll never reach everyone, not even close, but I think it's far too easy to sit back and uncritically resolve that it's "sell-out" to work with a mainstream media source.

AND we should all ask ourselves what we ever really knew about Riot Grrrl that wasn't tainted by the biases of the mainstream press. Yes, it sucks that RG, as a function of its form and content, has been almost entirely inaccessible and that it has been impossible for almost any source with a large readership to really disseminate information about it. Does that effectively rule out dialogue on the Riot Grrrl movement, except among the few with insider privilege? Perhaps--so let's start talking about a Girl Power movement, the new (rather than third) wave of the feminist movement. Yeah come on, Intervention Grrrl-Style Now and Forever! S Thanks a ton to everyone who answered the survey. —S

It's somewhat difficult to summarize fifteen pages in a zine. If you would like a copy of the paper, send me a few stamps and I will send it to you. But of course you must first prove to me that you will use it only toward the promotion of honest and thorough dissemination of RG information. Thank you.

cont. from p.13

All such academians are not hippies. They are older and misguided and often chauvinist despite pledges and disclaimers at the beginning of the term that it's for important reasons that we are not studying George Eliot this term, even though she was a great Victorian novelist and this class is Victorian Literature. These professors think that because they say "HE/SHE" now as second nature that they are liberated. It takes more than a pronoun change. They reminisce outloud about past student bodies who were full of vigor and energy (those of the sixties, to be exact...no joke. If they weren't part of it themselves, they long to teach the kids of the sixties, AGAIN) , openly insulting a room full of living, thinking , young people. Come on, you were also 30 years younger then. That probly has a lot to do with your fondness for 1969.

After hearing about it for 30yrs, we gotta believe a little that the sixties was a groovy time to grow up. But I don't attend class to witness living icons from the era telling what would have been thought about texts then. Or to be sold the idea that America is creepy and sneaky. I have my whole life to find that out.

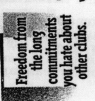

CUPSIZE gives you **Freedom from the long commitments you hate about other clubs.**

Back Issues: $1 and 2 stamps for each issue, please.
CS#1: subway anxiety, mike kaniecki interview, the truth about our cupsizes, the color brown, and much more.
CS#2: squatter interview, women writers, stonewall reflections, the legendary snapple/ fruitopia debate, long island coffee scene.
In every CS: music and laughs.

28

Beware. When you least expect it, you may be victim to the Zen Stare. But them be grateful, for it will make you a more honest, true, and articulate human being.

I first experienced the zen stare three years ago. I was super-hyper and nervous, all set to beg and bother a certain professor to get into his class. I thought the class would change my life. The class didn't-the zen stare did. Upon entering his office, he turned with a look of total peace and attention on his face. Shook my hand. Asked my name. Emitted a magical sense of peace and power that demanded that my own demeanor fall in line. He let me into the class. The zen stare stopped my anxiety right en route. I was stunned; silenced; awed. That is the zen stare.

Since my first exposure to the zen stare and my gradual maturing, I have cultivated my own power of zen stare that is essential to my existence, survival, and unique expression of goodwill to others. I use the zen stare on girls who are not pro-girl. Who are stuck in 3rd grade gossip/back-stabbing behaviour and want to share it with me and drag me into it. Basically all people who engage in bogus converstaions as a way of life that goes beyond the pleasures of flirting and socializing. And especially passive-aggressive types.

Other zen stare situations:gooey, kissy, super-hyper people running up to me all "hey" and what's up" just for the hell of it. They had better chill. You can't be that happy to see me. → The ALL POWERFUL

Other potential targets- people who cannot interact unless they are somehow entertaining me and getting a reaction. I take this as an insult after a while, like I am just there to be provoked. If I wanted people to constantly make me laugh, I'd go to comedy clubs and be a groupie. This is so oppressive and demands so much of my energy and I just want to say "fuck off"...but the zen stare works even better than that cathartic phrase.

When you use the zen stare, you refuse to be manipulated. You keep eye contact with the person, smile, and listen, as if you are taking them seriously. YOU ARE NOT ACTING in this behaviour. You are giving them the benefit of the doubt, trusting them, telling them you are not bullshitting. You become a spiritual mirror; they see themselves and calm down. They get real. ★ ☺ ☺ ★ ZEN STARE!←

Using the zen stare is delightful. It truly incapacitates and it is GOOD FOR PEOPLE. It feels good. They know when it's happening. It's disarming. It may sound a bit cruel, but in the end it is good for others. It is more gentle and constructive towards people that in the past you may have written off as just worthless. And it allows you to exist in the world and not be a total hermit or thorn-in-the-side cynic.

I think I actually assaulted my entire english class once with the zen stare. It was just when my zen stare powers were getting really fine-tuned. One particular meeting was so boring and outa whack when it's usually a great class. It was a waste of everyone's time that day and I was definitely exuding a "get real" zen stare vibe. Next thing I know, class is being dismissed 1/2 hour early.

Sometimes the zen stare requires compete and brutal honesty. Other times, you respond to the person's bogusnesss as if it were spoken with integrity so they

feel really stupid having to prolong their act. It is hard to pinpoint. But when you feel it you know it, and when you use it , you improve the world. E   18

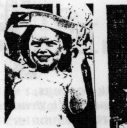

Sasha   Emelye

Sasha and Emelye Out on the Town in Baby Doll Wear

"We felt so liberated!"

When women dress like girls (not grrrls): *the Village Voice* set out to tell me what infantile garb on mature women is all about. The *Voice's* article argued that for some women, girl fashion represents a return to early adolescence, the period that precedes the command to shut up and simper. Pigtails are somehow empowering because they harken a pre-oppressed playground, an age of innocent liberation. To promote this one page article, I might mention that the *Voice* also didn't hesitate to include a scantily clad model on the cover.

I think there is a certain element of truth in the sociological studies that have isolated the period around 12 years of age as a time when American girls start to lose a sense of themselves and become less assertive, more quiet and removed. Pre-hesitation girlhood was an era of less inhibited existence. But for me, being a girl was not about wearing provocatively tight clothing and pigtails. The beauty of that period cannot be invoked by carrying a lunch box around with me. If I choose to adorn myself with girl-child clothing, my uniform will suggest youth, but cotton candy outfits are not going to transform my spirit into a nostalgic girl emancipation.

I see the girl-woman baby tee as more a Lolita sex creation than a form of empowerment. This is the fashion INDUSTRY, a profit-motivated enterprise that co-opts fashions that sincerely signify girl-power and sells them back to alterna-stores and mall outlets for maximum profit. The politics get watered down somewhere between the riot grrrl signifying aesthetic and the SKU coding of the price tag. Let's face it, tight t-shirts scream little girl fetish before they do girl's game on the playground.

At 99X, a hipkid downtown retail outlet, every article of "women's" clothing this summer was shrunken to pre-high school proportions. The fabiric allotted in the "women's" section was half that in the "men's." **Prominently displayed:** a tiny pink tee with **"Baby"** inscribed in the form of the Barbie logo. "Baby" doesn't quite speak girlpower to me. We are not creating these signs, insignias, dress codes to express our own return to girlhood. They are being created for us, from the hierarchy above, to fatten corporate dividends. It's pretty simple really, I don't think anyone really pretends to buy empowerment at the cash register. Tight clothing sells because it's sexy. Not that there's anything wrong with dressing sexy—I would just rather that the *Voice's* commentators don't couch the trend in absurd liberation metaphors to justify putting models on the cover.

It'smre than a little silly to call a trend of tight shirts and short skirts a meaningful return to "pure" girlhood. Baby tees no revolution make. ∫

 25

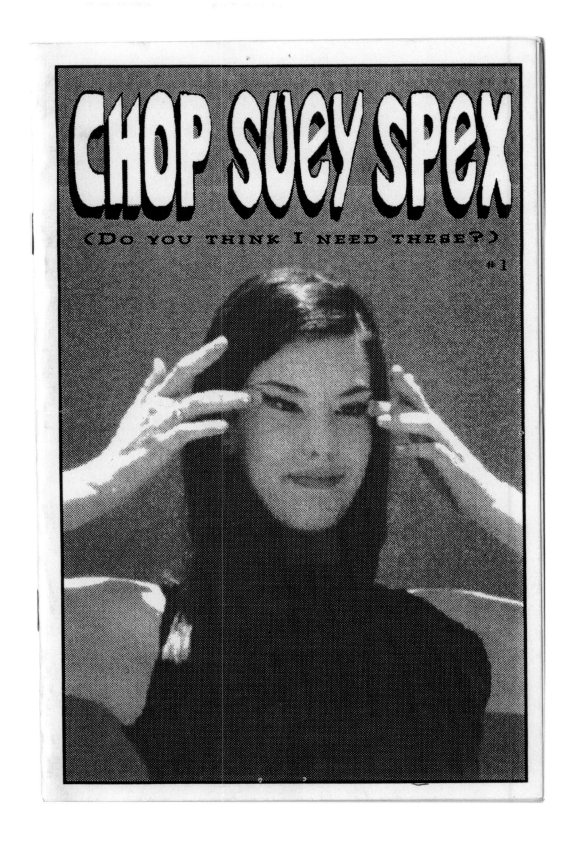

CHOP SUEY SPEX 1 (EXCERPT)

CHOP SUEY SPEX

February 1ˢᵗ, 1997
Happy Chinese New Year
y'all! don't forget to wear
red & eat an orange.

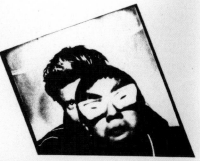

We made this zine to document our experiences, call shit out, have some fun, and most importantly, start some conversations.

It's really fucked that so many white folks in punk communities don't think or talk critically about racism. As a result, a lot of racist shit goes unchecked, and some of it even gets laughs. There's a big difference between something that "offends" (ie: something that is in "Bad Taste") and something that is racist-- something that reminds you that your ass is fair game for verbal harassment and physical attack.

We recognize that racist representations are integral to the maintenance of a white supremacist power structure. In other words, if Exene didn't sell Chop Suey Specs, someone else would. It's racism filtered through white liberal capitalism. But let's call it Amerikkkana.

Introduction, Greeting and/or Is there a purpose for this beyond "exene-bashing"?

I'll be honest with you: I didn't do a lot of soul searching about wheter it is a waste of time to do a zine about something that happened to me. I mean, my favorite zines are exactly about someone's personal experiences. What if one particular experience involved a "celebrity" (Exene Cervanka)? What if that celebrity, who is known as having progressive politics, does something fucked up that affects me directly? Should I just chill out because, after all, we're in the same corner? But we are not in the same corner, really. Sure, I don't eat meat or wear fur, I recycle, I love animals, plants and minerals alike and I want to save the whales. Come on, I still haven't met anyone who doesn't want to save the earth. But I'm so sick of these (mostle white) liberal types who think they can get away with racist crap. They have to be called on their shit. Especially when, by virtue of their celebrity status, they have access to a public forum (bands, spoken word Cds, books, stores)..

Exene Cervenka is the owner of a store in Los Angeles. That store sells "toys" that poke fun at Asian people. I'm Chinese, I can't "play" with these toys. I talked to Exene about how excluded and (sigh) hurt and yes, angry I felt by these toys. She didn't give a fuck. These are my facts. Am I supposed to protect this "progressive" celebrity? And who protects me?

KARLA: I've had a few encounters with the Chop Suey Specs. My first was at a Tribe 8 show at "You've Got Bad Taste" on Sunset in Silverlake. Before the show I

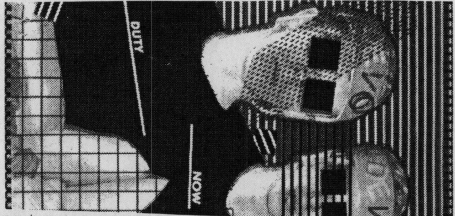

was hanging out with Lala and Kelly. I was really excited to see Tribe 8 live because they are punk rock <u>and</u> there are women of color in the band. Anyhow, Lala

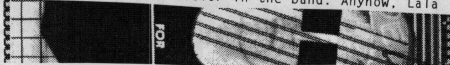

found a bunch of racist glasses for sale. We were like, "What the fuck is this?" We were wondering what we should do and then we realized Exene (store owner) was

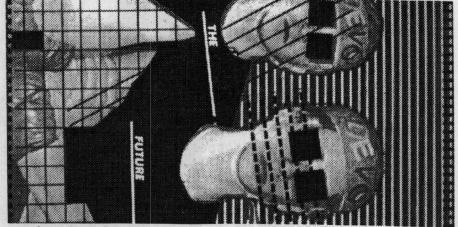

nearby. We thought an Asian chick delegation was in order. But as typical Asian women, we were too timid to approach. Then Exene came toward us and I spoke up.

CHOP SUEY SPEX 1 (EXCERPT)

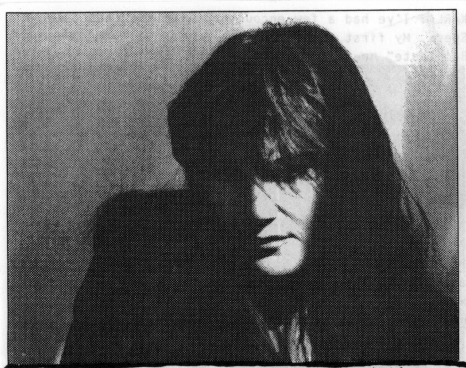

KARLA: Excuse me. Hi. We were wondering what's up
with these glasses.
LALA: (to Exene) Do you think I need these?
EXENE: What?
LALA: Do you think I need these?
KARLA: What's up with these glasses? This is racist.
EXENE: The store is called, "You've Got Bad Taste."
They are in bad taste.
KARLA: This is more than bad taste. How do you think
Asian people feel when they see this?
EXENE: It's bad taste. We specialize in Americana.
I'm sure a lot of women are offended by the nudie
stuff.
KARLA: Maybe, but the all the nudie stuff you have
glorifies white women's sexuality. These glasses are
██████████ racist. They take it too far.
EXENE: Whatever. I don't care. You can steal them.

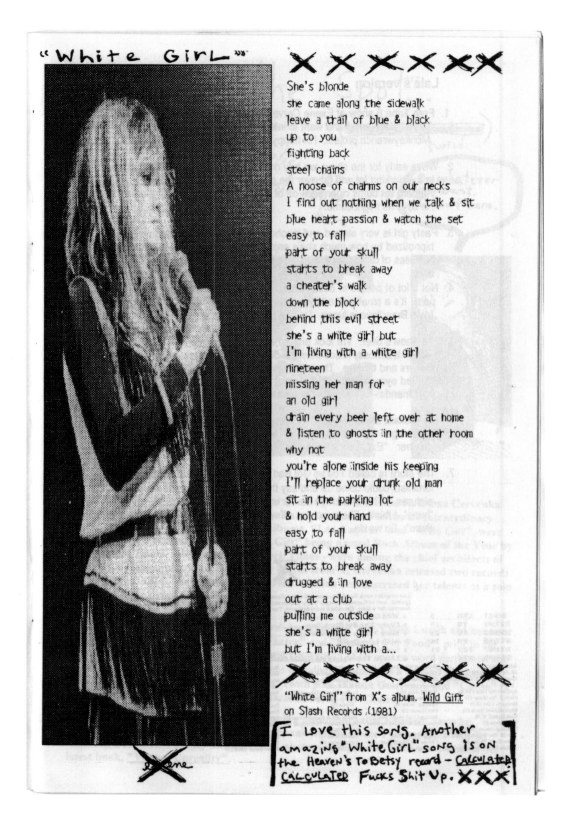

"White Girl"

XXXXXX

She's blonde
she came along the sidewalk
leave a trail of blue & black
up to you
fighting back
steel chains
A noose of charms on our necks
I find out nothing when we talk & sit
blue heart passion & watch the set
easy to fall
part of your skull
starts to break away
a cheater's walk
down the block
behind this evil street
she's a white girl but
I'm living with a white girl
nineteen
missing her man for
an old girl
drain every beer left over at home
& listen to ghosts in the other room
why not
you're alone inside his keeping
I'll replace your drunk old man
sit in the parking lot
& hold your hand
easy to fall
part of your skull
starts to break away
drugged & in love
out at a club
pulling me outside
she's a white girl
but I'm living with a...

XXXXX

"White Girl" from X's album. Wild Gift
on Slash Records. (1981)

I love this song. Another amazing "White Girl" song is on the Heaven's To Betsy record — CALCULATED. CALCULATED Fucks Shit Up. XXX

eXene

CHOP SUEY SPEX 1 (EXCERPT)

Lala's version

1. Free Tribe 8 show at Exene Cervenka's Silverlake store You've Got Bad Taste. Kelly and Karla want to interview Leslie Mah for their Monkeywrench project. I'm happy to be in L.A.

2. We're early for the show, we buy drinks at the 7 eleven nearby. We sit in the parking lot and go over the questions for Leslie. A homeless Vietnam vet bums cigarrettes off of Karla. We tell him about the show. He says he might come.

3. Pasty girl is very stoned and incoherent (am I being redundant?) We're hipnotized by how much she's enjoying her tofu delight ice cream and her tales of dead Carpenters.

4. Not a lot of people in attendance. Die hard fans and Exene's hipster pals. It's a small and oddly-shaped space for a show. Tribe 8 rocks. Lynn Breedlove is funny. I'm in a good mood.

5. The show's over. We look around the store while we wait to talk to Leslie. It's mostly kitsch from the 50's, plastic dolls and game boards and stickers and the like. There's a pair of costume eyeglasses with fake slanted eyes (made out of plastic) --Don this oriental disguise and fool your friends!-- It's a party toy meant to be worn by non-asian people.

6. I'm hesitant about confronting Exene. Karla is pumped and she encourages me to speak up. We ask Exene if we can have a word with her. "Excuse me," I begin, "do you think I need these?"

7. "The store **is** called You've Got Bad Taste. It's bad taste. A lot of feminists could come up and say that it's sexist to have all the girlie pictures." This she offers as her cocky version of an excuse. More like "lame", I think. She sends us off with something like "Whatever. Steal them". So we do.

X

Los Angeles rock band: Christine "Exene" Cervenka (vocals), "John Doe" Nommensen (vocals), Tony Gilkyson (guitar, son of Canadian singer Terry Gilkyson) and D.J. Bonebrake (drums). Cervenka and Doe were married for a time. Cervenka recorded with The Knitters.

6/6/81	165	5	1 Wild Gift	812	Slash 107
7/17/82	76	15	2 Under The Big Black Sun	88	Elektra 60150
10/8/83	86	23	3 More Fun In The New World	88	Elektra 60283
8/17/85	89	14	4 Ain't Love Grand	88	Elektra 60430
7/11/87	107	11	5 See How We Are	88	Elektra 60492
5/14/88	175	5	6 Live At The Whiskey A Go-Go On The Fabulous Sunset Strip......[L]	810	Elektra 60788 [2]

Adult Books (1)
All Or Nothing (4)
Anyone Can Fill Your Shoes (5)
Around My Heart (4.6)
Back 2 The Base (1)
Because I Do (2.6)
Beyond And Back (1)
Blue Spark (2.6)
Breathless (3)
Burning House Of Love (4.6)
Call Of The Wreckin' Ball (6)
Come Back To Me (2)
Cyrano De Berger's Back (5)

Dancing With Tears In My Eyes (2)
Devil Doll (3.6)
Drunk In My Past (3)
4th Of July (5)
Have Nots (2)
Holiday Story (5)
Hot House (3)
House I Call Home (6)
How I Learned My Lesson (2)
Hungry Wolf (2.6)
I Must Not Think Bad Thoughts (3)

I See Red (3)
I'll Stand Up For You (4)
I'm Coming Over (1)
I'm Lost (5)
In The Time It Takes (5.6)
In This House That I Call Home (1)
It's Who You Know (1)
Johnny Hit & Run Pauline (6)
Just Another Perfect Day (6)
Left & Right (5)
Little Honey (4)
Los Angeles (6)
Love Shack (4)

Make The Music Go Bang (3)
Motel Room In My Bed (2)
My Goodness (4.6)
My Soul Cries Your Name (4)
New World (3.6)
Once Over Twice (1.6)
Painting The Town Blue (3)
Poor Girl (3)
Real Child Of Hell (2)
Riding With Mary (2.6)
See How We Are (5)
Skin Deep Town (6)
So Long (6)
Some Other Time (1)

Supercharged (4)
Surprise Surprise (5.6)
True Love (3.6)
True Love Pt. #2 (3)
Under The Big Black Sun (2)
Unheard Music (6)
Universal Corner (1)
Watch The Sun Go Down (4)
We're Desperate (1)
We're Having Much More Fun (3)
What's Wrong With Me... (4)
When It Rains... (5)

When Our Love Passed O On The Couch (1)
White Girl (1.6)
World's A Mess (6)
Year 1 (1.6)
You (5)

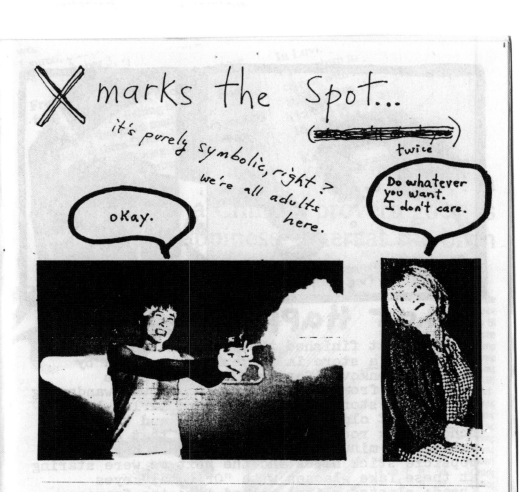

As the vocalist and lyricist for the seminal Los Angeles rock band X, Exene Cervenka has rightfully established her reputation as a performer and writer of extraordinary conviction and skill. X, whose first two albums, "Los Angeles" and "Wild Gift", were released to wide critical acclaim - "Wild Gift" being named Rock Album of the Year by both the Los Angeles Times and New York Times - were among the chief architects of the Los Angeles punk sound. During her hiatus from X, Cervenka released two records - "Old Wives' Tales" and "Running Sacred" - which demonstrated her talents as a solo performer.

In 1982, Cervenka co-authored **"Adulterers' Anonymous"** with **Lydia Lunch** and has since self published two books, **"Poetry Loves Poetry"** and **"Thought For Food"**, prior to her first book with 2.13.61 Publications, **<u>"Virtual Unreality"</u>**. As a spoken word performer, she has also appeared on various audio recordings including **"English as a Second Language"** (a spoken word compilation), **"Two Sisters"** (with poet **Wanda Coleman**), and **"Cause"** (a benefit compilation for the pro-choice organization **Rock For Choice**).

In 1992, Cervenka, along with award winning photojournalist Kenneth Jarecke, published **<u>"Just Another War"</u>** - a somber examination of the Persian Gulf War by means of Cervenka's poetry and Jarecke's photographs, and in 1993, she released her latest book, **<u>"Virtual Unreality"</u>**.

CHOP SUEY SPEX 1 (EXCERPT)

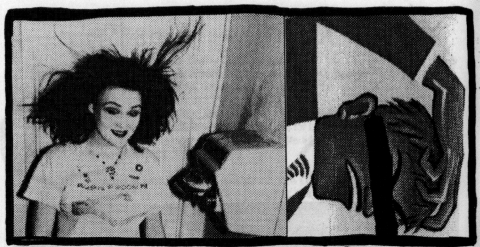

What Happened?

Tribe 8 just finished their set at "You've Got
Bad Taste" a store in Silverlake co-owned by
Exene Cervenkova (formerly known as Exene
Cervekanka from a band called X). I was wandering
around the store with my Lala and Karla, looking
at a lot of old stock merchandise and the old
school punk rock flyers and photos that cover the
walls. One minute we were looking at harmless
popsicle stick houses and the next we were staring
at these fake glasses with "Oriental" eyes
(read: slanted slits) molded into the frames.
They were sick and fucked up and we couldn't
understand why Exene would want to stock them.
We saw her walking by so we stopped her to ask.
Lala pointed to the Chop Suey Specs and asked,
"Do you think Ineed these ?" Exene maintained a
borderline blank stare. Then Karla told her we
thought the glasses were racist. Exene reminded
us that the store is called "Youve Got Bad Taste"
We told her that this was not an issue of of
GoodTaste-Badtaste. Then she told us that her
store specializes in Americana. Karla argued
that the Specs were Alienating to Asian customers.
This comment got us dismissed. Exene shook her
head and said, "Whatever. I don't care. ~~Something~~
Steal them." Then she walked away.

(XO)

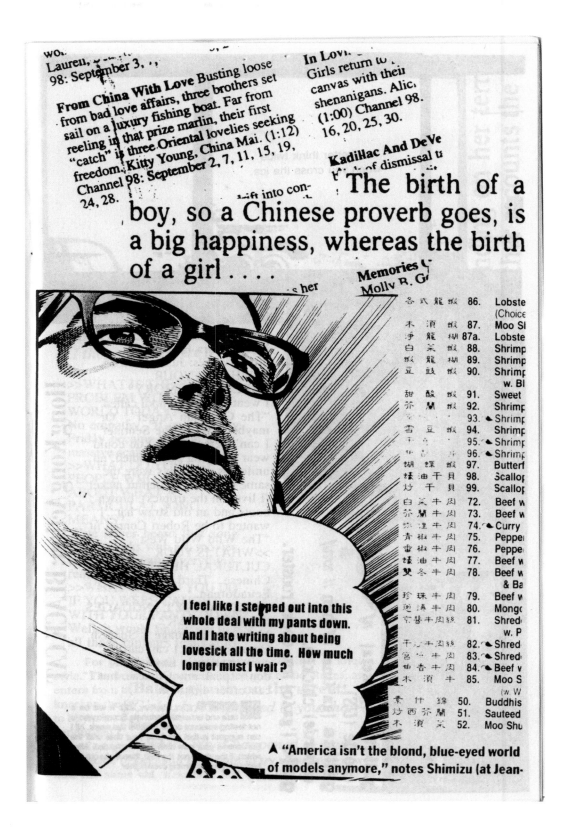

CHOP SUEY SPEX 1 (EXCERPT)

This rad Hawaiian girl named Barbara heard about the Chop Suey Specs and wanted to form an Asian delegation to storm the store and seize the entire box and tell them that Exene said we could steal 'em. Instead Barb braved the store by herself.

BARB: Do you have Chop Suey Specs?

WHITE GUY AT THE COUNTER: We sold out of them.

BARB: You did? I heard you had them.

GUY: We got rid of them because a bunch of people came in and said they were offended.

BARB: That's good cuz I know a lot of people that thought they were fucked.

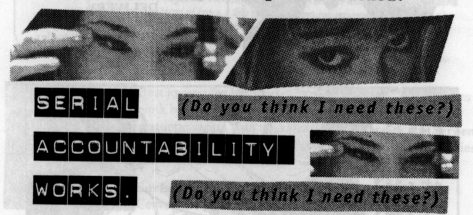

SERIAL *(Do you think I need these?)*

ACCOUNTABILITY

WORKS. *(Do you think I need these?)*

(Do you think I need these?)

my mom is chinese my dad is a whiteguy I'm the eldest my brother is a year and a half younger than me when we were kids we used to play games together and pretend we were race car drivers or the two boys from "flipper" and we wouldn't have pretend names we'd just ask each other "hey, amigo, are you allright?" my parents thought their firstborn would be a boy so they had already picked a name I got mine by default among all my chinese cousins my brother is ranked first in the "least chinese category" I get fourth place.

CHOP SUEY SPEX 1 (EXCERPT)

CHOP SUEY CHEX

by: Sabrina (age: 24, Echo Park)

Kelly: You went back?
Sabrina: Yeah.
K: Tell me what happened. Take yr time.
S: OK. I went in to steal something for you but I couldn't do it. You know me. Anyways, they put them back out again.
K: Where were they?
S: They were laid out on one of those middle rack things. ~~They weren't in the box.~~ They weren't in the box.
K: I thought you were gonna tell me they # were on the white sales dude.
S: There was a white sales dude. It's even more fucked up that the Chop Suey Spex are the only racialized ~~thing~~ thing in the store.
K: I know—those and the glorified naked white women.
S: Don't get me started on white wimmin...

01/97

no credits, it's more fun

Don't forget to check out recent developments in the continuing saga of that box of chop suey specs.

NEXT TIME:
An in-depth investigation into the politics of the new wave of white indie kids embracing the "Free Tibet" movement!

Kelly thanks The Fourth Wave - Diana, lala, Sabrina & Karla. (and my main man ~ York)

LALA WANTS TO THANK THE FOLLOWING:
Kelly, Karla, Barbara, De, Garrick, Laura, Ian, Sabrina, Heeyeon, Sasha, Alan, Diane and my Digital Imaging classmates, Juancho and my mom.

Send mail to = lala chop suey spex c/o
332 E. 4th #63
NY, NY 10009

OH YEAH, WE'RE ASKING ONE BUCK FOR THIS PIECE OF FINE LITERATURE. IF YOU DON'T THINK OUR "PRODUCT" IS WORTH IT, WHATEVER. WE DON'T CARE. STEAL IT. ☆

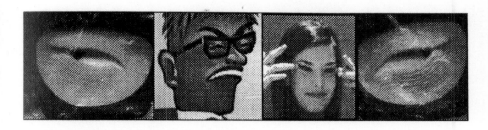

Fool your friends with this Oriental disguise??

The slit-eyed, bucktooth Jap thrusting his bayonet, thirsty for blood. The inscrutable, wily Chinese detective with his taped eyelids and wispy mustache. The childlike, indolent Filipino houseboy. Always giggling. Bowing and scraping. Eager to please, but untrustworthy. The sexless, hairless Asian male. The servile, oversexed Asian female. The Geisha. The sultry, sarong-clad South Seas maiden. The serpentine, cunning Dragon Lady. Mysterious and evil, eager to please. Effeminate. Untrustworthy. Yellow Peril. Fortune Cookie Psychic. Savage. Dogeater. Invisible. Mute. Faceless peasants breeding too many children. Gooks. Passive Japanese Americans obediently marching off to 'reclocation camps' during the Second World War.

—Jessica Hagedorn, NYC 1993 (editor, <u>Charlie Chan is Dead: An Anthology of Contemporary Asian American Fiction</u>).

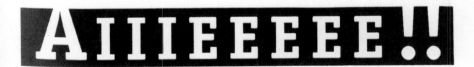

CHOP SUEY SPEX 1 (EXCERPT)

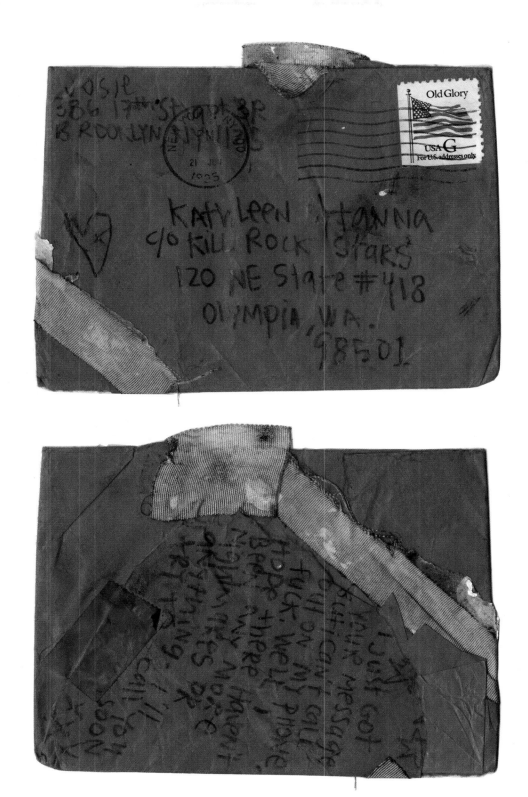

ENVELOPE

"SLY" Stallone (213) 828-8988
«Hi i just called to say: FUCK your
genocidal maniac movies."

July 14, 1994

→ Dear Big Hair Lady

1. essay smarty pants style about Patti Smith and Rimbaud that my teacher gave me. ~~[struck out]~~

2. i am really frustrated because i paid $40 for this piece of shit type-writer that worked really good in the store. and you know, this is not the first time.

3. "it grosses her out" is this thing i made two years ago but never printed + i finally did ~~#~~ last week because ONE: i realized that ~~i didn't put it out for fear of~~ i had been successfully intimidated by a certain contingent into believing that i was too much of an asshole to make photocopies. and i'm so over it. two: i didn't want to put out this new, more epic-like work without ~~this~~, documenting this certain period of my writing. It feels good to not be scared but also weird to print up something i'm sort of removed from. But also, who cares because i'm giving it to like 5 people. Its mostly just a favor to my future critical biographer ha ha.

4. THE OPPOSITE, PART I is my work-in-progress. I am sending you a big chunk (about half). It will hopefully be done on August fifth. That's what i pencilled into my filo-fax planner. I am not punk, I carry a Filofax. Its going to have a lot more drawings, color copies of my paintings + Dasha's video stills, more writing about art etc. I mean, who knows. But you gotta ~~[struck out]~~ dream.
   I would be grateful for any feedback, criticism. I ~~am~~ have tried to keep myself unattached to its present state and am willing to do surgery, trash parts etc. And, because you are both a subject w/in it and a major, major influence on me artistically i totally value your thoughts on it. AND on the same note: i realize that i am this total sponge that assimilates + regurgitates stuff that i look at/read/hear so please let me now if i am copping your style (or anyone else's that you know of) in a way that is not cool or should be credited. I lose perspective, you know, and i don't want to be creepy in that way that we both know about.

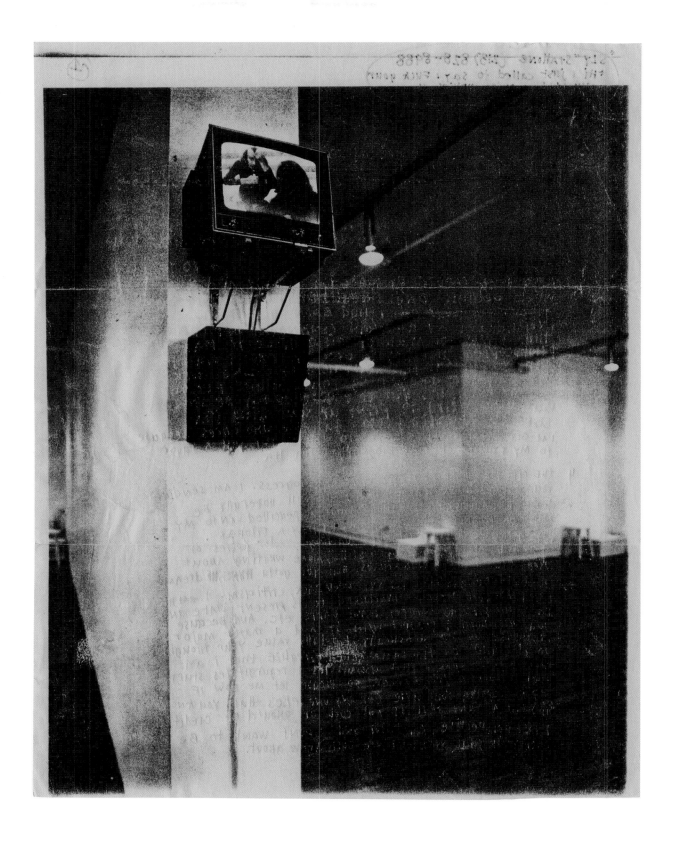

LETTER

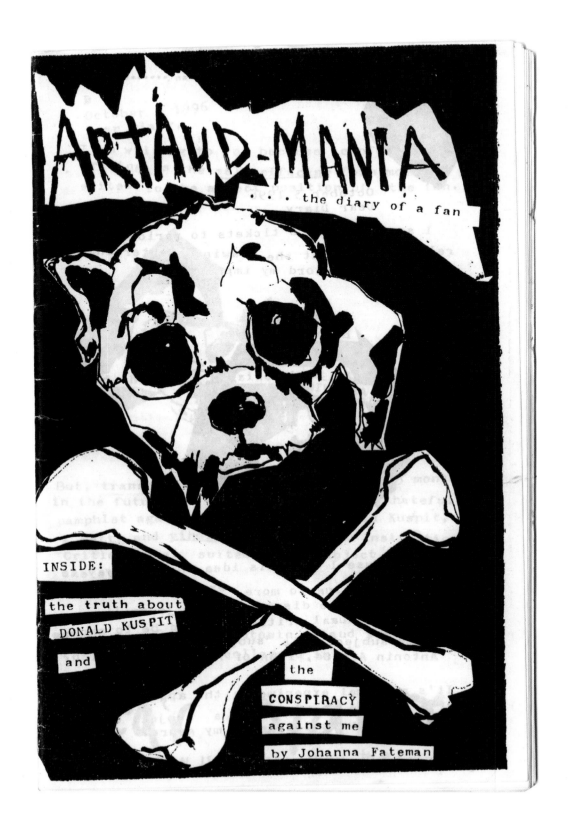

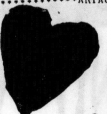

October 5 1996
Dear Diary,

I spent $50 on 6 tickets to various Artaud-related events at the Drawing Center and resolved to record my impressions.

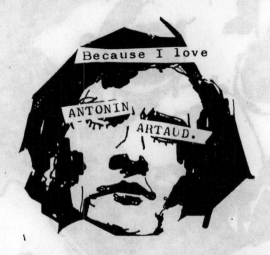

Because I love ANTONIN ARTAUD.

And because I had this idea that one way to get my writing to more explicitly mimic/depart from the disciplines of journalism and/or cultural criticism would be to choose as my subject this "subjectivity," Antonin Artaud, icon of Modern alienation.

It's a formal experiment: the application of a fanzine aesthetic to a subject outside the usual jurisdiction of my genre.

October 6 1996
Dear Diary,

I am writing to you because confessional
writing is the <u>self-effacing</u> form most
suited to the abject position of the fan.

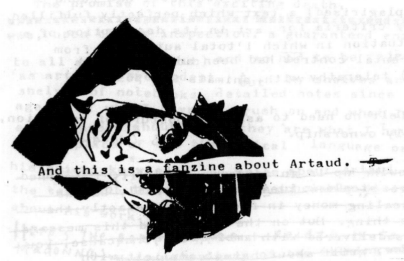

And this is a <u>fanzine</u> about Artaud.

But, transcribing these diary entries 3 months
in the future I will add: this is a hateful
pamphlet against the critic   Donald Kuspit,
a <u>petty</u> and <u>vindictive</u> strain of Institutional
Critique most suited to the abject position of
the student .

This is a letter to Antonin Artaud ~~from~~ written
from Art School   collapsed into

Dear Diary

cuz the pen is mightier than the sword, right?

I once wrote a novel called "Black Beauty" based
on the movie "Black Beauty"

I was unconcerned by my sister's critique
of the project based on a false notion of
originality and undeterred by the already
existing novel of the same name upon which the
movie had been based because I had found
(plagirised) a text which perfectly fulfilled
my criteria for art in its description of a
situation in which 1)total autonomy from
parental control had been achieved, and
2) telepathy with animals was possible.

I felt no need to assume a posture of invention,
only ownership.   THIS WAS CHILAHOOD.

~~Growing up in an academic community I learned
that stealing ideas was as morally bad as
stealing money in fact it was exactly the
same thing. But on the other hand this message
was delivered with ambivalence because, you
know, guilt about being complicit with
capitalism and, after all, it always depends
on who is stealing whax money from who, etc.~~

The lasting lesson of this was that even the
most menial methodologies conceived of as "in
homage" cannot excise imagination;
transcription was revealed as interpretive
and territorial.

ANTONIN aRTaud: aNother excuse to talk
aBouT MYSeIF...

Subsequent writings were no longer epic in their
aspirations. I got this new relationship
to culture as a white middle-class female,
narcissistic consumer. All artistic
production was/is for me a vanity or a therapy
and so takes this form:

ARTAUD—MANIA: THE DIARY OF A FAN

3 "Go Ask Alice," a canonical work of my literary
tradition, the diary of a young girl on the
Road to Ruin.   This pre-teen cult classic
circulated my junior high as a warning or a
dare to normal girls with moderate eating
disorders that we may very well end up
drug-addicted and dead.

The promise of this exciting death,
xpxnxxixaxexxxxpxxixanxxwxxxxnxhxxxixxxxndxxd
was, upon closer inspection, a guaranteed end

to all adventure (duh) and so had to be rejected
as artistic precedent. But My shelves and
shelves of notebooks, detailed notes since
age 12 of who I have a crush on and what I
am depressed about are they are what I have
in the place of the theoretical language or

historical knowledge to write about Artaud in
the terms of the established scholarly discourse
about his work.

Here's the PART WHeRe I ReLAte It to
MADONNA: Madonna's diary of the filming of
"Evita" in Argentina is published in the new
Vanity Fair. Her intimate disclosures as she
"gets into character" as Eva Peron seem relevant
to my Artaud Project if only for the mainstream
cultural example of a personal diary conceived
of from the beginning as a document for publica.

But also as a study of the psychology of
fantasy identification with a historical
figure (Madonna's strategy of ~~~~~~~~~~~~~~
renewing herself through icons of the past)..

She knows that evoking a pre-existing set of
references is inevitable to an extent, plus
it is economical. Madonna does not want to
reinvent the whe l.

Neither do I. xxxxx

dear diary,

It's two days before the first official Artaud event (Jacques Derrida and Gayatri Spivak at the Drawing center). I'm sitting at the Pick-a-Bagel near school with the new Village Voice.   Just finished reading Peter Schjeldahl's column, "MASTER OF MADNESS: Antonin Artaud: Works on Paper," a review of the Artaud drawings at the Museum of Modern Art.

The only way that he can identify with Artaud is in the tackiest possible way, theAmerican hippy affinity for Artaud's exploration of hallucinogens and his"trippy"poetics:

"I recognize an impulsive principle from my own chaotic experience in the 1960six, the most Artaudian of epochs. It was usual then to hear people say they needed to take more drugs and get their heads together."

(This xxxxxxixkxxx is clearly a sloppy reading of Artaud's
   position on drugs)

ARTAUD: My pointof view is clearly anti-social. ~~There is the~~ There is only one reason to attack opium. This is the danger that its use can inflict on society as a whole.
   But this danger is nonexistent   WE ARE BORN ROTTEN IN BODY AND IN THE SOUL, WE ARE CONGENITALLY   MALADJUSTED. . .

(THIS is NoT a HiPPY idea.)
ARtaud was diagNosed with heReditARY SYPHilis aNd was presCRiBed the opiate laudanuM wHich got hiM Hooked. But here, SchJeldahl must Be referriNg to ARtaud's coloNial experiment iN third-woRld mind expaNsioN. IN 1936 ANToNiN ARtaud, A white FreNcH MaN, traVels to MEXICO MotiVated BY 1) his racist NotioNs tHat "tHe LatiN-AMericaN psycHe" is someHow NaturaLLy predisposed to suRreaLIST aesthetics 2) his hoBBYistic iNterest iN astrology + pre-coLoNial CiVILIZatioN, aNd 3) tHe peyote rituals of the TarahuMara iNdigeNous people.
So wHile it's ridicylous to ~~iM~~ imply tHat aRtaud goT wasted to "get His Head togetHer," the NoRth- AMericaN 60's (+ its coUNtercultural LegacY) is for sure "ARtaud-iaN" iN its iNVolVemeNt with NoN- westerN culture Via patterNs of westerN coNsumer- culture + tHe proyectioN of coNtext-specific oppositioNal ideals oNto other cultures, "fiNdiNg" tHem alReady tHere. tHaT'S oNe waY to uNiVersaLize a value.
LoNg BefoRe Jim MorrisoN there was ANToNiN Artaud .

ARTAUD—MANIA: THE DIARY OF A FAN

Peter Schjeldahl writes the way that <u>Jerry</u> Springer wraps up his
talk show (the psychologically unified/stable, ~~text~~, benevolent last
word), the way that <u>Jerry</u> Seinfeld brackets his sitcom with those
stand-up comedy sequences, and of course, the way that <u>Jerry</u> Saltz
writes art criticism as well (NOT TO MENTION DONALD KUSPIT)

SANE COMMENTARY ON AN
INSANE WORLD

Its just boring to me.

Interestingly, Dan Savages's sex column this week is all about
allergic reactions to come. Artaud's ~~■■■■■■■■■■■■■■■~~
~~■■■■■~~ concern that ~~in~~ the attendants at the mental institution
were stealing his semen and shit (his soul, his ideas, his self)
and his virulent spells against such thievery ~~■■■■■■~~ come to
mind. I WISH MORE PEOPLE WROTE MORE like DAN Savage .

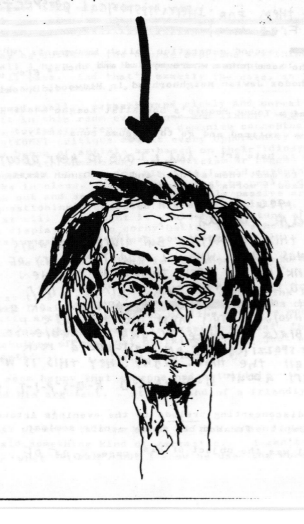

October 10, 1996
I was thinking of trying to get to Derrida's Artaud lecture
at the MoMA tonight but I didn't get off work until 7:30 and
the one of the heels of my shitty payless shoe source high
heels was wobbling. It cracked off entirely as soon as I
got in the door of my apartment. I think the lecture would
have been sold out anyway. I think Bella's there so she can
tell me about it. I feel bad about missing the inaugural event
of Artaud season, but hopefully I won't be so exhausted tomorrow
night.
My grandma called to see if I wanted to go to the Jewish
museum with her on Sunday. Something about clandestine
photography during the German occupation of Denmark. She
agreed to meet me at the Modern first to see Artaud's drawings.
She was reluctant at first: "Artaud? The schizophrenic woman-hater?
Is that what you want to see? "

I'm excited to see the exhibit with my grandparents.

**I exploit them for their historical perspective
and a free meal.**

They're ▰ second generation Polish immigrants who
live in the same house where my dad and uncles grew up
in an orthodox Jewish neighborhood in Midwood, Brooklyn.

They met at a Young People's Socialist League meeting.

Now they're retired and go to museums constantly.

They love to hate art. **And I love to hear about it!**

So I'm going to meet them at noon and have lunch first before we
check out Artaud's works on paper.

**October 11, 1996
Dear diary,
I know this is boring but diaries always
are. I was bored when I read "The Diary of
Anne Frank" in my early teens, bored when
I read Bob Flanagan's "Fuck Journal" last
night. But in both cases it was somehow ok and
I stayed involved. This must be because I
have a black + white tv and no cable so
I am not spazzing out on fast-paced rock
videos all the time, right? Hey this is where
the part about D-O-N-A-L-D K-U-S-P-I-T starts:**

As a disconcerting prelude to the evenings Artaud event,
Donald Kuspit freaked out in my senior seminar.

Sadly, I was the object of his rage, **Sort of.**

ARTAUD-MANIA: THE DIARY OF A FAN

The story with Kuspit's class is that he wrote this book recently
called "Idiosyncratic Identities" that is a collection of essays
about artists that I have very little interest in ~~(with the notable
exceptions of Marcel Duchamp and Jackson Pollock)~~, discussed in a
theoretical framework that ~~was~~ is, at best, pretty useless, and at
worst, creepy and ~~reactionaryxxxxx~~ politically conservative in its
implications. ▬▬▬▬▬▬▬▬▬▬▬▬▬▬▬▬▬▬▬▬▬▬▬▬▬▬▬▬▬▬
But content aside, Kuspit has structured the class with his book
as the only assigned text, and each week a couple of students
give class presentations on the artists he deals with in the book.

ITS AGONIZING.

Students at SVA are pretty accustomed to this type of academic
shoddiness, and it didn't really seem to bother anyone that
Kuspit's concept of "the idiosyncratic" ~~wxx~~ would serve as the
organizing principle and ideological monolith of the entire
semester. A lot of kids really dig Kuspit's style

To me it seemed like mind control, MAN.
▬▬   X
▬▬▬▬▬▬▬▬▬▬▬▬▬▬▬▬▬▬▬▬▬▬▬▬▬▬▬

From the way he outlined the course everyone was thinking: This
is great, all I have to do is summarize a chapter of this guy's
book and I'll pass. And that's exactly the case, so I don't know
why I opened my big mouth. . .

It just seemed really ~~pxthxtixxxnd~~ sickly and unreal that we could
all just sit in this room every week and listen, with no apparent
resistance, to this rotten ~~old~~ man demonize conceptual photography
and institutional critique ▬▬▬ at every opportunity whi'e
promoting a bunch of artists ~~xx~~ based on their"idiosyncratic "
involvement with numerology or mysticism or rugged individualism.
It was almost out of pity for him that I said anything the first
time I spoke in class. I thought it must be really depressing for
him to look out and see rows of completely passive art students who
either unquestioningly accepted his expert opinions, or who weren't
listening at all. I thought it would be a gesture of respect, or
at least a display of some corny belief in "scholarly exchange"
or "critical engagement" to say something..

I know you are thinking: "this is not about Antonin Artaud" but it
is somehow.

So the first time I said anything in class (I think it was like the
second week) I said that ▬▬▬▬▬▬▬▬▬ his concept of the
Idiosyncratic Artist sounded to me like a Genius model of
  artistic identity rephrased in ~~xxxxxxbxixxxxxf~~ the less
lofty vocabulary of"personal quirkiness", but just as
  deterministic.   He handled it ok.

  He did seem happy that someone had actually
considered his argument.   It was kind of a friendly discussion.

  BUT TODAY we were talking about Alfred Jensen. And first
  Jason said something kind of sarcastic.   I can't exactly
  remember what he said, but I know he used the word "mysterious"

in mocking reference to Jensen's work. Kuspit kept his head but seemed kind of irritated..He went on in his explanation of some painting that was these concentric circles XXX loosely painted with some accompanying script indicating their transcendant meaning to the artist. *The meaning of the circles, that is.*

Kuspit made some comment emphasizing the importance of the painting's "hand paintedXX, not computer generated" quality, implying thatXX this was a more immediate expr ssion, crucial to Jensen's id_iosyncratic identity."

Oh, I forgot to explain that idiosyncracy is the polar opposite' of Cynicism in Kuspit's terms. *I don't know why really.*

So this is what I said. I wish I had just kept my mouth shut becaus it's not like I really care about XX Alfred Jensen one way or the other, but I said: "I think it's kind of silly to see painting as a less mediated form of expression than the use of a computer to draw concentric circles. It seems like you are naturalizing painting." *←But I said it valley girl-style and not so concise.*

He remained calm but there was something weird about the way modulation of his voice and he addressed me with a gaze of pure hatred in the guise of bemused annoyance. I can't really figure out what exactly it was that provoked this response, but anyway, he first started to reiterate his argument and then he sort of broke off and said " and if you think it's silly, which is the position you've held since the beginning of this class, you should find a different class to be in." *Too late for that, Fuck-face. Drop/add week is over.*

I'm not communicating the drama of it. It was so unexpected unexpected and inappropriate, so personally attacking and insulting like it was highschool and I was getting thrown out of class for spitting gum at him. *Which, of course, is what I really wanted to do.*

People gasped in disbelief. He was so pissed. I froze up. I thought about grabbing my stuff and leaving and dropping the class (as he had suggested) and just never coming back but the consequences of this flashed quickly before my eyes (not graduating) and I just sat there paralyzed. Everyone kept glancing at me nervously and I started getting this crazy feeling like I was going to do something really bad, like I was going to escalate things beyond reconciliation and really get kicked out of the class. (I used to have a violent streak.) I was focusing intently on a complex fantasy about just how sorry Donald Kuspit will be some day andalso mentally composing a formal letter of complaint to the SVA administration and also worrying a little about getting to the panel discussion about Artaud on time when things got even weirder...

Somebody asked a question, it wasn't even a particularly smart-ass question. I think it was something questioning the difference between Jensen and a more conventionally modernist painter. I don't know really because, like I said, I really wasn't paying attention at this point.

Kuspit just closed his book and said "I cannot continue in the face of such cynicism." So class was dismissed almost an hour early. It was really disturbing. We were stunned. I was glad that I was going to have time to get a cup of coffee before the artaud event, but I felt bad like if Kuspit suicides tonight it will be my fault.

I mean, you know, like, partially my fault.

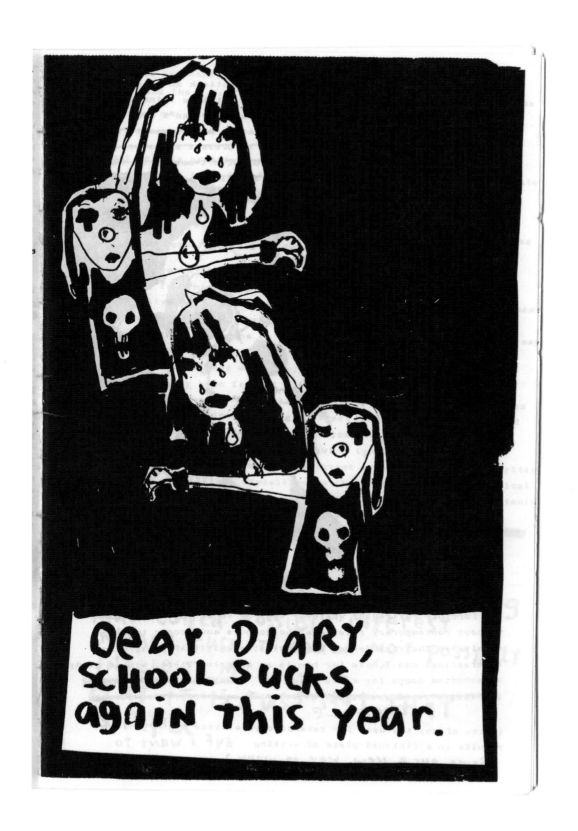

I am not without compassion for his bleak outlook on my generation and his generally depressive personality, but I do think he's got no business teaching a senior seminar if he can't deal with a 22-year old girl being a pain in the ass. ~~And it was infuriating to be called a cynic for caring enough to present a gesture of challenge or restitution to the endeavor of art-making in the face of his bitter nostalgia for a defunct idealism.~~

He
MISread
MY
SINCeriTy
totally.

But because I really have no power in this situation to have him forcibly retired or whatever they do to ~~be~~ big name academics without contemporary relevance who go nuts and become totally abusive to their students, the most strategic(self-preserving/ interesting) use I have for him is as a period piece, a case study of embodied dogma for me to react to. ~~XXXXXXXXXXXXXXXXXXXXXXXXXX~~

~~XXXXXXXXXXXXXXXXXXXXXXXXXX~~

aSSHoLe

(Quite often, the need for revenge crystallizes my thoughts and results in a finished piece of writing BYt I WaNt to Figure ouT a NEW way to work)

And this incident, ¶ punctuates my consuming interest in Antonin
Artaud and the N.Y. reception of his theorists, raising questions
about " my own critical approach to ▓▓▓▓▓▓ Artaud. "

Kuspit selects artists and theorizes their artistic practice
according to a taste-based promotional agenda justified by (ultimate
conservative) notions about individual/authentic expression,
using an artist and his or her work as the objectified and mute
illustration or evidence of a theoretical model but of course
this is precisely what I am doing with Artaud.

        I couch this ~~rhetorically (facetiously)~~ in the underdog
terms ^of the fan which always rely on ~~max~~ media fiction, and which
necessarily dehumanize ~~th~~ their object, and ~~itxix~~ it is through these
facts of fandom that I ~~prepare a xxcritique of xx~~ hold a mirror to
my underlying intentions as "critic." That is to say that when I say
"I love Artaud" I mean that I couldn't give a shit about Artaud
beyond his usefulness within my personal aesthetic and political
program. And my hope is that this honesty ~~▓▓▓▓▓▓▓▓▓▓▓▓▓▓~~
~~▓▓▓▓▓▓▓~~ plus the content (values) of my agenda differentiates
my project from normal-boring analyses routinely churned out and
attached ^to specific ~~xxixx~~ cultural icons.
So as I walked downtown to the Drawing Center ~~still somewhat~~
~~stunned and angry~~, attempting to invent myself as a cultural critic
                       explicit
in direct and ~~factual~~ opposition to the writing style and critical
values of Donald Kuspit, I started to question my choice of Antonin
Artaud ~~ax~~ as a subject. He is, after all, a figure of clinical
"idiosyncracy" to say the least and a repository ~~for~~ various ▓▓▓▓
~~genius x models x~~ distasteful ~~x~~ accounts of genius (pathological,
supernatural, etc.).

I WOULD liKE TO SAY: "ANYTHING
THAT COULD POSSIBLY INTEREST
DONALD KUSPIT COULD NOT POSSIBLY
INTEREST ME . . . "
BUT IT IS JUST NOT THAT
SIMPLE.

With Artaud's well-documented insistence upon̄ his s̄iñgularitȳ absolute singularity, and h̄is the subsequent fetishization̄ of his illness, addiction, and misanthropy, he seems like Kuspit's cup of tea. I kind of felt like dropping the project before I had even begun in earnest.

aRtaud: DoNald kuspit's cup OF Tea

But all that changed as soon as I arrived at the Drawing Center. I had never seen anything like it in SoHo. There was a line down the block. Everyone was speaking French. A tall girl wore a cardboard Artaud mask. But she was the only readily apparent Artaud f̄r̄m̄ f̄r̄m̄ freak. I judged the rest to be Derrida groupies. Indeed, the crowd went wild when Derrida showed up, ̄hīsxwhītexhaīr followed by a camera crew, his white hair backlit like a halo. I never ī̄m̄āgī̄n̄ēd̄ imagined he would be so handsome.

As 7pm approached people without tickets gave up hope and began to leave. The truly devoted waited to see if there would be some last minute miracle.

I got a ̄s̄ēāt̄ seat in the middle of a row about four from the front next to two girls who seemed like bestfriends. They s̄ēēm̄ēdxī̄īkāwere very serious about the event, each with a stack of books and papers on her lap. From their conversation I learned that the main attract for them was Gayatri Spivak. They sort of scoffed at undue exciteme about Derrida. On the other side of me was a woman who's voice I recognized from p̄hōn̄ēxx̄ān̄sxwēxxx̄tī̄n̄ answering the phone at my job.

She tried to get me to switch places with her husband so they could sit together and I refused. The Columbia girls (I decided they were Columbia students) shot her mean looks and the one closest to me whispered to her friend "of course the single woman in public is expected to accomodate the heterosexual couple." I was really glad to be with them.

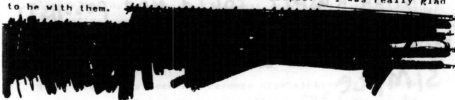

Sylvère Lotringer, in master of ceremonies, first introduced
Margit Rowell, curator of the Artaud drawing show at the ~~Modern~~
Modern. Her take on Artaud is one of traditional fascination/with
~~the tormented soul~~ the tormented soul, the afflicted brilliance
etc of the artist. It was pretty funny that she was on the same panel
as Derrida and Spivak. She described an encounter with ~~A's drawings~~ A's drawings
at the Centre Pompidou in 1993 in which she was "stripped bare by the
penetration of the eyes staring back at me." It reminded me of one
of the first times I got high and I freaked out because I was convinced
that my sister's David Bowie poster could see me naked through the wall
that separated ~~out~~ our bedrooms. Rowell concluded with a comment abo
the skepticism of the French toward an exhibition of Artaud's drawing
in the U.S. she described the dominant sentiment in France as one of
pessimism regarding the ability of Americans to "truly understand"
Artaud. Her response to this nationalistic possessiveness was to sta
that Artaud's ~~work~~ drawings were legible to all, expressions of a
"universal language". The Columbia girls hissed audibly! I couldn't
believe it. They were so cool.
Nancy Spero was the next speaker and I was really interested to bette
understand her use of Artaud ~~forxa~~ within an explicitly feminist art
practice, given his reputation as (to use my grandmother's phrase)
a schizophrenic woman-hater. From 1969 to 70 she executed a series o
"Artaud paintings" and from 71-72 a piece called "Codex Artaud." She
explained that ~~iax~~ Artaud's work was somehow resonant for her even as
she was well aware how he would have hated her appropriation.
~~His~~ Fortunately, it just doesn't matter what Artaud would think as
for Spero, ~~his work provides a harmonious~~ his worth is symbolic -- an
example of a male hysteric, a Crazy Bitch with male authority. I am
always ~~intere~~ fascinated by commitments to ~~mixed feelings~~ complex
~~mixed feelings~~ mixed-feelings which ~~existence~~ in rejection of the
love/hate terms of patrilineal art-making. I find myself in the
same boat as Spero: I am not crazy, a dope fiend, a theoretician of
theatre or a misogynist, and yet somehow I like Artaud.
Gayatri Spivak spoke next insisting throughout ~~kx~~ that she ~~kx~~ knew
very little about Artaud, and yet she definitely stole the show.
What became clear to me from her presentation was that Artaud's
egomaniacal, ~~in~~ vehement ~~that~~ conviction in his unique alienation and
persecution prevented his counter-conjuring from becoming a counter-
politics (he was his own category of marginality, ~~if and not to~~

his "oppression" not describable in the terms of systematic
hierarchy, but by the specific ~~xxxpixx~~ magic conspiracies
against him, ~~and~~ discernible only through his clairvoyance)
~~XIXXKIXXX~~ Whatever existential and ~~dx~~ artistic dilemmas
~~texuxa~~ embodied by Artaud's tormented predicaments ~~Th~~ ~~~~ there
can be no model ~~xxxstruxted~~ for action constructed around his
artistic production. Artaud begins with a loss, with a theft.
Each spell is a response, a counter-spell. His drawings exist
defensively, ~~xxxpxyxhix~~ Spivak: "Something has been done to me,
my politics are a counter-politics, and therefore cannot be a model."

Derrida had not prepared a talk, he had come with the idea that the
event was to be a less formal conversation between the scholars
present. and so he shared some anecdotes about Artaud. It was
entertaining, especially when he told the story about a psychiatrist
who stated that with todays state-of-the-art psychopharmaceuticals,
Artaud could have been "corrected" in a week...

He did add a ~~few~~ thoughts about ~~B~~ Artaud's politics, ~~that~~ his
~~██████████████████~~ disturbing (lack of coherent) politics . . .
namely that ~~whttxhtx~~ ~~htx~~ the terminology of his analysis (curses,
spells, charms, spectres, and evil doubles) was indisputably
inadequate ~~xxxx~~ to describe the political climate of his time, but
still may have had (may still have) potential for articulating radical
insight ~~██████████████~~

Did You see last year's movie "The Craft"
in which a gothy/punk girl slays a jock with
Magic? She, like artaud, ends up
Muttering and thrashing around in
an institution, but before things go all
wrong she and her highschool girlfriends practice
~~████~~ witchcraft according to a politically
progressive program of Revenge. The
racist cunt girl's hair falls out in
Big blond chunks in her bathing cap
in the locker room. And, like I said
before, a jock (played by the not-yet-famous
skeet ulrich) gets killed. Its pretty entertaining.

October 12

1 met my grandparents at noon in the lobby of the Museum of Modern Art
feeling weak and in a fog ,from desperate for food and coffee.   XX
They have a real problem with the cafeteria at the museum, but its
inconceivable to them to eat anywhere else : "Let's go buy a sandwhich
from these bastards." They had gone to SoHo the the day before xx to
see the the Francis Bacon show ("really stupid stuff. a sick guy.")
and complained that they were the only old people there. They also ha
plans to go to the XX Jasper Johns opening at the museum on Friday and
kept grimacing at the promotional posters for the exhibition ("I don't
know why we're going. Who needs to look at the American flag?")
They interrogated me about Artaud while I tried to drink enough
coffee to get a grip on the situation.They were particularly concerned
with his relationship to the Surrealists (they hate surrealism) and
I said I didn't know much except that he could hardly have been a
Surrealist in any ~~SUSTAINED WAY~~ as he was incapable/unwilling to
be subsumed by any collective description or aertistic movement althou
he was kind of a darling of ~~theirs~~ ,exhibiting/embodying aesthe
ic affinities ("oh, so he was their stooge. A puppet.").   I pulled out
my Artaud reader edited by Susan SOntagx and and read parts of his
formal critique of the Surrealists,"In Total Darkness" (1927)xwhih
which was based upon his objection to the Surrealist embrace of the
Communist party, "External metamorphosis is, in my opinion, something
which can xxixx only be given as a bonus. The social level, the mat
l level toward which theSurrealists direct their pathetic attempts a
action, their forever ineffectual hatreds, is for me no more than a
useless xxd and obvious illusion." There was an anxious lull in the
conversation in which thexf they found themselves momentarily alligned
with the Surrealists against Artaud's dismissal of thexrexximtimnx
the transformation of material conditions as basis for revolution.
Bella suddenly appeared at the cafeteria and they bought her a sandwhic
too. Then we all went th the second floor gallery to see the exhibitio

XHXXXXXXXXXXHHHXXXHXHXHXHXXHXXHXXXXXHHXXHXXHXXHHXXXXXHXXXHHX
XXXXHHXXXXXHHXHHX

(Artaud's official involvement with the Surrealists ixx lasted only
a few years, beginning thxxugh with an introduction through his frie
the artist Andre Masson.   He edited the third issue of th La
Revolution Surrealiste in 1925 before ixx his dramatic excommunication
from the group in the following year)

....

The drawings exhibited were all executed during his 8 year
internment in various psychiatric institutions. In 1936̷7, Artaud,
no money, no drugs, is deported from Ireland as an"undesirable"
to the hospital of Ville-Evrard, Paris. The first group of drawings
are from this period: the spells. It seems wrongxto misleading to
call them drawings as they are clearly intended to function as
documents of incantations, symbols or props within a defensixe
scheme of psychic warfare defense. Their cosmological significance
is not that of "art-objects" per se. X Scrawled upon, torn, burned
and otherwisexwer decorated,they appear within the conventions of
anthropological display of ritual objects,form Encased upright ꟷꟷ.
thatxbothxsidexxarexxisible away from the wall so that both sides
are visible.byxwaikingxxxund   Each one is for a specific friend or
enemy,XX Leon Fouks, for example("keep this spell against your heart.
in case of danger touch your heart with the Index and Middle fingers of
your f right hand and THE SPELL WILL ILLUMINATE", he writes and adorns
the paper with scars and pentagrams). And there is one to Hitler.
"The Rodez Drawings" are them 2nd group of drawings, produced between
1943 and 1946 around the time that Artaud was subjected to early
experiments with XIxelectroshockxtreatment electroshock therapy. 51 treatments knocked teeth
out and fractured vertebrae. XXXXXXXXXXXX Artaud's body is the literal and
physical site of fragmentation, and his drawings, more free than ever
before from the conventions of sanity,consistency, style, are the
mediated representation, the analogous images. Here we see someone
 physiologically driven to pastiche. ▆▆▆▆▆▆▆▆▆▆▆▆▆▆▆▆▆▆▆
▆▆▆▆▆▆▆▆▆▆   Artaud, unstable and under extreme duress, is still
ell aware of the art of his time and^of the recent past,and references
t randomly and/or vindictively. The drawings are nicely XX scattered
nd clutzy.
The third group of drawings are the portraits. While the spells are th
most clearly rooted in a performative practive of magic, these drawings
of Artaud's friends and associates arex contextualized by a curious
mythology about their production, as well. According to the museum
brochure for the exhibition: " He stood before a table covered by a she
of paper, changing, humming, and shrieking while gouging his pencils an
crayons into the paper."
I liked the portraits the best of the drawings I think. There was a
real sense that Artaud was representing his admirers and peers as
faithfully as he could to his standard of psychic realism. His lack of
facility for traditionally representational sketching makes his insiste
upon his own distorted, expressionistic version of it all themx more
unsettling.

Any romantic claims about the xix ingenious insight or visionary
clairvoyance of Artaud as conveyed by the relentless, piercing
gazes of his subjects is just total drivel, though. He drew them
frontally with their eyes open in this fucked-up way that communica:
a complete disregard forbx bourgeois portraiture. It's no more
special or mysterious than that. I really liked the One that's
:rather spare and black and white except for xxxxx an obsessively
articulated and colored-inxx mass of hair. Its so punk.

October 15, 1996
Another night at the Drawing Center MCed by Sylvere Lotringer.
The evening was billed as xx readings of Artaud's works by
Susan Sontag, Vincent Kaufman and Claytbn Eschelman. It was xxxxxxx
 considerably less crowded than the first event and it puzzled me .
I figured that the city was crawling with Sontag fanatics. I persox
am a longtime fan. I have a red xerox xx copy of her with an arm
around Richard Hell from an old poetry magazine tacked to my studio
It was my first time seeing her in person. She is really beautiful +
she's got a natural white skunk stripe in her hair.
xThxxfixxx Her introductory observation was that Artaud is frequently
enlisted xxx into an anti-intellectualist position under the faulty
premise thatxx madness and passion are necessarily xxxxxxd in polar
opposition to xx traditional artistic or literary bconcerns. She
suggested that Artaud's hysteria or fringe mental states were often
organized around issues of formal purity.xx
    I was somewhat disappointed by the selections she read of his
writing -- a 1922 love letter to Genica Ahhanasiou and then pieces
of his correspondence with Jacques Riviere, editor of La Nouvelle
Revue Francaise. The letter to Athanasiou which Sontag insisted was
xx incredibly beautiful didn't do a lot for me, but it was interesti
in the xxxxx articulation of a generalized objection or obstacle to
the expression of interior states. Artaud writes to her that a
to him even the effort of the articulating feelings constitutes a
betrayal, "all wordsxx are a lie." Here, Artuad's disatisfaction with
given language (which remains a constant problem and subject of his
throughout his life) results inx a paralysis and silence toward his
lover: "My mind was very sick for 5 days, a recurrence of my nervous
diseasein which I was fx robbed of all tangible expression of my
cbnsciousness,xIxdxxx. . . I had no material thought, so to speak, f
within myself I was more profound, expressing myself, paralyzed. . .
His "nervous disease" ix becomes, in this light, not so much a sickness
or a fault, but an involuntary censorial function of his person with
positive function of guarding him against compromise.
And yet he is compelled to speak.
THe correspondence with Jacques Riviere begins with Artaud's submiss
of a group of poemsxxhixhxxxxxxxjxxixd to the Review edited by Riviere
The rejected poems are accompanied by a suggestion that the two men Meet
They do, and afterwards Artaud sends Riviere a letter to clarify a poin
of their discussion.xxdxthixxix The ensuing correspondence becomes A's
y first published writing., Sontag read passages of the letters xxt
a deep calm voice. It was very relaxing.
By coincidence, Vincent Kaufman (mousy xxx and French) chose many of the
same letters of this particular correspondence, and viewed the inter:
much more xyxixxity skeptically. He seemed to see Artaud intentions
kind of opportunistic and egomaniacal regarding Riviere regarding x
a maybe). He identifiew Artaud's xxx objective upon his intiation of
cobmunication as publication of his work. The letters bxxxxx exist as
a substitution for the poems xhxxhxdixxppxxxxfxxmxthxixxdixxxxx

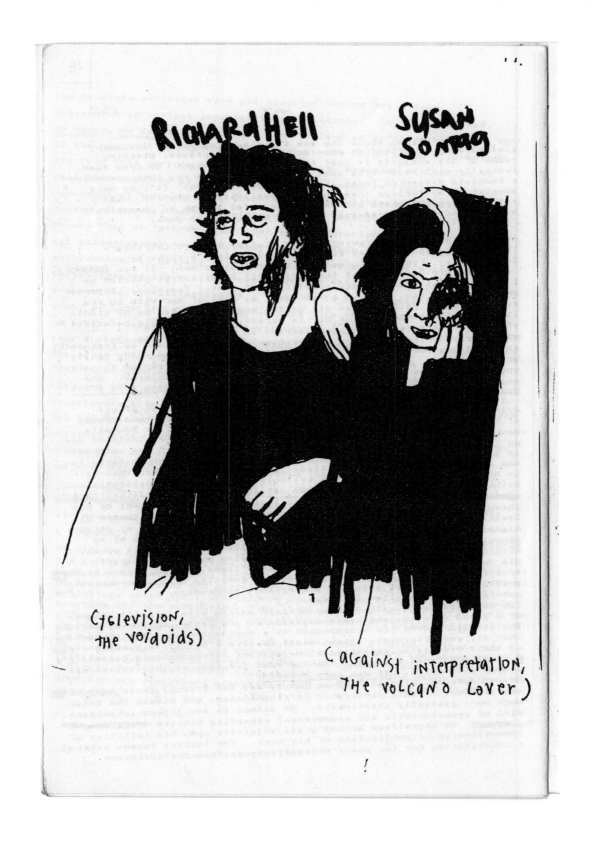

RICHARD HELL

SUSAN SONTAG

(Cyclevision,
the Voidoids)

(Against interpretation,
The Volcano Lover)

the letters, the documented discourse supposedly about the poems,
is published in stead of the poems. This of course is emblematic
of Artaud's attitude. . . all tangible communication is defiled
telepathy. Materiality signifies substitution.
Artaud's audience/objects/recipients/victims of his letters or spells
are always the inferior/evil doubles to his true audience... they ar
complicit in a circuit of imperfect communication. They are impost(
zombies or false twins emptied of their true souls which cannot be w.
n to.   Artaud's insistence upon his singularity and unique spiritua.
predicament within his correspondence with Riviere serves to erase
Riviere's subjectivity, to dissolve it into generically damaged publi
reception of Artaud's own invetnion.
I got tired and couldn't really follow all of Kaufman's talk. My
lasting impression of him though was that through his veneer of scho;
detachment, he found Artaud irritating and und over-rated. XXXXXXX
Unlike Sontag, not an Artaud "fan."
Clayton Eschelman is more than a fan, he is an impersonator. His
               certain
leather vest and subtleties of his demeanor even seemed to reference
the tradition of Elvis-impersonatoation in his mx reading of Artaud':
works. He yelled and shrieked and inflected, shaking people awake
from their VIncent Kaufman-induced stupor. I wasn't sure what to t|
l mean, I thought it was good. My friend Kirstin hated it,felt it
was an aggressive affront to the spirit of Artaud;" he wasn't like t|
I know that Artaud did not perform like that." There was something
sort of embarrassing or distasteful about Eschelman's performance, I
s.   But I thinktxx that Artaud was embarrassing probably. Xxtxxxxt
, certainly he was annoying.
,

October 22, 1996

Tonight I tried to go see Carl Dreyer's film "The PAssion of Joan of Ar
, the & 1928 silent film featuring Artaud as the monk Massieu.
My night was ill-fated. My friends left a message for me that they
had decided to go to the Stereolab show instead. I went to Anthology
Film Archives anyway taxfix only to have the last xxx ticket sold jus
as I reached the box office.   A big disappointment.
But it was interesting from a sociological stand point to mx super-
ficially examine and make judgements about the swarm of people
lined up outside of the theatre to see Artaud caught on film.
Whereas the people at the Drawing Center events so far xh have been,
for the most part, visual artists and downtown art workers -- a
large percentage of youngish front-desk people from Soho and Chelsea
galleries -- the people at Anthology reflected another demographic of
Artaud fan: tormented poets and actors who feel they experience a
kindred pain. Or who romanticize such pain as a   . symptom of genius.

XXXXX (This is all just a prejudicial impression based on my observat
of, and juvenile bias against, the East Village Goth aesthetic which
dominated the crowd's collective fashion sense) This wasn't the same
crowd at the Spivak/Derrida talk because this crowd xxx does rxdid no
need to examine its "deep" affinity for Artaud through a theoretica
filter. This crowd "gets" Artaud in a kind of spiritual or intuitive
way.

Later I found out that the Stereolab show sold out as well and
my friends did didn't get in. Oh well.

Dear diary   JAN. 15 1997
3 MONTHS AFTER I aBANDONED
THIS project, more interested in
painting again all of a sudden,
Donald kuspit Has a review of
artaud's drawing SHOW IN the
January ArtFORUM. Decided on
the plane Back to New York to
Paste up this diary as a pamPHlet
and xerox a BUNch so that if
some version of THIS does end up
IN SPEX I will also Have it IN
English For MY Friends.
kuspit's dumB review is so perfect
To end with. Because its such a clear
Illustration of HIS Sucky Humanist
essay writing style and HIS
retrogressive values. And Because
its publication   Has   such
a shockingly poetic Meaning For
Me. kuspit's PUBlic   judgement of
artaud's drawings as theatrical
and inauthentic (or whatever) profoundly
validates MY FANdom, as IRONIC
as MY Love might ultimately Be.

"ANTONIN ARTAUD: WORKS ON PAPER"

MoMA

DONALD KUSPIT

"Few graphic expressions in the twen-: tieth century show the power and authentic inner necessity seen in the drawings of Antonin Artaud . . . they show the heightened sensibility and critical lucidity of a mind at odds with society and unable to compromise with its conventions." That is the standard Artaud defense, put forward by Margit Rowell, curator of the MoMA exhibition. The reason he needs defending is the stark diagnostic probability offered by Rowell: Artaud (1896–1948) "suffered from confabulatory paraphrenia, a delusional psychosis which is not accompanied by intellectual deterioration and in which some symptoms—hallucinations and confabulations—are close to those of schizophrenia."

Rowell invites us to view Artaud as one of the great "spiritual revolutionaries" of modern art, as Wassily Kandinsky called them—"solitary visionaries" articulating "the internal truth which only art can divine . . . which only art can express by those means of expression which are hers alone." Does Artaud belong among them? Or are his works on paper the visual ravings of the Artaud who "screamed deliriously as his argument disintegrated into crazy acting" during a lecture, and the Artaud who regarded "cruelty [as] a sort of rigorous discipline" that would be the basis for a new "physical and spatial poetry that has long been lacking in th...... "?

Art and "aggressive cruelty," to use Rowell's phrase, were one and the same for Artaud. But the issue is whether Artaud was a prophet of social catastrophe, or whether it served his personal catastrophe, which had been in the making since the "nervous disorders" and "depression" of his adolescence, when he was diagnosed with hereditary syphilis and given the laudanum that began his lifelong drug addiction. (He eventually turned to heroin.) Apart from an early self-portrait (ca. 1915), the works in the exhibition were made immediately before, during, and after the Second World War, but it is equally important to note that they were made during Artaud's confinement in mental hospitals, where he received fifty-one electric shocks over a nineteen-month period and was diagnosed as suffering from "incurable paranoid delirium." The exhibition begins with the so-called "Spells," 1937–39, which seem, in their violence and terror, to herald the trauma of war. They are angry letters to real and imaginary friends—Artaud tried to bewitch them with cryptic emblems as well as words—written on paper that has been all but destroyed: ripped, punctured, and burned; splotched and smeared with ink and gouache. The second group of works (1944–46) carries the destruction into the image, which becomes a nightmarish "bouillabaisse of forms in the tower of Babel," to use the inscription on one of them. Finally, there are a number of portraits (1946–48), of varying degrees of expressive uniqueness, which seem to bespeak postwar—post-traumatic—exhaustion, ruin, depression. The self-portrait of May 11, 1946, and *La Tête bleue* (The blue head), another self-portrait made about the same time, are particularly extraordinary: what Artaud did to the paper of the "Spells" he now does to himself. He in effect shows the death throes of his psyche.

these works are simply cultural and aesthetic curiosities—the symptomatic products of a delusional psychotic—or whether they have an important place in modern art, where they hold their own intellectually, morally, and stylistically. The relation of art to madness has been an issue since antiquity—Plato assumed their inner connection in the *Lysis*—and has become an open issue in modernity, where the art of the insane has been celebrated as, in the words of Bernard Dorival, "equal in dignity, in quality, even in financial value" to any "major art." Are Artaud's works on paper "major art" because they are insane and insanity is disturbing to the bourgeoisie, or because their quality resides in the uniqueness of the artistic methods with which they mediate insanity? It is this question that is at the core of an evaluation of Artaud's visual art.

To an extent, Artaud's visual work was an attempt to put into practice his theory of cruelty, which he was not able to do in the theater and cinema, despite the fame his portrayal of Marat in Abel Gance's film *Napoléon*, 1927, brought him. *The Cenci*, 1935, a stage adaptation from Shelley, which he wrote and directed, and in which he acted, was his most ambitious effort to do so, but it was a financial and critical failure. (In 1927 he wrote "Manifesto for a Theater That Failed," as if in anticipation of the event.) So he was reduced to drawing, all the more so because of the breakdown he suffered not long after his theatrical failure.

Artaud seems to have literalized Rimbaud's "disordering of all the senses" ("*Lettres du Voyant*," 1871), and indeed, Artaud's *Fragments of a Diary from Hell* (1926) emulates Rimbaud's *Une Saison en enfer* (A season in hell, 1873). Both—as well as Artaud's works on paper—are examples of what Jean Dubuffet called "*les œuvres des irréguliers*" or *art brut*. He contrasted its "instinct, passion, caprice, violence" (primitive . . . values of the savage") with "*l'art culturel*" or "official art"—the "art of museums, galleries, salons," with its "vacuous" value of "beauty." Dubuffet undoubtedly concurred with Artaud that "Culture isn't in books, paintings, statues, dances: it's in the nerves and the fluidity of the nerves." For both Rimbaud and Artaud art was a record, or kind of trace, of the process of disordering and the final nervous state of disorder: the process of going insane, that is, going to the hell of instinct, passion, caprice, violence, where one could be unequivocally primitive or savage—"naked, natural, excessive," as Artaud says.

After the "Spells," the barely coherent bouillabaisse drawings are the most emotionally primitive of Artaud's works on paper. "Composites" of imagistic fragments, mostly of parts of the body, they suggest that Artaud had reached the final stage of disorder. Throughout his life he was embarrassed by his body, and now he no longer had to be: he had shredded it—undermined the very idea of the integrity of the body, male or female. Ironically, this gives the drawings their artistic integrity and radical character: they carry Surrealist incongruity to its (il)logical conclusion. Where the Surrealists tried to hold on to unity, in whatever distorted form, Artaud abandoned corporeal continuity altogether, radicalizing the picture in the process. Instead of making a picture of the body—that basic subject matter of art—Artaud implies that it is impossible to picture it with any finality.

The body's unity becomes unthinkable—just as it is for infants, who experience the body as a disordered sum of emotionally raw fragments. Thus, Artaud's bouillabaisse drawings fulfill the project of his theater of cruelty (the title, in fact, of one of them). The process is painful, but, unexpectedly, the result is not particularly pleasurable and liberating: where the alchemy worked for Rimbaud, it unfortunately didn't for Artaud. He

never found paradise, for he had in effect drugged himself to death—the death he repeatedly talks about in his letters and manifestos.

In 1927, Artaud wrote that "what divides me from the Surrealists is that they love life as much as I despise it." His portraits, of himself and others, do nothing to belie this statement. Artaud's portraits are supposedly his most lucid, undeteriorated, intellectual works, as Rowell suggests, but they too have a disturbing symptomatic dimension. "In my unconscious it's always other people that I hear," Artaud wrote in 1946, and in

ARTAUD'S PORTRAITS LACK THE EMPHATIC INSIGHT OF VAN GOGH. ARTAUD IDENTIFIES WITH HIM. BUT HIS PORTRAITS ARE MORE BELABORED AND MUCH MORE THEATRICAL.

his portraits they become the "inexplicable crimes inside [him]self," incarnations of the "evil forces" of zeitgeist, as he wrote in 1933, that persecute him. To exorcise them by projection is not enough—he becomes the "torturer-executioner" that he conceived the director-author of the theater of cruelty to be. They are in effect effigies he cruelly abuses, explicitly, as the *Portrait of Paule Thévenin* or *Paule with Irons*, May 24, 1947, indicates, or implicitly, as the *Portrait of Yves Thévenin*, June 24,

1947, suggests. The more straightforward, dull faces—figures whose faces haven't been cruelly treated (all but defaced) have the inert look of discarded masks. They remain intact, but their existence has been completely devalued.

In June 1947 Artaud wrote: "Not a single painter in the history of art, from Holbein to Ingres, has su-

ceeded in making it talk, this face of man. . . . Van Gogh only could make of the human head a portrait which has the bursting flare of a throbbing, exploded heart." This can be regarded as a standard avant-garde repudiation of tradition and argument for modernism's greater authenticity—the same made in favor of primitive art by Dubuffet, and Paul Gauguin before him. But Artaud's portraits are nowhere as spontaneously expressive—authentically instinctive, passionate, primitive, irregular, nervy, unconventional—as those of Van Gogh. They lack not only the empirical power of those of Holbein and Ingres, but the emphatic insight of Van Gogh.

Artaud identifies with him, as is clear from his essay *Van Gogh, le suicidé de la société* (The man suicided by society, 1947) indicates, but his portraits are more belabored and above all much more theatrical than those of Van Gogh. Compared to the people in Van Gogh's portraits, those in Artaud's portraits appear to be acting—posturing, the way Artaud did on the stage and screen. They are like stone heads of medieval saints, and in fact form a theatrical tableau not unlike that of the saints at the portal of a medieval church. Only where they open the way to eternal life, Artaud's portraits "provide," as he said, "access to death."

Artaud's theater of cruelty is a posture meant to do away with all postures—a desperate attempt to escape from acting that becomes the ultimate act. It was an effort to elude what Lionel Trilling described as "the characteristic disease of the actor, the attenuation of selfhood that results from impersonation," and arrive at authentic selfhood, but it was, after all, just more theater—impersonation. The heritage of Artaud, especially in his works on paper, is his pathetic self-deception and unremitting theatricality, which did exactly the opposite of what he intended it to do—break down the difference between art and life, or rather enlist art in the service of a more authentic self and intense life than seemed possible

Artaud's theatrical writings raise, however unwittingly, the question of whether art can really serve the self and life without falsifying them—the same modern question that, according to Clement Greenberg, Franz Kafka raised. The works on paper make the dark side of his theatrical ambition explicit: they leave us with a very modern sense of the angry futility of it all—no doubt a reflection of the angry futility of his effort to free himself from drugs—which turned into nihilistic hatred. Hatred ate him away from the inside: he, not other people, punched the holes in his face, and above all made them so theatrical. This, no doubt, is why his works on paper can be seen to have a peculiarly exemplary relevance in modern visual art. □

Donald Kuspit's most recent book is *Idiosyncratic Identities: Artists at the End of the Avant-Garde,* Cambridge University Press.

JANUARY 1997 **81**

I ended up getting an "A" in his class because I gave a really great slide presentation on JACKSON POLLOCK.

You can get my performance notes for $3 cash or check.

MY FANZINE "THE OPPOSITE" COSTS $2.

THE End

JOHANNA FATEMAN
250 NORTH SIXTH STREET, #5
BROOKLYN, 11211

ARTAUD—MANIA: THE DIARY OF A FAN

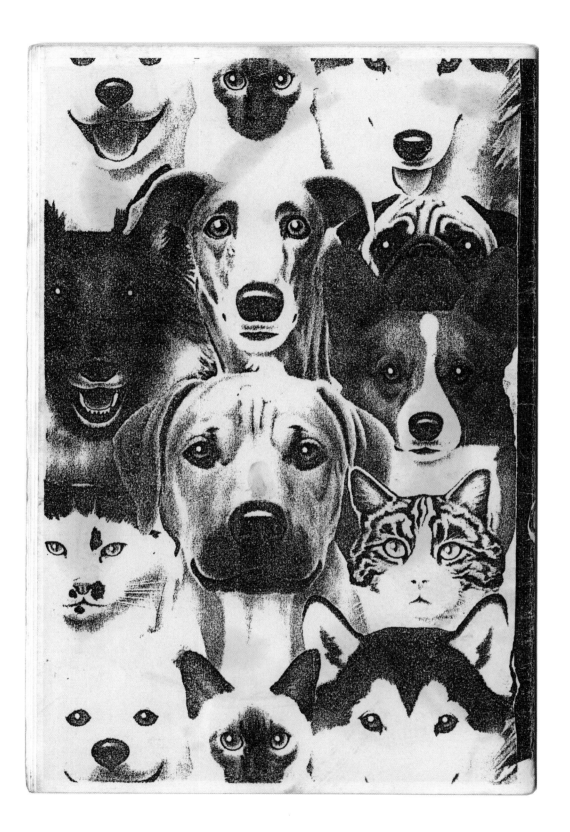

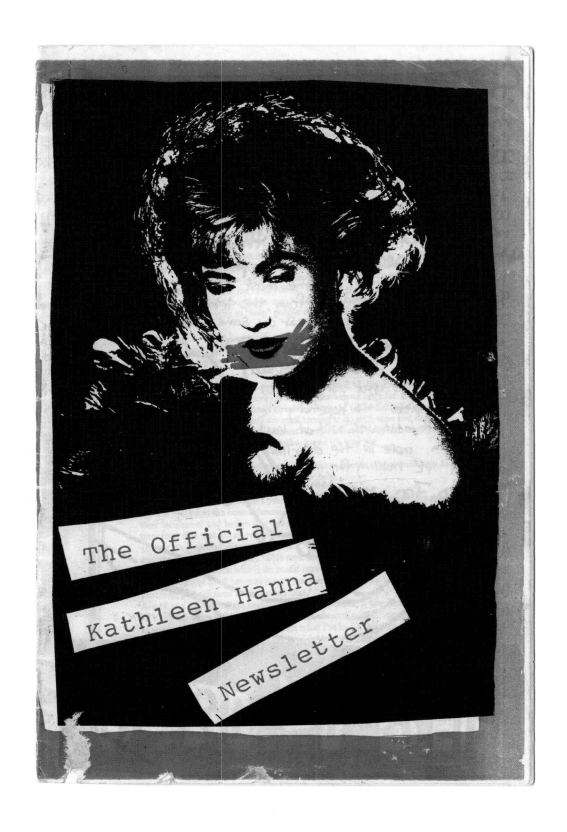

The Official

Kathleen Hanna

Newsletter

THE OFFICIAL KATHLEEN HANNA NEWSLETTER (EXCERPT)

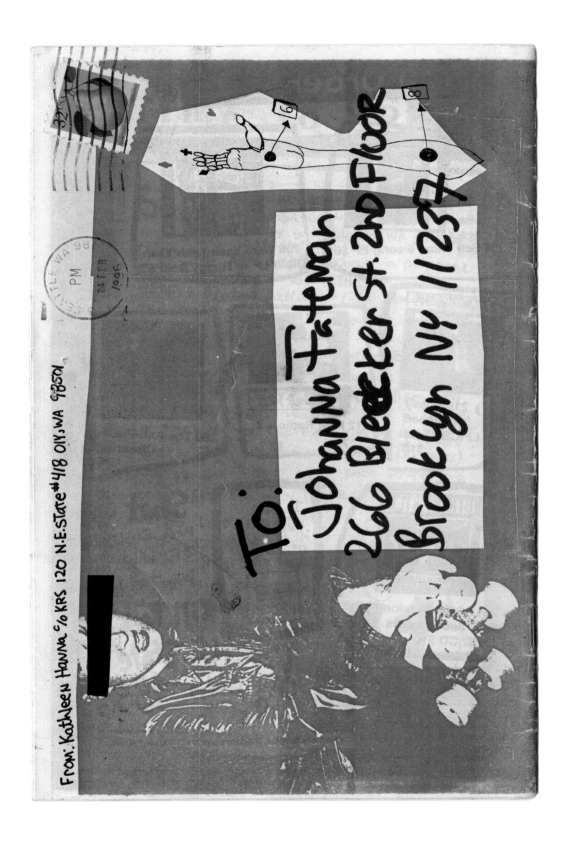

From: Kathleen Hanna c/o KRS 120 N.E.State #418 Oly, WA 98501

To:
Johanna Fateman
266 Bleecker St. 2nd Floor
Brooklyn NY 11237

Magic animal

1. the wheelie is ephemeral
It happens in but a moment and yet is beautiful, uncontainable, you never know when one might happen.

2. The wheelie cannot be televised.
Trust yr brain above and beyond mechanical intrusions. Remembering the wheelie is enough to make some cum. It need not be sanitized thru photography.... tho' there really are no rules.

3. Don't fear the wheelie. In witnessing someone else's wheelie: allow yrself the sheer amazed thing that's happening. Even if you don't understand their particular wheelie aesthetic or even know what they're about, kick back and enjoy. Don't compare their wheelie to yr own, all wheelies are different and beautiful.

4. The Wheelie is power. Many of us have been trained to immediately record/define/discuss "the magical" because we are afraid of sheer untameable power. A gaping mouth in the face of a wheelie and witnessing another stunned set of eyes (mutually witnessing a wheelie rules!) without needing to speak....... Yeah, silence equals death.... except for during wheelies.

5. The Wheelie must not stand in opposition to "flat" riding. Popping a wheelie, who knows when it'll happen.... when the conditions will be just right, when the urge will hit you. The fact that a wheelie could happen should not be used to distract from the distinct pleasures involved in "flat riding" (like just a basic trip to Safeway or something) It is important to not set the wheelie apart → the idea is to live in the moment, no matter what.

6. Wheelies are different than bike tricks. Even just getting yr front tire off the ground for, like, 5 seconds constitutes a wheelie. The whole BIKE TRICK thing is cool but that's a whole other thing than, just the, say, Random Wheelie. when girls do Bike Tricks or like heshers, and form gangs around this.... But I'm getting ahead of myself

1. I would you like smoking or NON?

2. I feel some performance art coming on.

3. whatever

The Answers

7. The wheelie, performance art connection.
It was 3 in the morning & I was sitting in my apartment window looking down on the street, contemplating suicide when this hesher kid came riding down 4th Ave. In the middle of the night w/supposedly "no one watching" the boy popped a wheelie all the way down the Ave.

8. Colonization and the Wheelie. Attempts have been made yet always fail. The kids know one need not destroy other wheelie gangs in order to enjoy themselves.

I WHEELIE WHEELIE MEAN IT.

NOTES

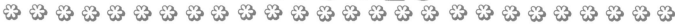

zines, artwork, flyers, and other documents. Those who had donated to the collection at the time the book was produced are: Becca Albee, Ramdasha Bikceem, Tammy Rae Carland, Johanna Fateman, Zan Gibbs, Kathleen Hanna, Milly Itzhak, Kelly Marie Martin, Molly Neuman, Mimi Thi Nguyen and the People of Color Zine Project, Lucy Thane, and Matt Wobensmith. Becca, Ramdasha, Tammy Rae, Johanna, Kathleen, Kelly, Molly, Mimi, and Matt also graciously gave me permission to reproduce zines, flyers, and other material they created. Thank you!

A huge thank you to all of the other zine writers and artists who gave me permission to reproduce their work: Margarita Alcantara, Sasha Cagen, Cindy Crabb, Donna Dresch, Felix Endara, Andrea Fernandez, Gary Gregerson, Angelique Hart, Elena Humphreys, G.B. Jones, Bill Karren, Nomy Lamm, Diana Morrow, Tinuviel Sampson, Corin Tucker, Rachel Lee Walsh, Kathi Wilcox, Allison Wolfe, and Molly Zuckerman-Hartung.

I also want to thank those who gave feedback on the project: Becca Albee, Elizabeth Keenan, Liza Harrell-Edge, and my stellar editor Amy Scholder; to Emily B. King for her last-minute fact-checking, and to Barnard Zine Librarian Jenna Freedman for helping me contact zine writers. A special thanks goes to Sam Huber, who did the bulk of the scanning for this project. Thank you, Herb Thornby, for this amazing design. And thank you to Daniela Capistrano of the People of Color Zine Project for her collaborative role in bringing in Mimi Thi Nguyen's collection.

I am particularly grateful to my greatest allies, David O'Neill and Johanna Fateman, for making themselves available for endless hours of editing, fact-checking, and general cheerleading as I agonized over every decision.

Finally, I am indebted to Amy Scholder, Elizabeth Koke, Jeanann Pannasch, and the Feminist Press for their commitment to publishing this book of primary texts that takes the theory and practice of riot grrrl seriously, and for understanding the value of preserving these documents and making them accessible to everyone.

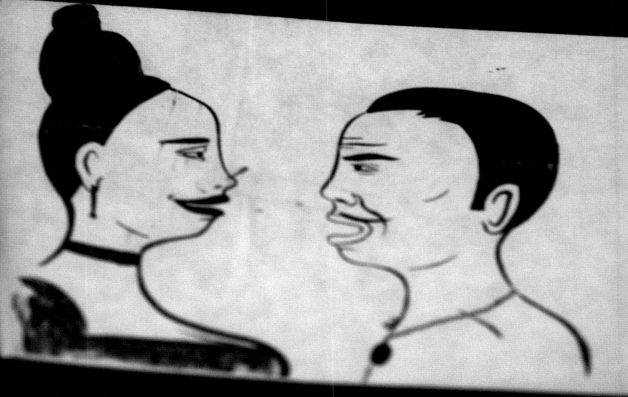

The Feminist Press is an independent, nonprofit literary publisher that promotes freedom of expression and social justice. Founded in 1970, we began as a crucial publishing component of second wave feminism, reprinting feminist classics by writers such as Zora Neale Hurston and Charlotte Perkins Gilman, and providing much-needed texts for the developing field of women's studies with books by Barbara Ehrenreich and Grace Paley. We publish feminist literature from around the world, by best-selling authors such as Shahrnush Parsipur, Ruth Kluger, and Ama Ata Aidoo; and North American writers of diverse race and class experience, such as Paule Marshall and Rahna Reiko Rizzuto. We have become the vanguard for books on contemporary feminist issues of equality and gender identity, with authors as various as Anita Hill, Justin Vivian Bond, and Ann Jones. We seek out innovative, often surprising books that tell a different story.

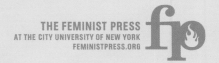

THE FEMINIST PRESS
AT THE CITY UNIVERSITY OF NEW YORK
FEMINISTPRESS.ORG

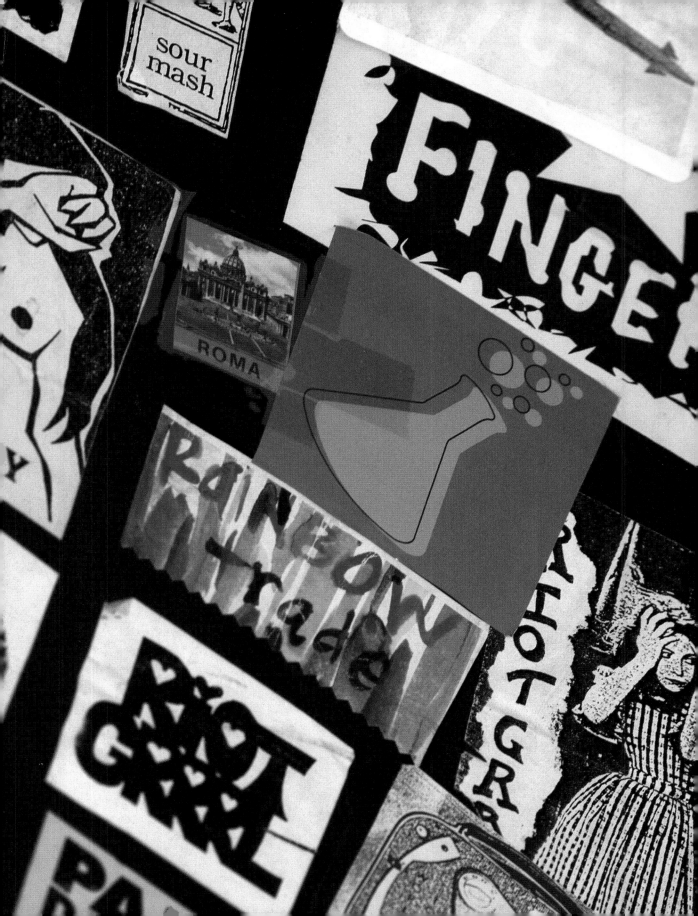

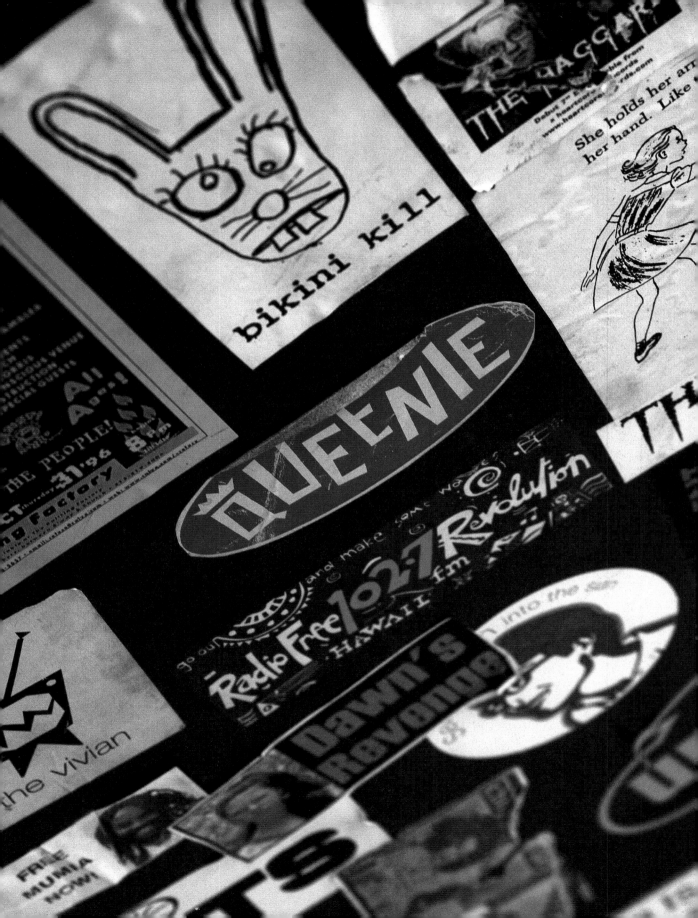

the
end

Things i made ♥